Isabel Orleans-Bragança

abel Orleans-Bragança

The Brazilian Princess
Who Freed the Slaves

JAMES MCMURTRY LONGO

McFarland & Company, Inc., Publishers
Jefferson, North Carolina, and London

Library of Congress Cataloguing-in-Publication Data

Longo, James McMurtry.
    Isabel Orleans-Bragança : the Brazilian princess who freed the
slaves / James McMurtry Longo.
      p.   cm.
    Includes bibliographical references and index.

    ISBN-13: 978-0-7864-3201-1
    softcover : 50# alkaline paper

    1. Isabel, Princess of Brazil, 1846–1921.   2. Brazil — History —
Empire, 1822–1889.   3. Slaves — Emancipation — Brazil.
4. Brazil — Kings and rulers — Biography.   5. Princesses —
Brazil — Biography.   I. Title.
F2536.I8L66   2008
981'.04092 — dc22   2007041497
[B]

British Library cataloguing data are available

Cover photograph: Princess Isabel prior to her 1864 marriage to a
French prince (courtesy Imperial Museum/ Iphan/Ministry of
Culture, Petrópolis, Brazil)

Manufactured in the United States of America

McFarland & Company, Inc., Publishers
Box 611, Jefferson, North Carolina 28640
www.mcfarlandpub.com

Para a minha mãe
e todas outras mulheres
que nunca usaram a coroa que conquitaram

For my mother
and all the other women
who never wore the crown they earned

The history of every country begins in the heart of a man or a woman

— Willa Cather

Women are found between the lines of history, kept in the shadows.

— Isabel Allende

I think that every strong woman in history has had a difficult path to walk. She is a threat.... I think it's the strength and the fear. Why is she strong? Where does she get it from? Where is she taking it? Where is she going to use it? Why does the public still support her?

— Diana, Princess of Wales

History has always been written by winners, those who survive or triumphed in their battles. It is the official history. It helps us understand that, in a conflicting world, the history is not neutral. It reports one version of the facts to safeguard present and future interests.

— Maria José da Conceição

Acknowledgments

Writing is a singular activity, yet no writer can write without the help and understanding of others. I have been blessed with the support of family, friends, and strangers during this project. To thank all of them would fill another book. I will thank only a few here, but I appreciate all those who assisted Isabel and myself during this journey.

I want to begin by thanking my wife Mary Jo Harwood, who, since Princess Isabel joined our family eleven long years ago, often referred to Isabel as my mistress. The three of us have traveled many roads together through Portugal and Brazil, Michigan, Pennsylvania, Missouri and North Carolina, and through the woods of Massachusetts and mountains of New Hampshire. Sometimes it got crowded with three along for the ride but I am grateful for her helping me better understand Isabel and the other strong women in this book.

Next I would like to thank my colleagues and friends at Washington and Jefferson College, Rosalie Carpenter, Diane Day Brzustowicz, Matt North, and Richard and Patti Easton, for their unwavering support, assistance, and help with this project. In the early stages of my research I am especially thankful to Anna Luísa Orleans-Bragança and Luís Felipe Orleans-Bragança for introducing me to their great-great grandmother and sharing their time and family stories with me.

I owe a special debt of gratitude to Dr. Iêda Siqueira Wiarda, Specialist in Luso-Brazilian Culture of the Hispanic Division of the Library of Congress for her enthusiastic and consistent help, support, and belief in this project. Dr. Ernesto Sweeney S.J. of the Department of History at Loyola Marymount University in Los Angeles, Maria Angela Leal, Assistant Curator of the Oliveira Lima Library at The Catholic University of America in Washington, D.C., and Monica Salam de Zayas of the Imperial Archives and Museum in Petrópolis, Brazil, have all generously shared their time and expertise with my research. To Gloria Kaiser of the Austrian-Brazilian Cultural Initiative, I offer special thanks for her belief in this project from its inception. Professor Kaiser's knowledge and writings on Princess Isabel's grandmother, aunt, and mother helped me understand and appreciate the influence these and other royal women had on Isabel's life.

Finally, my research would have been impossible to complete without the many translators who helped guide me through hundreds of books and thousands of words in several languages. And as always a special thanks in closing to Patrick Right, Jeanne Norberg, and Dr. Virginia Peden, whose friendship, love, and support have allowed me to share whatever gifts and talents I have with others. Muito obrigado!

Table of Contents

Preface:
Introduction to a Princess

In the summer of 1995, I was sent by Michigan State University to São Paulo, Brazil, to teach a graduate course in education at the international school there. Four days a week I taught my students, many of them Brazilian, in modern classrooms that looked out on gardens filled with flowers and large hummingbirds. On three-day weekends my wife and I explored the Brazil that the school's high walls and armed security hid from us.[1]

One of our weekend excursions was to Rio de Janeiro, and Petrópolis, a resort in the mountains north of the city. My fourth grade geography teacher first had introduced me to Brazil, Rio de Janeiro, and Petrópolis by describing a palace in Petrópolis that had been home to Brazil's last emperor. Her story of a European royal family fleeing war and then peacefully ruling the largest country in South America captured my young imagination and never let it go.[2]

Our mountain trip up the winding razorback roads to Petrópolis was an adventure in itself; but the fairy tale city, with its pink palace and picturesque gardens, were just as my fourth grade imagination had pictured it. A short walk from the palace stood a large Gothic church promising shade from the warm sun. In its cool, darkened interior we found the impressive tombs of Pedro II and Teresa Cristina, last emperor and empress of Brazil.

A steady stream of visitors made their way in and out of the church. They didn't stop at the altars or light candles or linger in front of the statues of Catholic saints. Instead, they quietly walked past the tombs of emperor and empress to a smaller tomb almost hidden in the shadows. There they prayed, laid flowers, and lovingly touched and kissed the carved figure on the sepulcher. Most of the pilgrims seemed to be poor and black, but all ages and shades of skin were represented.

When there was a small break in the procession, I walked back to the tomb. In marble almost obscured by flowers were carved the words "Princesa Isabel Christina, Leopoldina Augusta, A Redentora." I had no idea who this woman was or why she was the object of so much veneration. Outside the church I

1

found a street vendor selling post cards and cornstalk doll souvenirs. I asked him about Isabel. He smiled and told me, "Isabel is our redemptress." My confused expression must have told him I still didn't understand. He patiently explained in broken English, "In North America Abraham Lincoln freed the slaves, but in South America Princess Isabel freed us. She is Brazil's Abraham Lincoln."[3]

The next Monday my students wanted to know where we had traveled over our three-day weekend. I told them about our excursions to Rio de Janeiro and Petrópolis, and shared my story about our visit to the palace and church, and my conversation with the street vendor. My mention of Princess Isabel's name immediately sparked a strong emotional reaction among my Brazilian students.

"She was a bad woman! ... No! No! She was a good woman but didn't know her place... She was a tool of the Church and the Pope... No! No! Her French husband, not the Church, used her... She pretended to be a friend of the slaves and the poor, but used them to gain power for herself... No, she was an enemy of the army and wanted Brazil to be weak and powerless... Isabel championed the constitution, but was used by others to destroy it!"[4]

Patricia, the youngest and quietest student in my class, a nineteen-year-old teacher's aide, surprised everyone by offering her own opinion. It was nearly the first time we had heard her shy voice since the class began weeks earlier. In slow, halting English she declared Isabel "the greatest woman in Brazilian history." Her bold statement momentarily silenced her more talkative senior classmates.[5]

Seizing the moment, she explained, that like many others in the class, her first introduction to the princess was in school. Then she added, "People who learned about Isabel before Brazil's last military dictatorship viewed her one way; those who learned about the princess during the dictatorship years [1964–1985] saw her differently."[6]

Patricia continued. She had been a student *after* the fall of the last military dictatorship. Government-selected textbooks had always taught about the past through the lives of powerful men, but her teacher taught differently. She was a woman who taught history through the experiences of women, and the poor and powerless. As part of Patricia's course of study, she had to interview people from all walks of life to learn about Brazil through their eyes.[7]

In a voice that grew stronger, Patricia shared what she had learned from her interviews: "To many Brazilians who would never attend school or have their own stories appear in history books, no man or woman was greater than Princess Isabel. They learned of the princess not through books, but through the memories and hearts of their ancestors."[8]

I don't think Patricia's statements converted any of her classmates to the "Isabelist" cause, but her bold words transformed her in the eyes of her classmates. By the end of our heated discussion, I was happy to see that she had become a respected, valued, equal member of the class.

Patricia's minority position on Isabel further aroused my curiosity about the princess. I visited the international school library, then the library of the University of São Paulo, and many bookstores to learn about Isabel but found little if anything about her. I was told most books on Princesa Isabel had been removed during the twenty-one years of military rule and never replaced.[9]

Back at school, one of the administrators heard of my interest in Princess Isabel and asked if I would like to meet Isabel's great-great-granddaughter, an alumna of the international school where I was teaching. I quickly accepted the invitation and met Anna Luísa Orleans-Bragança on July 29, 1995, the only day we both had available. It turned out to be the one hundred forty-ninth anniversary of Princess Isabel's 1846 birth. Anna Luísa was an intelligent, attractive, modern career woman who edited one of Brazil's leading interior decorating magazines. I invited my class to join us and we spent a memorable afternoon as Anna Luísa shared family stories about her great-great-grandmother, who had died in 1921.[10] The first person I introduced Anna Luísa to was Patricia.

At the end of our visit Anna Luísa gave me the telephone number of her brother Luís Felipe in Boston and urged me to visit him if I wanted to learn more about Princess Isabel. That January, Luís Felipe and I met. I discovered his love of history and storytelling matched his sister's.[11] By the end of the Boston visit, I knew I wanted to tell Isabel's story. At the time I had no idea it would take over ten years of research, hundreds of hours of interviews, another trip to Brazil and two trips to Portugal before I would be able to piece together Isabel's story and those of other royal women who played significant roles in the rise and fall of Brazilian slavery.

In a biography of Anna Roosevelt Cowles, Teddy Roosevelt's remarkable sister, her friend Henry Adams wrote, "American history mentioned hardly the name of a woman, while English history handled them as timidly as though they were a new and undescribed species."[12] He might have also been speaking about women in Latin American history. I discovered in many ways their influence was as difficult to discover as someone in North America looking for the heavenly constellation of the Southern Cross. The stars of the constellation can't be seen by most people in the northern hemisphere without travel, effort, and a willingness to go above or below the familiar horizon.

Women, even royal women, are often invisible, just beyond the surface of history. If they are featured, they are too often dismissed or portrayed as caricatures in historic narratives. Most of the scant references I initially found on Isabel turned out to be distorted by a biased perspective or factually wrong.[13] She and other royal women were often mentioned only in footnotes, even in describing historic events in which they played the major role. My research revealed time, and again that women, are the nearly invisible strands holding the tapestry of history together.

On a recent trip to Brazil I visited dozens of large and small, modern and antiquarian, bookstores searching for anything I could find on Princess Isabel. I discovered dozens of books on the men in Isabel's royal family — even books on their mistresses — but only one Isabel biography, and it was critical and dismissive. Yet, Princess Isabel served as Brazil's head of state three separate times and was the national leader who signed the law abolishing slavery.[14] Everyone there knew her name and seemed to have a strong opinion about her, but few had any facts to support that opinion. She may be one of the best-known invisible women in history, the most famous of her family's invisible royal women.

In North America, dozens of books continue to be published every year on Abraham Lincoln, "the man that freed the slaves." Some are pro and some are con, but they are found everywhere. My search for the story of this Latin American abolitionist has been a frustrating but fascinating hunt for pieces of a surprising puzzle.[15]

Many people I spoke to, interviewed or corresponded with saw different Isabels — some believed her a saint, others a sinner. Some labeled her a traitor, others a dupe, some continued placing the mantle of redeemer on her shoulders.[16] She may be parts of all those things, but mostly the person who emerged from my research was an intelligent, thoughtful and headstrong woman — a daughter, wife, mother and princess trying to balance her responsibilities to family, church and country. Isabel was right about some things, wrong about others. But she was a consistently astute politician — a national leader who placed herself and her government squarely at the forefront of a popular revolution.[17]

To her enemies in nineteenth century politics, Princess Isabel was a dangerous woman — bright, independent and uncontrollable. If she were alive today, opponents would still consider her dangerous. I think that is one of the reasons her legend continues to live in Latin America; and part of the reason the person, the woman and the politician has been hidden or lost.

Slavery in America began and ended in Brazil. To tell the story of Isabel's role in ending slavery, the roles other royal women played in its beginnings had to also be told. Power brings out the best or worst in human nature. The history of slavery is a history of power — an abuse of power. In many ways slavery is about selective blindness, the coexistence of good and evil within people. Some recognized slavery for the evil it was; others ignored that evil. Some used the power they had to oppose human bondage; but a significant number of princes, priests, popes, kings and queens sincerely convinced themselves slavery was a good thing. They rationalized the good that came from slavery as outweighing the bad.

Early in my research I discovered the published diary of Thomas Ewbank, a North American traveler to Rio de Janeiro in 1846. His diary provided me with one of my first introductions to Isabel in his record of the joyful public reaction to her birth. "Yesterday a princess was born, and today hundreds are off to the São Cristóvão Palace; not only army and navy officers, priests, monks, and diplomats; but almost all that can raise a suitable dress, and hire or borrow a carriage for the occasion. The road is thronged with parties hasten-ing to leave their salutations for 'Her Serene Highness,' the Imperial Princess Dona Isabel Christina Leopoldina Augusta Michaela Gabriela Raphaela Bra-gança — a lady one day old!"[18]

Ewbank's eyewitness narrative also included a description of Rio de Janeiro's nearby slave market. The very week the city welcomed the addition of Princess Isabel as a member of Brazil's royal family, Ewbank wrote of the destruction of a slave family being sold at auction. His description of the appear-ance and mood of the doomed slaves provides a dramatic contrast to the rev-elers celebrating Isabel's royal birth.

> They were of every shade, from deep Angola jet to white or nearly white, as one young woman facing me appeared. She was certainly superior in mental organization than some of the buyers. The anguish with which she watched the proceedings, and waited her turn to be bought, exposed, examined, and disposed of was distressing.[19]
>
> A little girl, I suppose her own, stood by weeping, with one hand in her lap, obviously dreading to be taken away. This child did not cry out — this was not allowed, but tears chased each other down her cheeks. Her little bosom panted vio-lently, and such a look of alarm marked her face as she turned her large eyes on the proceedings that I thought at one time she would have dropped.[20]
>
> The head, eyes, mouth, hands, trunk, legs— every limb and ligament without are scrutinized, while, as aught within to be ruptured, the breast and other parts sounded.... One fact was most palpable — no more regard was paid the victims than if they had been so many horses.[21]

Ewbank's diary provided me with one of the common threads found throughout Princess Isabel's story. Her own life could not be separated, under-stood, or appreciated without placing it in the context of Brazilian slavery and the role of slavery in the lives of other royal men and women.[22]

It became impossible for me to understand or appreciate the life, deeds, choices and decisions of Princess Isabel in legally ending slavery in Brazil with-out also addressing the deeds of those men and women who brought slavery to the "new world."[23]

How other royals used power and the institution of slavery to achieve their personal and political goals is an important part of her story. This book attempts to tell some of that history. It begins and ends with exile. There is no other way to write about slavery.

It is my hope this book will foster further interest, research, dialogue and inclusion of women in history so that someday Stendhal's famous quote, "All geniuses born women are lost to the public good," can be forever relegated as a footnote in history books. I also hope the lives of the women and men found in these pages will help others like Patricia, my quiet Brazilian student, find the courage to use their own voices in the classroom and throughout their lives.

1

Exiles Under the Southern Cross

"It was a nightmare. We had not enough mattresses or blankets to go around, so most of us spent the cold nights in the stuffy hold. Water was our principle need; we thought about it all the time. The food became worse every day, and we had so little of it as to fear for our lives. In fact, our situation was so horrible that I could not wish it upon my worst enemy."[1]

The writer was one of thousands who fled Lisbon with the Portuguese royal family on the morning of November 29, 1807. Stiff winds filled the sails of their escaping fleet just as the invading army of Napoleon entered the city.[2] The last ship of the line was disabled by enemy cannon fire, causing the French general to "stamp his feet in rage" at how close he had come to capturing his prey.[3]

Thirty-nine years before her birth, Princess Isabel's family journeyed from Europe to Brazil as exiles, royal exiles. They traveled under the banner of Isabel's great-great-grandmother Queen Maria I with thousands of Portuguese nobility and their retainers. Never before in the history of western Europe had a monarch with her entire government sought refuge in a royal colony.

For three frustrating days winter winds and high seas forced the fleet to sail north away from Brazil. On the third night, winds shifted and the ships finally turned south. Many anxiously watched as the last tip of their homeland disappeared. As long as anyone could remember, the jagged outcroppings of Portugal's coast had been called "the end of the world." The name must have seemed painfully true to the fleeing exiles.[4]

After refueling in the Madeiras, the exiles sailed toward Brazil guided by the starry constellation of the Southern Cross. For nearly two months they would not see land again. Ten thousand people crowded onto a fleet of thirty-six ships.[5] Most had never traveled more than a few hours from the place of their birth. Half their luggage, most of their families, and all of their memories remained in Portugal.

The royal flagship built for three hundred passengers carried eleven hundred men, women, and children.[6] Fierce winter storms followed by the stillness of the equatorial doldrums provided contrasting nightmares. Hunger, thirst, seasickness, dysentery, lice, fear and uncertainty traveled with the homesick exiles during the three-thousand-mile voyage.[7]

Claustrophobic conditions on the ships made it appear the decision to flee had been a spontaneous one, but the evacuation had been carefully planned. Queen Maria's son acting as regent decided on the night of November 24 to put prearranged plans into action. By the morning of November 29 despite heavy rains the entire machinery of Portugal's government had been dismantled and packed into the ships, and sailed with the royal family.[8]

Periodic proposals for moving the seat of the vast Portuguese empire from Europe to America had been made for over two centuries. Napoleon's invading army made political rhetoric a military necessity.[9]

In early November, Prince Regent João discovered that Napoleon planned to invade Portugal, depose its royal family, and partition the country.[10] A French army soon crossed the Portuguese frontiers looting farms and towns, monasteries, churches and cathedrals on their way to Lisbon. The escape plan to Brazil was immediately implemented.[11]

A "previously prepared diagram of the number, size, and location of rooms available in the fleet" was matched with pre-selected people and artifacts to be evacuated.[12] Inventories of "everything belonging to the ministry of state" had been prepared. Thirty-seven large boxes were quickly filled to remove all "papers, books, maps and prints."[13] Movable assets including the treasury, the contents of the royal library, the royal chapel and even horses from royal stables were rushed to waiting ships.

Included in the packing was a new printing press. Queen Maria's government had never before allowed the colony of Brazil to print its own books or newspapers. A month earlier the secretary of state for overseas dominions forbade Portuguese ships in Brazilian harbors to sail home. His order saved the merchant fleet for the future use of the crown.[14]

The escape was accomplished with a minimum loss of life. No ships were lost during the crossing, but those experiencing the journey remembered it with horror. Still there is no record, no single letter or diary entry, showing that any of the passengers connected their own terrible experience with the sufferings of the millions of African slaves the Portuguese crown had exiled to Brazil. Now they too had become exiles under the Southern Cross but without the chains, whips and branded flesh.

Three hundred years earlier, Portuguese seafarers became the first Europeans to visit Brazil. They were financed in part by Portugal's wealthiest slave trader, Bartholomew Marchionni, the first recorded person in history to label America "a new world."[15] Brazil was named for the rare brazil wood found there that made the voyage profitable. Its great harbor was designated Guanabara or "arm of the sea" and its crystal-like sand beaches Copacabana or "luminous place." The city that grew there was named the River of January or Rio de Janeiro because the bay was discovered on January 1, 1500. Brazil's temperate climate below the equator and safe harbors soon became a welcome destination for weary travelers crossing the cold Atlantic.[16]

Brazil beckoned adventurers, missionaries, immigrants, artisans, craftsmen, musicians, planters, merchants, and eventually even kings and queens. Its reputation as a safe haven became famous. Many emigrants and exiles looked toward Brazil as a golden paradise — a land of opportunity. But the arrival of Europeans made the native peoples exiles in their own land. And for Africans, Brazil became one more destination in a nightmare world of slavery, betrayal, exile and death.

Inland legends of gold and diamonds taunted the Portuguese, but thick rain forests, rugged highlands and uncharted rivers blocked interior exploration. For centuries, the Portuguese depended on slaves to do their work. Brazil's native population seemed a natural source for slave labor, but the Catholic Church stood in their way. The pope viewed Brazilian natives as potential converts to the faith.[17]

Jesuit missionaries were dispatched to Brazil. Given the choice of settling on Jesuit run plantations or being hunted down and killed by the Portuguese invaders, many natives embraced baptism. As newly converted Catholics, they were placed under the protection of the Church beyond the control of the state. King João III of Portugal did what he often did when his political goals were frustrated — he turned to his queen for help. As often happened in Portuguese history, the queen, the cross and slavery offered a solution to the crown's problems.

2

"Swords from the Hands of a Woman"

Portugal's queens often came from other countries, sacrificed as hostages in dynastic marriages, pawns of political or military alliances among suspicious rivals. At the time Portugal decided to colonize Brazil, the queen of Portugal was Catherine of Austria. Some dynastic marriages worked, others did not. The marriage of João III and Catherine of Austria was considered successful. The king was not known for his intelligence or diplomatic skills, qualities synonymous with his queen. Catherine, a stealthy politician and diplomat, dedicated her considerable skills and talent to the service of Portugal. She was the king's closest adviser, wise enough to never flaunt her domination over him or his government.[1]

Catherine was not the first wife or queen whose influence changed the course of a family or a nation's history. It was the encouragement of an earlier Portuguese queen that paved the way for the country's initial involvement with the African slave trade. Philippa of Lancaster, the formidable granddaughter of the Plantagenet kings of England, was sent to Portugal to marry João I. Under the leadership of her husband, and with the support of her family, Portugal freed itself from Castilian domination.[2] The queen brought discipline, order and the code of medieval chivalry to the Portuguese court.[3] She also fueled her son's belief that it was their Christian duty to invade Moorish north Africa.[4]

Philippa presented them swords to fight and enslave the African Moors. Prior to their sailing to Africa she told them, "I give this sword with my blessing and that of your grandparents from whom I descend. Though it be strange for knights to take swords from the hands of a woman, I ask you not to object, for, because of my lineage and the will which I have for the increase of your honor, I think no harm can come to you by it. Nay, rather I believe that my blessing and that of my ancestors will be of great help to you."[5]

Philippa's sons and a Bragança stepson returned from Africa with gold, ivory, spices and "shiploads" of African slaves."[6] The swords brought Portugal wealth, power, and prestige, but not the honor she sought.

Prince Henry the Navigator, fourth of Philippa's five sons, knew he would never sit on the Portuguese throne. Without a crown of his own, a wife or children, he focused his passions and ambitions elsewhere.[7] The capture in 1415 of the African city of Ceuta was for him only the first step in creating a great Portuguese empire. For the rest of his life he relentlessly pushed for further exploration and conquest of the west coast of Africa. The slaves he captured and sold helped pay for his expeditions, but his ambitions proved costly. After the death of his mother, his father discouraged further African adventures fearing they would bring disaster to Portugal. With little personal wealth of his own, Henry's dreams of Africa seemed doomed.

In 1433, King João I died, bringing his oldest son Duarte to the throne and renewing the hopes of Prince Henry. He flew to his brother "like a falcon," but Duarte also feared Africa.[8] He asked members of the court and the Holy See to put into writing the pros and cons of future African wars. Their responses revealed that Prince Henry's plans had "almost unanimous opposition at court." Even Church lawyers rejected claims such wars were "just."[9]

Henry refused to be discouraged and quietly began courting Duarte's wife Leonora of Aragon as an ally.[10] The king had never been in robust health, and many believed his Spanish born wife would outlive him. Nine years of marriage produced eight children. Five survived; but they were all young, leaving the foreign born queen vulnerable if the king died.[11]

Leonora's constant pregnancies and Spanish birth kept her isolated, with few friends or allies at court. Henry offered protection, friendship and to make Leonora's second son his heir if she would embrace his cause.[12] A first son could become king, but a second son would inherit little without a royal sponsor. Henry promised a rich inheritance, "all his possessions," but his wealth depended on African conquests and expanding the slave trade.[13] With Leonora's support for his "explorations," he pledged to serve as her protector and her son's benefactor.

Leonora of Aragon became a powerful advocate for further expeditions to Africa, gathering a war party around her to lobby the king. For two years Leonora, Henry and their supporters worked to wear down Duarte's opposition. Finally during the difficult delivery of another royal child, Leonora extracted a promise from her comforting husband to support Henry's voyages.[14] If Henry the Navigator was the father of the African slave trade, Leonora was its midwife.

Duarte's new Portuguese invasion of Africa ended in disaster at the gates of Tangier.[15] Henry's youngest brother Fernando was taken hostage. The demanded ransom was the surrender of the African port of Ceuta. Despite intense negotiations Fernando's "piteous appeals to his brothers" went unanswered. Portugal's war party refused to surrender the city. The youngest son of João I and Queen Philippa died in a Moorish prison.[16] Even a royal brother could not compete with the African ambitions of Prince Henry and Queen Leonora.

Shortly after the Tangier debacle, five unhappy years after he ascended the throne, the dispirited Duarte died, elevating Leonora to queen regent in the name of their first-born son.[17] Prince Henry rallied to her side, as did his half brother Afonso, the count of Bragança. Despite the support of her two brothers-in-law, Leonora's Spanish birth and fears of foreign influence undermined her position. Portuguese nationalists wanted the regency passed to Pedro, the royal brother closest in age to the dead king. The death of the king, shifting public opinion, political uncertainty and riots in Lisbon caused a suspension of Henry's African expeditions.[18]

Pedro suggested that Henry and the Count of Bragança would have no regrets if they supported his regency over that of the queen. The message and threat were clear and Leonora found herself abandoned. Without the protection of her brothers-in-law, deprived of access to her children, she was forced to flee to Spain.[19] Once there, she was promptly murdered.[20] For his assistance in helping depose of the inconvenient queen, Prince Henry's plans of African conquest became the cornerstone of Portugal's foreign policy.[21] It would remain so for centuries, paid for in part by the blood of the African slave trade.[22]

Leonora's body was returned to Portugal to be buried next to her late husband in the royal burial vaults of Batalha. Like the abbreviated lives of the dead king and murdered queen, the tombs were never finished. The uncles who destroyed the lives of his parents raised the orphaned prince who became known as "Afonso the African" for his firm commitment to Africa and its slave trade.[23]

Nearly a century after the death of Prince Henry, Portugal's King João III and Catherine of Austria continued seeing slavery as a solution to the throne's problems. African slaves made up ten percent of their court, many "purchased" by the queen or given to her as gifts.[24] Other royals, even political and military rivals, accepted slavery as the natural order of the universe. Catherine's brother Charles, emperor elect of the Holy Roman Empire, was also the king of Spain. In that position, he found himself Portugal's neighbor and rival in both Europe and Latin America. The rival brothers-in-law shared not only a relationship with Catherine but also a firm belief that slave labor was essential to maintain their American empires.

Despite the Catholic Church's interdict against enslaving America's indigenous population and a similar ban from Spain's Queen Isabella in 1503, following her death, enslavement of Amerindians spread from the Spanish Caribbean islands to the mainland.[25] Over five million died in the process, mostly through disease, causing an ever-rising demand for slaves and the displeasure of the pope.[26] The Catholic Church, however, was in a weakened position as it struggled with the Protestant Reformation in northern Europe, an armed Muslim invasion in eastern Europe, and ongoing political and military conflicts with Charles V.[27] The Church continued condemning slavery, but failed to enforce mandates against nations, kings, emperors or priests supporting it.[28]

Bartolomé de las Casas, a priest in the court of Charles V, was a powerful

advocate of protecting the dwindling Amerindian population by the importation of African slaves.[29] Sending African slaves, many of them Muslim, to America appealed to the military, political, economic and spiritual instincts of Charles
V. For centuries Christians and Muslims used slavery as a weapon in the wars
they fought across Europe, the Mediterranean and the Holy Land.[30] To Charles,
exiling Muslim slaves to America worked to the benefit of all. It eased labor
problems in his struggling colonies, saved New World Christians from slavery,
removed thousands of Islamic infidels from Europe's door and provided their
souls with their only possible chance at redemption and salvation.[31]

Just fifty-seven years earlier, Spain's Queen Isabella and King Ferdinand
had captured one of the last great Moorish cities on the Iberian Peninsula. At
that time, over four thousand Muslim slaves in Europe were exchanged for a
similar number of enslaved Christians in Africa. Four thousand additional
Muslim slaves were sold to pay war debts. And regardless of Church teachings
another four thousand were presented as gifts "throughout Christendom...—
a hundred went to Pope Innocent VIII, fifty girls were sent to the queen of
Naples and thirty to the queen of Portugal."[32] Isabella lined the massive walls
of the church where she planned to be buried with chains removed from Christian slaves. The heavy shackles remain in Toledo today, a reminder to Christian Europe of the role Isabella played in ending Islamic enslavement. In the
first half of the fifteenth century, when João III ruled Portugal and Charles V
ruled Spain and much of central Europe, the subcontinent remained an armed
fortress surrounded to the south and east by powerful Islamic enemies.

The problem confronting Charles was not the Church's condemnation of
slavery, but the trading monopoly it had granted Portugal in 1452. That year,
Pope Nicholas V gave Prince Henry the Navigator and the Portuguese exclusive trading monopolies for all commercial goods taken from west Africa[33]—
the primary "goods" exported being enslaved men, women and children.[34] A
traveler to Lisbon in 1466 wrote that the Portuguese king made more money
buying and selling slaves "than from all the taxes levied in the entire kingdom."[35]

It was this trading monopoly that stood in the way of Spain's plans to send
African slaves to America. Then a surprise alliance was announced. Portugal
agreed to supply slaves, and the ships to carry those slaves, directly from Africa
to Spanish America.[36] The quiet influence and diplomacy of Catherine was
believed to be the force behind an agreement that on the surface seemed to
favor Spain, but in reality most benefited Portugal. Within a few years, Portuguese bankers and slave traders dominated large portions of the economy of
Spanish America. By 1588, frustrated observers in Buenos Aires reported the
daily arrival of "Portuguese vessels ... with blacks and merchandise."[37]

Portugal continued to grow rich through the slave trade. Spain had its
slaves but its chief rival came to control a major portion of Spanish America's
economy. In the process Brazil became the destination for four out of ten

African slaves sent to America.[38] Perhaps only the Austrian queen of Portugal could have brought all the pieces together for such an alliance; but even royalty could not control the future. Only one of Catherine's nine children, one sickly son, lived to marry. And he died before the birth of his own sickly son. Nineteen years later the death of Catherine's only grandson witnessed the violent end of her royal dynasty. It ended where so much of the wealth of Portugal and the royal family came from — Africa. Portugal's unmarried king Sebastião and the cream of his country's nobility were massacred in a disastrous 1578 African invasion. Not even that tragedy weakened Portugal's insatiable appetite for Africa and its slaves.

The death of the king and so many nobles destabilized the country, bringing Isabel's family a step closer to the throne. Since the ascension of João I in 1385, the Braganças had been related to all of Portugal's monarchs but had never worn the crown themselves. Following Sebastião's death, and that of his sixty-eight-year-old bachelor uncle two years later, the Portuguese throne sat empty. No one in Portugal had a stronger claim to it than Catherine Bragança, a royal niece married to her own royal cousin, the sixth Duke of Bragança.

Many Portuguese supported Catherine as their queen, but her cousin Phillip II of Spain did not. He believed his gender and the fact that both his mother and first wife had been princesses of Portugal gave him the right to the crown.[39] Phillip tried persuading Catherine and the nation's nobles to support his candidacy with generous bribes and ominous threats. At one point, he offered her the throne of an independent Brazil, but she refused to relinquish her claim. Phillip then took crown and country by force, boasting, "I inherited it. I paid for it. And I conquered it."[40]

Catherine remained the Duchess of Bragança, retaining her wealth, lands and titles. She brought the Braganças closer to the throne than at any time in their long history. Three more kings and sixty years of Spanish occupation passed until 1640 and opportunity presented itself.[41] In that year civil war in northeastern Spain forced Phillip III to focus his attentions there. To rule Portugal in his place, he appointed another formidable cousin, Margaret of Habsburg. Many believed the time for Portuguese independence had arrived, but Catherine's grandson João did not. Since Sebastião's death, the Braganças were the first family of the land, the hope of the future. The current duke of Bragança did not believe the future had arrived, but his wife did.

Luísa, Duchess of Bragança, believed she was born to rule. As a descendent of a long line of Spanish nobility who had fought the Moors for centuries, she used every opportunity to convince her husband to lead the fight for independence. The duke feared losing the peaceful life he relished, but it was too late. His wife offered him no peace until he agreed to lend his name and prestige to the revolt against the Spanish.[42]

On December 1, 1640, Portuguese troops under the Bragança family banner stormed the Lisbon palace of the Spanish viceroy. Margaret of Habsburg was arrested, her secretary of state killed, her bodyguards scattered. In an elaborate, but hasty ceremony the Duke of Bragança was proclaimed João IV of Portugal. Not since the last Portuguese king had there been a royal coronation. Tradition dictated only the king, not his queen, be crowned. The irony must not have been lost on Luísa or the Portuguese nobles. Regardless of the ceremonies, Spain promptly declared war.

At the time of the revolution, an English traveler observed, "The King is an honest plain man, changing nothing of the Duke of Bragança by being king of Portugal ... but for the Queen, she has more of the majestic in her, and if she be not king, her ambition 'twas that made the king.'"[43] During his entire

Portrait of Luísa de Gusmão (1613–1666) at the time she became the queen of Portugal. Luísa gained the throne of Portugal for her husband and two of her sons, the throne of England for her daughter, and Brazilian exile, slavery, and death for thousands of African slaves. Courtesy the Catholic University of America, Oliveira Lima Library, Washington, D.C.

reign of sixteen years, the peace loving João IV never knew a day without war. Portugal found itself fighting Spain for independence, and the Dutch for the rest of the Portuguese empire including Brazil.[44]

On November 15, 1656, João died, leaving his wife, three children, and a country at war. He had fathered seven children but only three survived. His oldest child Catherine provided the Braganças the best opportunity to gain an alliance through a royal marriage. Afonso, his thirteen-year-old son, was physically and mentally weak. Few expected him to live to adulthood. The future of the dynasty rested on João's third child, Pedro, a healthy eight-year-old boy.

Luísa, queen regent in Afonso's name, was determined to achieve Portugal's independence and maintain its overseas control of Brazil's sugar trade, Asia's spice trade, and Africa's slave trade. She denied opponents an opportunity to exploit her Spanish birth by becoming more Portuguese than the Portuguese.[45] Even her allies conceded she "delighted in authority," but her enemies declared, "[she became] ... so much the state ... she almost ceased to be human."[46]

She worked tirelessly to win by marital diplomacy what she was unable to achieve on the battlefield. Following years of revolution and Puritan rule in England, the restoration of its monarchy caused Luísa to intensify her efforts. A successful royal marriage with its new king Charles II might tip the balance of power toward Portugal. When he reclaimed the throne in 1661, Charles was in need of a wife, a queen, and money. Luísa promised her twenty-three-year-old daughter would provide him all three. Catherine of Bragança arrived in England on May 13, 1662, to marry a man she had never met. She was an intelligent, well-educated, convent-bred princess who spoke no English. Charles was a worldly survivor who spoke no Portuguese.

After a difficult period of adjustment culminating in the bride's acceptance of her husband's many mistresses and thirteen illegitimate children, a workable marriage developed. Charles thought his wife a good woman. She proved to be loving and loyal to her new family and country, and smart enough to hide her intelligence at a time feminine intellect was perceived as a threat.[47] Politically and financially she supported her husband in all endeavors, including expansion of England's slave trade that had begun years earlier under the reign and sponsorship of Elizabeth I.[48] By the time Catherine arrived there, "virtually every black in Britain was a product of the African slave trade."[49]

She brought to England the custom of drinking tea and a dowry of $2,000,000 in hard currency, British trading privileges in South America and the ports of Bombay in Asia and Tangier in Africa.[50] Tangier had cost Portugal the death of a prince, but Luísa handed the city to the English as a wedding present. It was the largest dowry in the history of Europe, paid in part by a special levy on Lisbon's slave traders.[51] Sixty-two years later, twelve years after Catherine's death, it was still being paid.[52] To Portugal's queen regent, the loss of an only daughter and the dowry was worth the cost.[53] Having the king of England as a son-in-law promised to help Portugal finally gain its independence.[54]

The year Catherine Bragança traveled to England her sickly brother Afonso turned nineteen. Partial paralysis hobbled his movements and his mental growth and emotional maturity remained stunted. Most doubted his ability to govern or continue the dynasty. Still, he was alive and, since his father's death, legally king. His mother Luisa ruled only through his name. With Portugal's independence within her grasp, Luisa became increasingly fearful of her simpleminded son. For the good of all concerned, she decided he must never rule.

As Luísa plotted to change heirs to the throne, finance her daughter's dowry and continue Portugal's war for independence, help appeared from an unexpected source. In January 1662, the famed Jesuit Antônio Vieira preached a powerful sermon in the royal chapel echoing the spirited diatribes that once made Bartolomé de las Casas so influential at the Spanish court. Vieira, born in Portugal but raised in Brazil, had a well-deserved reputation for making the scriptures bend to his will.[55]

Enslavement of the new world Christians was driving them to extinction, he thundered; only the increased importation of African slaves could save Brazil's indigenous peoples. The power of his sermon seemed to inspire Luísa, but she may have been as attracted to his African solution as she was by the plight of her Indian subjects. Since the time of Prince Henry the Navigator, one fifth of the sale and *resale* of every African slave went directly to the crown. Almost as an answer to prayers, a man of God had once again come to the aid of the crown offering the chains of slavery as a solution to its problems.

Portugal had long since lost its slave trade monopoly, but it still maintained historic and geographic advantages over other slave trading nations such as Spain, France, Denmark and even her son-in-law's England. The center of the slave trade had gradually moved south of the equator toward Angola, a movement caused in part by repeated colonial slave uprisings led by Islamic slaves. The non–Islamic Africans of the south seemed more willing, at least outwardly, to adapt to the rituals of the Christian faith.[56] Luísa and the Portuguese continued believing the forced baptism of slaves not only saved the spiritual lives of those in chains, but somehow cleansed the souls of the slaveholders in the process.

Religion provided a moral veneer justifying slavery. Vieira was only the latest in a long line of churchmen who found scriptural and spiritual justification where none existed. In one of his most famous sermons he proclaimed, "When I compare the present with the future, time with eternity, that which I see with that which I believe, I cannot accept the idea that God, who created these people as much in His own image as He did the rest of us, would have predestined them for two hells, one in this life and another in the next. But when I see them so devout and festive before the altars of Our Lady of the Rosary, all brothers together and the children of the same Lady, I am convinced beyond any doubt that the captivity of the first transmigration is ordained by her compassion so that they may be granted freedom in the second."[57]

Physical salvation also mattered to the Portuguese, especially when it came to safeguarding profits. By the 1600s royal decrees had been issued to protect all aspects of the slave trade. The numbers of captives carried in each ship, their food, drink and exercise requirements, were all specified and carefully supervised, reducing the middle passage death toll to one in five slaves.[58] To the crown, and other investors, a twenty-percent loss seemed acceptable. It was the same loss sustained by the sailors transporting the slaves.

Luísa's late husband had attempted to curb the slave trade by renegotiating long-standing treaties with African kings and queens.[59] Luísa reversed his policies.[60] A priest assigned to the royal court noted it had once taken traders three weeks to travel to the interior of Africa to find slaves for Brazil — now it took three months.[61] To Luísa the extra effort was worth the trouble.

The spiritual benefits of saving souls, sweetened by the practical benefit of increased revenues, proved to Luísa and others the ancient adage that the end justifies the means. Luísa's oldest son used similar reasoning to seize the throne from her. In 1662 he demanded she immediately surrender the crown to him. He abandoned the palace they had shared, set up a rival court, and threatened to take his birthright by force. Civil war seemed inevitable. Dueling letters were exchanged with competing salutations and signatures. Luísa addressed Afonso as "Most High and Mighty Prince" and signed herself "I, the Queen."[62] He addressed her as "Most High and Mighty Queen of Portugal" but signed his letters "The King."[63]

Luísa used all her considerable powers of persuasion to convince Afonso to meet with her, but he refused. Fearing civil war would cost Portugal its independence, Luísa surrendered and was soon imprisoned. In time she was banished to a distant convent where she died after a lingering illness.[64] In the last weeks of her life she begged to see her sons, but neither visited. She died without the physical chains and violence of African slaves, but like them she ended her life an exile — separated from family, friends, and home — buried away from all she loved.

One of her last public acts was to negotiate a marriage for her elder son with Maria Francisca of Savoy, Princess of Nemours, niece of King Louis XIV of France. The marriage may have been a cynical attempt to wrest Afonso's birthright from him since his infertility would inevitably give his younger brother the throne. Maria Francisca initially refused to marry "a paralyzed idiot," but the decision was not hers. France's powerful Sun King approved the proxy marriage in 1666, the year Luísa died.[65] Portugal's new queen had much in common with the mother-in-law she never met. They both had strong ideas on what was best for themselves, for others, and their adopted country.

The French princess was assured she would quickly dominate Afonso and Portugal.[66] The predictions proved correct. Within two years Afonso's frustrated inability to consummate the marriage allowed Maria to have the marriage annulled, and her husband declared insane, imprisoned and exiled. She soon married his younger brother Pedro, and through him ruled Portugal.[67] Despite the public embarrassment, hard work, and the expenditure of considerable energy, she believed everything had worked out for the best. As queen, she continued the policies begun by her dead mother-in-law, including pursuing the African slave trade.

Afonso VI was eventually confined to the mountain palace of Sintra. History remembers him as Afonso the Victorious because during his brief unhappy reign, Portugal finally won its war for independence. He is also remembered for the path he wore on the stone floor of his tiny cell, restlessly pacing back and forth the last nine years of his life.

Sintra, Afonso's place of exile, was the palace where Prince Henry first proposed invading Africa. Its oldest portions dated to the time of Moorish rule, but nearly all the Portuguese monarchs left their imprint on the ancient palace. Even today the roof of its great entrance hall is painted with one hundred and thirty-six magpies dating from the reign of Queen Philippa and João I. The beak of each pestering bird holds a banner with the royal motto—"Por Bem"—"For the Good."[68] In the final moments of his freedom the magnificent roof may have been the last sight Afonso VI saw before being led away to his cell. The motto captured the noble goal of Afonso, his wife, his mother, and other kings, queens, princes and slave traders, who struggled to do what was best in deciding the fate of others.

Over the centuries Portugal's kings and queens came and went, but the slavery they brought to Brazil endured. When the court fled to America in the winter of 1807-1808, the neglect and blind ambitions of Maria's royal ancestors confronted the startled eyes of the Portuguese.

3

"It Is Impossible
to Rule Innocently"

None of Princess Isabel's royal ancestors could have imagined the world they discovered sailing into Brazil's Guanabara Bay on March 7, 1808.[1] Nor could they have dreamed of the undercurrents tugging at them from all sides. Royalty born to absolute rule and others born to serve them had been the foundation of their lives for centuries; but those foundations were crumbling.[2]

In Haiti, the largest slave revolt in the history of the Americas had driven France out of the Caribbean in 1804. Following twenty years of debate, the English parliament in 1807 passed a law ending the British slave trade over the objections of their own king. That same year the Catholic Church canonized its first black saint.[3] And in 1808 the new republican government of the United States headed by Thomas Jefferson outlawed the slave trade to North America.[4] Jefferson was the third elected president of his nation, deriving his power not from divine right, but from a written constitution and the citizens who elected him.[5]

Thousands of miles to Thomas Jefferson's south, Isabel's ancestors sailed past the dragon teethed mountains guarding the sleepy city of Rio de Janeiro. Their world must have seemed turned upside down. Still one woman held the entire entourage, the government, and royal family together. She was Her Most Faithful Majesty, Maria, Francesca, Isabel, Josepha, Antônia, Gertrude, Rita, Joanna Bragança, the queen of Portugal. To many of her fellow travelers it was Maria's divine right as a hereditary monarch and as the head of the royal family that legitimatized the transfer of the Portuguese government to America.

Like Portuguese royalty for well over a century, Maria was designated a princess of Brazil at birth, but she was the first of her family and the first European monarch to visit America. As the oldest of four royal sisters with no living brother, she was also the first woman to rule Portugal in her own name. Her entire life, she had made history.[6]

Maria's father had been His Most Faithful Majesty José I and her mother Queen Maria Victoria of the Spanish Bourbons. As a child Maria showed signs of exceptional intelligence but was not provided the education expected of a royal heir because of her gender. Still, she loved to study and showed a special talent for music and the visual arts. She was sixteen when her father became king, but was kept from involvement in affairs of state by order of the prime minister.[7]

Prime Minister Pombal, the Machiavellian dictator of Portugal, plotted to have Maria's son usurp her position in the line of royal succession, but he underestimated his opponent. Although not personally or politically ambitious, Maria saved her birthright by making a forceful personal appeal to her father, effectively ending attempts to change the royal succession.[8] In 1777, a year after the American colonies declared their independence, José I died and his forty-two-year-old daughter Maria Bragança became queen. It was a time of high hope and great achievements for women rulers. Catherine the Great was empress of Russia and Maria Theresa, empress of the Holy Roman Empire.

Maria, promising to "govern with peace and justice," quickly ordered the release of hundreds of Pombal's political prisoners. Young boys imprisoned in their youth stumbled onto the streets as old men. So many ghostly captives emerged that the Spanish ambassador wrote the scene was reminiscent of the "resurrection of the dead."[9]

Twenty-four hours after the death of the king, for the first time in twenty-seven years Pombal was refused entrance to the royal palace.[10] He was respectfully informed, "Your Excellency no longer has anything to do here."[11] The queen's dismissal of the feared prime minister triggered a public outburst of suppressed rage.[12] Despite calls for his arrest, she merely banished him to the humble village of his birth where he died in his own bed.

Maria's coronation on May 13, 1777, provoked a genuine outpouring of emotion. Crowds overwhelmed guards and tumbled through barriers to see and touch their queen.[13] Years later, Maria remembered the celebration as the happiest day of her life. A poet wrote of the event:

> A dawn of brightest ray has boldly promised the returning day
> of Lisbon's honors, fairer than her prime...
> now Heaven-taught Science and her liberal band
> of Arts, and dictates by experience plann'd,
> beneath the smile of a benign Queen
> boast the fair opening of a reign serene.[14]

Many of Pombal's most capable administrators were kept in office, but Maria appointed a new prime minister "of irreproachable character and moderation" to supervise them.[15] She also purged the harshest sections of Portugal's criminal codes, ending many of Pombal's most repressive policies.

The ascension of the new queen raised hopes for better times. Maria did not disappoint, reigning with humanity, moderation, and common sense.[16] For most Portuguese it was a time of unparalleled peace and prosperity, creating the foundations for an emerging middle class.[17] Her handpicked prime minister strengthened Portugal's finances, cut expenditures, paid off the national debt, and reversed the country's crippling balance of trade deficit. The Portuguese affectionately proclaimed the "golden reign of Dona Maria I."[18] The court emerged as a dazzling center of energy, activity, and culture. One contemporary wrote, "Everything was done with great magnificence, great profusion, good taste, and good order.[19] Music was at the center of all royal events. The world's best operas, the finest musicians and singers, all performed there."[20]

Music, flowers and visual spectacles became the order of the day. In 1780 a visitor described "one hundred and fifty illuminations, fourteen dozen stars, eight dozen vases of flowers, ten containers of sparklers, one hundred flying diamonds, twelve dozen pistols, sixty dozen mortars, and two hundred flying bombs ... Ninety eight large lanterns, one hundred twenty-eight small lanterns, and one hundred thirty round lamps" illuminating the royal gardens.[21]

Portugal's queen promoted the arts, education, and the sciences. She founded the Royal Public Library, the Royal Academy of Science, the Royal Naval Academy, and the Royal Academy of Fortifications, Artillery, and Design. She encouraged expeditions to "record the natural history of the Amazon, Angola, and Mozambique" and funded charities devoted to the poorest of the poor, the nation's widows and orphans.[22] In 1778 she traveled to the Spanish-Portuguese border to sign an economic, political and military treaty with her uncle Charles III to ensure peace between the longtime rivals. Maria I was determined to be a peacemaker. During the American Revolution, Portugal remained neutral. Despite strong pressure from England and intense lobbying from the persuasive Benjamin Franklin, Maria held firm. With Catherine the Great of Russia, she signed an alliance keeping both nations at peace when much of Europe was at war. Portugal's neutrality provided her subjects a rare respite from the violence plaguing their history.

Maria Bragança was loved and admired for the peace, stability, and prosperity she brought to her country. But like her royal ancestors, she believed Brazil and other colonies were meant to serve Portugal, not the other way around.[23] Colonies were heavily taxed and their economies tightly controlled from Lisbon. At one point Maria ordered Brazilian looms capable of creating cloth and linens destroyed to keep the colony dependent on Portuguese manufacturing.[24] Her refusal to help her cousin King George III of England fight his own rebellious colonies did not mean that she would tolerate financial or political independence from her own.

During the early years of her reign an English visitor recorded his impressions of the young queen: "She looks born to command; but at the same time to make the high authority as much beloved as respected. Justice and clemency, the motto so glaringly misapplied on the banner of the abhorred Inquisition, might be transferred with the strictest truth to this good princess. During the fatal contest betwixt England and its colonies, the wise neutrality she persevered in maintaining was of the most vital benefit to her dominions ... hitherto, the native commerce of Portugal has attained under her mild auspices an unprecedented degree of prosperity."[25]

Maria's commitment to peace and prosperity did not extend to Brazil's slaves. Pombal abolished slavery in Portugal in 1773, but neither he nor Maria curbed Brazilian slavery. During her years as queen the importation of slaves to Brazil actually reached an all time high.[26] Brazil's need for additional slaves never ebbed because new slaves were needed to replace those worked to death.[27] Slave suicides, matricide, and self-induced abortions continually reduced the slave population. Like many Portuguese monarchs before her, Maria increased government revenues by expanding the importation of slaves.[28] Portugal's prosperity continued to be built on the backs of Brazilian slaves.

Despite her support of slavery, Maria condemned racism, and included African and mixed-raced attendants as members of her court.[29] During her father's reign, Pombal declared, "His Majesty does not distinguish between his vassals by their color, but by their merits." Maria shared his sentiments. Portugal made it a criminal offense to call persons of color "Niggers, Mestizos, and any other insulting opprobrious names."[30] The law was one of the first anti-hate acts ever legally mandated.

Maria also encouraged her church to recruit, educate, and ordain clergy of all races.[31] African or mixed race priests, brothers, monks, and even bishops were found in Portugal, Brazil, and other Portuguese colonies. In Lisbon, the first promotions to the "learned professions" for men of mixed racial heritages took place during her reign.[32]

Efforts to model tolerance, rule wisely, and reverse Pombal's most reactionary policies did not prevent Portugal's colonies from becoming restless after the successful republican revolutions of North American and France. When similar revolts broke out in Portuguese colonies, Maria's government crushed them unmercifully. In Brazil six leaders of a republican rebellion were condemned to death. Five were eventually exiled to Africa. Only one was executed, but his execution was gruesomely horrific. After being publicly hung, then beheaded, and drawn and quartered, his mutilated body was displayed throughout the colony.[33]

Such punishments were rare, but they troubled Maria's conscience, recalling unpleasant truths she had uncovered about her father.[34] Shortly after becoming queen an investigation into the ministry of her old enemy Pombal revealed the king's approval for everything undertaken by the prime minister. Whatever good and bad had been done during his reign was under the king's signature duly stamped by his personal seal. Maria was shaken by the findings. Clemency for her old enemy allowed a cover-up of her father's role in a number of unsavory events. A summary report issued in her name found Pombal "culpable and deserving of exemplary punishment, which however I do not order to be executed in view of his present grave illnesses and decrepit age ... and also because the Marquêse has begged for pardon and execrated the temerarious excesses he has committed.[35] A public trial would have destroyed her father's reputation.

She ordered the commemorative medallion of Pombal removed from the base of the magnificent monument dedicated to her father in Lisbon's main square, but she could not erase the memory of her father's role in Pombal's abuses of power. Her conscience continued to trouble her as she signed government decrees fearing she would be "condemned to very hell" for approving many of them.[36]

In 1786 Maria's life began to unravel. Her devoted husband died unexpectedly of a massive stroke.[37] The following year a smallpox epidemic struck Portugal. No disease was more feared in Europe. At the time only West Africans understood the power of vaccination in preventing the painful disfigurement and death caused by the disease. Portugal's royal family was offered the opportunity for inoculation practiced by Brazilian slaves, but the queen refused. One of Lisbon's first victims was her oldest son — heir to the throne. A sister also died. Then the queen's prime minister, her priest confessor, and dozens of attendants and court officials. Death claimed her uncle, King Charles III of Spain, and his favorite son and his daughter-in-law, Maria's own daughter and the only grandson she shared with the Spanish king. Political and social revolution shook France and Maria's gentle cousin King Louis XVI was publicly beheaded. Apologists justified the horror by claiming, "It is impossible to rule innocently."[38] Within a short time the French queen Marie Antoinette, Maria's own goddaughter, was also executed. Deep mourning overtook the court and the music and fireworks stopped.

Maria's emotional stability was further undermined by an undiagnosed case of epilepsy. Frequent seizures sapped her physical strength and mental confidence. Fear and anxiety triggered additional convulsions and sleepless nights. After each disabling attack Portugal's queen surrendered to longer periods of lethargy, depression, and prayer. Many thought she was losing her mind. The best doctors in Europe were consulted, including the famed physician who had treated the madness of her English cousin, George III. Dr. Willis was unable to diagnosis the cause of her attacks but suggested a long sea voyage to calm her nerves.[39] Portuguese doctors vetoed the recommendation, preferring instead to treat her with regular bleedings with leeches and physical restraints. Maria's health continued deteriorating.

She no longer had the strength to govern. Physical and mental exhaustion, epileptic seizures and terrifying images of her father, and his father, and his father before him burning in hell tormented her. Unrecognizable shadow people terrorized and haunted her, perhaps the ghosts of Brazil's slaves.[40] In 1792 Prince João, her oldest surviving son, took the reins of government. Seven years later he was formally appointed regent. Throughout his regency, he continued to regularly consult with his mother on public and family matters.[41]

Maria Bragança remained queen of Portugal. To her subjects and son, she was the recognized head of state, the respected head of the family. The Portuguese government fleeing to South America in 1808 carried nothing more valuable than Maria herself. Her living presence legitimized their journey. As Dr. Willis had predicted, the queen found the voyage beneficial to her health. Her almost serene demeanor during the difficult crossing calmed members of her frightened family. In the frenzy of their Lisbon escape, despite her supposed madness, it was Maria who had the presence of mind to repeatedly admonish her family and court to show no panic that would cause fear in the Portuguese remaining behind.[42]

As the government fled, threats against the prince regent were everywhere. Angry crowds stoned his carriage, taunting "death to the prince who abandons us."[43] Sight of the carriage of Maria I produced a dramatically different response. As it moved through Lisbon's freezing rain and muddy streets toward the ship taking her to America, surly crowds fell into respectful silence.[44] Along with their queen the Portuguese royal family brought many of their possessions and thousands of supporters. To keep the power and accumulated wealth of the court from falling into the hands of their French enemy, the English sent a fleet to protect them.[45]

Medallion over the tomb of Maria I (1734–1816), Lisbon. Maria I promoted the arts, education, science, and peace in Portugal at the same time the number of African slaves exiled to Brazil reached an all time high. Author's collection.

The Napoleonic invasion suddenly and dramatically reversed centuries of treasures traveling east. Determined to leave nothing behind to help their enemy the refugees took much of the best and some of the worst of Portugal to America under Maria's royal mantle. Even with her health broken, she remained the center of her nation's identity. When Portugal's royal family sailed into Rio de Janeiro's harbor, the queen's personal ensign fluttered in the breeze, heralding their arrival.[46]

A huge celebration greeted Prince Regent João and the royal family as they disembarked in Rio de Janeiro, but the queen was too ill to leave her ship. For two days her disappointed Brazilian subjects waited patiently. When Maria I was well enough to come ashore, they joyously repeated the entire welcoming celebration for her.[47]

The Rio de Janeiro Portugal's royal family found in 1808 was not the beautiful city it would become. One contemporary visitor described the city as "a false jewel in a magnificent setting."[48] Despite its breathtaking natural location its history had been one of neglect. Brazil's great wealth had only traveled through its unpaved streets on its way to Portugal. There was no adequate water supply, newspaper, bank, library, hospital, school or plumbing for sixty thousand residents. Not one bathtub could be found in the city. And there were no steam engines or mechanical machinery; slaves did all manual labor. Everywhere one looked were slaves. One million slaves, one of every four Brazilians, was held in bondage, the living legacy of long dead monarchs—and one living queen.[49]

Rio de Janeiro's largest building, the Carmelite convent near the old viceroy's palace, was requisitioned to serve as Maria's Brazilian home. During the eight remaining years of her life, she could sometimes be glimpsed through its windows or in its gardens walking with her ladies in waiting. A day never passed that the prince regent did not visit his mother or consult his queen. He never forgot that he ruled two very different countries and a large empire separated by thousands of miles of ocean through his mothers' name, position and title.

On December 17, 1815, the eighty-second birthday of Maria I, her son made the colony of Brazil a co-equal nation with Portugal. Uniting the countries on the queen's birthday strengthened his controversial decision by honoring the living symbol of both nations.[50] Three months later Maria Bragança died. For a full year and a half the entire Portuguese Empire went into official mourning in memory of their dead queen.

4

"Schemes and Plans"

Prior to 1808 few Euro-Brazilian women were publicly seen in Rio de Janeiro. The Portuguese and their Brazilian colony had selectively embraced many of the gender traditions and attitudes of their old Moorish enemies.[1] It was popularly said Brazilian woman only left their home on three occasions, "to be baptized, to be married, and to be buried."[2] In the exiled court of Queen Maria I, royal woman approached life differently, none more so than the wife of Maria's regent son, the free spirited Carlota Joaquina.

Portuguese tradition claims, "Bad winds and bad marriages come from Spain." The old proverb may have its bitter roots in Carlota's 1785 marriage to the future King João VI of Portugal. Despite centuries of suspicions and conflict, for dynastic, political, economic and military reasons the Portuguese and Spanish monarchies continued to intermarry. The oldest surviving son of Maria I and three of his sisters wed members of the Spanish royal family.

The prince was reportedly quiet, sedentary, introspective, and good-natured with a talent for remembering the names of people he had met years earlier. His voice was seldom raised, his anger rarely displayed. The Portuguese came to love him even if they did not always agree with his policies and decisions.

His faith was simple and sincere, and he preferred the peace and solitude of a quiet chapel to the noise and energy of a court reception. Gentle humor, good music, and food were his greatest comforts. The first two decades of his life were his happiest, until the smallpox death of his older brother made him heir to Portugal's throne. Two years earlier the shy eighteen-year-old became engaged to his Spanish first cousin Carlota. In almost all ways she was his opposite — energetic and athletic, restlessly extroverted, impulsive, cunning, opinionated, and as ambitious as her ten years of life allowed her to be.[3]

Carlota was sent to Portugal to live with the royal family until she was old enough to marry and produce children. She was always physically small, her adult height only reaching four feet six inches. At the time of their betrothal, João's seventeen-year-old sister was sent to Spain to marry that king's favorite son. Portuguese fisherman, noting the age, height and weight differences between the princesses, joked, "We sent them a cod and they sent us a sardine."[4]

Gender traditions of the time dictated young girls born into the aristocracy wear the same formal dress and tight corsets constricting adult women. Carlota was so active she continually broke the stays of her whalebone corsets.[5] Her nurse recorded she was never still, preferring the freedom of being out of doors to the confining walls of the palace. Even as a child Carlota resisted any constraint on her personal freedom.

In almost all ways she was like her mother Maria Luísa of Parma who at fourteen had unhappily married her own first cousin, the future king of Spain. Restless but iron willed, Maria Luísa ruled Spain and her weak husband through her protégé and suspected lover, Prime Minister Godey. Many believed Carlos IV a "royal cuckold" and Godey the father of several of the royal children.[6] Their cousin, the king of France, stated, "the poor man is a mere cipher, completely governed and henpecked by his wife."[7]

The famous Spanish court painter Francisco Goya, rumored to be one of Maria Luísa's lovers, recorded her grotesque features and those of her family for posterity.[8] By the time of Carlota's birth, the Spanish Bourbons had become infamous for their "dynastic degeneration."[9] Another royal cousin, Queen Caroline of Naples, called them "a family of cretins."[10] After meeting Maria Luísa and observing her relationships with her children Napoleon wrote, "What a mother. She horrifies me."[11]

Maria Luísa was described as a "passionate, unsatisfied woman bursting with ill restrained desires."[12] The description might have easily applied to her daughter. From her mother, Carlota received her sense of morality and propriety, her strong will, her ambition, and her nervous energy and temperament. She inherited her father's name, but not his throne. Had she been born a male, she would have ruled Spain and its great empire. That fact defined and dominated her life.

Sixty-two earlier, her great grandfather had changed the laws of royal succession, excluding women as heirs to the throne. Spain had a long history of strong female monarchs dating back to the pre–Christian era; but fears of national domination by a foreign born husband caused the crown to break with tradition.[13] By the time Carlota was born, a woman could no longer rule the country founded through the statecraft and military prowess of Isabella the Catholic.[14]

With no chance to sit on the Spanish throne, Carlota left a nation dominated by one strong woman to a nation ruled by another. Within the formal protocol of the Portuguese court, Maria Bragança treated Carlota as if she were one of her own royal daughters, but she found it chaffing to be treated like a mere princess when she believed it her destiny to rule.[15]

Carlota could ride horses, shoot or hunt as well as any man, and dance till the early hours of the morning. The next day, however, she was an immovable child. She refused to eat the food at the royal tables, and treated servants white and black, young and old, with equal contempt. To Carlota everyone but the queen was her slave. Still, when her future mother-in-law was not present, Carlota singled out the queen's black attendant and favorite, Dona Anna, for special torment.[16]

Maria I attempted to control her young ward with threats of keeping her indoors, away from her beloved gardens and horses.[17] Carlota recognized power and strength. As long as the queen of Portugal had both, she responded to her commands.

When court watchers reported Carlota's menstruation at fifteen, she promptly wed her Portuguese cousin. Following the ceremony João's attempt to kiss her was rebuffed with a bite. Aside from their wedding and family relationships, their only common bond was a mutual dislike for one another. Carlota's adult personality was described as "vulgar bad tempered, unscrupulous and malicious."[18] Her pacific husband was as sincere and easy going in private as he appeared in public. One was fire, the other water. Neither was physically attractive but both possessed talents and gifts. João's docile personality was frustrating, but disarming. His tentative nature consistently caused people to underestimate him, but his core judgments were sound. During a crisis he usually made the right decisions. He never lost his head or his crown as many of his royal relatives did.[19]

Carlota's strong will and verbal gifts could captivate and win almost anyone to her side.[20] But her hyperactive mind and nervous intelligence offered no rest. When she was still a child, a gypsy foretold her fortune in a song. The lyrics included the refrain, "Stubborn in my quarrels, with the malice of a gypsy, my schemes and plans never leave me in peace." Carlota liked the words so much she sang them her entire life.[21] The lyrics proved to be accurate. Like her husband, Carlota had a remarkable memory, but used it to remember only real or imagined slights. She wed her powers of recollection to a talent for revenge. Perhaps because of her own chaotic childhood, she had a keen instinct for creating and exploiting trouble. Like many unhappy people, the only pleasure she enjoyed was in making others unhappy.

As the daughter of one king, a future queen of another, and the possible mother to a third, Carlota's position afforded her influence and opportunities most people would never know — but it brought little satisfaction. Portugal was an absolute monarchy, its empire built on the backs of slaves. To Carlota, the system represented the natural order of the universe, with the possible exception that she should be its master. She was contemptuous of her husband and of any powerful person who did not flaunt their position. Whenever possible, Carlota's sharp tongue mocked and taunted Portugal's future king. His response was silence. Each knew the weapon to use against the other. Still, to be married to the heir to a throne meant someday she might rule. Portugal's queen ruled with or without a king, and the Bragança men were not known for long lives. At her parent's court she earned a reputation as a "born conspirator."[22] As illness overtook her mother-in-law, Carlota surprised many by becoming more civil to her husband — especially in public appearances. Tensions between the royal couple became buried under layers of etiquette and protocol. Carlota needed to be close enough to the throne to someday claim it for herself. To achieve that goal, she dutifully provided Portugal with royal heirs, three princes and four princesses. Her first son died, but her second and third lived, providing her status, security and independence.

She gave birth at the Queluz Palace outside of Lisbon. There in a gilded bedroom painted floor to ceiling with scenes from the Spanish novel *Don Quixote*, she presented her husband with royal princes.[23] Her oldest surviving son was christened Pedro de Alcântara Francisco Antônio João Carlos Xavier de Paul Miguel Rafael Joaquin José Gonzaga Pascal Cipriano Serafim de Bragança e Bourbon.[24] Fate would take him to Brazil where his own children, and his granddaughter Princess Isabel, would be born.

Once Carlota provided Portugal's crown its required male heirs, she asserted her independence by moving to Ramalhão, a secluded royal residence ten miles from Queluz. Her husband lived at his own favorite palace at Mafra. Their children remained at Queluz with their grandmother. Only when affairs of state made it necessary did the royal couple appear under the same roof.[25] Royal heirs allowed Carlota's husband minimal contact with his wife. The arrangement also pleased Carlota. After the birth of her first three children court gossips speculated about the father of her other offspring.[26] The wife of the French ambassador noted, "The interested thing about the Portuguese royal family is that one child never resembles the other."[27]

Gossip did not deter Carlota, who created a private life for herself apart from her husband. In it she refused to be ruled by any man, any king, or any social convention. In her public life, however, she was forced to remain subject to her husband. As the physical and mental health of Maria I deteriorated, governing the country and the empire fell to her son. The heavy workload and emotional strain of watching his mother physically and mentally slip away weighed heavily on him.[28] By 1806, exhaustion forced him to his bed at Mafra. Weeks passed and rumors at court circulated that the prince regent, like his mother, had lost his mind. The uncertainty of the prince's health caused fear, confusion and opportunity. Some whispered the time had come to declare him mentally incapacitated and make Princess Carlota regent.

The Marquês of Loulé, the prince regent's close friend, directed spies to discover the source of the rumors. Intercepted letters to the king and queen of Spain traced the conspiracy to Carlota. In one letter she wrote, "I appeal to you with greatest consternation to inform you that the prince is everyday becoming more deranged, and in consequence I am in danger of ruin... the time has come for you to help me, and your grandchildren.... The only remedy is for you to send intimidation that you wish me to enter government, and that you will not accept a refusal, or else your reply will be to take up arms to avenge the affronts and insults to which you know that I am constantly exposed.... This is the only means of preventing the spilling of blood in this kingdom, because the court wants to draw sword on my behalf, and the people also ... for it is obvious to all that the prince is out of his mind."[29] His wife's duplicity forced the prince from his sickbed. To the shock of the entire court he appeared at Carlota's official birthday celebration firmly in control of his senses and the government.[30] He had no intention of becoming another Afonso VI.

Carlota hastily withdrew to Ramalhão, denying any role in the conspiracy; but her husband never trusted her again. There she waited for another opportunity to gain power. She was not by nature a patient person — but she had learned from the Braganças the value of patience and the importance of timing. The failure of the Spanish royal family to rally to their daughter's defense did not indicate a lack of interest in Portugal. Hoping to save their own thrones, they secretly negotiated a treaty allowing Napoleon's armies to cross Spain, depose the Braganças and partition the country into several small pieces.[31] Carlota's mother, Maria Luísa, was not completely devoid of loyalty. Her suspected lover, Prime Minister Godey, was to become monarch of the Algarve section of Portugal.[32]

News of the secret treaty reached the prince regent and Carlota, who wrote her parents begging to be allowed to return to Spain with her daughters. She received no response from her mother. The Portuguese royal family gathered at Queluz, where Prince João shared his plans to evacuate the government to Brazil. Carlota was instructed to bring the queen and their daughters to Lisbon and to be prepared to depart as soon as possible.

The betrayal and rejection by her parents forced the unhappy Carlota to rely on the man she most hated — her own husband. She had no choice but to follow him into exile.[33] In one last plea she wrote her mother, "I cannot willingly fling myself into a well — if I should go, it will be my ruin, for if they have treated me here as they have done, how will they treat me away from you?"[34]

There is no record Maria Luísa replied. Spain's monarchy was busy making plans to relocate to Mexico if Napoleon betrayed them. Family feuding and public riots against Godey provided an opportunity for him to do just that. He deposed the Bourbons and their government on the way to Portugal.[35] Carlos IV abdicated and his entire family was arrested and exiled to France. The disintegration of the Spanish monarchy allowed Portugal's own unhappy royal family to flee to Brazil.

5

"Restless Intrigues"

Portugal's prince regent was enchanted from the first moment he glimpsed Brazil's lush green coastline, whispering, "I have lost a kingdom, but found a paradise."[1] Carlota, dependent in flight on the husband she despised, could not see beyond the dark skin she saw everywhere, dismissing Brazil as a place of "Negros and lice."[2]

Like a guilt-ridden father who discovers a lost, neglected child, the prince showered Brazil with attention and affection. He opened its closed ports to trade and welcomed ships and cargoes from around the world. New docks, wharves, and roads were constructed, and manufacturing and industrialization encouraged. Soon new aqueducts and impressive public buildings appeared throughout Rio de Janeiro. Architects, musicians, artists and journalist were invited to join the exiled court. The Royal School of Medicine was opened, as was the National Library, the Royal Mint, the Academy of Fine Arts, print shops, museums, banks and a theatre. Princess Isabel's great-grandfather also created a botanical garden, filling it with thousands of flowering trees, plants, and flowers. In time it became world famous for its spectacular flora and the magnificent butterflies and hummingbirds it attracted. Within a decade, Rio's royal court transformed Brazil's capital into a city worthy of governing the vast Portuguese Empire.

The prince also took the first step away from Brazil's dependence on slavery. Under pressure from England and in gratitude for the protection of its fleet, he signed an agreement for the gradual abolition of the slave trade. By 1815 the trade would be banned north of the equator. At a time to be decided in the future, the ban would be extended south of that line.[3] As he worked to elevate and improve Brazil, Carlota pined for Europe and the power that eluded her. As soon as she was able, she built a life for herself away from her husband. She moved into her own palace away from the center of the city, declaring, "If I must vegetate in this forsaken corner of the world let my exile be complete. Take me away from half naked black apes that make me think of Africa."[4] A number of loyal supporters and all but one of her daughters joined her. In Brazil a wife living away from her husband was unheard of, but it gave Carlota the freedom she desired, and Prince João the peace he craved.

With the queen indisposed, Carlota became the most influential woman in Brazilian society. Her tastes were European and she continued wearing layered, heavy clothing despite Brazil's tropical climate and warm days and nights. Many Portuguese expatriates copied her dress. They were even joined by some Brazilian women, who began to appear at court functions wearing feathered hats, thick fabrics, high collars and layers and layers of suffocating petticoats.[5] The only concession Carlota made to practical fashion was slitting her long dresses fore and aft so that she could ride her horse like a man. Her influence was felt immediately. She had been forced to shave her head because of the lice and fleas she

Portrait of Carlota Joaquina (1755–1830) near the time of her marriage. Carlota could not see beyond the dark skin of her subjects when she and the royal family arrived in Brazil in the winter of 1807–1808. She dismissed Brazil as a land of "Negros and Lice" (Eul-Soo Pang, *In Pursuit of Honor and Power*). Courtesy the Catholic University of America, Oliveira Lima Library, Washington, D.C.

acquired during the long ocean voyage; many Euro-Brazilian women followed her example and short hair became fashionable.[6]

Brazil's new trendsetter introduced Rio de Janeiro to European-style balls. When her husband did not attend she hosted them herself. Her desire to recreate a European-style court expanded the social horizons for women. Carlota's behavior was sometimes shocking, even scandalous, but in her own way Carlota created social opportunities for women never before available in Brazil. Slowly in Rio de Janeiro some Euro-Brazilian women began to emerge from behind the cloistered walls of their homes. Increasingly they joined the wives of diplomats and foreign merchants at court functions and the theatre. Men ambitious for entry into the royal circle began urging their wives and daughters to publicly participate in a social life they had always forbidden.[7]

Despite becoming the center of such attention, Carlota remained miserable. Her husband had the political power she desired, and she soon focused her energies on gaining a crown for herself. Carlota's family remained exiled and imprisoned in France, Napoleon's brother Joseph sat on the Spanish throne, and civil war devoured Spain. In the misfortune of her family and homeland Carlota saw opportunity. From her palace in Brazil, she issued a manifesto to colonial capitals throughout Spanish America urging them to place themselves under "the immediate protection and government ... of the Infanta Dona Carlota Joaquina de Bourbon, ... as our Sovereign Regent."[8] Carlota followed her public statements with private correspondence to governors, bishops, military men and other influential leaders throughout Latin America, seeking support.[9]

Most royalists ignored her appeal. In La Planta, however, the region that later became Argentina, her proclamation was well received. Fueled by rivals competing for political advantage, a powerful monarchical movement swelled in her favor. The throne that had eluded her since birth finally seemed within reach. One obstacle, however, proved insurmountable. Spanish Americans wanted a constitutional monarchy and Carlota believed royals accountable only to God. For a king *or* a queen to be bound by laws or constitutional restraints was unthinkable. Refusing to compromise her absolutist beliefs, the throne she had desired her entire life slipped away.[10]

Political uncertainty spread across Spanish America. Carlota made one more attempt to gain an American crown by helping to finance revolution in Argentina. A British naval squadron agreed to transport her to Buenos Aires, but when the plot was discovered Carlota's co-conspirators were arrested.[11] A English admiral was recalled to London amid rumors he was politically and romantically involved with the wife of Portugal's future king. Prince Regent João was a realist. He might be able to build a great nation in Brazil, but he would never be able to control his unhappy wife. One court watcher observed, "Had it not been for the baneful influence of his despotic consort, — her restless intrigues of all hues, political as well as private — her wanton freaks of favoritism and atrocious acts of cruelty, — his reign would have gone down to the latest times in the annals of his kingdom surrounded with a halo of gratitude."[12]

Monarchists hoping to keep Spain's splintering South American empire together traveled to Europe in search of a more stable royal candidate, but their petitions were rejected. No European monarch would agree to have any family member sit on a throne supported by a written constitution.[13]

The American minister to Buenos Aires, exasperated by their search, wrote to Secretary of State John Quincy Adams; "I lose daily somewhat of my faith (which was never very great) in the susceptibility of these people of the perfect republican liberty. I see to my great mortification so much idolatry to everything European and such indifference, bordering on hatred, to things North American."[14] Many of South America's emerging liberators, including

José San Martín, believed only a hereditary monarchy could preserve the continent's peace and unity. The desire for monarchy was so strong that, in an almost desperate attempt to maintain the tradition, proposals were made to crown a descendent of the last king of the Incas. Carlota rejected an offer for the hand of one of her daughters to create a Euro-Incan royal dynasty. Her racism and hatred of constitutional government doomed the plan, and Spain's great South American empire shattered into warring factions.[15] Only in Brazil was civil war avoided and the monarchial ideal realized.

In 1816, the year following the death of Queen Maria I, Princess Isabel's great-grandfather was proclaimed King João VI of the United Kingdoms of Portugal, Algrave and Brazil. In a magnificent medieval ceremony in Rio de Janeiro's cathedral, European-style monarchy blossomed in America. Most Brazilian men and women, white and black, rich or poor, had never seen anything like it.

For Carlota, being in a king's shadow was no more satisfying than when the shadow was that of a prince. Carlota's restless energy grew and she used her own racism to sew discontent by creating a "Corps of Cadets" to do her bidding. Mixed race soldiers with fierce physical features and aggressive personalities were recruited to intimidate, frighten and bully her growing list of enemies.[16] Most Euro-Brazilian women were still seldom seen in public. But Carlota and her entourage, surrounded by her cadet bodyguards, appeared everywhere. As she was driven through the streets of Rio de Janeiro, she demanded people bow and kneel to pay her homage. Cadets were dispatched to discipline those who hesitated.

The American and British ministers refused to conform to such humiliations.[17] The minister from the United States became so enraged during a street encounter that he drew his gun, dispersed Carlota's cadets, and threatened to make an international incident of the altercation.[18] The harassed king alternately ordered and begged his queen to control her outrageous behavior. Despite his position as a ruler of an empire touching four continents, João VI spent much of his time keeping his restless wife from undermining his throne.[19]

Carlota's promiscuous behavior forced the king to finally act, after the wife of a rumored lover was publicly murdered. The investigation pointed to the involvement of the queen, forcing her to disappear within the walls of her private residence.[20] With Carlota temporally silenced, the king devoted his time to the welfare and future of his family, Brazil, and Portugal. For assistance he turned to his fourth daughter, Maria Teresa, the most intelligent and capable of his children.[21] Widowed in her teens from a Spanish prince and cousin after two years of marriage, she and her young son lived with her father and brothers.

Maria Teresa Bragança Bourbon was not only the favorite child of King João VI; she soon became his political confidante, private secretary and closest family adviser. In recognition of her public and private roles, she was appointed to the Council of State, a position denied both his sons.[22] With her appointment Teresa became the first woman in North or South America to sit on the governing council of a national government. Teresa's reputation traveled to Europe, where Austria's emperor Franz I approached João VI about marriage to his son and heir. The Austrian prince's poor health prevented the marriage, but royal matrimonial negotiations were not in vain.[23]

Recognizing the prestige of a marriage between a Habsburg princess and his own heir, João VI pursued a possible union between the two royal houses.[24] Such a royal marriage would allow him to distance his family from the Spanish Bourbons and consolidate and safeguard all he had built. He wanted his oldest son Pedro to have a non–Spanish wife who would be an asset, ally, and partner who could elevate and strengthen the dynasty — the opposite of what Carlota had been to him.

He found such a woman in the remarkable Archduchess Maria Leopoldina Josepha Carolina, daughter of Austria's emperor. Leopoldina was the niece of France's legendary Queen Marie Antoinette and the favorite sister of Marie Louise, wife of the French emperor Napoleon I. She had been raised and educated in the city of Vienna at the very center of culture and political power. The marriage was proposed, negotiated and agreed upon through intense diplomacy and generous bribes. It trumpeted the triumphal rise in influence, power and prestige of the Braganças. Leopoldina forever changed the history of Brazil and Portugal. To its Austrian princess and Portuguese prince it brought fame, national greatness and personal tragedy.

Brazil's ambassador to Vienna, rumored to be one of Carlota's lovers and the father of Prince Miguel, should have heeded the advice of his cynical queen. She secretly wrote him, "And don't contract this marriage if the Archduchess is ugly. Our Pedro, like you, is crazy about beautiful women. If he should see an ugly princess, it would be a great misfortune for them both."[25] Diplomacy rather than loyalty to his queen or prince dictated the ambassador's honest description of the Habsburg bride. He wrote, "In her presence sovereignty shines forth alongside the rarest virtues."[26]

Tragically for Leopoldina, the virtues Leopoldina exemplified were not qualities Pedro found attractive or appreciated. Without setting eyes upon her future husband, the nineteen-year-old archduchess was married by proxy to her Brazilian prince on May 13, 1817, the anniversary of the coronation of Maria I and the birthday of both King João VI and Maria Theresa — the greatest of all Habsburg rulers. It was also the anniversary of Catherine of Bragança's arrival in England following her own proxy marriage to Charles II, but no one mentioned that unhappy coincidence. Three months later Leopoldina sailed to America. She would never again see her own sisters or brothers, father or home, but became known as "the mother of their nation" for her leadership in Brazil's independence movement and for planting the seeds of abolition her granddaughter Isabel would harvest.

6

"We Unfortunate Princesses"

"We unfortunate princesses are like dice whose happiness or unhappiness depends on the throw.... Nothing remains for me to do except weep with you and curse the word politics for causing me so much suffering."[1] The words were Leopoldina's following her marriage to a man she had never met. They were written to her sister Maria Louise, who understood them only too well. She had been sacrificed in a dynastic marriage to Napoleon I, her family's most hated enemy. Leopoldina could have been speaking for both of them, or for many other princesses, including her new mother-in-law Carlota Joaquina.

In her young life both Leopoldina's mother and beloved stepmother died before reaching the age of forty. Now she was losing the rest of her family. As the date for her departure to Brazil approached, Leopoldina wrote in resignation to her maternal aunt and surrogate mother, Marie Amélie Orleans, "The journey does not frighten me. I believe it is my fate.... it may be predestination, but I have always had a strange curiosity about America and as a child I always hoped to visit there."[2] Fate brought the Austrian princess to America for far more than a visit. Toward the end of her ninety-two-day voyage, Leopoldina and other passengers feared a sinister looking ship bearing down on them was a pirate ship, but it turned out to be a Brazilian slave trader.[3] Its frightening appearance served to introduce Leopoldina to her new country. It was a fitting introduction.

Her apprehension was eased somewhat with her first glimpse of Rio de Janeiro. The words of a friend described what they both saw: "Nothing that I have ever seen before compares with the beauty of this bay. Naples, the harbor of Bombay whose beauty I thought to be perfect, all of them have to bow to [this].... Rio de Janeiro, the Bay of Guanabara, is the most charming sight that one can imagine."[4] The capital the Austrian princess discovered in 1817 was a vastly improved European version of the crowded slum the Portuguese court had found nine years earlier. To welcome his new daughter-in-law, King João showcased his recreated city to resemble a brilliant Brazilian carnival. Crowds cheered, music played, cannons roared and church bells pealed.[5] Citizens of Rio de Janeiro loved a visual and musical spectacle that overwhelmed the senses.

Their king did not disappoint them. From the moment of her arrival, Leopoldina seemed to bring out the glory of Brazil. Perhaps no other woman on earth was better prepared to accomplish such a feat.

In many ways, this young princess who was to become Princess Isabel's grandmother represented the best of European culture, education and tradition. To this she added her own personality, intelligence, wisdom and wit, built upon the strict Habsburg commitment toward duty. "Do not oppress the poor; be benevolent," she wrote at the top of each and every page of her school lessons.[6] Throughout her young life a dedication to the needs of others, a genuine passion for learning, and a deep mystical belief in her Catholic faith sustained and cursed her.

Portrait of Leopoldina (1797–1826) near the time of her marriage. Leopoldina, the first empress of the New World, became known as the mother of the nation for her leadership in Brazil's independence movement and for planting the seeds of abolition her granddaughter Princess Isabel would harvest. Courtesy the Catholic University of America, Oliveira Lima Library, Washington, D.C.

This trinity of beliefs was prescribed for all Habsburg children by her great grandmother Empress Maria Theresa, whose administrative talents helped create a multi-national multi-ethnic empire in the heart of Europe.[7] Maria Theresa believed a successful leader must possess all three qualities to withstand the storms and turmoil of public life.[8] Even by Habsburg standards, Leopoldina was not a typical princess, woman, or student. As a child she was captivated by the sciences, mathematics, and linguistics. Already fluent in ten languages, after her betrothal she added the study of Portuguese to her learning regimen. The nineteen-year-old princess brought to Brazil her own librarian, a zoologist, a botanist, a geologist, an entomologist and numerous other scientists, artists, teachers and tutors to continue feeding her passion for learning.

The moment she saw her new husband she fell under his spell. She was not the first to do so. Years earlier the French ambassador described the Portuguese royal family to his wife, writing, "My God! How ugly they all are! There is not a comely face among them, except the Prince Royal."[9] Pedro looked like neither of his parents. He was sun-bronzed, dark-haired and athletically handsome. Somehow within his person their combined features became attractive. Leopoldina was also athletically built but light skinned and fair. Like her prince she excelled in sports and was a natural athlete. His new wife may have been one of the few people alive, man or woman, able to match his equestrian and marksmanship skills. Pedro and Brazil had never seen anyone quite like her.[10]

Yet despite her education and athleticism nothing prepared her for the impulsive, rough side of her husband. As daughter of an emperor who ruled over one of the most cultured empires in Europe, she had been strictly chaperoned her entire life. Her brothers were raised in separate nurseries and she and her sisters were only allowed female pets to shelter them from developing an unhealthy interest or knowledge of sexuality.[11] Leopoldina was a virgin in mind and body. She had been raised to respect, honor and obey the men in her life in the strict religious customs of the nineteenth century. Leopoldina wrote, "I admit that the sacrifice of leaving my family, perhaps forever, is more than painful, but this alliance makes my father happy, and I have the consolation of knowing that I have bowed to his will, being persuaded that God has a particular way of ruling the destinies of princes, and that submitting to our parents is submitting to his will."[12]

Pedro viewed life and duty differently. During his childhood he had been chaotically indulged. Attractive, bright, charming, a born musician and gifted athlete — everything seemed to come easily to the Portuguese prince. Nothing had been denied him, but still he was prone to sudden, sometimes-violent mood changes. Without warning or provocation, he would become short tempered, caustic, and harsh. As a child he had been alternately ignored or spoiled by his ill grandmother and feuding parents. Pedro had few positive teachers to instruct him in the responsibilities of his position. Self-restraint and self-discipline had never been rewarded. The only tutor able to instill discipline into his life was murdered by a disgruntled slave.[13] Pedro was never again exposed to structured learning. His youth was spent in the company of sycophants, stable boys, slaves, and women, all of whom gave him what he wanted.

The heir to Portugal's throne lived the privileged life of a prince with none of the training or discipline. His passion was not duty or service — it was making love to women — many women. He once bluntly wrote, "I worship God and am afraid of the devil, but if God or the devil were to confront me when I am making love, I should kick them both into the street."[14] The quote is also attributed to his mother. It accurately describes the attitude of both. This was the man the virginal Leopoldina married.

Leopoldina was everything King João and his Brazilian subjects could hope for in a princess. Everyone loved Leopoldina but her prince. Although

Pedro was initially intrigued by his new wife, he would never limit himself to one woman. At times, he could be like his uncomplicated father. But in his nervous energy and marriage vows, he was his mother's son.

The first years of their marriage were difficult, but there were also times of great happiness.[15] Pedro's family life had been filled with competition and strife. Leopoldina attempted to create a safe, stable home life that served as a sanctuary from the pressures and competition of court. New things always appealed to Pedro and the novelty of home as a respite from chaos proved temporarily appealing. Leopoldina had grown up in such an environment and tried her best to recreate it for her husband. But it was not easy. Her letters described the handsome Pedro as a "living Adonis" but also as restless and unpredictable. To her sister Maria Louise she wrote, "My husband's character is violently eccentric. Because of a great degree of hard and unjust treatment, he is inclined toward all change, and he wants everything that even suggests freedom. I can only watch silently and weep."[16] Following their first year of marriage, she wrote her sister, "My poor heart and a German background suffer a great deal.... You think that Brazil is a golden throne — but it is an iron yoke."[17]

The "melancholy songs of the slaves" heightened her homesickness.[18] To Leopoldina, slavery was an abomination. To Pedro it was an accepted part of life. Over time he came to see slavery through the fresh eyes of his wife; but neither he nor Leopoldina had any influence over government policies — including slavery. Profits from the slave trade obscured its horrors for most Brazilians. Investors and slave traders earned a 500 percent profit on the safe return of one slave ship, making them the wealthiest men in Brazil. In turn they provided loans and capital for the nation's agriculture, business, and even the government. Slave traders held half of the mortgages on plantations and financed the speculators holding most of Brazil's uncultivated land. The government's dependence on the slave tax solidified an unholy alliance with the traders. Despite their small numbers, they had a disproportionate influence in the affairs of Brazil. Portugal's staunchest ally, England, wanted Brazilian slavery restricted, but slave traders fiercely opposed government regulation of their business or profits. Still the Crown managed to limit the number and size of slave ships and tried to outlaw the practice of branding slaves to identify ownership.[19] Ship captains and surgeons were required to enforce royal laws and health mandates, but money and profits often overcame scruples and legal guidelines.

Dealing with the conflicting agendas of England and his empire's slave traders claimed much of the king's time. Leopoldina had little contact with him, and even less with his queen. Her father warned her to avoid Carlota, whom he described as a devilish schemer.[20] Leopoldina's new life found her surrounded by strangers and slaves. Her husband was seldom home, but when he was his unpredictable moods and nervous energy created tension and confusion.[21]

Despite her best efforts Leopoldina irritated and confused him. He had known many women but none that nurtured their mind at the expense of their personal appearance. To Leopoldina her physical attributes meant little. To her husband, they meant everything. She believed Pedro's erratic behavior was caused by his own neglected childhood, not her neglectful image. Throughout their marriage she clung to the hope that her love and patience would change him, but nothing she did overcame his desire to bed other women. Their time together was spent pursuing their few shared interests such as horseback riding, music, drawing, and even occasionally reading. Such quiet interludes provided happiness for Leopoldina and brief diversions for her husband who found relaxation moving from one physical activity to another. The freshness of his wife's goodness encouraged him to try to become a good husband, but the concept eluded him.[22]

One powerful bond drew them together. They both loved children and understood their dynastic responsibility. Leopoldina was pregnant nine times during the first ten years of their marriage. She surpassed her mother-in-law, but fell short of her mother's thirteen pregnancies, and her great-grandmother Maria Theresa, who birthed sixteen.[23] Despite the exhaustion caused by her pregnancies and frustrations with her husband, her children became the joy of her married life. Leopoldina's first child, a girl, was destined to be queen of Portugal. Even before the umbilical cord was cut, high-ranking members of government, ministers of state and the diplomatic corps who witnessed the birth welcomed the new princess. The assemblage reported the weary mother whispered for all to hear, "I receive my daughter for the glory of God and the royal house of Bragança."[24]

The American born princess became known as Maria da Glória, a name honoring the patron saint of Brazil's slaves. She was baptized in the small hilltop church dedicated to her namesake that overlooked Guanabara Bay. It was the favorite place of worship for Leopoldina and her husband.[25] Their daughter's entire baptized name was Maria da Glória Joana Carlota Leopoldina da Cruz Francisca Xavier de Paula Isidora Michaela, Rafaela Gonzaga. The happiness of Maria da Glória's birth stood in nightmarish contrast to the unhappy ending of another royal pregnancy.[26] Pedro's sister Maria Isabel Bragança had married her uncle Ferdinand VII, who reclaimed the Spanish throne after his acceptance of a written constitution. Maria Isabel was an intelligent, cultured patron of the arts, still remembered in Spain as the founder of the world famous Prado Museum. She inherited from her father an easy-going nature and from her grandmother, epilepsy.

Toward the end of an uneventful pregnancy doctors mistook a severe epileptic seizure as a death coma. The helpless mother was butchered in a misguided attempt to save the child. Flesh, arteries, and vital organs were slashed. By the time the seizure ended, Maria Isabel was bleeding to death. In her death throes she was told she had failed her family and country; the child was a stillborn daughter.[27] Failure and disgrace followed her to the grave. In an isolated corner of the Escorial mausoleum Maria Isabel was buried away from the royal family in a wing reserved for childless queens.

The successful birth of Maria da Glória quickly eclipsed the Spanish tragedy. Leopoldina and Pedro were thrilled with their first child and were affectionate loving parents. Within six months, Leopoldina wrote her Aunt Amélie. "My little daughter is the prettiest and most intelligent child I know; she is already beginning to babble and to stand on her feet showing extraordinary strength in her legs. With pleasure entirely new to me, I observed her daily progress and I can proudly say that she knows me and my beloved husband because when we are at home, we do nothing but carry her around in our arms by turns."[27]

Leopoldina's next two pregnancies ended in miscarriages, leaving her depressed and weak, but a fourth pregnancy resulting in the birth of a son in 1821 revived her spirits. With the royal succession assured, change came rapidly for Leopoldina and the rest of the royal family in Brazil. João VI looked again to Europe. Napoleon had been defeated at Waterloo in 1815; but it wasn't until his death six years later that most European royalty felt safe. Within weeks of the birth of his first grandson, the king prepared to return to Portugal. Carlota was recalled from seclusion, and thousands of the royal family's entourage prepared to return with them. Pedro and Leopoldina were told they and their children would remain in Brazil.[29]

7

"My Soul Has Never Been Enslaved"

Change again seemed to be in the wind, and thrones needed to be secured. Portugal's population had been reduced by two-thirds, its economy shattered.[1] After years of war, military occupation, and neglect its people wanted to again be at the center of their empire. The Portuguese who had remained behind to fight for king and country expected Brazil to revert to the status of a royal colony and to pay for reconstruction of the motherland. Brazilians thought otherwise. João VI hoped to relieve the growing tension between Portugal and its former colony by returning to Portugal, but leaving behind his heir, daughter-in-law and grandchildren to reassure Brazilians they were not abandoned. Pedro was appointed prince regent of Brazil. In the event of his death, Leopoldina would assume the regency. The appointment of a woman regent to lead the largest national territory in North or South America was unprecedented. It showed confidence in Leopoldina, but also the reality of Pedro's reckless lifestyle. At their final meeting together, the king secretly told his son that if Brazil sought independence, Pedro should become its leader rather than its casualty.[2] João wanted to keep crown and country in the family.

On April 26, 1821, fourteen ships sailed from Rio de Janeiro's harbor carrying the king and queen of Portugal, their younger son Miguel, their four daughters, four thousand of their supporters, the two surviving sisters of Queen Maria I, and the body of the dead queen. João VI had his mother's coffin carried aboard his flagship with all the pageantry and military honors befitting her position in life. Once on board, the coffin was placed in a cabin decorated as a royal chapel.[3]

No one was as happy at their departure as Carlota, who announced she was delighted to be returning to "a white man's climate" and a "land of people" after being surrounded by Africans for twelve years.[4] Still, she refused to depart until she was reassured that adequate food, water, and soap were onboard. Then in a parting gesture of contempt she removed her shoes and threw them into Guanabara Bay. Carlota refused to take even one particle of Brazilian soil back to Europe with her.[5]

During their years of Brazilian exile the political landscape in Europe had shifted beneath the Braganças throne. They sailed from Portugal as absolute monarchs, but returned to a population demanding greater voice in government and a written constitution.[6] Napoleon and revolutions on both sides of the Atlantic had rewritten the foundations of kingship. Prince Pedro, whose lifestyle brought him closer to the people than any other member of the royal family, helped persuade his father to accept the principles of a constitutional monarchy.[7] As a king and as a Bragança, João VI understood the necessity of reinventing himself for the times. Following the advice he had given Pedro, rather than fight a social revolution, he placed himself at its forefront. Prior to sailing for Europe he renounced his absolutist past. The king of Portugal agreed to become a constitutional monarch even before a constitution was written. His declaration appeased leaders controlling the government and silenced critics who wanted a greater voice, but traditionalists seeking a return to the privileges of the past felt betrayed. Portugal was deeply divided.

When João VI returned to Lisbon, constitutionalists leading the government gave the royal family a proper but cool reception. Unsure of the sincerity of their returning king, they lined the streets with troops; but cheering crowds overshadowed the military presence. Carlota immediately recognized the deep divisions below Portugal's thin political surface. As the royal carriage made its way through enthusiastic crowds, João VI and his son Miguel waved at the welcoming throngs. Like his mother, everywhere Miguel looked, he saw fault lines of opportunity.[8]

Following a celebration in the fortress-like Lisbon Cathedral, João VI swore to uphold the principles of the unwritten constitution. Prior to the oath taking, Carlota, citing poor health, departed for her palace on the outskirts of the city.[9] The king moved to a convent to be close to the seat of government and away from his wife.

Months after their return to Portugal, the burial vault that had been prepared for Maria I was ready. Her heavy coffin had been carried from convent to convent throughout Lisbon until her tomb was completed in the great hilltop Church of the Sacred Heart. Years earlier she had ordered the church built as an answer to her prayers for a healthy male heir. It was still being constructed when her twenty-seven-year-old heir died of smallpox. Maria was the only member of the royal family to be buried there. The three-day burial ceremony began with a nighttime torch-lit procession carrying her remains to the massive church. The royal family followed in state coaches. Behind them trailed representatives of all the great noble families on horseback wearing mourning cloaks, then the bishops, priests, and monks on foot, and finally the army and its many regimental bands playing funeral dirges.[10]

At the church, the queen's body was disinterred from the three coffins that had held her body for six years. It was cleaned, and redressed with all her royal orders, medals, and sashes carefully replaced. Then her corpse was laid in a new open-faced coffin. For two days thousands of her Portuguese subjects came to say their final farewells.[11] Nearly everyone present was overcome during the long carefully orchestrated ceremony, either by grief, or by the smell of decaying flesh. By the time Maria Bragança was laid to rest in her large black marble tomb, many must have prayed their dead queen find the peace that eluded her in life, and death.

For Portugal itself, there would be no peace. The Cortes meeting in 1821 to write the new constitution was the first parliament convened in the country since 1689. The constitutional ideals many hoped would heal their nation proved too radical for those wed to the past.[12] One of its basic tenets proclaimed, "Sovereignty resides essentially in the Nation"—not the king. For the first time in the history of Portugal the crown's power would be limited, the monarchy would "reign but not rule."[13] To the queen of Portugal such words were blasphemy.

All citizens, white and black, were guaranteed the right to vote with the exception of "women, illiterates, and friars." A representative general assembly was also created to write laws, protect individual rights, and provide the people with a unified legal system. Rights of landowners were protected as were the religious and economic interests of the church. But for the first time in Portugal's long national history, the Inquisition and other ecclesiastical courts were abolished.[14] Reactionary members within the Church hierarchy were incensed.

In November, a government delegation traveled from Lisbon to witness Carlota Joaquina's swearing of allegiance to the new constitution. Wearing black and standing firmly erect during the entire meeting, the queen, who continued claiming to be ill, spoke in a surprisedly strong voice. She announced that as a child she had promised to never swear an oath, and as an adult and a queen she would never go back on her word. Delegates respectfully reminded Carlota that article 11 of the constitution stated that refusal by any member of the royal family to swear to support the charter "invoked penalty of exile."[15] Carlota replied that she would abide by the law of exile once she was well enough to travel.

A second attempt by the Cortes to persuade Carlota to support the constitution was also rebuffed. She responded in writing, addressing her comments to the king, but knowing her real audience was elsewhere. Her manifesto revealed her Bourbon roots, her sense of entitlement, and her belief in a divine right to rule. Carlota's letter was a carefully crafted declaration of war on the constitutional government and an emotional appeal to return to the past. She hoped and prayed it might finally give her the throne.

Sire,
I have last night received by the hand of one of your ministers, the order to depart from your territories. Its purport was to banish me; you have requested me to descend from the throne to which you once elevated me! I pardon you. I feel compassion for you from my inmost heart. All my contempt, all my hatred shall be reserved for those who surround you, and who have betrayed you.

I shall be freer in my banishment than you in your palace. My liberty, at least will attend me. My soul hath never been enslaved, it hath never humiliated itself in the presence of those rebel vassals who have dared to impose laws on you, and who have endeavored to compel me to take an oath that my conscience rejected. I have not cared for their threats. I have obeyed the voice of Heaven, which has announced to me that if the epoch of greatness has passed, that of glory was now to begin. The world shall yet exclaim, "The Queen has preserved unspotted the majesty of the diadem, she has not suffered that its splendor shall be dimmed. While those potentates who held alike the scepter and the sword, I have crouched down before the storm, she alone hath remained firm and unquailing."

As thy obedient wife, I will obey thee, Sire, but my obedience shall be to thee alone. To your Majesty I will only remark that my infirmities and the rigor of the season, at this moment render my immediate departure impossible. They have not as of yet required that you should pass the sentence of my death. I will go soon but whither shall I find a place of rest? Whither alas shall I direct my steps? My country, our country is a prey to the spirit of revolutions: my brother, like you is a crowned captive!...

Ye shall not then deny me leave to take my daughters with me. Among the laws that have been imposed, there is none that separates a parent from her children; and though the rights of a Queen may be despised, surely some regard will be paid to those of a mother. With the arrival of spring I will quit these states, this land wherein I have reigned, and in which I have done some good. I will take part in the perils of my brother, and tell him that they can never vanquish me! I am a banished woman, but my conscience is unstained, for I have ever remembered the blood that runs in my veins. Farewell Sire!

The Queen[16]

Carlota's letter and secret correspondence with reactionary leaders in Portugal and Spain rallied family and political support around her. The Bragança and the nation divided between king and queen. Prince Miguel and three of his four sisters supported their mother's call for a return to a simpler time — a time of absolute monarchy. Teresa, the king's favorite daughter, widow of one Spanish prince and mother to another, sided with her Spanish born mother. Carlota successfully drove a wedge in the political center of the nation her husband hoped constitutional monarchy would bridge.[17]

The disenchanted, the fearful, and the ambitious supported Carlota. Reactionary leaders of the Catholic hierarchy joined forces with many of Portugal's most ancient noble families in hopes of retaining power, position and privilege. They recruited farmers and villagers afraid of a changing future. Many city dwellers, middle class merchants, Portuguese Masons, students and younger sons and daughters of aristocrats supported the constitutional monarchy, hopeful they could find a voice in a new Portugal.[18] For four years Portugal and its royal family were consumed by civil war. Across the Atlantic Prince Regent Pedro and Leopoldina tried to keep a similar fate from destroying Brazil.

8

"Fire from Two Sides"

With Portugal once again at war, its government turned to Brazil to pay for its arms and debts. Prince Regent Pedro wavered. Anger toward his mother and siblings and a sense of loyalty pulled him to the cause of his father. Yet like most Brazilians he was reluctant to become embroiled in the feuds of Europe. War had already cost the French and British their colonial possessions in North America. In South America, Brazilians warily listened to the war news from Portugal and from their near neighbors. Spain's former colonies were still warring a full decade after declaring independence.

At the center of the storm were the Portuguese prince and his Austrian archduchess—both only twenty-four years of age. Those wanting to continue political union with Portugal and Europe saw the royal couple as natural allies. Those seeking independence believed them the best hope for a united independent Brazil. Each group recognized the danger the royal pair would present as enemies. Austria's ambassador wrote, "malicious people stir up the fire from two sides."[1] Leopoldina explained the precariousness of her position in a letter to her father: "the unhappy situation in which I find myself ... being surrounded on one hand by a revolutionary spirit and on the other hand by a civil war which will blossom forth at any time. I, as a European and representing military potential, am suspect because there exists a rivalry and hatred between both parties.... How all this will end only God knows."[2]

Pedro, whose childhood was battled by rivalry, confusion, and disorder, was at his best at such times. Having survived his feuding parents and chaotic youth he bluntly wrote, "I know my mother is a bitch, but she brought me into this world without fear."[3] Brazil's prince regent was not afraid of life's uncertainties. He had never known anything else. Leopoldina, grounded by her own keen political instincts, had a talent for recognizing the short- and long-term implications of events. She hated politics, but she was a gifted politician. Brazil's royal couple made a formidable team.

After four years of marriage Leopoldina knew her husband's strengths and weaknesses. The most dangerous part of his character was his inability to stay focused. Behind the scenes, his wife fought with all her power to steady his resolve. As her influence grew, spies and enemies attempted to isolate and silence her. Leopoldina's letters and correspondence were delayed or censored and most of her entourage sent home. She secretly wrote her father, "Everything here is confusion. My husband, who unfortunately likes anything new, is enthusiastic, and I'm afraid he will pay dearly for it. As for me, they don't trust me, for that I am thankful because I don't have to give my opinion and thus have fewer arguments. Don't worry because, come what may, I won't lack anything, since I have my religion and my Austrian principles."[4] Leopoldina would need both.

In December 1821, as factionalism and calls for independence spread throughout Brazil, Portugal's embattled parliament determined to assert its authority. Brazil's delegates to the Cortes had been ignored, insulted, and alienated. Those slights and a proposal to divide the huge colony into smaller, controllable units further brought them together.[5] Then, in an attempt to subdue Brazil, the Cortes recalled the prince regent. Their stated purpose was to allow him to complete his education, but many saw the effort as a way of removing him as a rallying point for dissent.[6] The order caused excitement, dismay, and anger in Brazilians. Most believed their autonomy and independence would end the moment Pedro and Leopoldina sailed for Portugal.

Leopoldina longed to return to family and friends and to spend the rest of her life in the cultured lands of her birth. Her marriage contract stated she was to return to Portugal when political conditions permitted safe travel. Yet perhaps even more than her husband, she realized the political consequences of Portugal's recall of the prince. As a Habsburg whose family united much of Europe under its dynastic mantle, she understood the personal power of monarchy in keeping a diverse empire united and at peace. Leopoldina feared that without strong central leadership Brazilian unity would end and foreign intervention or civil war would follow. Despite weariness from yearly pregnancies and the neglect and mercurial temper of her husband, a homesick Leopoldina urged him to remain in America. In order to support and strengthen her position, she also encouraged him to recruit native-born Brazilians as allies and advisors.[7]

One supportive letter from São Paulo seemed to speak to the heart of her concerns. It read in part, "They [the Portuguese] aim at no less than disuniting us, weakening us, and in short, leaving us like miserable orphans, tearing from the bosom of the great family of Brazil the only common father who remained to us." Many of São Paulo's most prominent citizens signed the letter, including José Bonifácio Andrada, vice president of the province, an internationally respected educator, scholar, lawyer and scientist.[8]

The first days of January 1822, Leopoldina wrote, "The Prince is decided, but not so much as I would wish; the ministers will be changed for native-born men who have insight, and the government will be of the kind in the United North American free states. To achieve this has cost me much — I only wish I could inspire him with greater firmness."[9] On January 9, 1822, Pedro publicly announced his refusal to return to Europe, declaring, "As it is for the good of all and the general felicity of the nation, tell the people I will remain."[10] The words electrified the already intense political debates. Brazilian nationalists were thrilled, but many Portuguese denounced him as a traitor. As his father had secretly advised, Pedro placed himself at the front of a popular revolution. In the process he reinvented himself and the monarchy.

That night, Portuguese troops in Rio de Janeiro rioted and fighting broke out throughout the capital. The commanding officer of the Portuguese army threatened to forcibly return the prince to Lisbon as a prisoner.[11] Leopoldina, nearly eight months pregnant, fled the capital with her small children.

One of her most frightening childhood memories had been the similar royal flight she and her pregnant stepmother had made from Napoleon. Pedro escorted his wife and children part of the way south toward the royal planta-tion of Santa Cruz. He then rushed back to Rio to rally supporters. The abrupt temperature change from city to country and the journey itself over mountain-ous rutted roads caused their infant son to fall ill. Still Leopoldina did not allow herself rest. Leaving her children at Santa Cruz she set out to recruit José Bonifá-cio to join her husband in their hour of need.[12]

The friendship between the teacher-statesmen and homesick princess was born from this meeting. Individually and together they did much to create the Brazilian nation.[13] Returning with Bonifácio to Santa Cruz, Leopoldina intro-duced him to her children, saying, "These two little Brazilians are your com-patriots and I beg you to care for them with paternal love."[14]

Although Bonifácio had been born into one of the most influential polit-ical families in São Paulo, three decades of teaching and traveling abroad had earned him fame and respect. In Europe he was known as the Benjamin Franklin of Brazil, but he returned to his homeland to serve the land of his birth.[15] The violence and excesses of the French Revolution had led him to believe the ideals of the Enlightenment needed to be tempered by a strict constitutional monar-chy. He and Leopoldina shared many of the same views.[16]

As the political situation between Brazil and Portugal deteriorated, the Austrian government became concerned for Leopoldina's safety. The memory of Marie Antoinette haunted her father's court, and Prince Metternich demanded Leopoldina return to Europe.[17] To his surprise she refused. Leopold-ina wrote the Austrian emperor, "Our return to Europe has now become an impossibility because the noble spirit of the Brazilian people has become excited and it would be the greatest measure of ingratitude and the grossest political error if we did not extend all of our force and energy to guarantee a just lib-erty and flowering empire.... I am certain my dear father that you desire all that is good and noble of me and that you will not refrain from giving us all the help that is in your power and force during this emergency."[18] To her Aunt Marie Amélie she revealed how aware she was of the implications of her decision. She privately wrote, "It is necessary to endure the sacrifice of remaining in America and regardless of what this might cost me, I have decided to submit and part forever with my dear ones in Europe."[19]

Brazilians recognized Leopoldina's sacrifice and loyalty.[20] Austria's ambassador reported, "This sublime princess, Dona Leopoldina, has received the greatest evidence of a boundless affection from all classes of people. They now exhibit a devotion and a veneration that are well deserved, but that I would not have expected of this people."[21] Whenever Leopoldina was seen in public, she was enthusiastically cheered. To some, their Austrian princess seemed more popular than their Portuguese prince. People began to refer to her as "nossa mãe- our mother."[22] Leopoldina convinced Pedro the public support signaled the people's desire to become an independent nation under his leadership. With his popular wife at his side, Pedro's resolve strengthened and more Brazilians rallied to their cause.

Members of Brazil's Masonic lodges were well-educated social activists whose opinions influenced society well beyond their small numbers. To them the Prince Regent appeared their best hope for a united government built upon enlightened constitutional principles. Masonic leaders circulated petitions proclaiming Pedro the "Protector and Perpetual Defender of Brazil." With the support of the influential fraternal lodges, and with Bonifácio and Leopoldina steadying him, Pedro's confidence and stability grew. He began corresponding with Thomas Jefferson and other statesmen and sought advice from a broad spectrum of enlightened advisors. For a time he actually seemed to become the man Leopoldina believed him to be.[23]

9

"The Apple Is Ripe"

Pedro's transformation was fleeting, and within months he was clashing with the equally strong-willed Bonifácio.[1] By the close of 1822, Brazil's prince regent had dismissed his chief advisor in a burst of anger. Public opinion and Leopoldina refused to support him. For the first time in their married life Leopoldina openly disagreed with her husband. She reasoned, pleaded, and argued that a political rupture with Portugal was imminent, making Bonifácio's support more important than ever.

With his wife at his side Pedro traveled twice to Bonifácio's home to persuade him to return to their side. At the close of their second visit, Bonifácio joined them on his second floor balcony announcing his return to government. Waiting crowds responded with celebrations. Perhaps only Leopoldina could have persuaded her prince to humble himself in such a public manner. Bonifácio rejoined the royal couple at the moment of their greatest need.[2]

Revolts in provinces to the north and south and rumors of an invading Portuguese naval force threatened from three sides. In the midst of the growing political crisis personal tragedy struck. Leopoldina and Pedro's infant son died. He had not been well since the royal family's traumatic flight from the capital, but they were not prepared for the loss. Leopoldina blamed Portugal's "damned scoundrels."[3] Broken hearted, she wrote her aunt Marie Amélie. "The poor little one who had a weak nervous system, caught some sort of inflammation of the liver and poorly treated, or rather improperly diagnosed, died after two weeks of continuous suffering, and a final epileptic siege that lasted twenty-eight hours. I assure you, dear Aunt, that in my whole life, I have never known greater grief and that only my religion and the passage of time will console me."[4]

Six weeks after the flight to Santa Cruz, a month following the death of her son, Leopoldina delivered another royal daughter. She was named Januária for the Brazilian city of her birth. The following day Leopoldina was seen standing at her desk writing government reports to her husband.[5] In the next two years two additional daughters were born. One was named Paula for the city of São Paulo and the other Francesca to honor Leopoldina's father. Then a son was born. He was named for his father and would grow up to be emperor of Brazil, and the father of Princess Isabel.[6]

Much of Leopoldina's personal popularity was centered on the devotion she showered on her children. To Brazilians it seemed to mirror her relationship with them. But she was more than the nation's most beloved mother. She was unlike any woman in Brazil, certainly any royal woman they had ever known. Queen Maria I was seldom seen. Maria Teresa was known only in the inner circles of government. And the frenetic Carlota Joaquina had been defined through scandal. Leopoldina's first public appearance was attending church not in a curtained sedan chair carried by slaves but riding her own horse to the Glória Church.[7] She soon became a familiar figure in the city and countryside, smiling and bowing to those she met.

Even with nearly uninterrupted pregnancies and political turmoil, Leopoldina sponsored educational and scientific expeditions, personally collecting, cataloguing and publicizing Brazilian gems, minerals, plants, flowers, birds, butterflies, insects and wild animals. She brought artists from Austria and scientists from Bavaria to paint, sketch, collect and report Brazil's glories to an amazed and fascinated Europe. Brazil became famous throughout the world as an exotic showplace of unspoiled beauty, a treasure house for scientific research and investigation. Leopoldina's promotion of its natural wonders and sponsoring of scientific investigations elevated Brazil's status on both sides of the Atlantic.[8]

In one of her first letters from America she wrote, "The country is charmingly full of delightful places, high mountains, green prairies, forests of the rarest and most magnificent trees that are strewn with the most beautiful flowers around which birds with incomparable plumage flutter. I must say that Portuguese America would be an earthly paradise if it were not for this unbearable heat."[9]

Following her well publicized marriage, the nations of central Europe began importing Brazilian products popularized by the artists and scientists Leopoldina brought to Brazil.[10] In doing so she helped break the economic stranglehold Portugal and England held on Brazil and helped shatter the gender stereotypes of the invisible Brazilian woman. Unlike Carlota Joaquina, she quickly adapted her heavy European-style fashions to the realities of the tropical climate. Practical, comfortable linens replaced layers of petticoats, stiff collars, and silks and satins. Leopoldina's outfits caused some to whisper she looked more like a Gypsy than a princess, but such comments only made her laugh. She refused to wear makeup or accessories in the sweltering heat. People who judged others by outward appearances were confounded and confused by such behavior. Her husband was one of them.[11]

Pedro understood on some level the political value of his wife, and he appreciated her devotion to their children, but he never stopped enjoying the company and beds of other women. To most Brazilians he and Leopoldina presented an image of a model husband and wife. They appeared together at the theatre and church and were seen horseback riding, swimming, boating, and hiking the hills around their country palace.[12] Brazil had never before seen a marriage where partners shared their time and activities so openly or equally. It sent a powerful message to married and unmarried men and women throughout Brazil. Their partnership did a great deal to energize and personalize Brazil's emergence as a nation in the years ahead, including their wearing of the patriotic colors of their respective royal houses to public events. Leopoldina personally designed matching blue military uniforms with silver spurs and high leather boots to wear when they reviewed their troops.[13]

Brazil's newly created cavalry was designated as Leopoldina's own lancers. Many recruits were former slaves of every shade of skin handsomely dressed in light colors that stood out in the bright tropical sun.[14] In contrast to Carlota's cadets, whose purpose was to terrorize, Leopoldina's lancers celebrated racial diversity.

Leopoldina also took a special interest in the creation of the Brazilian navy, regularly inspecting all new ships of the line and personally greeting naval recruits and officers. Brazilian sailors, many of them of African descent, were placed under her royal protection and patronage.[15] She and Pedro accepted the respect and affectionate hand kissing of Brazil's "naval, military, civil officers, and private citizens" without regard to color.[16] Court observers were struck by the sincerity of their respect and genuine acceptance of all Brazilians.[17]

Racial tolerance, celebrations, and any challenging physical activities came easily to Pedro, but details of governing bored him. Many day-to-day decisions of government were turned over to José Bonifácio, who understood and appreciated Leopoldina's political assets more than her own husband. In addition to tempering Pedro's nervous energy, Leopoldina helped legitimize Brazil in the eyes of a conservative, militarily powerful Europe.[18] Although in a state of undeclared war with Portugal, the country legally remained a part of that kingdom. Austria was bound by military treaty to come to Portugal's aide if and when Brazil formally declared independence. Bonifácio counted on Leopoldina's family influence to keep her father neutral. His confidence was not misplaced.

Brazil's independence could only be achieved if Portugal was separated from its political and military allies—including Austria. Leopoldina worked behind the scenes to isolate Portugal, writing her father about the potential economic benefits a free Brazil could bring Austria's own troubled provinces. The "non-political" Austrian archduchess wrote, "Brazil's power and greatness should be of major interest to the European powers particularly with respect to trade and commerce and we want nothing more than to establish such relations with the Austrian possessions in Italy and to give their ports exclusive preference which would be adventitious to the land of my birth."[19]

Pedro appointed Leopoldina regent, freeing him to travel through Brazil to gather support for the difficult times ahead. Leopoldina became the first female head of state in America since the ancient days of the Mayan monarchy.[20] She wrote her father, "God knows that I have never wanted to rule." And in another letter to her Aunt Marie Amélie, she wrote, "I am in charge of all the affairs of state which is only a small sacrifice which I can make for Brazil."[21] Leopoldina was no Carlota Joaquina.

Leopoldina was princess regent when Portugal moved against Brazil. A dispatch arrived from Lisbon denouncing her husband as a traitor, declaring his acts as regent null and void, and demanding his immediate return to Europe. Failure to submit would result in war, invasion, and imprisonment. Unconfirmed reports also reached Leopoldina that a Portuguese force had landed in the north. It was the moment Leopoldina had dreaded, but for which she was prepared. She summoned the council of state into emergency session then sent a letter to Pedro, traveling near São Paulo, detailing the crisis. In part she wrote, "I regret to send you this disagreeable news and I do not know if all that it contains is true. If it is, it disturbs my heart to know that a troop of Portuguese soldiers has landed at Bahia.... Yesterday there was a rumor that a squadron of Portuguese ships was seen off our coast and I gave the order to receive them with cannon fire."[22]

The following day Leopoldina appealed for Pedro to return to Rio. "The news from Lisbon is most discouraging: fourteen battalions are ready to disembark aboard three ships. Your letters to Portugal have been published and the people of Lisbon have manifested indignant expressions against your person. Six hundred men have already landed in Bahia aboard two or three war ships and our traitorous squadron remains paralyzed with open mouths."[23]

With the council of state meeting around the clock, one weary counselor asked Leopoldina what options they had. She replied, "There is only one possibility: the immediate declaration of independence of Brazil!"[24] Bonifácio wrote, Leopoldina's response "filled the cabinet members with the inspiration and courage to take this irrevocable step."[25] In her role as princess regent, Leopoldina signed Brazil's declaration of independence.[26] She sent her husband Portugal's demands and her blunt response. "Pedro, Brazil is like a volcano.... this moment is the most important one of your life.... Brazil wants you as its monarch. With or without your help, independence will be achieved! The apple is ripe; pick it now or it will rot."[27] With those last eleven words, Princess Isabel's grandmother forever closed the door on her life in Europe.

10

"Cancer"

When Pedro read Leopoldina's letter witnesses reported his face turned dark crimson. His shouted response on September 7, 1822, was, "Independence or Death."[1] By the time he returned to Rio de Janeiro, Bonifácio and their supporters had proclaimed Pedro and Leopoldina emperor and empress of Brazil. A formal coronation was celebrated on December 1, 1822, in Rio's cathedral and the Paço Imperial, the former palace of royal viceroys. On that day a select honor guard of four Brazilians—one white man, one black, one Amerindian, and a man of blended racial heritage—escorted the royal couple, representing the multiracial composition of the new Brazilian empire.[2] It was the one hundred and seventy-eighth anniversary of the revolution that first brought the Braganças to Portugal's throne. Once again a Bragança had placed family and monarchy at the forefront of social revolution.

With their new nation preparing to fight for independence, Pedro, Leopoldina, and José Bonifácio waved from the balcony of the Paço Imperial to thousands of saluting Brazilians. To many it seemed the royal couple had become the living embodiment of their country—the human face and soul of an independent Brazil. Church bells and cannons boomed but were drowned out by human cheers. The former prince, archduchess and teacher set out to create a new nation as their tiny army and navy prepared to fight. The three founders of Brazilian independence were different in many ways, but shared a common dream. They wanted a united, peaceful country, free of slavery.

Leopoldina's attitudes regarding race could be traced to an enlightened branch of her family. The Habsburgs were not traditionally associated with liberal thinking, but her great-grandmother Maria Theresa, and grandfather and namesake Emperor Leopold, had taught, "princes must be convinced of the equality of human beings."[3] Empress Maria Theresa wrote, "All men are equal and must have the same rights."[4] Leopoldina was their spiritual and lineal descendent. As the niece of Marie Antoinette, she was an unlikely revolutionary but did not have to look as far as Europe to know about the violent consequences of revolutions. Brazil's Haitian neighbors on the French Island of Santo Domingo and to the north in Dutch Guinea and British Guinea overthrew established governments, defeated well-trained armies, and massa-cred thousands.[5] Slave revolts sparked all three revolutions.

Brazil's slaves also rose up against their bondage, some to fight, others to flee. The country's deep forests held thousands of runaway slaves who would rather die deep in the interior than live in bondage. Their numbers had grown so large the army feared pursuing them. Still Brazilians thought nothing of attending the ballet in Rio where complexions of the dancers ranged from "deep black to a *café-au-lait* tint," and then returning home attended by similarly complexioned slaves.[6] A British visitor noted, "I sometimes saw groups of well dressed females here, shopping for slaves, exactly as I have seen English ladies amusing themselves at our Bazaars."[7] To Leopoldina slavery was an abomina-tion.

No one knew the exact number of slaves held in Brazil, but Leopoldina was determined to find out. She proposed each Brazilian household create a family book to record the name, birth, gender, legal status and relationship of everyone on their properties. Slaveholders feared such a national census was a step toward emancipation and stopped the proposal from being implemented.[8]

In a more direct move against slavery Leopoldina quietly advocated free-ing the children born of slaves once they reached maturity. Pedro implemented the idea within the royal household, but not as official government policy.[9] As with most things in his life, Pedro viewed slavery through an erratic lens. He came to genuinely abhor slavery and could sincerely state, "My blood is the same as that of the Negro's." His statement may have been more than mere rhet-oric. Many believed the Portuguese royal family itself had a strong "Negro strain" dating from João I and the nation's Moorish roots.[10]

Still Pedro did not free his own slaves.[11] He insisted no one had the right to own another human being, but continued giving his children slaves as gifts.[12] Many of his childhood playmates and friends were of African descent, and as emperor his personal physician, members of his court, and several of his mis-tresses were people of color.[13] Pedro's conflicting racial attitudes were just one of many parts of her husband that confused and bedeviled Leopoldina.

Shortly before convening his country's first general assembly he anony-mously published a newspaper article condemning slavery as a "cancer gnaw-ing away at Brazil."[14] In it Pedro detailed the economic and moral evils of forced servitude. A plan was presented ending the slave trade in two years, gradually replacing slaves with an immigrant work force of free skilled laborers. He argued that emancipation could be accomplished "little by little" without destroying the economy, disrupting national unity, or disturbing the nation's peace. Pedro's anonymous testament was widely read and became one of the earliest aboli-tionist statements ever presented in Brazil.[15]

Urged on by Leopoldina the young emperor may have originally planned to present the proposal to the General Assembly, but some believed José Bonifá-cio persuaded him to publish it anonymously. Like many in Brazil Bonifácio believed independence must come before emancipation. Once Brazil's struggle for independence turned in their favor, he, the emperor and empress hoped abolition would quickly follow.

Brazil's forces eventually defeated troops loyal to Portugal on land and sea. With the help of his ship the *Leopoldina*, the brilliant British mercenary Thomas Cochran forced the surrender of rebellious provinces in the north, causing the Portuguese fleet to return to Europe.[16] Portugal's military threat to Brazil gradually faded, but the economic and political realities of nation-building blocked steps toward abolition. Pedro's council of state fiercely resisted addressing the slavery question or even allowing it to be discussed in the General Assembly. They insisted that with independence nearly within reach, the major crisis facing Brazil was a labor shortage that would overwhelm the government if emancipation took place. After long and bitter debates, the young emperor was persuaded to postpone any reform of Brazil's slave system.

Government ministers did agree to create a national policy to encourage immigration. It was hoped increasing the number of free, skilled workers would lessen the need for slaves. Leopoldina wrote, "If no more population comes and the ground is not broken through great effort and patience, change will be difficult."[17] She redoubled her own efforts with European contacts to increase immigration, encouraging thousands of German and Swiss farmers, merchants, herdsmen, and families to come to Brazil.[18] Once they arrived she financially supported them through their first difficult years.[19] Several of these early European colonies were named in her honor.[20] In time Leopoldina's communities laid the foundation for Brazil's industrial future, providing the country with its first modern flourmills, tanneries, quarries and factories.[21]

Disappointed by the postponement of abolition and perhaps hoping to please his wife, Pedro freed a small number of personal slaves, providing them farmland on royal estates.[22] He also attempted to fulfill the promise his father made by ending the slave trade south of the equator. Brazilian diplomats were instructed to begin secretly negotiating a treaty with European powers to set a firm deadline after which no additional slaves would be imported to Brazil. He and Leopoldina continued sharing a dream of ending slavery, but their hopes regarding abolition were overwhelmed by marital problems.[23] Pedro had fallen in love with a married woman on the trip to São Paulo on which he declared independence. Unlike his other lovers and many of his ideals, she did not quickly fade away.

Domitila de Castro was intelligent, worldly, seductively beautiful, and politically ambitious. She understood how to please Brazil's emperor in ways his wife was unable or unwilling to do. In his earlier indiscretions, Pedro protected Leopoldina's feelings and position. With Domitila, he protected neither.[24] By January 1823 Pedro's new mistress moved from Santos near São Paulo to Rio de Janeiro. To many Brazilians she became that "Santos Woman." The Austrian ambassador noted her immediate influence, writing, "This unfortunate alliance causes the Emperor to lose respect and trust daily. On the other hand the Empress wins these same things ... through her boundless patience and her constant goodness toward everyone."[25]

With his mind and heart elsewhere, the twenty-five-year-old emperor grew increasingly frustrated, bored, and impatient with the details of government. A political observer noted Pedro was "at his best during a revolution and at his worst when governing a state."[26] He began avoiding his counselors, including his wife, to spend more time with his mistress. As Pedro's personal behavior deteriorated and Domitila's influence increased, his political thinking became more reactionary. He began holding ministerial meetings in the home he built for his mistress within sight of the royal palace. The lines between the public and private life of the emperor became blurred.[27]

An English governess in Brazil wrote, "At first different women refused to visit the Santos woman. Soon they perceived that their recalcitrance would not improve the situation of the Empress, but would certainly ruin that of their own families."[28] When Domitila was refused admittance to a theatre in Rio, Pedro ordered it closed.

The deterioration of his relationship with Leopoldina was echoed in his faltering political partnership with his mentor José Bonifácio. Pedro tolerated scolding from the prime minister regarding his royal duties, but reprimands regarding the neglect of family responsibilities precipitated a public rupture. Bonifácio resigned as prime minister but remained an elected representative in the General Assembly from the powerful state of São Paulo. No one had a better understanding of Pedro's strengths or weaknesses and he became a formidable opponent. When the assembly took up the task of writing the new Brazilian constitution, Bonifácio led the fight to limit the powers of the emperor.

Domitila reportedly urged Pedro to seize the opportunity to crush his enemies.[29] He ordered the military to forcibly dismiss the legislature. Opponents were ordered arrested, including José Bonifácio, who was then exiled to Europe. One Brazilian writer lamented. "The nation lies prone ... weeping at such base ingratitude."[30]

In Portugal, despite the fact that the political and military tide had turned against Pedro's mother, Carlota must have smiled. She and three of her daughters had been imprisoned at Queluz and Pedro's autocratic brother Miguel had been exiled to Vienna. Now her "liberal" son seemed to be siding with their political leanings.

Shortly after Pedro and Leopoldina declared Brazilian independence, Carlota reportedly hired an assassin to kill him. Pedro discovered the plot, arrested and executed the man, cut off his hand and sent it to his mother as a gift.[31] In her own motherly fashion Carlota appreciated the gesture. It always pleased her when she saw some of herself in her children, but nothing pleased her more than Pedro's latest reactionary behavior.

Then Pedro waffled. In an attempt to calm the people's anger against his dictatorial behavior he announced he would personally supervise the writing of a new constitution. He promised it would be more liberal than the one the legislature proposed. In many ways it was, but he deleted the portion mandating equal educational opportunities for women and presented the constitution to the people, rather than the people presenting it to him. Pedro declared, "I will do anything for the people, but nothing by the people."[32] Despite his best intentions, the hopes of his wife and many of his fellow Brazilians he had within him the heart and soul of an autocrat.

Brazil's new constitution included many civil liberties such as freedom of the press, but was balanced by conservative safeguards against social and political change. The role of emperor as royal arbitrator was the core of Brazil's constitutional government. Pedro was to be the nation's moderating force, balancing opposing forces to find the common good. He had once again remade himself and his monarchy, now becoming the protector of the status quo, the moderator of change in Brazil. The greatest challenge to the new constitution was its dependence on the wisdom of its emperor. In creating a new constitutional order Pedro turned away from the advisors and supporters who had brought him his throne. His new role positioned him in an alliance with Portuguese merchants, wealthy slave traders, and Brazil's tradition-bound planter class. All three groups had a vested interest in maintaining the existing social order — especially slavery.

The emperor did not completely surrender his ideals. England and the United States demanded an end to the African slave trade as a price for the recognition of Brazil's independence. Pedro used their demands as political leverage against his nation's slave traders. In November 1826, under pressures from all sides, they reluctantly agreed to ban the importation of slaves to Brazil by 1830.[33] It was one of the few consolations easing Leopoldina's aching heart.

11

"First Empress of the New World"

In the next four years the number of slaves brought to Brazil and their price doubled. But by the time the 1830 deadline ending the slave trade arrived, Pedro's government no longer had the support or willpower to enforce the ban.[1] Still Pedro's attempt to end the trade entailed a major financial sacrifice on the part of his government. A foreign diplomat noted, "A slave pays to the government 20 percent on the first price and the same amount every time he is purchased again.... To consent then, to the abolition of the slave trade, attended with such a serious deduction from the embarrassed revenues of the country, was no small sacrifice on the part of the government, and affords a strong presumption that the Emperor is very sincere in his humane wishes for the extinction of the traffic."[2]

The emperor's abolitionist beliefs were genuine, but few Brazilians outside his wife and Brazil's slaves shared them. Pedro initially placated proslavery forces by assuring them the economic and political benefits of an independent Brazil would offset short-term revenue losses. They were temporarily appeased when the United States became the first nation to recognize Brazilian independence, followed by England and Leopoldina's Austria. Recognition from the great powers should have strengthened Pedro's position, but public opinion had begun turning against him.

In European exile, José Bonifácio, free of government responsibilities, published his long anticipated anti-slavery manifesto. His stinging words mocked the emperor he once served. "How can there exist a liberal and lasting constitution in a country constantly inhabited by a huge multitude of brutalized and hostile slaves? Let us therefore begin at once this great work for the expiation of our ancient crimes and sins. Yes we must not only be just, but also repentant. We must prove before God and the rest of mankind that we are sorry for all we have done over the centuries to justice and religion, that we are moving forward in harmony with the precept of not doing unto others that which we do not wish done to us."[3]

Economic uncertainty and political unrest spread across Brazil. Bonifácio's blistering anti-slavery rhetoric stirred one end of the political spectrum; doubts and fears regarding banning the slave trade stirred the other. For the first time in months, emperor and empress were seen everywhere together; even riding in blinding rainstorms. But when Brazilians recognized Leopoldina's riding companion, their cheering stopped.

Bonifácio continued railing against the poison of slavery, writing, "Generous citizens of Brazil who love your country, recognize that without the total abolition of the infamous African slave trade, *and* without the subsequent emancipation of the present slaves, Brazil will never affirm her national independence and assure and defend her liberal constitution."[4] The words must have been especially bitter to the young emperor who more than ever needed the support of his nation's slaveholders.

Pedro tried ignoring his growing numbers of critics, but soon sought refuge in the home of Domitila de Castro a short walk from his own palace. It was there he fathered their first daughter, and their other children that followed. The emperor's reckless affair threatened to become a public scandal and he asked Leopoldina to appoint his mistress as one of her ladies in waiting. An appointment from the popular empress would place Domitila under a mantle of respectability and allow him to remain physically close to both women in his life.[5]

Leopoldina unhappily agreed. The Austrian ambassador noted, "The most extreme self control prescribed the behavior of the Archduchess. Such clever behavior endured for her the greatest approval of her husband."[6] But the English ambassador condemned the emperor and his behavior. "He is young, utterly non-instructed and inexperienced in business, impetuous and warm in character, seeking ardently ... in the most violent and boisterous amusements."[7]

Half a year later on his birthday, Pedro elevated his mistress to the ranks of Brazilian nobility, naming her the Viscondessa de Santos. The following year, she was appointed the Marquêsa de Santos. Then in the Brazilian tradition of the time, he brought his "natural" daughter to be raised in the same nursery as his children by Leopoldina. Brazil's empress was consumed with anger, but publicly remained silent. Privately she wrote, "I could bear anything, as I have in the past, except seeing the little one treated as my children's equal. I tremble with rage when I look at her and it is the greatest sacrifice on my part to receive her."[8]

The humiliated Leopoldina secretly wrote her aunt Marie Amélie, "I would have many things to tell you and would beg you not to refuse me your advice, but since I am certain that they open all my letters, I must be prudent and remain completely silent about everything that has to do with politics; and there are other matters where the advice of a second mother, which you have always been, dear aunt, would have been indispensable."[9]

In December 1825, Pedro's wife and mistress both gave birth to sons named for their emperor. The birth of a legitimate male heir afforded Leopoldina an opportunity to issue an ultimatum. She demanded Pedro end his relationship with his mistress, or his marriage with her. Surprised and stunned, Brazil's emperor refused to consider his wife's demands. Leopoldina responded by formally petitioning to be allowed to return to her father's court. She signed her letter "Maria Leopoldina, Archduchess of Austria."[10]

Pedro was furious, but perhaps for the first time in his life, also frightened. He returned to Leopoldina's side, but refused to dismiss his mistress. Alternating periods of charm with outbursts of fury, he did whatever he could to change his wife's mind. Their short reconciliation ended in a violent quarrel and another pregnancy. Leopoldina had difficulty eating and sleeping, and the Prussian ambassador wrote, "How amazed I was to find the sublime princess so pale, almost fading away, in the flower of her years."[11] The royal marriage became the major topic of gossip throughout the capital and the nation.

A journey to the restless northern provinces was planned to direct the nation's attention away from the emperor's personal and political problems. In recognition of her continued popularity and perhaps in an attempt to calm scandalous rumors, Leopoldina accompanied him. He also brought Domitila.[12] By the time they returned to Rio de Janeiro the royal marriage was irretrievably broken. Pedro prepared to travel south in an attempt to keep one of the nation's southernmost provinces from declaring independence. A public reception was planned for diplomats to wish him well on his expedition, but Leopoldina refused to appear if the Marquêsa de Santos attended.

As guests gathered in the diplomatic reception room they were able to hear Brazil's emperor, empress and his mistress engage in violent argument. Pedro physically attempted to force his wife to join them, but Leopoldina loudly and physically refused. Members of the palace staff, and foreign diplomats and their embarrassed wives, heard the entire incident. In the end Pedro received his guests with the Marquêsa de Santos served as his official hostess. The Austrian minister wrote a full report to his government concluding, "The Emperor forgot himself." Leopoldina's father upon reading his minister's correspondence, stated to Metternich, "Through the enclosed reports ... I have learned, alas, how miserable a scoundrel is my son-in-law."[13]

The last heated words between the emperor and empress of Brazil were in the royal apartments. During their disagreement, Leopoldina reportedly fell or was thrown to the floor. Pedro immediately left the city to deal with the military revolt in the south. He never saw his wife again. Despite their bitter estrangement Pedro once again appointed Leopoldina regent in his absence. Although she had sunk into a deep depression, she presided over public ceremonies and Council of State meetings.[14] Four days before the birthday of her son, Leopoldina began running a high fever. On December 2, 1826, on her infant son's first birthday she miscarried a three-month old fetus. Court doctors were unable to stop her subsequent bleeding, fevers, or infection.[15]

With health and pride broken, Leopoldina's brilliant mind shattered. Delirious and incoherent, she repeatedly screamed and murmured the name of the woman representing her torment. The Marquêsa made repeated attempts to enter Leopoldina's bedroom, but was rebuffed by attendants. Reports that the empress's illness might be life threatening caused civil unrest fanned by rumors the emperor's violence had caused the miscarriage. Austria's ambassador noted, "It must no longer be concealed from the Emperor that the masses are in an alarming state of ferment. The long duration of the Empress's illness is the greatest contributing factor in maintaining peace."[16]

In moments of lucidity Leopoldina dictated her final letters, begging her attendants to save her children from her rival.[17] To her sister, the widow of the Emperor Napoleon, she dictated, "My adored Marie! Reduced to the most deplorable state of health and brought to the last moment of my life amidst great suffering, I also have the misfortune to be unable to explain to you in person all the sentiments that have so long been inscribed on my soul. Hear the cry of a victim who begs of you not vengeance, but pity and help, sprung from your sisterly affection for those innocent children who are now orphans, yet will remain in the power of the same persons who were authors of my misfortunes.... For almost four years, my adored Marie, as I have written you, for love of a seductive monster I have been reduced to the state of greatest slavery and totally forgotten by my adored Pedro. Lately I have received final proof that he has forgotten me completely, mistreating me in the presence of that very one who is the cause of all my afflictions."[18]

Her thoughts also wandered to José Bonifácio. In one of her last lucid moments she dictated a letter to him pleading for reconciliation with her husband and imploring her old friend to return to Brazil to tutor her children.[19] By the time Bonifácio received Leopoldina's letter she was dead. Death came two weeks to the day after her husband held his last diplomatic reception. The empress of Brazil, archduchess of Austria, birth mother of five small children and the adopted mother of her nation was twenty-nine years of age. The emperor's popularity and reputation did not survive her death.[20]

During her final illness churches were kept open day and night as Brazilians prayed for her recovery. Large crowds gathered in pouring rains outside the palace keeping a silent vigil. When word spread of her death, people reacted with an outburst of anger and grief. The military were called out to prevent riots and control the surging mobs. Rio's chief of police reported, "all measures have been taken to prevent the possibilities of ill intentioned people from going to extremes because of the fatal event which has just occurred."[21] Newspapers were soon filled with the rumors surrounding Leopoldina's death. In the days that followed, hundreds of letters were printed from Brazilians on what her loss meant to the nation and their personal lives.

One man wrote, "I render my humble and due homage to the virtues of the Empress. Disinterested, retiring, her character was kindness, her conduct modesty, a dutiful consort, an affectionate mother, an affable princess, a friend to the sciences, generous, just, and full of sensibility. She loved the human race and did good to all of whom her arm could extend. She never saw distress without a corresponding feeling of affliction and an effort to relieve it.... The virtues that adorned her—her wisdom, her moderation, her prudence, her charities, her very sufferings, have endeared her memory to a sincere people. This is not the language of adulation or the tactic of a court. It tears into the eyes of every citizen, and clothes them with spontaneous mourning."[22]

A mourning woman wrote, "I never supposed that any motive would compel me to leave the privacy and retirement in which I lived and become a correspondent of the public press: but I am a Brazilian woman, a wife, and a mother, and I cannot restrain the impulse which urges me to give utterance to what I feel on this melancholy occasion. Though I want words in which to express myself; and when I attempt to write, the only expression of my grief is tears. Still I cannot rest in my apartment if I do not publicly avow the affliction with which my heart is bursting. Who, imbued with the feelings of our common nature, and gifted with a human heart, that does not weep when the best of women, the most dutiful of wives, and the kindest of mothers, has ceased to exist among us? To women, wives, mothers, I would appeal to join their tears with mine. Would that they could restore her life! Would that my blood could revive her! Every drop should be shed for that purpose, in testimony how dear in person and valuable in character she was to all Brazilians."[23]

A Protestant clergyman visiting Rio de Janeiro from North America was struck by the outpouring and sincerity of such letters. He wrote, "The writers ... were the simple, sincere and unsought tribute of respect and affection from persons in the middle ranks of life. They all praise her, not for her high station, but for her moral worth and personal qualities."[24]

He also felt moved to comment on the direct and indirect influence her life might have had on women and other Brazilians had she lived. "I have been more particular in noticing the death and character of this lady, because she was the first Empress of the New World. Had she lived, her conduct might have had an important influence on that of her sex here ... and excited a correspondent feeling among those who have hitherto taken no kind of interest in them."[25] His comment might also have addressed Leopoldina's influence in helping Brazilians rethink their attitudes toward slavery. Her death may have delayed the abolitionist cause by a generation or more in Brazil.

Like his nation Pedro grieved. In his self-centered but sincere way he wrote, "She loved me with the greatest of loves and I admired her honesty; I feel my heart breaking with pain." Austria's minister to the Brazilian court contrasted the personal with the cold political implications of the passing. "Her death was sincerely and unanimously bemoaned. She leaves a dangerous vacuum."[26]

Perhaps the most prophetic of all epitaphs came from her father. The emperor of Austria sadly but philosophically wrote, "It would appear that a special destiny summoned my daughter to America."[27] It remained for her infant son, who would become Princess Isabel's father, and for her unborn granddaughter Isabel, to fulfill Leopoldina's "destiny."

$\mathscr{A}$ 12 $\mathscr{A}$

"My Beloved Son and Emperor"

Nine days after his first birthday Leopoldina's son kissed his dead mother goodbye for the final time. The young prince never remembered the kiss or any other moment with his mother. Her laugh, her voice, her touch were all beyond his recall. He only knew her face through her portraits and her personality through the stories told about her. Yet in almost all ways he was his mother's son.[1]

Of all his ancestors Pedro II seemed most like his mother. Physically, mentally and temperamentally, Leopoldina lived through him. In time his father's grace and handsome features would become his own; but they would be displayed through his mother's blond hair, deep blue eyes, and fair skin. His passion for languages, mathematics and the sciences, and his keen ability to understand large and small details were also maternal gifts. Pedro himself seemed to recognize and respect her influence. For sixty years, the second emperor of Brazil made a pilgrimage to her grave on the anniversary of her birth.

Childhood ended with the death of his mother. Within a short time political turmoil and intrigue in Brazil and Portugal claimed his father, his oldest sister, and even the first teacher who nurtured his learning. While still a child Pedro was called upon to assume the position to which he had been born — the "Constitutional Emperor and Perpetual Defender of Brazil." Leopoldina had wished to give Pedro and his sisters a gift that could never be taken away — an education to sustain them in the uncertain times ahead. It had been her greatest desire to devote herself to that end. With that in mind, like her great-grandmother Empress Maria Theresa, she wrote out the dictums by which each of her royal children should be raised. Determined they have an education completely different from their father's, she analyzed their individual strengths, interests, and personal traits and provided each with an individualized curriculum. From her deathbed, Leopoldina asked her friend José Bonifácio to return from exile to serve as their tutor.[2]

Pedro I did his best to deal with the emotional and political backlash caused by the death of his empress. Even before Leopoldina died, the Brazilian and

Portuguese thrones had been shaken. Months earlier, shortly after finally recognizing Brazilian independence, Pedro's father suddenly and mysteriously died. Rumors of murder could not be proven, but many suspected poison and Carlota.

Portugal's king had selected Isabel Maria, the only daughter to remain loyal to him, to serve as regent in the event of his death. His designated heir, however, was Brazil's embattled emperor. When his choice became known, it was greeted with riots in Rio de Janeiro. Pedro used his army and paid mercenaries to keep order. The time had passed when he, or anyone, could wear the crown of both countries.[3] Neither Brazil nor Portugal would tolerate a united monarchy, but he waited as long as possible before making any public statement that could cost him one throne or the other.

Without Leopoldina everything was more difficult. He attempted to calm the political storms by avoiding contact with the Marquêsa de Santos and by ending his feud with José Bonifácio, who was recalled from Europe. In a whirlwind of activity he publicly swore to uphold the new constitution, created a two-house parliament, abolished the death penalty for political crimes, and granted limited male suffrage. Still his crown, and the crown of others, was not secure. The latest French revolution drove his Bourbon cousins from the throne, replaced by his Orleans cousins Louis-Philippe and Marie Amélie, Leopoldina's much-loved aunt. The revolution did more than exchange one branch of the royal family for another. His Orleans relatives were recognized as king and queen *of the French*—but not of France.[4] Power and position no longer came by divine right, but from the people.

In Brazil, the press continued attacking Pedro as they lionized his dead empress. Months after her death, one Brazilian newspaper wrote of Leopoldina, "What Brazilian does not know how much she advocated our interests, how much effect the attractiveness of her sublime virtues had, and in the end how much her family relationships to the great monarchs of Europe contributed to making known our efforts for independence and freedom. Today they revere Dona Leopoldina in Brazil as the 'Mother of the Nation'; they describe her in Brazilian schools as the 'model for Brazilian mothers.'"[5]

As his dead wife's legend grew, Pedro was unable to regain his political equilibrium. In 1828 Brazil's southernmost province gained independence, becoming the country of Uruguay.[6] Revolts in other provinces further threatened Brazil's unity and peace. In an attempt to overcome the lingering bitterness over Leopoldina's death, Pedro decided to again marry. He and his advisors hoped a royal wedding might stabilize his throne, but few royal houses were willing to accept the risk. Finally Amélia de Leuchtenberg, the seventeen-year-old daughter of Princess Augusta of Bavaria and Prince Eugene de Beauhaunais, agreed. Her father was the son of Empress Josephine of France and the loyal stepson of the fallen French emperor. Forced to remove the name Napoleon from her title, Amélia exacted her own price in exchange. She demanded the

Marquêsa de Santos be banished to São Paulo. Pedro reluctantly agreed, but it was not enough to save his throne.[7]

In Portugal Princess Regent Isabel Maria struggled to fulfill her role as a constitutional monarch, but neither she nor her nation's politicians were experienced in the process.[8] The Portuguese Cortes, England, and foreign governments demanded Brazil's emperor return to Europe to claim the throne or appoint a permanent successor. Pedro proposed a Bragança compromise to keep crown, country and family together. He announced he would abdicate the Portuguese throne in favor of his young daughter Maria da Glória. He would also recall his twenty-year-old brother Miguel from exile if he renounced his absolutist past, swore allegiance to the Portuguese constitution and agreed to marry the ten-year-old Maria if a papal dispensation could be obtained. Urged on by his mother, Miguel acquiesced to his brother's demands, and on October 29, 1826, with the consent of the pope a proxy marriage ceremony was performed uniting uncle and niece in matrimony.[9] Miguel promised to serve as prince regent until his bride came of age at fourteen, when he would become her consort.

European powers were troubled by Pedro's plan, not because of a marriage or age difference between niece and uncle, but because an emperor had willingly embraced the ideals of constitutional monarchy. England's prime minister wrote, "The abdication of Dom Pedro in favor of his daughter and her betrothal to Dom Miguel, was in accordance with the advice of England, France, and Austria ... but the Constitutional Charter was really unforeseen by all the governments of Europe, including Great Britain."[10] The dangerous precedent of a crowned head freely accepting a written constitution troubled Austria and Spain. Austria in particular found itself in an awkward position. In order to protect the birthright of Leopoldina's daughter and uphold the "sanctity of legitimacy" it could not question the decisions of a legitimate sovereign, but they were unhappy a constitution was involved. Reluctantly it approved Pedro's plan.[11]

Spain did not feel honor bound by such principles. Its government supported Miguel as a candidate for the Portuguese throne, but not as a constitutional monarch. Spain's position, like Austria's, was influenced by family considerations. Its government was in secret communication with Portugal's dowager queen. Carlota's brother Ferdinand still sat on the Spanish throne long after renouncing the constitution that had allowed him to regain it. Carlota insisted Miguel promise whatever it took to return to Portugal. Once there, he could repudiate the constitution, reject the marriage, and seize power.[12] Old age and failing health had not dimmed Carlota's appetite for intrigue. She devoted her considerable wealth, family connections, and remaining energy to giving her favorite son the crown she had always wanted.[13]

Shortly after returning to Lisbon, Miguel reasserted his absolutist beliefs. His mother and three sisters rallied to his cause. British observers soon reported prisons overflowing and a "reign of terror" sweeping across Portugal.[14] Carlota demanded, "Cut off their heads for me. The French Revolution cut off forty thousand, and ... the population did not diminish."[15] One of Miguel's first victims was the Marquês of Loulé. Two decades earlier his spies had uncovered Carlota's plot to declare her husband insane. It had been a long wait, but Carlota forgot nothing.

Turmoil also rocked Brazil. Pedro's political and personal popularity had nearly vanished. All of Pedro's energies were consumed with holding onto power. To do so he depended on the loyalty of his army, paid mercenaries, aristocrats, and businessmen with strong economic ties to Portugal. Suspicions he was preparing to reunite Brazil with the homeland triggered spreading violence.

When his personal honor guard joined anti-government demonstrators he recognized the end was at hand. He had always believed there was one "queen of the world" even kings had to obey — the queen of public opinion.[16] In the early hours of the morning he abdicated the Brazilian throne to his son, announcing he would return to Portugal to reclaim its crown for his daughter. He privately concluded, "My son has the advantages over me of being Brazilian and the Brazilians like him. He'll reign without difficulty and the constitution will guarantee his prerogatives. I'll descend from the throne with the glory of ending as I began, constitutionally."[17]

His written declaration read, "Using the right that the constitution concedes to me, I declare that I have voluntarily abdicated in favor of my very beloved and esteemed son Senhor Dom Pedro de Alcântara ... April 7, 1831, Tenth Year of Independence and of the Empire."[18] One of his final official acts was to remember Leopoldina's last wish. José Bonifácio had returned to Brazil and Pedro asked a final favor from him. With Bonifácio's consent he made the following appointment: "Using the right conceded me by the constitution I appoint ... as the tutor of my beloved and esteemed children the very upright, honorable, and patriotic citizen, José Bonifácio de Andrada e Silva, my true friend."[19] Reclaiming the ancient title Duke of Bragança, Pedro prepared to sail for Europe. His wife Amélia, his oldest daughter Maria da Glória, and a small retinue of friends and supporters joined him. The French charge'd'affaires wrote, "He knew better how to resign than to reign."[20]

Even as he departed, Pedro's inconsistencies were in evidence. The only anger he displayed during his final hours in Brazil concerned his slaves. After deciding to not grant them freedom, he was furious his quick departure forced him to sell them below his full asking price.[21] It was Pedro at his worst. His best side was displayed by his peaceful abdication. He understood a throne was secure only when it rested on the trust and support of the people. To attempt to hold power by arms, threats, or terror was the worst betrayal of kingship. It was a principle his brother Miguel failed to grasp.

In a farewell letter, Pedro saluted his heir, addressing him as "My beloved

Son and Emperor."[22] He pledged fatherly love, but also his loyalty as a good citizen to the ruler of Brazil. The night before their departure, Pedro and Amélia silently kissed his sleeping children goodbye without waking them.[23] Brazil's new child emperor had always been quiet and introverted. He became more so when he discovered his charismatic father had abandoned him without a parting word or embrace.

In addition to his children by Leopoldina, Pedro left behind several mistresses including the Marquêsa de Santos and a dozen children of all colors, races and backgrounds.[24] Several of his descendents became highly successful and were remembered by Pedro in his will. But only his son by his dead empress became Brazil's emperor. As he sailed from Rio de Janeiro the final sounds the Duke of Bragança heard were thousands of Brazilians acknowledging his son as Pedro II. On a balcony of the Paço Imperial the tiny boy stood on a chair next to José Bonifácio as his cheering subjects acknowledged him.[25] Early that morning he had been pulled in an open carriage through dancing crowds. Throughout the entire bewildering journey Brazil's five-year-old emperor cried uncontrollably.[26]

﹏ 13 ﹏

"Orphans of the State"

Empress Amélia composed an open letter to the "Mothers of Brazil" asking them to watch over her stepchildren as "orphans of the state."[1] She also selected Mariana Carlota Verna de Magalhaes Coutinho, former lady in waiting to Empress Leopoldina, as their governess. Coutinho had traveled to Brazil over twenty years earlier with the exiled Portuguese court and planned to return to Europe with Pedro I. The dowager empress persuaded her to remain behind to help raise the royal children.

The young Pedro affectionately called her "Dadama," a mangled childish version of the Portuguese word "lady." She was kind, strict but loving. To her royal wards she presented a simple Catholic world of good and evil where good deeds and Christian duty endlessly warred with selfishness and excess. She used their sainted mother and hero father as virtuous role models, not neglecting the power of evil. The devilish Marquêsa de Santos was presented as the source of all troubles to their family and Brazil.[2]

Among the positive habits she encouraged in her young wards was a love of letter writing, requiring them to regularly write their father, stepmother, and maternal grandfather. The practice began a lifelong love of letter writing in Pedro II. Family was always important to him although he only knew most of them through letters. Written communication became his principal form of human contact. His passion for correspondence was similar to that of his mother, who had seldom let a day pass without writing her family.

As Leopoldina had wished, Pedro I appointed José Bonifácio as her children's tutor. Following the departure of Pedro and Amélia, Bonifácio served as their surrogate guardian.[3] He selected all male instructors for the young emperor. Outside of school, his female companionship was made up of his governess and sisters. Bonifácio and Dona Mariana saw to it that the children ate meals together, studied, played, and went to the Glória Church every week as a family. This continued until adulthood and marriage separated them.

Neither tutor nor governess could protect them from events beyond their control. In 1830, their grandmother Carlota died. The priest presiding over her funeral mass in Sintra's royal chapel had been one of her personal favorites. He had once preached a sermon urging her to use her royal position to hang, jail, or poison liberal vermin who had the temerity to petition the crown for a Portuguese constitution.[4] He was Carlota's kind of priest. She had sincerely attempted to live up to their shared view of Christian responsibility. During Carlota's funeral sermon he remembered her as few others did. He intoned, "She had died as she lived; filled with peace, fortitude, and resignation.... Our hopes are founded upon the heroic virtues which she has displayed in many and momentous times of crisis."[5]

The words might have better described Carlota's ten-year-old granddaughter Princess Paula, who died in Brazil in 1833. Paula was the most quiet and gentle of Leopoldina and Pedro's children. She had never been robust or completely well since her birth, but seldom complained despite a life filled with physical illness. Her death was one more loss to her lonely brother and sisters.

Januária, the oldest of the royal children, inherited her father's physical handsomeness, coloring and mercurial temper. Francesca also physically resembled her father, but her mother believed her to be the most Habsburg of all her children. Francesca had her father's charm and verbal quickness, without his moodiness or frenetic energy.[6]

When they were younger royal position did not always take precedence. Playing church, the vivacious Francesca was the priest, her older sister and younger brother the acolytes.[7] Pedro however was quick to sometimes assert his authority. He once took it upon himself to hit his sisters because he felt they were not applying themselves to their studies.[8] After he refused to apologize, Dadama railed that members of the court were attempting to turn him against his own family. Even sibling rivalry was viewed through a political lens.[9] Perhaps because of such diatribes, Pedro learned to conceal his innermost thoughts and feelings. Few ever knew what he was thinking. As an adult, he was inscrutable, perhaps because he had been in the public eye since he was born.

Leopoldina had hoped Bonifácio's intelligence and loyalty to Brazil would guide, focus and ground her children. She shared his belief in the power of an enlightened monarchy to stabilize, uplift and humanize society. They both believed a government's role was to seek balance and fairness in a world of excess and uncertainty. Pedro II seemed to personify that vision. The young emperor's formal education did nothing to encourage the spontaneity that had been so much a part of his father. Learning was intense, strict and unrelenting. He was taught the liberal arts as well as Latin, Portuguese, German, and French, the languages of diplomacy and private family correspondence. Curriculum and texts came primarily from the extensive library his mother had brought from Europe. Her personal librarian was one of his first teachers. Few contemporaries royal or otherwise were provided a more grounded education, but he was seldom allowed to reflect or enjoy it.

Bonifácio carefully followed Leopoldina's educational dictums. Like Dadama he taught the royal children to admire and love their parents, but he wasted no time on his old enemy, the Marquêsa de Santos. Instead he directed his scorn toward two of the staunchest pillars of the Brazilian monarchy—the Catholic Church and Brazil's slaveholders. He feared both had self-serving agendas that would bring them into conflict with a reform minded government. He also shared the political hopes and abolitionist's dreams of their parents bringing him into conflict with the nation's conservative regents and council of state. The men who ruled Brazil in the young emperor's name were staunch supporters of slavery.

Politics were not the only differences Bonifácio had with Brazil's traditionalists. He believed women should receive the same education as men, teaching his own daughter and the royal princesses accordingly. It was one of many radical ideas that made him powerful enemies. In December 1833 he was removed as the royal tutor of "His Imperial Majesty, and his August sisters" because of suspected involvement in a "conspiracy against the Authorities and the Constitution."[10] Bonifácio was arrested. No proof was offered, no trial held. But he never again had direct contact with the royal children. For his confused students, the dismissal was one more broken link with their absent parents.

Brazil's child emperor withdrew further into his studies. A court observer wrote, "The love of books is the only passion he knows."[11] The French charge d'affairs observed, "It is impossible to know his private thoughts. The terrors that dogged his childhood ... have given him an outlook of suspicion which is belied by his awkward stance, his difficulty in making conversation, often replying with only one word, both in his public appearances and in private."[12] Years later Pedro remembered, "The people who came to speak with me ... always wanted to obtain something.... [Now] I am always forced to watch what I say and what I do and can never be spontaneous."[13]

Time not spent in his books found the young Pedro as the symbolic center of diplomatic receptions, parades, and government ceremonies. For someone as shy and reticent as he was, the constant attention must have been painful. Yet even when surrounded by curious crowds, he seemed alone. His governess reinforced this detachment by emphasizing Christian duty over personal pleasure and public responsibilities over privileges. Everyone, even his older sisters, deferred to him. He was taught to defer only to his constitutional responsibilities.

A court visitor presented a brief glimpse into the life, etiquette and ceremony surrounding Brazil's young emperor, writing,

> At the head of the stairs and entrance to the salon, stood a halberdier, dressed in a harlequin suit of green, checkered with yellow stripes half an inch wide.... In the first room, which was handsomely furnished, were several gentlemen of the foreign diplomatic corps.... From this we passed into a larger room, fitted up in much more elegant manner. Both were hung with portraits and paintings illustrative of Brazilian history ... when the right hand door opened, the ladies and gentlemen of the Brazilian Household entered. Dom Pedro II was accompanied by his sisters and

regents. The dresses of the members of the Court were splendid; that of the young emperor was neat and simple. As they passed through the rooms, every head was bowed in salutation.

Presently a flourish of trumpets followed by a grand march by a full band proclaimed the opening of the Court. We all followed into the anteroom. In a few moments the chamberlain informed the diplomatic corps that his Imperial Highness was ready to receive them. On entering the presence, we all bowed; and again when halfway up the dais, and repeated the reverence immediately before his Royal Highness. Then retreating, with our faces toward the throne, and making three bows, we made our exit through the right hand door....

Dom Pedro II, who bears a striking resemblance to his father, stood upon the dais—an elevation of one step, on which the throne is usually placed—with the regency on his right and his two sisters on his left hand. His large liquid eyes wandered from one person to another with the expression of half indifference. His salutations were stiff, and the princesses who are his seniors (he is not six years old) seemed to suffer a kind of Mauvaise honte.[14]

It was an unusual life for a child.

Everything he did was planned, watched, and orchestrated, even recreation. To familiarize him with other youngsters, children from all backgrounds were invited to the palace to play with him. From these early encounters, two lifelong friendships developed. One, Luíz Pedreira, a boy his own age, came from an aristocratic, scholarly, but poor family. The second was with Rafael, a young soldier and slave who had been especially close to his father. Like many white children in Brazil, Pedro was surrounded by slaves of every conceivable hue of skin. In some ways he became color blind to race.

In between long hours of study, Pedro and his sisters enjoyed drawing and reading and more active activities such as horseback riding and dancing. Part of their attraction to such amusements might have been stories told of their parents who enjoyed similar pastimes. The royal children were also given a plot of ground to farm behind the São Cristóvão Palace, where they cultivated a vegetable garden. Their mother had had a similar garden as a child. One of the few areas in which Pedro was taught a skill different than his sisters involved hunting. While he hunted, they were taught to cook. It was a strange reassertion of traditional gender roles since his mother's skills as a marksman and hunter equaled, and at times surpassed, their father's.

Political unrest periodically shattered Pedro's tightly controlled life. Most of Latin America continued to be battled by violent upheavals. Lima, Peru, and Caracas, Venezuela, lost half their populations during one fourteen-year period of continuous war. In Brazil, military uprisings, slave revolts, and anti-government riots would occasionally force the royal children into hiding until order was restored. A succession of regents struggled to hold the country together. Many Brazilians wondered if the nation would survive long enough for Pedro to wear its crown. Others clung to the hope Pedro I would return; but that was not to be.

In 1834 their father wrote them that the armies of their fifteen-year-old sister Maria da Glória had finally defeated those of their uncle. Miguel had fled Portugal, and their older sister had been greeted in Lisbon "amidst the shouts of her delighted subjects."[15] The royal children hoped the news meant their father would soon return. Three months later a letter arrived informing them he was dead.[16] Years of hard living and fighting had broken the health of the thirty-eight-year-old former emperor. He died in Queluz Palace, in the room where he had been born, surrounded by fading murals of Don Quixote.

His orphaned nine-year-old son and daughters were devastated. They had always expected he would return. José Bonifácio tried to comfort them in a letter, writing the role their father embraced in life transcended death. "They err," he wrote; "Dom Pedro did not die. Common men die, not heroes."[17]

Nearly sixty years later at the time of his own death, all the cherished letters his father had ever written Pedro II were discovered among his treasured possessions. They were written on an adult level, but lavishly illustrated with drawings to delight any child.[18] José Bonifácio's letter saluting Pedro I as a hero was also included. They were faded, folded, refolded and wrinkled, indicating they had been reread many times over the years.

14

"*Fairy Princess*"

In 1834, the year their father died, death also claimed the royal children's grandfather, Austria's emperor. Observers noted Pedro and his sisters seemed increasingly withdrawn. The deaths of Pedro I in Portugal and Franz I in Austria also had political repercussions. With the passing of their father and grandfather, the Brazilian monarchy's two most powerful protectors were gone. At times the huge country seemed held together only by the fragile attachment the nation felt toward its "royal orphans."[1]

The French Prince of Joinville, once mentioned as a possible marriage partner for Maria da Glória, visited Rio de Janeiro in 1838 and wrote, "The emperor and the princesses are blond and small, the emperor has a lot of the Austrian family, but the way of a forty year old man. As for the princesses, they are rung out from the devil. Dona Januária is shy. Francesca is straight, with a dry wit and is extraordinarily alert. They sought all opportunities to bring me closer to and stick me with Francesca, these were amusing maneuvers.... I share plenty of pity for these abandoned children."[2]

By the time Princess Januária approached her eighteenth birthday, pressures mounted to make her regent until her younger brother came of age.[3] The constitution stated that in times of troubled conditions, the relative nearest in age to the heir should assume authority, but also mandated the regent should be at least twenty-five years old. Other factors may have undermined Januária's candidacy including mood swings that echoed those of her father. Patriarchal slaveholders and the hierarchy of the Catholic Church might have feared entrusting their future to a female Pedro I. They hoped for someone strong enough to lead the government, but flexible enough to defer to their wishes. Januária failed to fit that profile.

In 1840, the nation's instability provoked intense debates in the Brazilian senate on whether to declare the fourteen-year-old Pedro of age. Months of heated arguments spilled onto the streets and police units were put on alert. A government delegation petitioned Pedro to assume the full powers of the throne.[4] The adolescent emperor agonized over the proposal and consulted with his family, advisors and teachers. His entire life he had been preparing to rule, but the task was formidable. The position was a powerful one. Once he assumed power he could dissolve parliament and appoint or dismiss almost anyone in the government. Yet, his primary legal responsibility was to be the country's conciliator, its "poder moderator," the nation's moderating influence.

Pedro I saw the emperor as peacemaker, someone able to find the common ground where opponents could come together to solve problems and create consensus. He had to be above partisan conflicts, able to balance and unite the diverse country behind his unquestioned honesty and leadership. The words of the constitution were his father's but the spirit behind them was his mother's. As a true Habsburg, she had understood the need to unite a people through identification with a leader. The task had been beyond his father's considerable talents and energy. To one of the royal couriers, the young Pedro asked, "but can you be certain that with little more than fourteen years of age, it is possible to possess such wisdom?"[5]

His own family history did not reassure him. His father had surrendered his own position, his country, health and life to give his son the throne of Brazil and his daughter the crown of Portugal. By the age of thirty-eight he was dead, buried an ocean away. Pedro's mother also died thousands of miles from her birthplace, broken in mind, body and spirit when she was just twenty-nine years old. Pedro knew the life of a prince did not always end happily, but there seemed no other alternative than to assume the throne. With more resignation than enthusiasm, eight months after his fourteenth birthday he agreed to accept the full responsibilities as emperor of Brazil. Years later he sadly recalled his single regret was not having more time to prepare for what lay ahead.[6]

The coronation was a spectacular affair. Pedro's solid gold crown was encrusted with 639 diamonds and seventy-seven perfectly matched pearls.[7] To most Brazilians, their young sovereign became a rallying point uniting people and country. Yet even at the beginning of his reign slavery caused division. One of his first public acts was to free the slaves serving him since birth. Slaveholders reacted with anger. In a country struggling with labor shortages it seemed a bad start. To others it represented a hopeful beginning.

The search for suitable royal marriage partners began at once. To ensure dynastic, national and political stability, Pedro and his sisters had to marry quickly and produce heirs. His sisters had to wed a prince of equal rank, but precautions needed to be taken so that no foreign-born brother-in-law might create political mischief. Pedro's position required him to begin a family at once.

He loved his sisters and would miss them both but he was especially close to the beautiful and witty Francesca. He enjoyed her extroverted personality. They understood each other's moods and shared a similar sense of humor even if Francesca's sense of fun sometimes bordered on the outrageous. Pedro quietly enjoyed her antics—but never emulated them. It was this sister he lost first. Louis Philippe, King of the French, was concerned Pedro's marriage might bring

Brazil under the influence of his enemies. His own "family matrimony agency" actively pursued a royal match for his twenty-four-year-old son, the Prince of Joinville, and seventeen-year-old Francesca.[8] Joinville remembered the princess from his earlier visit. He had not disliked her and agreed to consider the marriage on two conditions. The first was that he could take as much time as he wished to travel to Brazil. The second was that he had refusal rights to the marriage if he found Pedro's youngest sister had become repulsive since their last meeting.[9]

Joinville, known as the sailor prince, had recently basked in the reflected glory of Napoleon I when he returned the body of dead emperor to France for burial. As part of his reward for considering marrying the Brazilian princess, he leisurely explored the coast of West Africa where for centuries the Portuguese had traded slaves.[10] He visited Freetown, Liberia, the Gold Coast, Dahomey, Benin and other slave ports. The French prince was impressed with the prosperity of the American, Danish, and Dutch slave traders and made note of the escalating attempts of the English navy to end the trade by force. He recorded the slave trade was so entrenched that when hundreds of slaves rescued by the English were put ashore in Liberia, they refused to return home, fearful of being enslaved again by their fellow Africans.

In Dahomey, he was repeatedly offered the sexual favors of slave women but refused, much to the disgust of chanting crowds of blacks and whites. He had seen enough of slavery to know he wanted no part of it.[11] If he married Francesca, he decided they would leave Brazil and its slavery behind as quickly as possible.

Joinville found Francesca to his liking and began an intensive courtship. Both governments rapidly negotiated the marriage contract. On April 22, 1843, Brazil's young emperor wrote the King of the French, agreeing to the match between "my beloved sister the Princess Françoise Caroline on behalf of My Lord, the Prince of Joinville." In the letter he explained, "The desire to strengthen the bonds of blood and friendship that unite me to Your Majesty have made me welcome this request with eagerness."[12] The marriage took place on May 1, 1843, the birthday of Louis Philippe. If Pedro and Francesca's mother had been alive nothing might have pleased her more than marriage between her youngest daughter and the son of her favorite aunt. Marie Amélie had known Leopoldina's children through years of letter writing and had loved and prayed for their happiness even before their birth.

A visiting American sailor described his events of the royal wedding day.

> Everything is an uproar today. Guns, squibs and rockets are blazing away. Bells are ringing and colors flying, all in honor of the marriage of the Prince de Joinville, to the emperor's sister.... The knot was tied at the residence of the emperor and a signal being made from the shore that, the two had been made one, the French ships in the harbor commenced firing, being followed by all the National vessels lying here.[13]

"This evening we had a most splendid aquatic illumination in the harbor ... a constant blaze of fireworks as far as the eye could reach ... and in an instant, (when Dom Pedro and the princesses and prince appeared) as if by magic, every French vessel of war in the harbor, numbering eight to ten, became one brilliant illumination, and each of them fired a twenty-one gun salute. This was, without exception, the most brilliant spectacle I have ever beheld, each vessel represented a wreath of the most variegated lights, and a blue light was burnt at each of the yard arms, this with the thunder of the great guns, the flashes of which rendered the whole harbor a mass of illumination, was a magnificent sight to behold.[14]

The sailor also described the bride. "The Princess Francesca is the prettiest as well as the youngest of Dom Pedro's sisters, and is said to be the most amiable and intelligent in the family. I saw her some eighteen months ago.... I was at that time particularly struck with her wholesome appearance ... — since then, she has, if possible, improved on her beauty."[15]

The only controversy marring the celebrations was Francesca's request that all her personal slaves be granted their freedom. Francesca's new husband was not independently wealthy, but despite the financial loss, Joinville heartily approved. Others did not. It was not unusual for a wealthy Brazilian girl to free a favorite personal slave at the time of her marriage. But many felt Francesca was making a political gesture — a signal from the royal family regarding their attitude toward abolition.[16] Although she was moving to a nation that did not permit slavery, critics believed she would never have made such a sweeping request without the approval of her brother.

For some Francesca's action sent a winter chill through the body politic. For others it promised a hint of spring thaw. Pedro purchased and freed Francesca's slaves, ignoring the accompanying criticism, and on May 13, 1843, Francesca, Princess of Joinville, and her new husband sailed for France. The date was the wedding anniversary of her parents and the birthday of her paternal great-grandfather.

She was quickly engulfed in the love of her new family. During a visit with her English cousin, Queen Victoria wrote, "Little Chica [the family name for Francesca] is a charming, sprightly, [and] lively creature, with immense brown eyes."[17] They soon became friends. Joinville, the most unconventional and independent prince of the Orleans royal house, proved to be a good match for Francesca's own spontaneous personality. After settling into the Tuileries Palace in Paris, Francesca continued preferring Brazilian over French cuisine, burst into song at will, and snuck out of the palace whenever court protocol stifled or bored her. At times she exasperated Queen Marie Amélie and scandalized her conservative sisters-in-law, but delighted her husband and the king. Through frequent correspondence Francesca and Joinville remained close to her brother in Brazil, but they never again returned to the land of her birth.[18]

Januária, his oldest royal sister and next in line to the Brazilian throne, could do nothing until Pedro wed and produced heirs. This put additional pressure on him to marry quickly, but their father's scandalous reputation and the tragic death of their mother made brother and sister unattractive marriage candidates. In Joinville, Francesca found a prince who cared little about what others thought. But he also had two healthy older brothers in line to the throne before him. Januária and Pedro had no such luxury.

European royalty refused to consider marriage to the young and untried emperor until they knew whether Pedro took after his faithless father or sainted mother. His stepmother, the Dowager Empress Amélia, had come from the divorced and exiled family of Napoleon, but no sitting king or queen would consider such a match for one of their children. Even Pedro's Austrian cousins refused to consider marriage. They had never forgiven Brazil for Leopoldina's death.

A solution was found by marrying both Pedro and Januária into the royal family of the Kingdom of Naples and the Two Sicilies. The king was a Bourbon but his mother a Habsburg. The queen was their own great-aunt, a much milder version of her sister, their dead grandmother Carlota.[19] Januária would marry Louis, Conde of Áquila, her cousin and uncle once removed, but three years her junior. To the politically ambitious count his closeness to the Brazilian crown made the marriage extremely attractive. He readily agreed to become a Brazilian citizen and accept the title of admiral in the Brazilian navy. Januária and her husband would be allowed to live abroad; but if Pedro and his wife produced no heirs, they would return to Brazil and their children would inherit the throne. Pedro would marry Louis's sister, the Princess Dona Theresa Christina Maria Bourbon. Theresa was several years older than Pedro and also his first cousin and aunt once removed. As the youngest unmarried daughter from a family of twelve, she was available and more than willing to accept a marriage proposal.

Neither marriage was a perfect arrangement, bringing together cousins, aunts and uncles, and two sets of sisters and brothers, but they made political sense and provided a practical solution to an embarrassing situation. The convoluted marriage proposal was presented to Pedro along with a beautiful portrait representing his Neapolitan cousin. Diplomatic correspondence reported, "Theresa Christina is an attractive princess, with the best training and education."[20]

Brazil's emperor thought his prospective bride looked like a "fairy princess" and happily agreed to the proposed marriage. In fact, Theresa had received little in the way of education and the attractive captivating woman in the portrait was not Theresa Christina Maria Bourbon. By the time Pedro discovered the deception, it was too late.

15

"A Brazilian with All My Heart"

Pedro looked forward to finding a marriage partner to help replace the family he was about to lose. Since he and Januária were closely related to their future spouses, Pope Gregory XVI issued a special dispensation permitting the weddings to proceed. Like his star-crossed parents, Pedro and Theresa were married in a proxy marriage ceremony prior to a face-to-face meeting.

Their actual meeting was further delayed because Brazilian authorities feared sending a ship to Sicily with a nearly all black crew. Court officials worried the crew's "color might cause surprise" to Pedro's Italian relatives. [1] Finally enough white sailors were found to make the eighty-day voyage to Italy. The emperor's bride-cousin-aunt finally sailed from the beauty of the Bay of Naples to the magnificence of Rio de Janeiro's Guanabara Bay accompanied by her brother, dozens of diplomats, and several Brazilian and Neapolitan ships of the line.

On September 3, 1843, "the vessel containing the precious person of the future Empress of Brazil" was sighted. An American sailor wrote, "Such an excitement, as this discovery produced among the already frantic Brazilians, I do not believe was ever seen.... It was about four o'clock in the afternoon when the sea breeze sprung up, and the squadron entered the harbor all under full sail. Their entrée was the signal for a grand salute. Each and every vessel of war in the harbor hoisted the Brazilian ensign at the fore, and the Neapolitan at the main, and blazed away right and left for nearly half an hour.... When the ships anchored, every vessel in the harbor once again gave a twenty-one-gun salute. The concussion and echo of exploding shells in the bay was so great that despite it being a cloudless sunny day, it started to rain." [2]

The brief unexpected shower did not dampen the spirits of the citizens of Rio de Janeiro who believe rain a sign of fertility. They loved celebrations, and the marriage of their handsome emperor to a beautiful princess was the perfect excuse for a party. Rio was brilliantly decorated with flags, banners and archways of tropical flowers. Mobs of cheering, happy Brazilians dressed in their brightest colors danced, sang and cheered.

His entire life, Pedro had longed for an intellectual companion, a soul mate offering him the private sanctuary he had never known from his dead parents or departing sisters. His would be a very public life. To sustain and nurture his private self, he looked forward to sharing himself physically and intellectually with a woman who would be his romantic ideal and mental equal. He was to be bitterly disappointed on both counts.

As the sun began to set, Pedro surprised everyone by impulsively embarking from shore on his royal barge to welcome his bride to Brazil. His subjects exploded in cheers and war ships in the harbor boomed deafening salutes at the boy-emperor's romantic gesture. Against the sense numbing thunder of guns, the smell of spent powder, and cheers of faceless voices, Pedro first laid eyes on his new wife. The encounter was brief. Within minutes a nearby British sloop-of-war surprised the waiting ships and crowds by firing its guns to signal the emperor was departing Theresa's ship.

A twenty-one-gun salute greeted Pedro's silently returning barge pulled by forty strong oarsmen. "Fireworks," "rockets," and "burning blue lights on the mastheads, yard-arms, and head booms" illuminated the sky to light his way to shore. The brilliant display excited and pleased all the observers but one. Burst of lights in the evening darkness revealed the focus of the massive celebration, Pedro II, staring silently into the distance.[3]

His new wife did not look like the beautiful portrait or the idealized woman of his dreams. Theresa was short and wide, lame of walk, and as plain and open faced as a common peasant on the streets of Naples. Her mind and faith were simple, uncomplicated, and dull. The Neapolitan princess was thrilled when she saw her handsome husband. Pedro's reaction was horrifyingly different.[4] With one glance, his youthful dreams collapsed. It was as if he knew in a flash of the exploding fireworks that he would never feel desire for this woman, intellectually engage her mind or be able to share his deepest thoughts or private dreams with her. The youthful, athletic emperor who loved dancing and horseback riding realized he had married an old but child-like cripple. His knees buckled and he turned away. Theresa never blinked, but she knew.[5]

Brazil's emperor was seventeen years old. Theresa seemed a very old twenty-two. In the age in which they lived, she would have been considered an old maid. Pedro was growing taller everyday and had not yet reached his full height of six feet two. Still, as a married man he was expected to quickly father children with a woman who repulsed him. It was to Dadama, his faithful governess, he turned. The night he met his bride he returned to his palace and cried for the first time since he was a small boy. He felt he had been bitterly betrayed, misled by politicians and diplomats. It took all her influence and arguments to convince him that he must fulfill his responsibilities as a gentleman, an emperor, a Catholic and a bridegroom.[6]

That same evening Theresa discovered that the portrait Pedro had fallen in love with had not been of her. Theresa wept too, but not in front of her husband or any of their subjects. She contemplated suicide by drowning.[7] Then in a sad letter home she confided she would instead dedicate her married life to a personal creed. "I know that my appearance is different from what has been announced. I will make every effort to live in such a way that nobody will be misled about my character. It will be my ambition to resemble the nature of Dona Leopoldina, my husband's mother, and to be a Brazilian with all my heart in everything I do."[8]

The following morning the elite of the Brazilian Empire filled twenty magnificent barges "painted and decorated in the most expensive, and gaudy style" to meet their new empress. Unseen in the spectacular three-mile long procession were the slaves who powered the barges. One eyewitness wrote, "The 'Triumphal' barge intended for the use of the future empress was universally admired ... an exquisite piece of workmanship. Her length is a trifle over 60 feet, beam six feet. Her ... cabin is the most perfect thing of the kind I ever saw — surpassing in elegance, even the emperor's own barge, and that surpasses in turn the most expensive and luxuriously furnished drawing rooms on shore."[9] The entire time the launches were rowed to and from shore, the Brazilian and Neapolitan ships in the harbor and the forts surrounding the city fired thundering salutes.

A North American visitor recorded the splendor of the occasion. He wrote in wonder about "the grand triumphal entry, and procession from the landing place at the Navy Yard to the Imperial Palace. There were at least one thousand coaches in this procession, some private, and many public; each crowded with the nobility and gentry of the land, and with a 'great sprinkling' of ladies among them. The Imperial carriages, for the accommodation of the Royal family, were the richest ... I ever saw. There were three of them, all perfectly new, and, it is said, imported expressly for this grand occasion. They were most magnificently painted, gilded, decorated, and furnished with light *green* [Brazilian] and *white* [Neapolitan] silk and satin, trimmed with gold, each drawn by eight richly caparisoned horses."[10]

"The princess was dressed remarkably plain, wearing a dress of white lace over white satin, with a single band of splendid large white Brazilian diamonds, to confine her jet black hair, which was parted in front, smoothed over her temples, and gathered up behind ... 'ala Victoria.'... The Emperor ... was dressed in the uniform of a Colonel in the army — green dress coat, pants of the same, with the usual appurtenances to a military dress, including an immense pair of gold epaulettes." He also noted, "Dom Pedro looks thinner and more careworn than when I saw him last."[11]

Despite the fact that the royal couple had already been wed by proxy, a second elaborate ceremony was performed in Rio de Janeiro's cathedral allowing over one hundred Brazilian priests and bishops to officiate at the public event. That ceremony, the parades, and the nine days of celebrations that followed were patterned after the wedding of Leopoldina and Pedro I twenty-six years earlier. Theresa's smile, gentle demeanor and sincere enthusiasm captivated the crowds.

Waves of affection greeted her on the first day of her life in Brazil, and all the days that followed. Like the Austrian mother-in-law she never knew, everyone seemed to love her, except her own husband.

The parties and parades brought forth large numbers of women and girls from their usually reclusive lifestyles. They too wanted to "welcome with their bright eyes their future empress."[12] Local customs and traditions continued excluding unmarried Euro-Brazilian women from "appearing in public or even venturing beyond their own threshold."[13] But the unique occasion of the royal wedding filled the streets with men and women, masters and slaves enjoying themselves. In their midst, only the royal couple knew the reality of their sadness, but others soon suspected there were problems.

Royalty knows no privacy. One of the members of the Chamber of Deputies recorded in his diary, "No sign of copulation has been found on the sheets."[14] The Council of State officially requested Januária and her husband delay their departure for Europe, fearing the emperor and empress might not consummate their marriage.[15] But Pedro and Theresa fulfilled their dynastic duty. Ten months after the wedding the empress became pregnant. Over the next four years four children were born to them. Two sons died before their second birthday, but two daughters lived.

In time, Pedro came to respect and care for Theresa and they became comfortable partners. She closed her eyes to his infidelities, never professing knowledge of them or discussing his extramarital affairs. His life became her life and she lived in his reflected glory. She never publicly disagreed with her husband or her emperor, supporting him in all matters including his tolerant views regarding race. Mindful of his dead mother's pain, Pedro publicly and privately treated his empress with respect and discretion.[16] In their years together, he never felt passion for his wife, but he came to feel an attachment and affection toward her. They remained together for nearly fifty years as husband and wife, and as parents.

Pedro's own mother was remembered in the naming of all four of their royal children, Leopold for both sons and Leopoldina for both daughters. The first royal daughter was named Isabel Cristina Leopoldina Augusta.[17] Three of the names were to honor her mother and grandmothers, but Isabel was also the name of Portugal's most famous queen, peacemaker and patron saint. In England she would have been called Elizabeth, in Spain Isabella, in Hungary Erzsebet — the names of those countries' greatest queens — all of them Isabel's ancient cousins.

16

"Heir to the Throne of Brazil"

On November 15, 1846, Princess Isabel made the first of a lifetime of public appearances. The date had been carefully selected. It was the feast day of St. Leopold, the patron saint and name day of Isabel's beloved grandmother Leopoldina. Pageantry and traditions of family, church and monarchy came together to dedicate the infant's soul to God and her public life to Brazil.

Even before she was born, Isabel's christening served as an opportunity to unite family, church and state. On May 2 Pedro wrote his brother-in-law, the king of Portugal, asking him to serve as his daughter's godfather. Ferdinand Saxe-Coburg-Gotha was the consort of his sister Maria da Glória and cousin to both England's Queen Victoria and her husband Prince Albert. Pedro also asked his mother-in-law, dowager Queen Maria Isabel of the Kingdom of the Two Sicilies to serve as godmother.[1]

Neither would attend the ceremony, but both graciously gave permission to be represented. In his response Ferdinand addressed Pedro as "dear brother." Maria Isabel referred to the Brazilian emperor as her "dear nephew and son-in-law" and Empress Theresa as "my dear dear daughter."[2]

The day of Isabel's baptism the plaza next to the Paço Imperial, the City Palace, was filled with thousands of Brazilians hoping to glimpse the royal family and their newest princess. A magnificent elevated walkway had been built from the palace through the plaza to a large open-air pavilion allowing people to share in the visual spectacle of what was both a religious and state occasion.[3]

At 5:00 P.M. the head steward of the imperial household, dressed in the velvet and satin of an earlier age, entered the royal nursery followed by the Marquêsa of Marceio, representing the dowager queen of Naples, and the Marquês of Itanhaem, a former regent representing the king of Portugal. The steward gently received the princess in his arms then solemnly carried the royal infant to the waiting emperor and empress.[4]

The bishop of Rio de Janeiro and the assembled Catholic bishops of Brazil took their places at the front of the large procession. Slowly they made their way through the cool dark palace into the bright warm sunlight of Rio's central plaza. The parade of dignitaries formed a visual and living tapestry representing the

Brazil's imperial family in 1861— Princess Isabel (1846–1921), her sister Princess Leopoldina (1847–1871), her father Emperor Pedro II (1825–1891), and her mother Empress Theresa Christina (1822–1889). Despite his own abhorrence of slavery, Pedro II could not protect his royal daughters from the slave culture that permeated Brazil. Courtesy the Catholic University of America, Oliveira Lima Library, Washington, D.C.

power, traditions, and history of European monarchy and imperial Brazil. No other country in North or South America had anything to compare with the powerful imagery or majesty the Bragança monarchy brought to America.[5]

Dressed in the medieval robes of the Catholic Church, the bishops were followed by royal archers in traditional uniforms dating from the Renaissance, musicians playing solemn religious hymns, a military honor guard with drawn lances, justices of the courts, and provincial and municipal officials from throughout Brazil. Members of the Council of State and the General Assembly, noblemen and women, foreign dignitaries and distinguished literary personages followed.[6]

Three other officials of the court also solemnly walked in the procession. The first carried a velvet pillow on a silver tray. Upon it rested the magnificent Imperial crown of Brazil with its sparkling diamonds and shimmering pearls. The second carried the emperor's ceremonial robes of state, including a brilliant

cape made of the bright feathers of the Amazon toucan bird. The third carried
the large Pascal Candle used during Easter, the most sacred of all Catholic religious holidays.[7]

Attendants carrying the imperial crown, the robes of state and the Easter
candle paid their prayerful homage before a jeweled monstrance carrying a
consecrated host believed by Catholics to contain the body and blood of Christ.
Then the robes of state were placed on a table to the right of Pedro II, Theresa,
and Princess Isabel. The imperial crown was placed to their left.

At the open-air pavilion, Empress Theresa lifted America's only princess
into her arms as the emperor and other important dignitaries took their assigned
spots. Isabel was presented to the vice president of the Senate, the vice president of the House of Deputies, the president of the Supreme Court and the
Council of State. Pedro II then raised his daughter in his arms and with the
empress at his side presented the baby to the waiting crowds. The people in the
great plaza acknowledged the imperial salute with waves of applause as the
national anthem written by Pedro's father was played.

Earlier at the Glória Church the sweet smell of burning incense and candles had filled the sanctuary as the presiding bishop with great pomp and ceremony asked in a clear and rhythmic voice, "What name would this child take?"
Then using water blessed from the River Jordan in Palestine, he intoned, "I bap-
tize thee Isabel Cristina Leopoldina Augusta Michaela Gabriela Rafaela Bragança in the name of the Father, the Son and the Holy Spirit." The bishop then
officially welcomed Princess Isabel into the church.[8]

Later, guests were invited to approach the royal baby in the order of their
position in the empire. There they offered a prayer in celebration of the church's
newest member and the dynasty's first princess. Outside fireworks, so loved by
the Braganças, joined clanging church bells and booming cannons announcing
Brazil's princess had been baptized. Festivities continued till dawn.

On the same day as Isabel's baptism the British navy seized a Brazilian ship,
the *Paquetá de Rio*, off the coast of West Africa. The Sierra Leone *Watchman*
later reported its smuggled cargo of five hundred forty-seven African slaves had
been bound for Rio de Janeiro. The *Watchman*'s description of the human cargo
carried by the captured vessel provided a painful window into the world of slavery the year of Isabel's birth.[9]

> The slaves were all stowed together, perfectly naked, with nothing on which to
> rest but the surfaces of the water casks.... The slaves who were confined in the
> hold — it being totally impossible for the whole of them to remain on deck at one
> time — were in profuse perspiration and panting like so many hounds for water.
> The smell on board was dreadful.... the greater part of the slaves were chained
> together with pieces of chain, which were passed through iron collars round the
> poor creatures....
> I found they belonged to, and were shipped to, different individuals. They were
> branded like sheep. Letters were burnt in the skin two inches in length. Many of
> them ... were in a state of ulceration. Both males and females were marked as follows:

On the right breast "J"; on the left arm, "P"; over the women's right and left breasts, "S" and "A"; under the left shoulder, "P"; right breast, "R"; and "RJ"; on the right and left breasts, "SS," and on the right and left shoulder "SS."[10]

The "branded" slaves of the Paquetá de Rio may have been too exhausted to have celebrated their freedom, but in Rio de Janeiro nothing stopped the revelry accompanying Princess Isabel's baptism."

Slavery was an accepted fact of life in 1846.[11] People were bought and sold as property throughout Africa, Asia and the Americas. Slave markets auctioned human flesh to the highest bidder from Rio de Janeiro to Washington, D.C. The president of the United States and most of the people in the church during Isabel's baptism owned slaves, including the bishops and priests officiating during the ceremony.

Many of the same dignitaries had been present the year before when Isabel's older brother, Afonso Leopold, had been christened in an identical religious celebration. His strong, healthy appearance had not prepared his family or the nation for his sudden death seven months following Isabel's baptism. Pedro sadly wrote at the time, "This has been the most fatal blow that I could receive."[12]

Two more royal children were born to the royal family. Princess Leopoldina was delivered just weeks after Afonso Leopold's death. The following year a second son arrived and was christened Pedro Leopold. He immediately took precedence over his older sisters as heir to the imperial throne.

Eighteen months later Isabel and her younger brother were stricken by typhoid fever at the family's Santa Cruz plantation south of Rio de Janeiro. Pedro Leopold did not survive, but Isabel made a slow difficult recovery. The royal family never returned to Santa Cruz. The bedroom where the young prince died was sealed, frozen in time as it appeared on the last day of his brief life. With the death of Pedro Leopold, Princess Isabel became heir to Brazil's throne.

The emperor and empress, unhappy in marriage but joyful in parenthood, were in despair. In his grief the twenty-four-year-old emperor turned to the written rather than spoken word: "On me has fallen the saddest of fates. Father and mother I lacked in tender infancy, and now my tiny sons are dead."[13]

Following the deaths the emperor turned his fatherly attention toward Isabel and Leopoldina. He found in his daughters the happiness he felt with no one else. He and the empress would have no more children.

By July 1850, Pedro II had been emperor for ten years. Decades of provincial rebellion and lawlessness had finally been crushed and the empire was united and at peace. The thirty-one senators and seventy-nine representatives of Brazil's General Assembly responded to the occasion by passing a degree saluting Isabel's approaching birthday. It was an unofficial recognition of Isabel as Pedro's heir.[14]

That August lawmakers voted unanimously that in compliance with the 1824 constitution, "Her Imperial Highness Dona Isabel was heir and successor to her August Father for the throne and crown of Brazil."[15] In an unusual show of unanimity, every member of the General Assembly signed the decree.

The following day a committee made up of Brazil's elected representatives was received by the emperor in the throne room of the City Palace. With Isabel standing erectly by his side, Pedro II proudly and with uncharacteristic emotion stated, "I accept in the name of my daughter Isabel the degree of acknowledgment sent to me by the General Assembly recognizing the Imperial Princess as heir to the throne of Brazil."[16]

Pedro II was seen to smile at his small daughter. Isabel, dressed in a long white dress, stared solemnly ahead, but said nothing. At four years of age, she could not begin to understand the responsibilities descending on her shoulders.

September of that year, with the country at peace and the future of the dynasty assured, Pedro's government sought to complete unfinished business. After two decades of non-enforcement Pedro II and his justice minister moved to finally legally end the importation of additional slaves from Africa. The capture of the *Paquetá de Rio* the day of Isabel's baptism had been one of many escalating attempts by Queen Victoria's England to stop Brazil from trafficking in human flesh. By 1850 Her Majesty's ministers were threatening even more direct military intervention.[17]

Pedro privately abhorred slavery and believed the time right to enforce the ban on the slave trade. Internal political turmoil, provincial rebellions, economic self-interest, and nationalistic rhetoric had allowed pro-slavery supporters to postpone enforcement of the law for years. The newly confident twenty-five-year-old emperor was ready to fulfill the promise his father and grandfather made to end the trade once and for all.[18]

During his first decade as emperor, Pedro removed many of the obstacles preventing enforcement. In 1850, he and his ministers finally persuaded Brazil's recalcitrant lawmakers to abolish the trade "as a measure of social convenience, of civilization, of national honor, and even of public security."[19] The term "public security" referred to several harsh realities.

The British military threat, the fear of slave rebellions, and devastating epidemics brought by slave ships may have all helped persuade the country's legislators to act.[20] Whatever their motives, the ministry's proposal pleased a small but growing segment of public opinion. Slave traders in Brazil and West Africa were unhappy, but political reality forced them to comply.[21]

With the legal end of the slave trade Brazil entered into a golden age of peace and prosperity. Not since the reign of Maria I had Brazil known such a period of tranquility. Princess Isabel and her sister grew up in a stable, secure environment dramatically different from the one her father and aunts had known, and light years away from the childhood chaos of Pedro I.

17

"To Direct the Constitutional Government of an Empire"

At nearly the same time the slave trade was legally banned in Brazil, Princess Isabel began her formal education. Since her birth, her father had been her first and most influential teacher. Shortly after the death of his sons, Pedro wrote, "I would not have survived were it not that I still have a wife and two children, whom I must educate so that they can assure the happiness of the country in which they were born. That is also one of my consolations."[1]

Teaching his daughters not only comforted the emperor but also became his principle source of enjoyment.[2] From the time they were infants he shared his love of reading, writing and learning with them. His interest in their education must have been smothering at times; but for Isabel it was a significant part of the special relationship she developed with her father.

Pedro thought his daughters' "education should not differ from that given to men, combined with that suited the other sex, but in a manner that does not distract from the first." Duty and responsibility guided his thinking: "The character of both princesses ought to be shaped as suits ladies who, it may be, will have to direct the constitutional government of an empire such as that of Brazil."[3]

In order to achieve that goal he wanted his daughters taught by the best teachers regardless of their political viewpoints, race or gender. Their writing instructor was an avowed republican whose anti-monarchial political leanings caused him to address the princesses as "young ladies" rather than their "highnesses." To teach Isabel to play the violin, a highly cultured multi-talented Afro-Cuban musician was hired. Their dance instructor was a respected Englishwoman who also taught the daughters of wealthy Brazilians and foreign diplomats. The diversity of her instructors may have been a part of the "hidden curriculum" Pedro wanted his daughters to absorb.

Brazil's emperor had no intention of surrendering his own involvement in his daughters schooling, but he also sought a well-educated aristocratic lady to supervise their day-to-day instruction. He wrote his stepmother, the Dowager

Empress Amélia, for help in filling the position. His meticulously detailed job description specified a "German, Roman Catholic, religious widow with no small children. Someone over forty years of age, without interest holding her to Europe, able to speak several languages, with a sweet temper, delicate manners, and knowing the various occupations in which fine ladies spend their free time."[4]

Empress Amélia was unable to find such a candidate. But Pedro's sister Francesca suggested the Brazilian Condessa Barral, who had once tutored her own daughter at the French court. The Condessa did not completely fit the profile laid out by the emperor. Although she was aristocratic, well traveled and had an excellent education, she was also married with a young son. Her husband had been a French diplomat under the Orleans monarchy and her father the first Brazilian ambassador to France.[5]

Barral's wealth came from family owned sugar plantations in northern Brazil; but she had grown up in France and had a cosmopolitan perspective on life. She was intelligent, loyal, discreet, and well versed in court etiquette but not seeking or in need of the position. Francesca, however, believed she could be a genuine ally to her brother and nieces.[6]

The Princess of Joinville was aware of the gossips, sycophants and ambitious schemers attracted to royal courts. She cautioned her brother, "I think that it is indispensable to entirely change the people around your daughters and to deny them all access to them if Barral is to have a chance to be successful." To smooth the path of the appointment she wrote to "everyone in the palace recommending the Condessa Barral as being a person who is not only a very good friend of mine and a good Brazilian, but someone who deserves the entire confidence she needs to fulfill her mission."[7]

In September 1856, the Condessa met ten-year-old Isabel and eight-year-old Leopoldina. Following the meeting, she bluntly wrote the emperor, "Spoiled children aren't suited for my teaching. I certainly had not come to Rio to play the role of governess as a decoration, as staffage so to speak, here in the court, so that in the distant future somebody could be blamed if educational shortcomings or the lack of inner composure could no longer be concealed."[8] Pedro was immediately impressed. Barral was no sycophant. The emperor promptly hired her and they developed a close personal and professional relationship.

Luísa Margarida Barros, Condessa of Barral, effortlessly straddled several worlds at once. Still, she remained an aristocratic Brazilian woman cared for by three personal servants and fourteen slaves.[9] Diplomatic, insightful and respectful of traditions, she could still think for herself and be brutally honest in private. Few women in Brazil matched such a profile. The princesses loved their gentle mother and worshipped their demanding but emotionally distant father. With the introduction of the condessa, a third adult role model entered their private lives.

Barral managed to forge a bond with each member of the royal family.

With the empress and princesses she shared a deep religious faith guided by a personal God that loved them unconditionally, but held them strictly accountable for their actions. The emperor used the church when it suited him, but his only real object of worship and veneration may have been the constitution. He and Barral, however, shared a burning intellectual curiosity and a love of learning that bridged their differing views on religion.

Princess Isabel, drawn to the governess's strength and confidence, pleaded with her to move into the palace. Realizing access to the royal family would arouse jealousy Barral established a separate life for herself away from the court and its politics. Publicly she presented herself as traditional wife and mother, but privately she negotiated her own salary, the use of a private carriage, and a separate residence paid for by the emperor. She arrived at the palace every morning promptly at five fifty-five to oversee the education of Brazil's princesses. At the end of the day she returned to her own home and family.[10]

Pedro II respected Barral's independence and intelligence perhaps because she was unafraid to match wits or disagree with him. Few attempted such behavior, especially the empress. Still the condessa understood his position and ego, carefully treating him deferentially and with great respect. In the time and place in which they lived, nothing else would have been tolerated. Her intelligence, opinions and independence were carefully hidden under a mantle of femininity and charm. The emperor and Princess Isabel found her irresistible, Poldie and Theresa less so.

Theresa Christina must at times have felt a mere observer in the lives of her daughters. In one letter Barral wrote the empress, "The day before yesterday Poldie greeted me with the news that she could not ride into the mountains. She said she had a sore throat and that she intended to stay in bed all day. It was easy to see through it. Poldie does not like swimming at the waterfalls, nor does she like the dinners with the Argentine ambassador. She has tried to get out of a geometry exam that way. Both girls are inclined to use minor ailments as excuses. I shall drive the tendency out of them once and for all. Isabel already enjoys bathing in cold water, and I was satisfied with her performance during Dom Pedro's speech from the throne. She sat up straight for the entire two hours and listened intently to her father. Unfortunately Poldie's thoughts were only briefly focused on her the Emperor's words. These examples of carelessness, of course, are minor, and in one or two years they will no longer be evident."[11]

Brazil's princesses grew up under the watchful eyes and unrelenting demands of their governess and father. Pedro II selected and privately hired his daughter's teachers and the Condessa Barral supervised daily lessons. Six days a week for nine hours a day Isabel and Leopoldina were taught history, geography, philosophy, English, German, French, Latin, Greek, Portuguese, mathematics, physics, literature, music, dance, art, drawing and penmanship. Saturday studies included the Bible and scripture.[12]

Linguistics was a special passion of the emperor, and he believed his daughters should learn to think and speak in different languages. Their morning lessons were taught in Portuguese, afternoon arithmetic lessons in French, Spanish and German. Later in the day they were expected to converse, pray and read the Bible in Latin and Italian.[13] To their father's delight, Isabel and Poldie became multi-lingual.

In all ways but one, Leopoldina received the same instruction as her sister. Isabel received individual lessons in government, law and politics from the emperor. When she was older, she wrote and translated his correspondence into French and German.

Sunday mornings the family attended mass together, not in a royal chapel but at a local Catholic Church. Sunday afternoons the emperor reviewed and tested his daughters over their weekly lessons. Sunday nights were devoted to reading aloud as a family. Pedro II provided his daughters with a broad, democratic and rigorous education, through both its curriculum and the teachers who taught it.[14]

Despite his interest in the education of his daughters, the general state of education for Brazilian girls remained low. Brazil's constitution delegated education and its funding to state and local authorities, not the national government. Pedro, however, demanded the highest academic achievement from his own daughters and funded a school for orphan girls on the grounds of his São Cristóvão Palace. Eventually the enrollment grew to over two hundred pupils.[15]

Aside from their education, Isabel and Poldie had a childhood similar to many aristocratic Brazilian girls of the nineteenth century. In some ways it may have been less pretentious, due to the simple taste and quiet life style of their parents. Isabel and Poldie's childhoods stood in contrast to the strict protocol, family formality and sometimes-haphazard education most of their royal female cousins experienced. Pedro wanted to create a more democratic model of monarchy and protect his daughters from the temptations and corruption found in most royal courts.

There was one corruption, however, from which he could not protect them. Slavery was found everywhere in Brazilian society, including his own home. Tradition and law dictated crown slaves staff Brazil's royal palaces including the nurseries of his own children. Crown slaves were owned by the state, not the emperor. Even Pedro II dared not attempt to change such an entrenched custom. Nearly every individual of wealth in Brazil, including Pedro II and his family, the Condessa Barral, and the entire court were cared for by the bondage system Pedro privately detested.

As an emperor and as a man, Pedro was personally free of racism. His earliest role models dreamed of a nation free of slaves and he may have been one of the few Brazilians capable of imagining a slaveless Brazil. Theresa, as in all parts of her life, mirrored her husband's thinking. Both passed their racial attitudes onto their daughters.

Pedro's position as emperor was a powerful one, but he was by nature cautious and conservative. Still he was acutely sensitive to political realities and the shifts of public opinion. Although the Brazilian constitution forbade him from speaking directly on political issues, he had become adept at influencing opinion through actions rather than words.

In his first and in all subsequent cabinets and government appointments, Pedro II selected Brazilians for leadership positions regardless of their race.[16] Isabel and Poldie grew up seeing men of all races serving their father in positions of authority. As her father's student, daughter, and heir Princess Isabel followed his example. Race never played a role in her social life, political relationships, alliances or disagreements.[17] It may have been the most important lesson Isabel learned from him.

~ 18 ~

"A Living Symbol"

The empress of Brazil did not have the education or position of her husband or the personality or intellectual depth of the Condessa Barral, but she was a born caretaker. Theresa Christina Maria Bourbon Bragança mothered everyone — her husband, her children, and even the slaves attending them. Her sincerity, great heart and common touch softened court protocol and humanized the monarchy. Despite public scrutiny, she created for her family a home life that was secure, safe and predictable.

One of the greatest gifts Theresa gave her family was reconnecting them to the Braganças' longstanding love of music. Her singing and piano playing gave them an appreciation of the pleasure, relaxation and escape music provided. Outside the home Theresa saw to it that the court sponsored and attracted to Brazil noteworthy opera and classical performers. Pedro's musical conversion prompted his sister Francesca to write, "I was very pleased when I learned that you have been to an Italian opera and enjoyed the experience. It surprises me, you my brother, who has always been bored by music."[1]

Theresa gave freely of herself as a mother and a healer. As empress she dedicated her public life to charities supporting hospitals and helped create a health care system where almost none had existed. Brazilians came to affectionately call her "Mother of all Brazilians," the title once given her role model, Pedro's own mother.[2]

Pedro accepted and supported Theresa's public duties as long as they did not interfere with him as the center of her life. As emperor, husband and father, Pedro dominated the entire existence of his family. He believed it his role and responsibility to make all their decisions.[3] Theresa respectfully and affectionately concurred.

In 1848, Brazil's royal family began traveling to the mountains north of Rio de Janeiro to retreat from public pressures and responsibilities. In the capital, the family occasionally spent nights at the Paço Imperial in the heart of Rio, but their official residence was the São Cristóvão Palace on rolling green hills outside the city. The palace, a gift to the Bragança's shortly after they arrived in Brazil, was named for the patron saint of travelers. A visitor described it at the time: "The palace ... is placed upon a rising ground, and is built rather in the Moresco style, and colored yellow with white moldings. It has a beautiful screen, a gateway of Portland stone and the court is planted with weeping willows; so that a group of great beauty is formed in the bosom of a valley, surrounded by high and picturesque mountains.... The view from the palace opens to part of the bay, over an agreeable plain flanked by fertile hills."[4]

Pedro provided his children a plot to grow their own vegetables—a tradition begun by his mother. Isabel and Poldie also milked cows and cared for farm animals to familiarize them with agricultural life. In time, Rio de Janeiro grew and surrounded the palace, but for years it provided a quiet country retreat from the bustling capital.

Similar to the Braganças' Ajuda Palace, built on a hilltop in Lisbon, the family's living quarters on the third floor of the São Cristóvão Palace provided them spectacular views and seasonal breezes. Bottom floors included a museum, a library, a theatre and public rooms for meetings and entertainment. Within its grounds could be found not only the girls' school for orphans sponsored by the emperor but a hospital for the poor funded by the empress.[5]

The family's mountain home became what the mountain retreat of Sintra had been for their Portuguese ancestors. Its gardens and house were designed and built by German immigrants and paid for from Pedro's private funds. The town of Petrópolis, named for the emperor, grew around the royal estate.[6] Their two-story, forty-four-room home there was patterned after the Neapolitan villas of Empress Theresa's Italy. It was surrounded by a landscaped park filled with roses, rhododendrons and other perennially blooming plants. The palace and many of the city's surrounding houses were painted soft pastels of pink, yellow, blue or white, giving Petrópolis the fairy tale appearance of a child's Easter basket. Isabel and Poldie spent most of their childhood summers there.

Princess Isabel remembered, "We moved in the summer to Petrópolis. Embarking at the Navy Arsenal, in my father's steam launch, we sailed for an hour though the green and picturesque islands ... leaving behind us Sugar Loaf and the fortress ... guarding Rio Bay. In front of us we had beautiful mountains ... resembling pipe organs. At Mauá we boarded the railroad and two hours later we found ourselves at Petrópolis, our summer residence, a delicious residence: flowering gardens, canals that crisscrossed the town, pretty houses, wooded hills and mountains in the distance, some of them granite, whose flanks the setting sun turned purple."[7]

Pedro and Theresa wished their daughters to have as normal and simple a life as possible. In Petrópolis a favorite family recreation involved long walks after dinner with stops to admire the park-like grounds of friends and foreign diplomats. Residents competed with each other to create magnificent gardens, knowing that sooner or later the royal family would pay a call.

The royal family came to relish the pace of their life in Petrópolis. Aside from birthdays, family anniversaries or special occasions, Brazil's princesses did not attend parties or play with children outside their court circle. They were each others' playmates, joined by a large menagerie of pets and animals including brilliant macaws and other colorful Brazilian birds. Almost before they could walk they learned to ride horses. As they grew larger, so did the horses they rode.

Brazil's princesses entertained themselves and their parents by putting on their own theatrical productions or acting in French comedies playing all the parts. Isabel had a flair for acting, Poldie for verse and dialogue. Structured time away from their studies was spent reading, painting and practicing piano, violin or other musical instruments. It was a busy, happy, but solitary childhood.

In February or March they celebrated their own Carnival with masks and costumes; but their favorite celebration was the feast days of Saints João and Pedro. Bonfires and fireworks would be lit and the palace grounds would be open to all the children of court officials, servants and slaves. On those special occasions the emperor could be seen playing childhood games he had missed as a child.

Despite the rigid schedule and intense demands of their studies, individual personalities of each princess emerged. The emperor wrote, "Isabel it seems is going to be willful and her sister the opposite."[8] Poldie was usually very easygoing, less intense in her focus, and with a personality like her mother. Isabel was her father's child. Like her father she sought solitary escapes, but not in books or reading. She loved to be out of doors and was happiest when she was in a garden. As an adult she fondly remembered, "During my childhood the [palace grounds of São Cristóvão] notable above all for its shady alleys of mangos, tamarind and other trees; its alleys of bamboo of which the tops crossed so high as to form a true cathedral ceiling."[9]

Petrópolis afforded Isabel time to escape from some of the responsibilities of her royal childhood — but also opportunities for trouble. During one holiday celebration she nearly blinded a child with a lighted rocket. The emperor accepted financial responsibility for the visually impaired girl the rest of her life.

After the accident Isabel felt genuine remorse, but it failed to curb all her childish misbehavior or an occasional poor conduct grade from teachers. In situations when she disappointed her father, she was sincerely repentant. Following one such event she wrote him, "I ask a thousand pardons of you for all my faults.... Today I spent an hour in the confessional."[10]

Despite her best intentions she could still ruffle her usually unflappable father. Once when she was in the garden cutting wood with a small hatchet, Maria Amandinha, daughter of the Marquês of Paranaguá, surprised Isabel from behind and was hit in the face with an ax.[11] Screams from both children brought the frightened emperor and marquês rushing to them. The injury was not life threatening, but the court doctor, the marquês, and both girls spent a considerable amount of time calming down the distraught emperor. As "Protector and Perpetual Defender of Brazil" Pedro II was imperturbable, but as a nervous father he was all too human.

Maria Amandinha was left with a permanent scar, but the incident solidified her friendship with Isabel and she became one of Isabel's closest confidants and a lifelong friend. Amandinha's mother descended from a long line of Portuguese nobility. Her father, a respected Brazilian statesman, bore the distinctly handsome features of his African ancestors.[12] Isabel, like her father, did not see race in her fellow Brazilians.

On July 29, 1860, after years of quiet preparation, Isabel once again found herself the center of attention. On her fourteenth birthday, with neither parent present, she made her first solo public appearance. As heir to the throne she was required to publicly pledge allegiance to the empire's constitution and to her father as emperor.[13]

In 1846 following her baptism, Isabel had been carried as an infant to the cheering crowds gathered in the plaza of the Paço Imperial. Now before a joint session of the nation's elite and the entire elected General Assembly, she spoke for herself. The simple but important ceremony had the same solemnity as the one her father attended when he was nearly her age and assumed the powers of Brazil's constitutional emperor.[14] The General Assembly was filled to capacity with all thirty-six senators and the ninety-six elected deputies awaiting Isabel's arrival. Diplomats from Portugal, England, Prussia, Spain, Austria, and the United States were present. Even Pope Pius IX sent an envoy. Galleries overflowed with the empire's most important personages.

To usher Princess Isabel into the grand assemblage a military honor guard was created, made up of representatives from every battalion of the regular army and national guard. Like the honor guard of her grandparents, it contained Brazilian men of all colors and backgrounds. The national anthem played and crowds applauded as Isabel arrived in a royal carriage drawn by six matching horses. Her dress was a dazzling white gown intricately embroidered. A simple sash crossed from her shoulder to her waist and her ash blond hair was parted in the middle in a style favored by her mother and popularized by Queen Victoria.

When the young princess entered the chambers, the president of the Senate, the first secretary of the House of Deputies, and a wave of emotion from those in the galleries greeted her. People clapped, cheered, and waved scarves and handkerchiefs. Order was restored and Isabel solemnly sat in her designated chair in front of her father's large, empty throne. On her right sat the leader of the Senate, to her left the leader of the House of Deputies. The crowd grew silent as Isabel kneeled before the constitution, rested her right hand on a Catholic Prayer Book, and her left hand over her heart. Without further delay, with her face drawn of all color, Isabel spoke in a clear voice touched by emotion. In her first public oath as heir to the throne of Brazil she proclaimed, "I swear to preserve the Catholic religion, to follow the Constitution of the Brazilian nation, to be obedient to all laws and to the Emperor."[15]

Princess Isabel and the president of the Senate signed the oath to loud applause. The first secretary of the Deputies read the signed document aloud and the hall again filled with cheers. Moved by waves of support and affection, Isabel stood and bowed. Cheers from inside merged with those outside as her honor guard escorted her to her waiting carriage. It was a glorious day for the Bragança dynasty and the empire of Brazil.

That same afternoon Pedro II, Empress Theresa, Poldie, and Isabel received official delegations at the São Cristóvão Palace. For several long hours members of the Senate and House of Deputies, the foreign diplomatic corps, representatives of provincial and municipal governments, large and small business interests, and the leaders of the Catholic Church came to offer their respect, or pledge their loyalty and allegiance.

All segments of the nation were represented, rich and poor, black and white, men and women, aristocrats, slaves and former slaves. Hundreds of groups and individuals, planters, military officers and enlisted men, merchants, lawyers, engineers, and literary and educational associations pledged their loyalty to the their future empress, the third member of her family to rule the largest nation in North or South America.

One speech from a member of the General Assembly seemed to speak for all of Brazil when he proclaimed, "Today is not only your birthday but the day we salute you for the oath you have taken. Today you are a living symbol of the allegiance between the crown and the people."[16]

The emperor expressed gratitude to each delegation visiting the palace. At times, the affection and loyalty of so many Brazilians seemed to touch Pedro, and he was uncharacteristically open in expressing his feelings. The joy, pride, and happiness of the event would linger in the hearts of Brazil's royal family in the bittersweet days ahead.

19

"On the Surface of a Volcano"

The year 1860 was a high-water mark for Brazil's monarchy, but events outside of the country cast a troubling shadow. In North America escalating debates on slavery threatened civil war in the United States. Twelve years earlier republican revolutions swept across Europe, toppling France's monarchy. Pedro's sister Francesca with the entire Orleans family was living in English exile.[1]

European revolutionaries were again on the move. Giuseppe Garibaldi and his supporters were in the process of uniting Italy by overthrowing the monarchy of the Kingdom of the Two Sicilies. Garibaldi had earlier fought against Pedro's own government in southern Brazil. His defeat there by General Caxias had not extinguished his revolutionary zeal.

Pedro's older sister, Princess Januária, fled Naples with other members of Empress Theresa's family.[2] The Neapolitan royal family were besieged at the great northern citadel at Gaeta. King Ferdinand seemed overwhelmed by the rapid turn of events. The rallying point for royalists became the dowager queen. Her "courage, devotion, and spirit" held family and kingdom together. England's Victoria wrote that the only hope for saving the throne was if Ferdinand's mother had the opportunity to shoot Garibaldi herself.[3] But not even the queen of Naples could save the monarchy. By the end of the year the Italian Bourbons were also in political exile.[4]

In his final address to his people King Ferdinand declared, "As a descendant of a dynasty which has reigned over this country for 126 years, my affections are centered here. I am a Neapolitan, and cannot without feelings of bitter grief, speak words of farewell to my dearly beloved people. Whatever may be my destiny, prosperous or contrary, I shall always preserve for them a lasting and affectionate remembrance. I recommend to them concord and peace, and the observance of their civic duties. Do not let an immoderate zeal for my fate be made a pretext for disorder."[5] He would not be the last king to make such a plea.

Some believed the age of monarchy was passing, and Pedro made no effort to offer his exiled sisters and their families a home in Brazil. Exiled royalty could be an embarrassment to those who still wore crowns. In Portugal, Spain and France ambitious politicians proved more than willing to use one branch of a royal family against another. Pedro was never comfortable with anyone who might become a political rival, including a member of his own family. It sometimes seemed as if no crown was secure. Two of his three sisters had become political exiles. The fate of his third, Portugal's queen, was a painful reminder that intelligence and high birth did not ensure political success.

Maria da Glória sacrificed her childhood to the political ambitions of her father, leaving her sisters, brother and Brazil to become queen of a country she had never seen. An ocean separated her from the place of her birth and the grave of her mother. Portuguese "advisors" even forced her to surrender her name, thinking it too Brazilian, and she became Maria II to honor the great-grandmother she never knew.[6]

Portrait of Princess Isabel's Aunt Maria da Glória (1819–1853) near the time she became queen of Portugal. She became known as Maria II after she left Brazil to become queen. One of her first official acts was to move against the African slave trade her ancestors had begun. Courtesy the Catholic University of America, Oliveira Lima Library, Washington, D.C.

Her charismatic but erratic father controlled her early life proclaiming himself her "tutor and natural defender."[7] When she was ten he selected his twenty-year-old brother to be her husband. Her husband-uncle, grandmother and aunts then attempted to steal her crown. She became a political pawn fought over by the governments of England, Austria, France and Portugal, a queen without a throne, shuttled from one country to another but accepted by none.

During a stay in England she was initially ignored by her cousin, King George IV, and snubbed by his prime minister. Finally when her presence could no longer be overlooked, the king hosted a ball for her and his own niece and young heir, Princess Victoria. The two small girls became friends and corresponded for the rest of their lives. But as predicted on the occasion by Lord Grenville, their futures would be dramatically different.[8] He wrote, "I saw for the first time the Queen of Portugal and our little Victoria. The Queen was finely dressed, with a ribband and order over her shoulder, and she sat by the king. She is good looking, and has a sensible Austrian countenance. In dancing she fell down and hurt her face, was frightened and bruised, and went away. The King was very kind to her. Our little Princess is a short, plain looking child and not near so good looking as the Queen. However, if nature has not done so much, fortune is likely to do a good deal more for her."[9]

By the end of Portugal's civil war Maria became queen of a bankrupt, deeply divided nation. After her father's death she was left to contend with liberal and conservative politicians competing to create a national agenda. A third group, the defeated reactionaries, still hoped to exclusively retain power in the church, the crown and the ancient aristocracy. But since the death of Carlota Joaquina and the exile of Maria's uncle and husband Miguel, they were leaderless.

Outwardly everyone pledged lip service to the young queen, but a member of the Portuguese cabinet told the Belgian ambassador, "I ought to warn you that we are on the surface of a volcano, and that the eruption may break out at any moment. Looking at royalty, as you see it here, surrounded with honor and receiving homage from ministers, officers of high rank, soldiers, and palace guards, you would imagine, no doubt, that it is firmly established and secure from every risk. The fact is that the crown is lying on the ground. There is not man among all those whom you see bowing low before the Queen who could not upset her throne if he chose. They all do obeisance within the precincts of the palace; but they all begin to conspire as soon as they get outside."[10]

Prior to his death from tuberculosis, exhaustion and hard living, Pedro I requested the parliament recognize his fifteen-year-old daughter as queen without the guiding hand of a regent. Twelve days before his death he was granted his wish. He also arranged to have his daughter Maria's marriage to her uncle Miguel annulled by the archbishop of Lisbon. Portugal's peace and stability depended on Maria's quick remarriage and her prompt delivery of a royal heir.[11]

Many princes were considered as consorts including two from France: Louis, Duke of Nemours, and François, Prince of Joinville. Initially Maria was attracted to Joinville, who later happily married her younger sister, but a French marital alliance was rejected. Joinville confided he was relieved because being a husband to a reigning queen offered no chance for peace or happiness.[12]

With no more brothers to offer in marriage, Pedro I selected his brother-in-law as her next groom. The Duke of Leuchtenburg, German-French grandson of Empress Josephine of France, seemed an ideal choice. Maria dutifully agreed. The year she became queen, Maria lost her father, married a second time, and within eight weeks became a widow. Some believed the sudden death of the healthy young duke was caused by poison, but no evidence could be found. For the sake of throne and dynasty, Maria was told she must quickly remarry. It would be the third marriage for the fifteen-year-old queen.

Without her father's ambitious hand to guide her, Maria's stepmother Amélia and the Portuguese government acted as matchmakers. The French Duke of Nemours and other princes were again put forward and again rejected. The groom became Ferdinand of Saxe-Coburg-Gotha. Like her other two husbands, the rush to the altar caused a proxy ceremony to be performed before she was able to meet her marriage partner. Maria never did meet her first husband, Uncle Miguel, and barely knew her second. By the time Ferdinand landed in Lisbon, the populace had become bored with royal grooms and he was greeted with silence.[13] The young queen, however, was favorably impressed. Following the birth of an heir the next year, she elevated Ferdinand to the position of king-consort. Through prodigious letter writing, he became Pedro's favorite brother-in-law and later Princess Isabel's godfather.

At the time of Maria's third marriage, competing political groups put forth candidates for the position of commander in chief of the Portuguese army. Each hoped their candidate would receive the influential position. Maria appointed perhaps the only male in Portugal not interested in it, her nineteen-year-old husband. The appointment sparked civil war — the first of fourteen over the next fifteen years.[14]

Maria spent most of her time trying to establish a political center from which to govern. Her first speech from the throne presented her vision for the future of Portugal. "With full confidence in the virtues of the Portuguese people I trust they will rally around my throne, and aid me in our just object. Most glorious and memorable will be the day in which I see the members of the Portuguese family, forgetful of their old disagreements, embrace each other, never more to separate. The realization of this object is dependent on the fulfillment of justice and duty."[15]

A chorus of denunciations from those with their own political agendas denounced Maria as a vampire and viper with "peace in her mouth and poison in her heart." Ambitious opportunists assailed her as sitting on a throne built on "blood and bones." Her dream of a regime built on "justice and duty" was mocked.[16]

Despite fierce opposition, Maria proceeded with a reform agenda she hoped would unite and heal the country, beginning with a plan to end Portugal's involvement in the slave trade. Bernardo Sá da Bandeira sponsored legislation to legally outlaw the sale of slaves in the Portuguese empire. Maria signed the legislation into law, but opponents blocked all attempts to establish firm deadlines or enforcement procedures. Colonial governors in Mozambique and elsewhere resigned to protest the law and African leaders and merchants denounced it.[17]

In contrast to the political frustrations of her public life, Maria's marriage provided her a peaceful sanctuary, but at a high price. Ferdinand built her Pena Palace, a fairy tale mountaintop retreat near Sintra. Its architecture and gardens were a combination of Portuguese dreams and German fairy tales surrounded by Brazilian trees and flowering plants.[18] It was a magical setting, but Portugal and Maria needed more than magic.

Ferdinand assumed the parental role once filled by Maria's dominating father and stepmother. After visiting Portugal, Prince Albert's brother glowingly wrote of the queen, "Such an affectionate surrender is rarely to be seen. She knows nothing of obstinacy, moodiness, etc. and lives only for her family."[19] Unfortunately for Maria, a queen must also live for her country. Diplomats in Portugal soon reported she "received no one until her King-Consort Ferdinand first saw the visitors and arranged their affairs. Then they were admitted to her presence only to kiss her hand."[20] Such deference to her foreign-born husband did little to unite her badly fragmented country.

Empress Leopoldina once wrote that her oldest daughter was the brightest and most strong-willed of her children. But by the time Maria da Glória became Maria II, life, death, war, and the patriarchal culture of the time took their toll. Observers noted her intelligence, spirit and genuine goodness allowed her to keep her throne, but seldom permitted her to get her way.[21]

Still, Maria earned the respect of Europe. Napoleon III admiringly wrote that Queen Maria II of Portugal and Queen Victoria in England elevated queenship by mothering their families and successfully leading their nations. Maria personally supervised the education of her eldest son and heir Pedro, recognized by many as "the most promising prince" in Europe. By the age of nine he was translating Virgil, Livy, Sallust and Cicero. At twelve, he had mastered several foreign languages including English and French while displaying remarkable talent for science and the arts. He reminded many of his grandmother, Leopoldina.[22]

Like her brother Pedro II, Maria seemed happiest supervising the education of her children. She became known as "the teacher of the nation," but holding her contentious country together limited opportunities to implement her educational reform agenda.[23] Strongmen such as João Carlos Saldanha dominated her reign. Saldanha had been a friend and ally of her father Pedro I and was one of the army leaders that helped reclaim her throne. He came to dominate her in the same manner Prime Minister Pombal once dominated her own great-grandfather. While Pombal had been the chief nemesis of Maria I, Saldanha became Maria II's strongest ally. Ironically, he was Pombal's grandson.

During her father's final illness, Pedro I had asked his old friend to care for the young queen as if she were his own daughter. Saldanha more than respected the request, treating her as a daughter first, his queen second. He never encouraged Maria to assert her independence or assume a greater constitutional role that would limit his role as the most powerful man in the country.[24]

Still in time he reconciled many of Maria's enemies to her side and helped create a united, peaceful nation. Her gratitude can still be seen today in the royal mausoleum of São Vincente monastery overlooking Lisbon's harbor. There among Bragança kings and queens dating from the founding of the dynasty in 1640 is Saldanha's tomb, close in death to the queen he served in life.

The last years of Maria's reign were peaceful, but short. Two decades of struggling to balance throne, marriage, and motherhood took their toll. She died delivering her eleventh child when she was just thirty-four years old. Maria lived six years longer than her mother but three years less than her father. Her last breath was drawn on November 15, 1853, the feast name day of her mother and anniversary of the death of the first Bragança king.

That year a government official reported the throne "had never been so respected as at this present time; and that peace, order, and contentment reigned throughout the country. The people renounced politics, in order to busy themselves with their own affairs. Industry was never so developed. Never were salaries and payments made with so much regularity."[25] Maria had finally achieved the goals she set for her nation, but did not live long enough to enjoy them.

Maria's eldest son, Pedro V, followed her on the Portuguese throne. To many he represented the best of kingship and the hope of his nation. Queen Victoria called him "the most distinguished young prince there is," and Prince Albert admitted he loved him "like a son."[26]

Pedro dedicated his reign to finishing what "my good mother" had begun.[27] Almost immediately he forced out of office the politicians who had dominated her reign then turned to his mother's old liberal ally, Bernardo Sá da Bandeira. He asked Bandeira to end once and for all the Portuguese slave trade his mother had tried ending seventeen years earlier. The young king and aged politician used the full force of the government to fulfill Maria's delayed dream. In 1858, the Cortes passed a law abolishing slavery in all Portuguese territories and colonies in twenty years. The extended time limit allowed slaveholders and traders to "prepare for the economic blow." The popular young king estimated it would take that long to put in place all the necessary enforcement procedures his government would need to make the law work.[28]

As Maria's son fought to end the Portuguese slave trade, Queen Victoria was busy playing matchmaker. She encouraged her niece Charlotte, only daughter of King Leopold and Queen Louise of Belgium, to look to Portugal for a husband. Charlotte's stubborn refusal allowed Pedro the unusual luck of actually falling in love with another bride chosen by politicians for purely dynastic reasons.

Pedro's marriage to the beautiful Stephanie of Hohenzollern, a Catholic princess from the Prussian royal family, proved to be happy, but brief. Two months after her triumphal arrival in Lisbon she suddenly died of diphtheria. Heart-broken, Pedro refused to consider another marriage while grieving the death of his bride. Two years later the twenty-five-year-old king died of typhoid fever and rejoined Stephanie, even if only in the Bragança royal mausoleum. Queen Victoria wrote, "It is an almost incredible event! A terrible calamity for Portugal, and a *real* European loss!"[29]

Lisbon had experienced outbreaks of cholera and yellow fever during Pedro's reign, but he refused to leave the city, spending time visiting hospitals and the sick. Almost miraculously he escaped the pestilence. Then he and two of his younger brothers become deathly ill during a country-hunting trip with typhoid fever. Only one survived, but it was not the king.[30]

Luís, the oldest surviving royal brother, was at sea, unaware of the tragedy. Only when the prime minister met his ship as it entered Lisbon's harbor did he learn of his elevation to the throne. His first full day as the king of Portugal was November 15th, the anniversary of his mother's death.

Despite the terrible beginning of his reign, Luís used the sympathy caused by the death of his brother to fulfill the promise made to their mother. In 1875 he finally ended the slave trade begun four centuries earlier by Prince Henry the Navigator.[31]

20

"No Place for Women"

The tragedies besetting Portugal's royal family did nothing to reassure Pedro II about the future of his own dynasty. Both royal daughters were approaching marriageable age. For the good of the monarchy and for their future happiness the right marriage partners must be found. But as events in Portugal and the rest of Europe showed, unforeseen events could destroy the best-laid plans of queens, kings and diplomats.

In Spain, the Bragança royal cousins were plagued with the kind of scandals dynastic marriage brokers most feared. After years of civil war and nine years of unhappy marriage Queen Isabella II had produced eight children — none apparently by the man diplomats had chosen to be her husband. Following the birth of Isabella's first child, Queen Victoria confided, "It is a very good thing no one will be inclined to care as to who the *real* father is considering her very peculiar and distressing marriage for which she, poor thing, is no way to blame."[1]

By 1860, the year Princess Isabel turned fourteen, Victoria had been queen of England for over two decades. Since her ascension to the throne at eighteen Victoria had survived numerous assassination attempts, calls for an English republic, famines, epidemics, military disasters, several prime ministers and nine pregnancies. At just forty-one years of age she was a grandmother twice over and wanted nothing more than to retire to Australia with her husband. Victoria found happiness in her marriage, but the British press never forgave her foreign-born consort Prince Albert for not being English. Newspapers regularly savaged him, bringing Victoria endless frustration, anger and pain.[2]

Pedro II was in no hurry to lose either of his beloved daughters but wondered where he would find suitable marriage partners for them. Then the year Isabel publicly came of age, Brazil's royal family had the rare experience of being visited by a European relative in search of a royal bride.

Archduke Maximilian, brother of Emperor Franz Joseph of Austria, traveled to Brazil seeking a wife for their youngest brother Ludwig. Maximilian had once been engaged to Pedro's half-sister Maria Amélia, the only child born to his father and stepmother in Portugal. She had reawakened a fascination with

Brazil planted by his aunt, Empress Leopoldina. Maria Amélia's death by tuberculosis shortly before they were to wed was one of many tragedies in Maximilian's life.[3]

He then married Princess Charlotte of Belgium, who Queen Victoria once hoped would marry Pedro V of Portugal. Charlotte, however, had set her heart on Maximilian. Many royal observers believed Charlotte the most intelligent princess in Europe, but it was not intelligence that attracted her to Maximilian. Like nearly everyone else, she was taken with his handsome features and surface charm.[4]

Maximilian privately admitted what attracted him most to Charlotte was her dowry. His own attitude toward women was revealed in a letter he wrote shortly after their meeting. "She is short; I am tall, which is as it should be. She is dark-haired; I am blond, which is also good. She is very intelligent, which is a little tiresome; but I'm sure I'll get over it."[5]

The first years of their marriage Maximilian served as Austrian viceroy of the Italian provinces of Lombardy and Venice, but Austria lost those territories shortly before Empress Theresa's family was driven from the throne of Naples. Since then, he and Charlotte had lived in restless boredom. As an antidote, he decided they should travel to Brazil.

Their first stop was Madeira, where Maximilian's late fiancé had died. The visit triggered a glimpse into his thoughts and feelings since her death. He wrote in his diary, "seven years filled with ... pain and bitter disillusionment.... I am coming back to seek on the waves of the Atlantic the peace that tottering Europe can no longer give my worried soul."[6] The journey to Brazil represented to Maximilian more than a chance to play royal matchmaker. He seemed to be seeking a purpose for an unfulfilled life.

Winter storms delayed their departure from Madeira. By the time the weather cleared, Maximilian decided to travel to America alone. His decision allowed Charlotte to journey south along the African coast to visit her cousin Gaston Orleans, an army officer serving in Spanish Morocco.[7]

Once in Brazil, Maximilian confided in his diary that he felt he was standing "at the gates of paradise.... One would have to have a hundred eyes to take in the unknown wonders which are continually unfolding themselves on all sides."[8] To the absent Charlotte he painted another picture. "This country is no place for women, and you would have made such a long trip for nothing. Except in the filthy boring cities and villages, no decent woman can live here. This country rules out traveling for women. Only a man able to withstand great hardships can feel at home in Brazil."[9]

Maximilian was surprised by the near invisibility of Euro-Brazilian women. With the exception of the imperial family, he noted, "One scarcely sees white women on the streets, only on the rarest occasion do they tear themselves from their balcony windows and from their rocking chairs.... A Brazilian lady in town is the very impersonalization of weary idleness."[10]

Impressions of his royal relatives were more favorable. "Isabel, the oldest is somewhat reserved; she has clean cut features, and pretty blonde hair, is well built, and quite healthy. Leopoldina, the youngest, is visibly sprightly with a rather lively expression, genteel and very gay."[11] He concluded either princess could successfully grace the royal courts of Europe and be a genuine asset to dynastic fortunes.[12]

The simplicity and relaxed protocol of the Brazilian court shocked him, but he found the emperor a good family man, a gentleman and scholar and the empress easy to like. Despite strong physical similarities between Austria's archduke and Brazil's emperor, Pedro offered no marital or political encouragement to his imperial relative. The personal reputation of Maximilian's younger brother was poor and a political marriage with Ludwig offered little chance for stability or happiness.

It appeared Maximilian would return to Europe without a Brazilian sister-in-law or support for his own political career. Despite Pedro's discouragement, Maximilian urged Franz Joseph to order their younger brother to pursue the marriage, writing, "Owing to Ludwig's nature it is just such an order that would be most suitable.... it is not to be expected that he should of his own accord tear himself from his surroundings in Vienna, which are so harmful to him. It would take a powerful initiative.... I know the emperor of Brazil, and believe him to be the man who will be able by his intelligently directed energy to lead Ludwig into serious, sane and active ways."[13] Without the Brazilian emperor's support, Franz Joseph refused. It was just such a loveless dynastic marriage Pedro II was determined to avoid.

His unsuccessful journey nevertheless offered a unique perspective on Brazil in 1860. As much as the archduke was taken with its "primeval forests" and its royal family, he found much that disturbed him — especially the nation's acceptance of slavery. He wrote, "How a Catholic priest can have the courage to preach the gospel in Brazil, I cannot understand."[14]

Maximilian was horrified at the prevalence of slavery in all aspects of Brazilian life. Except for foreign sailors the only people he saw doing physical labor were slaves. The beatings, the chains, the mutinies, and the infanticidal killing of their children "to spite their master" sickened him. For many slaves their only escape was suicide. He sadly observed, "One can hardly imagine a more unhappy life than that of the Negros."[15]

He could not understand how his American cousin could privately detest slavery and not act against it. Pedro believed his aristocratic cousin failed to understand the political realities and legal restraints of a constitutional monarchy. As emperor, he had sworn to support and enforce all the nation's laws, not just those with which he personally or politically agreed. Brazil's government was flawed, but it was a nation of laws, not dictators. Most of Pedro's neighbors lived in political, territorial and military chaos. Since Brazil's constitutional monarchy had been adopted, its seven nearest neighbors had discarded thirty-seven constitutions through revolution, warfare and violence.[16] He feared a direct move against slavery would produce similar results.

Fourteen months after Maximilian's visit, just such a war broke out in the United States. The U.S. secretary of state wrote his minister in Brazil, "Slavery is the cause of this Civil War, and the debates upon the present treatment and ultimate fate of slavery give to its abettors and to the government which is engaged in suppressing it much of their relative strength."[17]

The war in North America did nothing to reassure Pedro II that the road to abolition would be easy or bloodless. The Prince of Joinville, serving as a military advisor to Abraham Lincoln's Army of the Potomac, sent him reports on the war's events.[18] Joinville's letters and official diplomatic dispatches only strengthened the emperor's resolve to find a peaceful end to Brazilian slavery. The best leaders of the United States failed to devise a plan for abolition or to prevent war. If Pedro II failed in the task, it would fall to Isabel and whoever her husband might be.

Brazil's emperor soon discovered Maximilian was not the only member of European royalty interested in his marriageable daughters.[19] Maximilian's own brother-in-law, the Count of Flanders, asked to be considered a suitor for Princess Isabel despite the opposition of his older sister Charlotte. She wanted "Fat Philippe," as she called him, to marry her favorite cousin, daughter of the Prince and Princess of Joinville.[20] Other suitors also came courting including Napoleon III. After seizing power in France he cast his ambitious eyes toward America. Diplomatic correspondence reported he hoped French holdings north of Brazil could be enlarged and strengthened through a royal Franco-Brazilian marital alliance.

Closer to home others saw political advantages in a dynastic marriage. To Brazil's south sat the landlocked country of Paraguay, ruled by dictators since the expulsion of the Jesuits in 1767. Paraguay's current strongman, Carlos Antônio López, had built his impoverished country into a formidable police state where he and his family ruled as uncrowned kings. His eldest son and heir, Francisco López, had recently returned from a trip abroad with dreams of military and imperial glory.[21] Visits to the Crimean War and the dazzling court of Napoleon III and Empress Eugenie inflamed his ambitions. The first Napoleon elevated himself in the eyes of the world by marrying the Habsburg daughter of Austria's emperor. His own marriage to the daughter of Brazil's "Habsburg" emperor might cause lightning to strike again and help him remake the map of Latin America.[22]

Following his father's death, López traveled to Brazil to meet Pedro II, supposedly to discuss a long simmering boundary dispute between the nations; but spies notified the emperor López planned to ask permission to marry fifteen-year-old Princess Leopoldina. The emperor was not impressed. López had already fathered nearly a dozen children by three separate women and lived openly with his Irish born mistress.[23]

Pedro recognized the marriage proposal as a cynical attempt to use his family, but understood the necessity of receiving López with diplomacy and respect. In order to minimize opportunities for the unpleasant subject to be broached, the agenda for all meetings was tightly controlled and protocol between the two leaders strictly enforced. López was treated with the courtesy afforded any foreign head of state, but given no chance to make his unwelcome request. Sweeping etiquette aside, López bluntly asked for Leopoldina's hand in marriage. Pedro II used the momentary lapse in protocol to inquire about the health of López's mother. The query seemed benign, but the dictator and others recognized its intent. López's estranged mother was the only person in Paraguay bold enough to publicly mock his imperial ambitions and his public affair with his mistress. López stormed from the palace in anger.[24]

Pedro, his dynasty, and nation were denounced. Newspapers from both nations graphically and in sensational detail publicized the diplomatic break. The Council of State, the Countess of Barral, and others urged the emperor to respond, but he refused. Pedro II never commented on personal or political attacks. Still it was increasingly clear his daughters would not be safe until they were safely wed.[25]

In Brazil, most girls Isabel and Poldie's age had already married and produced several children, but Pedro was not ready to lose his daughters. For the time being they continued enjoying a safe, secure and extended childhood. But they had become young adolescents, and social activities competed for their time. On Sunday afternoons the palace was opened to friends for visits. Within a short time, Isabel began pressuring her father to allow Poldie and herself to attend weekly dances in Petrópolis. Initially he adamantly refused, but Isabel with Poldie's quiet support eventually wore the emperor down.[26]

Pedro traditionally retired at nine in the evening. As the father of young daughters, however, he was obligated to chaperone them to all social activities. Accordingly, Isabel and Poldie with their parents, the emperor and empress of Brazil, began attending weekly public dances in Petrópolis. The royal family arrived at ten in the evening, listened to the music, visited briefly and departed by midnight. Neither princess danced but at least they were able to attend.

Some Brazilians were scandalized, but Pedro as usual ignored his critics. In addition to his official positions, he was a father of two adolescent girls. Seventeen-year-old Isabel and sixteen-year-old Poldie were thrilled — even if their official escorts were their ever-watchful parents and they never placed a foot on the dance floor.

By May 1864 the royal childhoods of America's only princesses drew to a close. In his annual speech from the throne, Pedro II declared, "I announce to you with pleasure that I am arranging the marriage of the princesses, my two dear daughters which I hope will take place this current year."[27] Speculation and excitement swept through Brazil. Elaborate wedding arrangements began even though no one, including Isabel and Poldie, knew who would be their grooms.

21

"Side by Side"

Despite his public announcement, Pedro II did not have a specific groom in mind for either of his daughters. The maneuverings of Archduke Maximilian, the aspirations of "Fat" Philippe of Belgium, and the transparent ambitions of Napoleon III and Francisco López forced him to act. His task was not an easy one. Queen Victoria confided, "There is nothing more difficult than marrying off a young princess."[1]

Pedro's first choice was to have his daughters marry within the family. He considered his Portuguese nephews, but Brazilian public opinion doomed that possibility. He then looked toward his nephews from the Prince and Princess of Joinville and the Conde and Condessa Áquila. As a child, Isabel had developed a crush on her Joinville cousin Pierre. Much to the family's disappointment, he expressed no interest in marriage, remaining a bachelor his entire life. Januária then volunteered her oldest son Luís.[2]

Such a match held the possibility of healing old wounds. Relations between Pedro and Januária had been strained since her husband's extroverted personality and brother's introverted nature clashed shortly after her marriage. Áquila's gregarious nature, easy charm and fierce ambition attracted equally ambitious men to his side, and he was drawn into Brazilian politics. Few things were as unforgivable to Pedro II, who was acutely aware of the havoc family rivalries played in the life of his father and grandfather. Despite his own democratic principles Brazil's emperor shared power only with those who deferred to his wishes. Fearing Januária's son might take after his unpleasant father, Pedro eliminated him as a potential son-in-law.[3]

He continued his search. The challenge was made more difficult by the restrictions he placed on candidates; they had to be Catholic in religion and liberal in politics. Family and political considerations dismissed suitors from the royal houses of Spain, Austria and Italy following the elimination of his Portuguese nephews.[4] The Prince of Joinville, Pedro's family representative in Europe, wrote many of their royal relatives in search of eligible princes. When no other candidates were forthcoming, he proposed two of his own favorite nephews, Prince Luís Augustus, Duke of Saxe-Coburg, and Prince Luís Gaston of Orleans, the Count of d'Eu.[5]

Luís Augustus had a solid reputation as an officer and gentleman in the Austrian navy. He had been decorated during military campaigns by the governments of Austria and Prussia, serving in the naval squadron commanded by their cousin Archduke Maximilian. He was handsome, morally and intellectually strong, and a recognized war hero. Although his father was Austrian, his mother was a princess of Orleans, making him an acceptable royal suitor and consort to the future empress of Brazil.[6]

Joinville wrote of his other nephew, Luís Gaston, "If you could get him to marry one of your daughters that would be wonderful. He is a strong, tall, blue eyed, beautiful fellow with a good disposition, very affable, well educated, and what is more, he has some fame as a soldier."[7]

Privately Joinville confided that Gaston would be ideal for Poldie and Augustus a perfect partner for Isabel. Gaston's mother was a German princess and Queen Victoria's favorite first cousin. His father, the Duke of Nemours, was twice a failed candidate to be husband and consort of Maria II of Portugal.

They were both first cousins to Isabel and Poldie, with exemplary personal reputations. Each was a decorated war hero, one in the navy and the other in the army, as well as being grandsons of Louis-Philippe, exiled king of the French, and his beloved queen Marie Amélie. Their grandmother had been the surrogate mother of Empress Leopoldina and was also the Princess of Joinville's mother-in-law. Such family ties were important to Brazil's emperor.

Joinville's nephews were quietly invited to visit Brazil, sailing from Southampton, England, on August 8, 1864, chaperoned by Conde Christian Dumas, a family friend of the Orleans family and military colleague of Lafayette in America and Napoleon I in Europe.[8] Three weeks later they arrived in Recife, the capital of the northern province of Pernambuco. Luís Gaston wrote home that the poverty and backwardness of Recife repulsed him.[9] Its narrow, dark streets reminded him of the poorest regions of Spain where he served in the military. Only when he visited the magnificent countryside did he fall under Brazil's spell. The lush vegetation, freshness of the air and perfumed scents of the forest enchanted him.

Brazil was full of surprises and contrasts. When attending mass, he was startled to meet an old black priest who greeted him in his own cultured French tongue. Then in Bahia, he was again troubled when he observed men and women being carried through Salvador's perpendicular crooked streets by human slaves.[10]

Everywhere he looked, he wrote his father, he was visually assaulted by "millions of bizarre things." Nothing shocked him more than the prevalence of slavery or the elevated social, economic and political positions attained by Afro-Brazilians whose descendents had been slaves. Brazilians, he reported, felt a great sense of national pride that the ability of former slaves to rise to the social levels of their one-time masters proved the superiority of their system. What amazed Luís Gaston was these same Brazilians were blind to the fact the rest of the world condemned them for their continued dependence on slavery.[11]

Still the French prince was deeply impressed by both the free Africans and the slaves he encountered. In letters home he contrasted them favorably with the blacks he saw in Africa, whose seeming lack of intelligence, native dress and grinding poverty confirmed his racial prejudice. Brazil caused him to reevaluate his African experience. For the first time since he left Morocco, he wondered if the people he had so easily dismissed might have been victims of their colonial circumstances.[12] He was especially impressed by the revered status and respect older Africans were held within Brazilian families. It reminded him of the best part of his own European culture. The overall confidence, charm, goodness and intelligence of Brazil's Africans began to undermine his earlier attitudes.[13]

On September 2, 1864, the sights, sounds and smells of Rio de Janeiro exploded upon his senses. The appearance and location of the Paço Imperial, where he and his cousin stayed, caused one more cultural shock. The former home of the Portuguese viceroys had not been remodeled or repaired for years. Its bottom floors were rented to various shopkeepers, fruit and fish vendors, restaurants and saloons. Adding to their royal discomfort was that from every window they saw and heard Brazilian slaves working on the city's waterfront. Neither prince had experienced anything in Europe like what they found within earshot of their own bedrooms. From painful personal experience they knew that even exiled kings and queens lived in better housing.

For Luís Gaston, who had been born in France, grown up in England, attended school in Spain, and seen military service in Africa, the layered aspects of Brazil's racial dynamics astounded him. His initial impressions of Rio de Janeiro were negative in part because of his conflicted feelings about race. He wrote his father about the "shabby" royal residence and his shock at finding the palace guard filled by "dark skinned" military officers. In Europe such positions were reserved for the cream of elite society.[14]

His own military reputation had been made in Africa, yet the very soldiers he once fought there might be his honor guard in Brazil. Africans seemed to be everywhere, from the slave market to the highest positions of honor in government and finance. Brazil seemed riddled by contradictions. Like most first time visitors, it took the French prince time to absorb all he saw. As troubling as he found the prevalence of slavery, he seemed more amazed by the acceptance of former slaves as social equals. He was not alone.

The United States minister to Brazil wrote Abraham Lincoln's secretary of state, "On the bench and in the legislative halls, in the army and in the navy, in the learned professions, and among the professors in her colleges, as also in the pulpit, and in the social relations of life ... descendants of Africa has his place side by side with the 'white brother' in Brazil, and not infrequently, he jostles him for his position."[15] This was the Brazil the two royal cousins found in 1864.

The day of their arrival, Luís Gaston and Luís Augustus made their way to the suburban São Cristóvão Palace in a royal carriage pulled by fine horses with gold accouterments. The officer assigned to conduct them to meet their imperial relatives was a soldier of African descent smartly "dressed in the royal uniform of green and gold braid, with handsome leather cavalry boots."[16]

As they approached the palace from a distance they were struck by its picturesque setting on rolling foothills against a backdrop of spectacular mountains. São Cristóvão Palace was in better repair than Rio de Janeiro's City Palace; but it too offered surprises. Former slaves had been allowed to plant vegetable gardens on parts of the estate. Those who could not own land in Brazil would never go hungry as long as Pedro II was emperor. Shacks and shanties of freed slaves, the emperor's school for orphan girls, and one of Theresa's hospitals shared the carefully landscaped palace grounds. By the time the royal suitors came face to face with their cousins, they had already glimpsed into their hearts and souls. It was clear this was not a traditional monarch or country.

The relationship between Brazil's royal family and its citizens always surprised visitors. Most were accustomed to governments kept in power by armed force, rather than affection and respect. When their Habsburg cousin Maximilian visited a few years earlier, he had been shocked at the absence of armed guards and lack of security at the palace. The Condessa Barral told him the emperor and his family was protected by the "love of his people."[17] The reply astonished him. Luís Augustus and Luís Gaston shared his amazement; but more surprises awaited them.

22

"God and Our Hearts"

Brazil's royal family made a more favorable impression on the visiting princes than the nation they ruled. When they met the empress they were charmed by her warmth but shocked by her ladies-in-waiting, whose skin colors ranged from dark black to pale white. Theresa's attendants were living examples of Brazil's diverse ideas of beauty.[1]

Empress Theresa always endeared herself to those she met, and her nephews were no exceptions. During their visit, she seemed as excited as her daughters and preened herself as if she too were being courted. Years of marriage and motherhood had softened her features. As she aged, her loving personality and general appearance merged. Luís Gaston described her in a letter home as "goodness personified."[2]

The emperor was also impressive. He seemed an enlightened ruler, loved and respected by his family and nation. Despite his somber appearance, they found him to be intelligent, kind and witty. He was deeply devoted to his tropical country, its diverse peoples and his own family. Gaston wrote that he was especially impressed with the emperor's "distinguished spirit."[3]

Princess Isabel's diary revealed her own thoughts and excitement. "We waited in the room with Mother until Papa came in with them. I liked them both and found them very entertaining. We had dinner with Papa at 5:00. My heart was beating so loudly as was my sister's and mother's that we could hardly breathe.... My sister didn't say a word."[4]

Life for the young princesses had always been a strict balance between intense public scrutiny and private family life. Suddenly their family expanded to include two new, equal members. Except for their older married cousin Maximilian they had never spent any amount of time with other relatives. Neither was accustomed to the personal attention of peers who were also princely cousins. It was a new adventure for them, one they relished. Even before they met, letters from Aunt Francesca raised their expectations about the possibility of a successful courtship.[5] They were not to be disappointed.

Isabel's diary provides a picture of the strict, formal royal courtship rituals of the nineteenth century. The four cousins were never allowed to be alone, spending their first full day visiting Rio de Janeiro's public plazas and historic buildings. One highlight was a stop at the city's most imposing new monument, a magnificent statue of Isabel's grandfather, Pedro I, heroically posed astride his horse. That evening they dined together at the São Cristóvão Palace as a family. Isabel never referred to her cousins by their names, only their titles.[6]

The following day, Isabel noted "Luís Augustus" missed the Sunday reception at the palace because of a headache. Monday's entry was even more informal, noting Gaston and Augustus talked and entertained the princesses while teaching them to play croquet. It was the first time she mentioned her visitors by name. From that day forward, Isabel referred to her two cousins as Gaston and Augustus.[7]

On September 6th, the royal party spent the day hiking, climbing and picnicking on Rio de Janeiro's great landmark, Mount Corcovado, where a huge statue of Christ would one day be built. The anniversary of the "Cry of Ipiranga," September 7th, was filled with pageantry and celebrations. Public prayers, music, processions and a trip to the theatre allowed the princes to wear their military uniforms and decorations, Gaston as a captain of artillery in the Royal Spanish Army and Augustus as a lieutenant in the Imperial Austrian Navy. Each looked every inch the descendents of kings.[8]

September 8th, the party traveled to the outskirts of Rio de Janeiro to the hundred-foot waterfall in the lush forest of Tijuca. It was a favorite picnic ground of the royal family, but it rained all day. Still Gaston kept the party amused by attempting but failing to learn the words to a popular song. Heavy rains the next day kept the four cousins indoors. Princess Isabel wrote that she had selected Gaston as her partner in playing cards. The selection proved to be prophetic. That night she revealed in her diary, "My father arranged this trip with the intent of marriage. He thought of the Conde d'Eu for my sister and the Duke of Saxe for me. God and our hearts have decided differently."[9]

The man Isabel set her heart upon was a fateful choice. He was quite literally a prince without a country. Two years after Isabel's birth, a republican revolution had overthrown the monarchy of Gaston's grandparents, exiling them to England. Napoleon III, nephew of the man that drove Isabel's own family into Brazilian exile, overturned France's republican government a short time later. During his reign, his fear and hatred of the Orleans family made him a more deadly foe than the republicans.

Perhaps because Gaston's life had been a succession of dramatic twists and turns, he seemed older than his years. To Isabel his quiet manner sheltered a gentle romantic soul. Some referred to him as "Chopin like," comparing him to the exiled composer he physically resembled. Tall and thin, Gaston was nevertheless physically strong from his military service in Europe and Africa. He had handsome features, fair skin, dark hair, and large, some thought sad, blue eyes. Publicly and with strangers he was quiet and reserved, but in private he was warm and charming.[10] The foundation of his life was the deep love he had for his family and his Catholic faith — the only two things he had not lost through revolution and exile.

Hopes he and Poldie would be a successful match were not to be. Isabel found herself attracted to Gaston and he found her quiet, strong personality compatible with his own. The eighteen-year-old princess fell in love with the twenty-two-year-old French prince christened Luís Felipe Maria Fernando Gaston de Orleans, the Conde d'Eu. For the rest of their life together, Isabel simply referred to him as "My Gaston."[11]

The equally handsome nineteen-year-old Prince Luís Augustus, Duke of Saxe-Coburg, towered physically over seventeen-year-old Poldie. As Isabel and Gaston became a couple, Augustus let it be known he found Poldie's wit and quick smile a perfect complement to his less serious personality.[12]

Isabel's attraction to Gaston pleased her father, who found him a more suitable match for his oldest daughter than the carefree Augustus.[13] He had many fine qualities, but the emperor may have been most impressed with what he did not find in him. Gaston showed no signs of personal or political ambition. The political star of the Orleans family had fallen, but that of the Coburgs was on the rise. Luís Augustus might be more susceptible to the ambitions of his family or others. Pedro II felt more comfortable with a son-in-law who would not have his head turned by political aspirations or intrigue.

By September 15th, less than two weeks after their initial meeting, Isabel proclaimed her love for Gaston in her diary. He and his cousin Augustus were soon waiting for letters from Europe granting them parental permission to marry. The letters arrived on the 17th. The following day both princes traveled to the palace to formally ask permission to propose marriage.

Princess Isabel recorded what happened next. "Gaston and Augustus came in the afternoon and spoke with Papa and then with Momma. They then came into the room and asked if we agreed to marry them and we both said yes.... My dear dear Gaston proposed to me! We trembled like sticks we were so happy. Gaston took my hand and kissed it. He then hugged me and showed me in many loving ways his devotion to me."[14]

Gaston's trembling may have been for reasons other than happiness. In the years ahead he became devoted to Isabel, whose love for him was intensely romantic. Gaston's feelings for Isabel were more complicated. His first thought upon meeting his cousins was how physically unattractive they were. He bluntly wrote his father, "The princesses are ugly."[15] When it became apparent Isabel and the emperor favored him as Isabel's marriage partner, he was initially flattered, naively believing he was in a position to refuse. As the days passed, Gaston realized a refusal was for all practical purposes impossible. A prince was born to duty and service, even more so a prince with no throne to claim and no future prospects. He convinced himself of the necessity of the match because it was best for his family. The deeply religious and fatalistic young man also felt that such a stunning turn of events had to be a part of God's will.[16]

He explained some of his thinking in a revealing letter to his younger sister, Princess Marguerite England. To him God had put this decision in his path and he must accept it as part of God's larger plan. Gaston also felt better after Poldie assured him Isabel loved him and would be a devoted wife. Living the rest of his life in Brazil away from his family troubled him. But he was promised he would be free to travel to Europe as much and whenever he desired. He told his sister he would soon bring Isabel to meet her and was sure she would come to care for her. He ended his letter frankly: "So you will not be surprised when you see my Isabel, I should tell you that she has no prettiness in her face, but she is a good person."[17]

Gaston and Isabel had a short engagement, setting the date of their marriage for October 15, 1864, less than a month after the official announcement. They would be wed on the name day of Empress Theresa's patron saint. Two months later Poldie and Augustus would follow with a December wedding. As family members heard of the coming marriages, their reactions varied.

Pedro's sisters immediately wrote their approval. Francesca happily wrote, "I'm sure the more you know of Gaston the more you will be satisfied that your daughter married him. He deserves to be your son in law and to marry the Princess Imperial." Januária agreed: "I know for sure that the young man is very well educated and has great courage and many good qualities."[18]

Not everyone was positive. Several Coburg relatives, especially Augustus's ambitious mother Clementine, were unhappy he would not become the prince consort. Clementine was considered the best politician in the family. Since she never achieved a throne for herself she was determined one of her sons would do so.[19] England's Queen Victoria, always concerned about family harmony, wrote Gaston's father for an explanation.

The Duke of Nemours was honestly disappointed Gaston's marriage would take his only son so far away but explained to Victoria the decision was a mutual one agreed to by all the major participants. His letter to the English queen revealed how similarly father and son viewed life's destinies:

My Dear Cousin,
    The arrangement as far as I'm concerned is not the one I had hoped for myself but I should not oppose it since both the Emperor and his daughter and even my son agreed with the arrangement. It is for my family and for me a huge sacrifice, but the sacrifice should not be considered since what is in place is my son's happiness. May he find happiness in the path that God has put before him.
    Your Devoted Cousin, Louis Nemours[20]

Victoria still worried the switch in fiancées might cause problems. Kinship among the royal houses of England, France, Belgium, Portugal and the lesser German states was closer than at any time since the seventeenth century, primarily because of dynastic marriages. After receiving further assurances Victoria gave her blessings.

Augustus himself privately confided to Gaston that he preferred a life in

Europe with Poldie without responsibilities rather than dealing with the difficult challenges facing his cousin. The cool reception that greeted Maria da Glória's foreign-born husband in Portugal and the struggles of Victoria's German husband Prince Albert in England were well known in family circles.

At the time of the official announcement, the São Cristóvão Palace was filled with laughter, excitement and anticipation. The young cousins enjoyed each other's company as they got to know one another before their weddings. Isabel played the piano or violin while sunny Poldie amused her sister and cousins with witty stories and songs. The chaperoned couples dreamed of a bright future as they walked arm in arm through the Royal Botanical Gardens built years earlier by Isabel's great-grandfather João VI.

For America's only princesses, the last days of their childhood were happy ones. On the surface Brazil seemed a peaceful and prosperous paradise, but beneath the polished veneer over a million Brazilians continued to live and die as slaves. Domestic and foreign violence was nearer than any of them could imagine. Even as plans for the royal weddings progressed, a large enemy army secretly prepared to invade Brazil. War, racism and claims of genocide would soon explode across the country.

23

"A Winter Is Before Us"

In Rio de Janeiro, frantic preparations kept merchants and the court bustling with the first royal marriages in twenty years. Visitors and diplomats bitterly complained that prices of everything from hotel rooms to cabs had been raised to take advantage of expected crowds. Three seamstresses worked around the clock creating Isabel's white lace and silk wedding gown. Finally, with family and government plans carefully in place, a picture perfect day provided the setting for the wedding.[1]

Prior to the ceremonies Isabel and Gaston received the Catholic sacraments of penance and communion and attended mass, asking God to bless their marriage. Isabel recorded in her diary, "My prayer and my wish is that God keep Gaston and myself happy and together."[2] The official ceremonies began at nine A.M. as the Brazilian Royal Calvary left the São Cristóvão Palace followed by ten imperial coaches carrying the prince and princess and their wedding party to Rio de Janeiro's cathedral.

Isabel's wedding provided an opportunity for city and the nation to publicly celebrate. The great waterfront square in front of the Paço Imperial was filled with flowers, flags and cheering people of all hues and backgrounds. Within the cathedral a rainbow of aristocratic Brazilian nobility were joined by diplomats representing nations from around the world. All available space was filled so that as many as possible could witness the historic event.[3]

The archbishop of Bahia performed the wedding ceremony, the same bishop who years earlier had officiated at the coronation of Pedro II. At the chapel doors, small boys held golden trays on embroidered velvet pillows with the wedding rings, marriage certificate and gold-chained Imperial Orders resting on them. The Order of the Rose was to be bestowed on the Count d'Eu. The decoration had been designed by Pedro I to honor his second empress, Amélia. The Latin motto read "Amor e Fidelidade" (Love and Faithfulness).[4] It was a pledge Isabel's grandfather had been unable to keep with the tragic Empress Leopoldina but which Gaston would religiously uphold during his marriage with Isabel.

An official royal degree was announced appointing the Conde d'Eu an imperial prince marshal in the Brazilian army. At his wedding in two months Louis Augustus would be made an admiral in the Imperial Brazilian Navy.[5] To the princes, descendents of ancient families with proud military traditions, the appointments were the perfect wedding gift.

Gaston presented Isabel with a set of pearl earrings with matching necklace. From her father, the bride asked for a more unusual gift. She requested he purchase the freedom of the nine crown slaves serving her since birth.[6] With schoolgirl earnestness she wrote,

Dear Papa,
    For the day of my marriage Papa, I ask that you free the slave girl Joanina. She has always served me very well. I would also like you to purchase a letter of freedom for these other slaves: Marta, the little girl and her mother Anna Sousa who works for me in the bedchamber, Francisco Cordeiroa and Maria d'Austria his wife, Minerva the laundress, Florinda and Maria my wardrobe maids who have done all my ironing, José' Luís the court musician and Antônia Santa Anna another black man who has worked for us for many years.

Portrait of Isabel's husband Gaston Luís Felipe Orleans (1842–1922) prior to his marriage. Gaston began seeing Brazil through the eyes of his wife and was called "Our Serene Protector" by Brazilian soldiers of color, much to the chagrin of white military officers. Courtesy of Imperial Museum / Iphan / Ministry of Culture, Petrópolis, Brazil.

    P.S. Daddy if you want the laundress and girls who do the ironing to continue working until I go to Europe then maybe you can give them their freedom on the 15th."[7]

Throughout her life, Isabel corresponded with her father in the submissive, respectful tones of a child. But it was not her tone that caused debate when the contents of her letter became public. Years earlier her Aunt Francesca sparked controversy when she asked that her personal slaves be freed; but Isabel was heir to the throne and her marriage officially ended her childhood. Court watchers wondered if the request was the last sentimental gesture of a child or the first political statement of an adult.

The joy of the royal wedding left the question unanswered. Even if anyone wanted to discuss politics, it was impossible. At the reception held in the Paço Imperial, Isabel and Gaston were loudly serenaded throughout the day and night. Sounds of singing crowds, booming cannons, church bells, and the ever present Bragança fireworks echoed across Guanabara Bay. The happiness people felt for the young couple manifested itself in sights and sounds overwhelming the senses.

Following the festivities the couple traveled to Petrópolis, where they stayed for a month in a borrowed cottage surrounded by magnificent mountains and gardens. The day after their departure Pedro wrote his daughter, "I just got up. It's six in the morning and my first thought cannot fail to belong to you both. I hope that you are well and that Gaston's cold has disappeared. We spent the rest of the yesterday very lonely; but, at the same time entirely satisfied to see you both indissolubly joined for your happiness."[8]

Gaston's cold was the first in what became a series of minor health problems usually corresponding to his participation in public duties. Once he retreated to the quiet of Petrópolis, the shy prince's symptoms disappeared. The lush vegetation and blooming flowers recalled the gardens of Isabel's childhood and the cool morning fogs, billowy clouds and gentle rain reminded Gaston of his boyhood home in England.

Isabel's husband never overcame his uneasiness at being in the public eye. As a child in France in 1848 he had watched at the windows of the Tuileries Palace as palace guards joined with mobs against the monarchy. His mother's quick thinking saved his life. Grabbing his hand and the hand of his younger sister, she pulled them through endless corridors, then through a hidden garden path to a deserted street. Louis XVI and Marie Antoinette had once attempted a similar escape but failed.[9]

Howling looters burned the palace behind them as his mother, along with the Princess of Joinville, his sister and terrified cousins finally found a hired cab to help them escape. The king and queen frantically followed. The French revolution of 1793 had sent Louis Philippe's mother to an insane asylum and his father to the guillotine. When his own coachman was killed, he and the queen fled to the same deserted street. There they made their way to the crowded cab holding his daughters-in-law and grandchildren. Ordering them out, he and the queen escaped in the cab, leaving Gaston and the rest of the royal family to hopefully follow.[10]

Gaston's German mother and Brazilian aunt saved their families by hiding in the homes of friends, and traveling at night toward the English Channel. Abandoned by the king and queen, with arrests warrants on their heads, they eventually escaped in a small packet boat across the North Sea in a winter storm. For days no one knew whether they were alive or dead.[11]

Gaston's aunt, Queen Louise of Belgium, described the suddenness of the event as comparable to "an *unbelievable* clap of thunder." She wrote Queen Victoria, "Who *could believe* that in *a day,* almost without struggle, *all would be over,* and the past, the present, the future carried away on an unaccountable storm!"[12] The exiled royals sought protection from Victoria, the much-loved first cousin of Gaston's mother Victoire Antoinette Duchess of Nemours, but hope to begin a new life in England ended tragically.

After safely delivering a baby daughter, Gaston's mother lost consciousness and died. A family member described the suddenness of the event. "Never did death seize a victim so quickly. The ways of God are mysterious; but life is but a valley of bitter tears! The poor queen! To submit to such a blow at her age! To see the happiness of her dear son reduced to nothing! It is too hard. And Nemours, so touching in his grief, so profoundly afflicted and yet so pious, so resigned — yes, resigned to the will of God! His dear children show much heart. Alas! They loved their mother so much! What a winter is before us, who were hoping for some bright days!"[13]

Queen Victoria mournfully wrote, "It seems *too* dreadful almost to believe it, — too hard to bear[14] ... We were like sisters, bore the same name, married the same year, our children of the same age."[15] She described Nemours and his family as heart-broken and in shock.[16] Many believed Gaston's mother provided the French court its real "grace and beauty." Her lovely features and natural warmth endeared her to all.[17] Gaston loved his vivacious mother, but he was in almost all ways his father's son.

Louis Charles, Duke of Nemours, was intelligent, handsome, and full of energy. Few people in their youth showed such promise. Fewer still saw so little of it fulfilled. When he was sixteen, Belgium's national congress had elected him king of their newly independent nation, but under political pressure his father refused the throne for him.[18] Later he was a candidate to become king of Greece, but again was passed over. Maria II of Portugal and Queen Victoria both considered and then rejected him as a marriage partner. When he was still relatively young, critics dismissed him as a man of the past.

Nemours's strengths never overcame his crippling weaknesses. With his family he was warm, thoughtful and affectionate, but his awkward shyness and quiet reserve made him seem stiff, aloof and haughty to outsiders. Such traits might cause few problems for some, but for a public figure, they proved disastrous. He lacked the ease and affability that endear a prince to his people. Louis Philippe confided, "I know that Nemours is disliked, he has no charm, and does not even try to make himself popular; but he is a good man, brave and above all a Frenchman."[19] After the revolutions of 1848, Nemours was a Frenchman living in English exile.

When Louis Philippe and the rest of the royal family fled Paris, Nemours dutifully remained behind rallying support for the monarchy. Despite his personal courage, he barely escaped with his life. Nemours saved his honor but not the throne.[20] With his brilliant future behind him, the love of his family sustained him. Life denied him much but blessed him with a loving wife and children. Few of his royal relatives on or off their thrones could make such a claim.

By word and example, Nemours taught his son about the importance of duty, family, and the uncertainties of royal birth. In exile Louis Philippe unashamedly told dinner guests, "If it were not for the generosity of the Queen of England, I should have neither this house to cover my head, or the plate, or anything on the table."[21] As a child Gaston had attended school at Claremont, a house Queen Victoria loaned to his grandfather. His classmates were his own cousins, various dukes, princes and counts with honored and ancient titles, but royalty without a country. Three-fourths of his young life was spent in exile. Revolution had driven him from France. Exile had taken him to England, then Spain to complete his education, and then to North Africa for military experience. Now duty and marriage took him to Brazil.

Gaston spent most of his life as a stranger in foreign lands. He never spoke of the blows his family had endured or the violence that had abruptly ended his childhood. Still, the disappointments of the past seemed always with him. In many ways the handsome prince saw the unpredictability of life through the melancholy eyes of his defeated father.

The short happy respite following his marriage was shattered when Paraguay invaded Brazil on December 15, 1864 — Poldie's wedding day. The events sent shock waves throughout the entire continent. Pedro II's military was unprepared for full-scale war. Although Paraguay was a small landlocked nation, its army was the largest, best-trained, and most feared in all of Latin America. The drums and banners of López's 100,000 soldiers were boldly emblazoned with the motto "Conquer or Die."[22]

Paraguay scored a number of strategic military victories before declaring war against Brazil and the neighboring countries of Uruguay and Argentina. The leaders of all three nations were confident fighting would quickly be over, but they were wrong. López was a formidable enemy who portrayed Paraguay as David fighting Goliath-like neighbors bent on military, political and racial domination.

Twenty-one years earlier, the elder López had signed a law of free birth granting male slaves freedom at the age of twenty-five and females at twenty-four.[23] Since the deadline had not arrived, his son was able to use the law as a powerful propaganda weapon against Brazil while drafting thousands of blacks mixed race and Indian slaves into his army.[24]

Following Poldie's wedding, Gaston and Isabel prepared to travel to Europe, believing the war would be quickly over. Poldie and Augustus remained safely behind until their return. The departure day was filled with lingering hugs and tears. After sailing from Rio, Isabel and Gaston traveled to São Salvador in Bahia and Recife in Pernambuco, where they were enthusiastically received with receptions, bands and fireworks. Within days Isabel began sending her father detailed dispatches on what she saw in the northern cities and suggestions on what the government could and should be doing there. Her reports continued throughout their tour of Europe.

Return letters from Brazil quickly dispelled initial optimism regarding a swift victory over Paraguay. By the time Isabel and Gaston returned home, Brazil would be bogged down in the largest, deadliest war in the history of Latin America — a war that would change forever the future of the monarchy, their nation — and slavery.

$\mathcal{L}$ 24 $\mathcal{L}$

"A Wife Should Not
Wish to Act Independently"

In the patriarchal world of the nineteenth century, most young girls went from a childhood dominated by a father to a marriage dominated by a husband. This was true for Princess Isabel's mother and grandmother despite each being the empress of Brazil. It was also true for her aunt, the queen of Portugal. Men decided what was best for women. Twin principles of deference and obedience dictated a women's public and private life.

Royal women, even Queen Victoria, generally conformed to the gender roles assigned them. Princess Isabel never outwardly questioned such restrictions, yet like many Bragança women, she kept her own counsel and remained her own person.[1] She learned to mask her independent thinking through humor, deferential language and the self–effacing behavior expected of her. Isabel worshiped her father and deeply loved her husband, but also understood their egos and the culture in which they lived. As a daughter and as a wife, Isabel conveyed her opinions, even when angry, in ways that did not offend or compete with the men she loved.

Her position as heir to the throne did not empower her to directly confront the gender stereotypes of her time. The suffocating traditions and political constraints felt by royal heirs may have been even worse for females. Isabel was not only under intense scrutiny by opponents of the monarchial system, but also people who believed only males capable of governing. Included in that number was her own cousin Queen Victoria, who privately thought women unfit to rule.[2]

In Gaston Pedro II saw an ally, strong enough to temper his daughter's willfulness, but compliant enough to respectfully submit to his own wishes. Shortly after their wedding, he revealingly wrote, "I am every day more pleased at having abdicated my power as father to him and at having in its place the love of one more child."[3]

Empress Theresa's interactions with her husband remained close to child-like throughout her marriage. The Condessa Barral strongly encouraged Isabel to follow suit. She wrote Isabel shortly after her wedding, "A wife should not wish to act independently even in thought, if that does not agree with her husband's contradictory message."[4] One of Barral's guiding principles to Isabel taught, "God made to men their share of work and another to women. Each should remain in that sphere, unless it is Joan of Arc inspired by God."[5]

Isabel was never allowed to forget that as a princess, a daughter and a wife it was her duty to cheerfully submit to the men in her life. To be good, to be successful, meant denying her own thoughts, feelings and wishes. Throughout her life she tried to serve others, but never completely surrendered herself. At her core was a strong independent spirit that sustained and strengthened her. Isabel was a survivor. She outlived both of her brothers and two of her Portuguese cousins, all victims of the typhoid fever she survived. The spirit that allowed her to survive as a child continued serving her as an adult.

When she was a student she had thrived under the tough regimen and rigid expectations of her father and the Condessa Barral. As an adolescent she turned the well-ordered routine of her father upside down as he chaperoned Poldie and herself to public dances. Even her choice of Gaston as her husband represented a personal victory over the conventional expectations of her uncle and aunt, her sister, and the powerful Queen Victoria.[6]

At times Pedro II and Isabel were willing co-conspirators, as when she selected Gaston over Augustus. In most important matters they agreed. Still the rules of society clearly made Pedro the unquestioned head of the family. Isabel as his daughter, even his adult daughter, never stopped seeking his parental attention or approval. When they disagreed, she retreated to the persuasive methods of her childhood, alternating emotional outbursts from the heart with appeals to reason. Women struggling to assert independent thinking in the nineteenth century had few other options.

By the time of her marriage and European honeymoon Isabel had outwardly mastered the traditional role expected of her. In Portugal she and Gaston visited their royal cousins, including King Luís I and Isabel's godfather Ferdinand of Saxe-Coburg. Coimbra University, and the shrine of Saint Isabel. They also met Pedro's stepmother, the dowager empress Amélia. Although only fifty-three years of age, ill health forced her to receive them from her sickbed. She was overjoyed with the visit and wrote Pedro, "They were very nice to come and see me.... I found Isabel very pleasant and sympathetic. She seemed to epitomize goodness, sound judgment, and intelligence and seemed very very happy. Gaston is a very distinguished prince. They seem made for each other."[7]

They then traveled to England but arrived at an awkward time. Brazil had recently broken diplomatic relations with Great Britain over the anti-slavery rhetoric of the British ambassador. It was hoped their trip would not aggravate an already tense political situation. Despite such concerns, Princess Isabel wrote home that they were "received with great friendship and joy."[8] She reported Gaston was like a small schoolboy thrilled to be surrounded by his loving family as he showed her every corner of Claremont and his father's nearby estate.

Queen Victoria's government had become the leading critic of Brazil's continued dependence on slavery, but to Isabel's surprise they received an invitation to Windsor Castle. Victoria's immediate predecessors hated abolitionists and privately supported slavery despite the fact that Queen Charlotte, wife of George III and mother of George IV and William IV, descended from a Portuguese king and his African mistress.[9] Victoria and her late husband broke from that past, quietly supporting the government's anti-slavery policies. The queen, however, justified the visit as a family affair between cousins. Victoria recorded in her journal, "Nemours arrived at two with ... Gaston and his Brazilian bride Isabel, who is the future Empress of Brazil. She is very quiet, simple and unaffected, and seems very good and kind."[10]

Isabel was received with the warmth and natural affection Victoria reserved for family. Shortly after the meeting England recalled its anti-slavery ambassador and diplomatic relations with Brazil resumed. Some traced the improved relations between the two countries to the family visit at Windsor Castle.

Her time in England afforded Brazil's princess imperial the opportunity to observe one of the world's great industrial powers. In the midst of social engagements, she and Gaston toured steel mills and industrial plants in Manchester, Mersey, and Birmingham. Isabel was soon sending her father detailed descriptions of modern machinery and agricultural equipment that might be adapted for use at home. From Birmingham she reported, "a great number of people surrounded our carriage.... It is not only in Brazil that there is unemployment and poor people."[11]

The more Isabel traveled, the more she came to appreciate all her father had taught her. She wrote him, "Oh, how many times I have thanked you in my mind for teaching me, and providing me with so many teachers, so that I can comprehend and appreciate all that I see here." Then she teasingly added, "Even though I ignored as much as I could when I was your student!"[12]

Isabel's European holiday provided her numerous opportunities to indulge in the dancing and social activities she had missed as a child. Shortly after meeting Isabel and Poldie, Gaston wrote home in amazement, "These poor princesses have never gone to a ball or theatre in their entire lives and they are crazy to do it."[13] In England, Isabel rode to the hounds and attended the parties she had always dreamed about as a girl.

Up to that point, Isabel seemed to comfortably fit into the traditional role expected of a young bride and princess visiting her husband's family for the first time. But a lavish costume ball hosted in her honor by Gaston's grandmother, dowager queen Marie Amélie, provided her an opportunity to showcase the independent side of her personality.

Queen Victoria had popularized themed balls with guests dressed as their favorite historic figures several years earlier. Prior to the war with Brazil, Francisco López's Irish mistress hosted one in Paraguay, appearing as Elizabeth I of England.[14] The night of the fete members of British society competed with exiled French royals and nobility to outshine one another. The Prince and Princess of Joinville appeared as the famed Sun King Louis XIV of France and his glittering queen.

Princess Isabel and Gaston did not dress as any of their illustrious ancestors. Instead they appeared as Africans. Gaston wore the uniform of a Moorish soldier from his days of fighting in Spanish Morocco. Isabel, her blond hair covered by bright scarves, appeared in the colorful clothing, clanging jewelry, and dark face of a Bahian slave woman.[15] Despite their aristocratic backgrounds, their choice of costumes provided a clue that they were not thinking along the lines of the typical prince or princess. There would be no more invitations to costume balls during their European travels.

Following their stay in England they traveled to the royal courts of Belgium, Austria, Spain, Bohemia and dozens of smaller German states. In addition to royalty they met local officials, went sight seeing, and drank beer with university students.[16] Dinners, hunts, receptions and parties blurred into one another as they were introduced to countless princes, queens, kings and even an emperor and empress, all royal relations. Whenever possible they expanded their itinerary to explore agricultural and industrial technologies that might be useful to Brazil. Isabel's endless questions echoed her father's schoolmaster style of interrogation. As they visited the cities and countries where manufacturing was remaking national economies, the contrast to Brazilian slave labor must have been painfully clear.

The war at home caused them to take a special interest in modern armaments and military hardware. Gaston toured Belgium's fortifications along the German and French borders and spent a great deal of time in Germany visiting the huge Krupp ammunition factories.[17] Princess Isabel regularly wrote her parents about the conflict. One typical letter read, "I was happy to read about the take over of Paicandu. It was reported here yesterday that the garrison at Montevideo had surrendered. Nevertheless, I am not going to take pleasure in the reports until I receive more positive news via letter and newspapers ... if only it is true."[18]

Six months of travel was enough for Isabel. She wrote her parents, "I am fed up with so many princes that do not interest me ... and the uniforms and cavalries to impress and please us, but in reality only bore."[19] Despite her royal pedigree, she disliked the stuffiness of European royal courts and missed the simplicity and informal manners of Brazil.[20]

In July of 1865, the travel-weary couple returned to Rio de Janeiro to be greeted by Empress Theresa and Poldie. Just days before, the emperor and Augustus had left for the war front in the hopes of lifting sagging morale there. Things were going badly for Brazil and its allies. Isabel and Gaston were both distressed; Isabel because she had missed her father by only a few days, Gaston because he was missing the war.

25

"The Far Reaches of Barbarism"

The war everyone predicted would be over in weeks showed no signs of ending. To Isabel's dismay, Gaston immediately prepared to leave for the front, precipitating their first argument. Isabel was overcome with fear, but he dismissed her dark premonitions. He saw the war as opportunity to make a name for himself in his new homeland.[1]

Three days after her nineteenth birthday Gaston left to join the emperor and Louis Augustus, but not before providing Isabel a list of instructions to follow in his absence. He reminded her not to leave the palace without her chaperones, not to slouch, to put things away when she was done with them, to take care of her personal appearance, and to lose weight.[2] Isabel's husband, like her father, continued to infantilize the future empress of Brazil.

From its very beginnings, many saw the war through a racial lens. Slavery in the United States had ended just three months earlier. Only the laws of Brazil and the Spanish colonies of Cuba and Puerto Rico continued legally protecting slavery. The majority of Brazil's soldiers were poor and black or from a blended racial heritage. Most of their officers were white and drawn from wealthy levels of Brazilian society. With their Argentine and Uruguayan allies they faced an enemy army composed almost entirely of Amerindian ethnic stock.

López presented himself to his people and the world as a courageous native leader fighting predatory racist neighbors. Paraguayans embraced him as their only hope for survival against enemies committed to their national extinction. Brazil's emperor rejected such rhetoric as racist propaganda, believing the war was about a military dictator willing to sacrifice human lives for a distorted sense of personal glory. Carlos López had owned half of all the land in Paraguay, but even that failed to satisfy his son.[3] Diplomatic correspondence reported the younger López planned to proclaim himself emperor, having placed orders for imperial "plate, fixtures, and paraphernalia" from Paris.[4]

One foreign consul wrote, "The masses ... believe that the Supreme Government is the rightful owner and the disposer of all they possess. And thus, without any exertion, but with the support of the clergy, which is entirely

130

dependent on it, the government can freely exercise its power of life and death, imprisonment, exile and confiscation. Military service, labor and private property are at its command."[5]

Although the allied armies defeated and eventually destroyed Paraguay's invading armies, López recruited younger and younger soldiers to continue fighting. Unsubstantiated reports that Elisa Lynch the dictator's mistress recruited and led female volunteers into battle enraged men and women in Brazil.[6] Brazilian propagandists, like their Paraguayan counterparts, knew how to appeal to emotional prejudice. Within a year mounting casualty figures made the war the bloodiest ever fought in Latin America. Isabel prayed it would end before her husband reached the front. Gaston prayed for the exact opposite.

With the fighting taking place over a thousand miles south of Rio de Janeiro, even traveling to the front presented dangers. A long ocean voyage, inland travel through uncharted jungles, swarming insects, flooding rivers, blood sucking leeches and deadly snakes all presented obstacles. "Endless thunderstorms and piercing cold" were constant companions.[7] Illness competed with swords, cannons and bullets in stealing soldiers' lives. One third of the Brazilian army was too ill to fight on any given day.

Only the threat of abdication persuaded Pedro's government to allow him to travel to the front. Despite all he had heard he was unprepared for what he found. The terrain, the weather, and the fanaticism of the enemy caused military engagements to frequently degenerate into suicidal hand-to-hand combat. More than once the emperor gave his own clothing to poorly clad soldiers, but he could not stop the massive suffering everywhere he looked.[8] His presence raised morale and inspired his exhausted troops to fight on, but the experience threatened his own health.

Gaston joined Pedro and Augustus just as Brazilian reinforcements were preparing to invade the territory of Paraguay. The conditions Gaston found caused him to write his former teacher, "We are truly in the far reaches of barbarism."[9] Once the armies met on Paraguayan soil the fighting intensified and Brazil's allies lost their resolve to continue.[10] Pedro again threatened to abdicate, vowing to fight on with or without his allies.[11] Argentina and Uruguay took the threat seriously. They feared the ex-emperor as a field commander supported by his equally vengeful daughter in Rio de Janeiro would threaten their own borders. Only when his allies agreed to continue the war did the weary monarch return to his capital.

Brazil's emperor left for the war a young, vigorous forty-year-old man. But when he returned his strawberry blond hair and thick beard had turned white and his athletic graceful movements had slowed and stiffened. Pedro's appearance shocked and frightened his family.[12] The horrors he had witnessed strengthened his resolve to rededicate his life to peace—*after* the war.

Pedro's time away from his wife softened his feelings toward her. To his surprise he missed her simple goodness and loving attention. Surrounded by homesick troops, everywhere he looked he saw Theresa's loving face. The war brought emperor and empress closer together, but threatened to tear Gaston and Isabel apart. To her shock, Gaston remained at the front, touring remote areas of fighting amidst his adopted country's Afro-Brazilian troops. Living with the soldiers further transformed his attitudes about race and slavery, but Gaston's evolving racial attitudes offered little comfort to Isabel. When she saw the effect the war had had on her father, she was overwhelmed with fears for Gaston.[13]

Isabel, with her sister and mother, worked tirelessly for the war effort, but no amount of activity or exhaustion comforted her. The empress devoted herself to caring for the sick, wounded and dying. More than ever the country's overburdened medical system needed her watchful eyes and caring hands. Poldie and Isabel helped, but the sights and sounds of the suffering filled Isabel with dread and anxiety.[14]

In early 1866 Brazilians were briefly diverted from the war. The ringing of church bells and the firing of cannon announced the emperor and empress had become grandparents. The birth of a prince is always a cause for celebration in a monarchy, but the announcement from the São Cristóvão Palace caused an uneasiness. The mother was not Princess Isabel but her younger sister Poldie.[15] The new baby was named Pedro Augusto to honor grandfather and father. Within months, it was announced that Poldie was again pregnant. The news made Gaston's lingering absence even harder for Isabel.

The princess imperial busied herself working with the war's growing numbers of orphans, but their sadness did little to distract her from her own fears. Gaston struggled with his own feelings. In Europe he was the grandson to the last king and queen of the French. In Belgium he was the nephew of King Leopold and Queen Louise. In England he was the cousin of Queen Victoria. And in Rio de Janeiro he was the son-in-law of the emperor and husband of the princess imperial. But in the Paraguayan war he was a soldier. It was the one identity that was his alone, and he clung to it with all his might.

He impressed the troops he met by his willingness to share their travails and listen to their concerns, and they in turn impressed him. The regiments from Bahia with their all black officer corps earned his special respect and praise.[16] Much to the chagrin of white officers, black and mixed race soldiers began calling Gaston "Our Most Serene Protector."[17] As his reputation grew with the rank and file soldiers, it diminished with some officers. But André Rebouças, an Afro-Brazilian army engineer, noted that the Conde d'Eu's sympathy, interest and respect for soldiers of color stood in marked contrast to the indifference and self-absorption of his cousin Augustus. During their time at the front the emperor also came to recognize that behind the pleasant personality of Poldie's husband there was little substance.[18]

Gaston began seeing Brazilians through the eyes of his wife and the emperor, but the revelation did not hasten his return to them. Generally he complained about his health, but being on the front seemed to invigorate him and he continued extending his stay. Gaston believed war tested and bonded men and nations together. In a steady stream of letters to Pedro II, he begged to be allowed to join the fight.

In Rio de Janeiro Isabel slept with her husband's picture under her pillow and wrote him letters twice a day pleading, and at times demanding, his return.[19] She worried constantly about his health, his lungs, the possibility of bronchitis, the threat of cholera, or his being wounded, captured or killed. Later, she admitted to being consumed with fears she would never bear Gaston's child. As a young married woman deeply in love, such a thought was unbearable. As heir to the throne, it was unthinkable.

Finally addressing the prince as son, the emperor ordered Gaston home, informing him he would never be allowed to lead troops in battle. He explained that the government and his allies did not believe Brazilian soldiers would follow a non–Brazilian officer.[20] As if to compensate him for his disappointment, he appointed Gaston to the position of commander in chief of artillery and inspector general of the army — both desk positions in Rio de Janeiro.

Pedro gently pleaded with Gaston to support the decision. Isabel's husband obeyed, but his barely concealed anger sent him into a deep depression, casting a deep gloom over his homecoming. He was furious and crushed. In a letter to his father he admitted, "I have been disconsolate to not have been able to take part in this expedition."[21] Later he remembered, "I did everything possible so that the Emperor would at least allow me to accompany the army that would pass through Uruguay and invade Paraguay, but [was] always refused."[22] Gaston, the nation's highest ranking army officer, was assigned to a desk at the very time the Brazilian government struggled to recruit soldiers. Short of impressments and kidnapping, the army had no effective way of filling its decimated ranks.

By the end of 1866 the situation had become so serious the emperor turned to the nation's slaves to fight, but insisted they be granted their freedom at war's end. Jefferson Davis, Robert E. Lee and other desperate Confederate leaders supported similar measures in the final months of the United States' Civil War.[23]

Pedro II announced the allocation of government funds for the purchase of slaves willing to volunteer and called on the nation's monasteries, convents and other large slaveholders to free their slaves if they joined the army.[24] As another incentive he promised to distribute government owned land to anyone, including slaves, who volunteered to fight.[25] It was the first time Pedro II had supported the idea of land redistribution as a government policy. Eventually 20,000 Brazilian slaves gained their freedom through such programs, but Pedro's ministers were alarmed that precedents were being set that would "open the door to a thousand misfortunes."[26]

Despite such predictions, Pedro II instructed his minister of justice to issue a statement that complete emancipation would begin once the Paraguayan war ended.[27] In his 1867 speech from the throne he asked parliament to begin considering ways of ending slavery that "would respect the rights of owners and not seriously upset agriculture."[28] The request infuriated slaveholders and sent rumbling aftershocks throughout the empire.

Gaston spoke of his own changing attitudes toward race only with Isabel and his father. He approved of the emperor's steps toward abolition, but continued brooding over his exclusion from the war. Three days after the birthday of the emperor in December, Poldie gave birth to a second healthy son. Following an earlier miscarriage, she had safely delivered two healthy sons within one twelve month period.[29] Isabel and Gaston remained childless.

The Princess of Joinville wrote the emperor, "They must be very sad for not having a child yet." After nearly three years of marriage, Isabel's childlessness had become a major concern for the royal family. Francesca wrote Isabel, "There is no reason for despair. There are many examples of people married longer than you and only later did they have children."[30]

Poldie and Augustus relieved the awkwardness presented by their growing family by traveling to Europe. Once there, they took up permanent residence at the huge gray Coburg Palace on Vienna's Ringstrasse.[31] Poldie's departure further increased Isabel's isolation and dependence on the men in her life.[32]

Reports from the battlefront offered no relief from the gloom filling the capital or the home of the princess imperial. The end of the war was not in sight. Political rivalries poisoned relations between the liberal prime minister and the conservative army commander in the field. The popularity of Field Marshal Caxias, a former prime minister for the Conservative Party, aroused the suspicion and jealousy of government ministers. Fear of political advantage through a military victory hampered and undermined the war effort.[33]

Gaston wrote his father that the intrusion of political infighting into military matters was the "worst of the worst."[34] Repeated attempts to affect a solution or compromise failed. Finally Pedro II dismissed the liberal ministry, replacing it with the conservative opposition. Gaston privately wrote,[35] "The Emperor has acted in a fashion contrary both to his own character and to parliamentary usage."[36] Others agreed. A firestorm of criticism descended upon Pedro for injecting himself into politics. Accusations of abuse of power thundered in parliament and across the nation, fanned by sensational battlefront reports of barbarity, atrocities and massacres.[37]

When the conservative ministry, like the one it replaced, failed to end the war anger and frustration grew. Staggering causalities demoralized even supporters of the conflict, and a growing national debt threatened the economic future of the country. Some claimed the war had become a personal vendetta of emperor against dictator. Pedro II stubbornly believed peace could only be achieved with the removal of López. In the poisoned political atmosphere a small group of Brazilians came to believe it was the emperor who needed to be removed. A Republican Party appeared, advocating replacing the monarchy with an elected president.[38] Some feared the government itself might become a casualty of the war.

26

"A Blind Alley with No Way Out"

Problems to the north did little to reassure Brazil's embattled royal family. Shortly before Isabel and Gaston visited England, Gaston's cousin Charlotte and her husband, Archduke Maximilian of Austria, announced they were accepting an offer to become emperor and empress of Mexico. The plan alarmed the Orleans family. Charlotte and Maximilian's safety was to be assured by their bitter enemy, Napoleon III.[1]

The family opposed the idea; no one more strongly than the family matriarch Marie Amélie. The former queen had always been superstitious. When Gaston was a boy, she frightened him with stories about the ghosts she saw at Claremont.[2] In her later years she was haunted by flashbacks of murderous mobs driving her family out of France. Such moments foretold impending family disasters. When Charlotte told her grandmother of the Mexican adventure, Marie Amélie experienced just such a premonition and begged her granddaughter to refuse Mexico's non-existent crown. She turned to Maximilian and fearfully predicted, "They will murder you."[3] The Austrian prince tried to reassure her, but tears filled his eyes. Gaston's youngest sister witnessed the confrontation and remembered, "It is usually the women who cried. This time is was the man."[4]

Charlotte seemed the most confident family member present. Although she spoke no Spanish, she was already calling herself Carlota, promising her grandmother all would be well.[5] Following their arrival in Mexico, she wrote Marie Amélie the situation was not nearly as bad as others claimed. Her grandmother did not believe her.

As the only American member of the family, Isabel found herself in a painful position. She had always felt safe in her own country, but Marie Amélie's gloom blanketed Claremont. Many European powers recognized Mexico's new emperor and empress, but Isabel's own father voiced his doubts.

Pedro II wrote the Condessa Barral, "My dear, in contrast to other countries, we, in Brazil, will not support the adventure of Napoleon III. I know that will make your blood boil! But the whole campaign seems premature to me.

The interests of Napoleon III are clear, but how will the Austrian Maximilian ... depend on free elections? He believes and has faith that the Mexican people have called him through an election! Margarida, you know how dangerous the combination of cool European mentality and passionate Latin soul is, how many generations it has taken and will surely yet take before the conquered and oppressed people will be spiritually free. Free elections to bring in an emperor?!! I cannot believe it."[6]

Brazil finally did establish diplomatic relations with the Mexican monarchy, but it was the only nation in North or South America to do so.[7] Although politically isolated, Maximilian and Carlota attempted to bring peace, unity and prosperity to their adopted country with little success. Large landowners and the Catholic Church opposed any reforms that threatened their privileged position. Rebel fighters fought just as bitterly for a share of the nation's wealth.

Maximilian appointed Carlota regent, allowing him to travel throughout Mexico to rally support. During her regency Carlota urged government ministers to recognize the "catastrophic squalor and abasement" of the country's Indians by passing laws to protect their human rights.[8] She was warned if Indians were allowed to be the equals of whites "we will see the moment of insurrection and vengeance at hand."[9]

Carlota refused to be swayed by such arguments and persuaded all but one of her husband's ministers to support laws abolishing corporal punishment and providing legal protections for Mexico's Indians.[10] Carlota proved herself to be an enlightened regent and able administrator. But Mexicans were not ready to accept a foreign-born head of state, especially one who was a woman.

Resistance, resentment and suspicion grew. Some observers began to believe Carlota more competent than her ineffectual husband — but such speculations helped neither of them. An American woman in Mexico wrote of Carlota, "It is more than likely that under her proud mien, she concealed a suffering spirit, or a least a consciousness of a superiority which has to efface herself."[11] Still the young emperor and empress worked tirelessly to create a stable banking system, reform the judiciary and build badly needed railroads and infrastructure. Schools were founded and immigration encouraged; but most of the population lived in feudal poverty, enslaved to land they would never own.

Maximilian sincerely chose as the motto for his monarchy, "Equity in Justice," seeing himself as the "savior of the oppressed." He seemed unable to believe that Napoleon III, disgruntled exiles, Mexico's large landowners and the local hierarchy of the Catholic Church had created Mexico's monarchy as a conservative bulwark against the very changes he sought.[12] Radical reformers, including leaders of Masonic lodges, offered support to the struggling monarch, but Maximilian rejected them, fearing further alienation from the Church hierarchy. The papal nuncio publicly proclaimed, "the clergy had made Maximilian's Empire." At the same time the bishop of Pueblo threatened excommunication to anyone supporting economic reforms.[13] In mounting frustration Maximilian wrote Napoleon III that the clergy and their reactionary supporters were "try[ing] to combat or obstruct my ideas of progress."[14] In a face-to-face confrontation with the bishops he bitterly complained, "The Mexican Church has with a lamentable fatality mixed up in politics and in matters of earthly wealth, forgetting thereby and neglecting the true maxims of the gospel."[15] The bishops resented a lecture from the man they had elevated to the throne to prevent just such dangerous thinking.

Carlota, considered a better politician than her husband, was asked by him to negotiate a truce with the papal nuncio. She wrote the French empress, Eugenie, about the experience. "I can tell Your Majesty that nothing has given me a better idea of hell than that interview, for hell is no more nor less than a blind alley with no way out. To try to convince someone, knowing that it is love's labor lost, that we might as well be talking Greek, since one side sees things black and the other white, is a labor fit for the damned. Everything slid off the Nuncio as if from polished marble."[16]

In the midst of their public struggles, Maximilian and Carlota's failure to conceive a child after nearly ten years of marriage doomed any hope for a future dynasty. Privately Carlota admitted having a child was "the natural and legitimate desire of every woman" and declared she and her husband might "still have children of our own." But the "barren empress" became the butt of jokes and gossip. Within hearing of the palace people called her "Mama Carlota" and sang crude songs mocking her infertility.[17]

Maximilian took matters into his own hands. Without consulting Carlota, he announced he was adopting a two-year-old Mexican boy, the grandson of Augustín Iturbide, a self-proclaimed native emperor executed years earlier by a firing squad. Maximilian accepted the child as his son and heir. Carlota and the nation did not.[18]

The weary twenty-five-year-old empress finally admitted her growing discouragement in a letter to her grandmother. "Today I am aging, if not in the eyes of others, in my own eyes I grow old, and my thoughts and sentiments are indeed far from what outwardly appears.... Among laborers, the wife contributes to the tilling of the field. There is here a great field of fallow land. The task is not too much for two who have no child.... They take me for a virago, when I am absolutely as you have always known me.... Ambition to do good, perhaps I have that, but it is only as Maximilian's wife"[19]

Napoleon III, under pressure from the United States, concerned about the direction of the "elected" Mexican monarchy, withdrew financial and military support. Uprisings spread throughout the country and Maximilian sent Carlota to Europe to appeal for assistance. As she traveled to the Mexican coast she was often serenaded by the refrains of a lewd song called "Adiós Mama Carlota."[20]

In June 1867 news reached Brazil that Maximilian's troops had been defeated and he taken prisoner as an enemy of the state. Despite pleas for mercy from crowned heads and even revolutionaries like Italy's Giuseppe Garibaldi,

Mexico's Habsburg emperor was placed on trial, found guilty and publicly executed. The republican leader of the rebels, Benito Juárez, a full-blooded Zapotec Indian, ordered the execution.

In Europe after a fruitless confrontation with Empress Eugenie and Napoleon III, Carlota traveled to Rome, where the pope also rebuffed her pleas for help. Alone without husband, child, country or throne, she physically and mentally collapsed. Maximilian's death by a firing squad ended her grasp on reality. Carlota spent the rest of her life under lock and key, protected from further harm, in a Belgium castle. Her grandmother Marie Amélie died before her worst fears were realized.

The tragedy struck close to home for Brazil's royal family. Moments before his execution Maximilian asked that the small religious medal he wore over his heart be sent to the mother of his first fiancée, Pedro's own stepmother. As he faced death, his thoughts traveled to Europe by way of Brazil. The medal, a gift from France's Empress Eugenie was meant to offer protection to him and his empire. It failed on both counts.[21]

The Condessa Barral wrote from Europe, "There is no name for this atrocity against the noble emperor. Dom Pedro, I shall spare you the details that they talk about here in France. Feminine vanity and plots played their role in driving that noble man to destruction. In what despondency this news will reach you, Dom Pedro. I hardly dare read the diplomatic reports about the situation in Paraguay. It is not possible to detect an imminent end to the war in a single sentence."[22]

The "feminine vanity and plots" Barral wrote about concerned the belief in patriarchal Europe that the political ambitions of three women sent Maximilian to his doom. Carlota his wife, Archduchess Sophie his mother, and the Empress Eugenie of France were held more responsible for Maximilian's death than Napoleon III or Maximilian himself.

The tragedy held its own significance for each member of Brazil's imperial family. Pedro II felt his own throne threatened as he was locked in a deadly military struggle against a popular native leader. Theresa, as a mother who had buried two sons, grieved for the families of Maximilian and Carlota. Gaston, like his cousins, was a foreigner and stranger in a land that viewed him as an outsider despite his best efforts to serve his adopted country.

Brazil's princess imperial may have been more affected by the Mexican tragedy than anyone imagined. Carlota and Isabel were close in age, background and religious faith. They shared similar hopes and dreams for their nations. Both were intelligent, accomplished women living at a time and place where such strengths and talents were more a liability than an asset. Mexico's empress attempted to break powerful social norms. Her time as regent proved her to be firm and decisive, perhaps more so than her husband. She championed the cause of oppressed native people, would not be intimidated by male ministers, and negotiated with the patriarchal hierarchy of the Mexican Church without the docility or deference expected of a woman. As a regent and as an empress, she tried to effect direct political change through her will, her intelligence and the righteousness of her cause. But unlike Maria Theresa of Austria or Queen Victoria of England, or even Brazil's Empress Leopoldina, she did so without the softening mantel of motherhood or the protection provided by a male heir. Not even the ambitious Carlota Joaquina dared be so reckless.

Princess Isabel was a Bragança by birth — a family known for their caution, sense of duty and remarkable political timing. Their ability to remake themselves was legendary; but who could Isabel become? She was surrounded by women and men bound to the stereotypes of the past. Her mother, her sister and even the strong willed Condessa Barral lived in the shadows of the men in their lives. Isabel's father and husband saw her as a child, not a young woman and heir to the throne of the second largest empire on earth. And then there was Carlota, an empress with no child, no heir and no future. Without a child of her own, Isabel remained a child in the eyes of her parents and husband. Unless she provided the monarchy an heir, how would she ever be able to become the empress of Brazil?

27

"Isabel's Lament"

The war with Paraguay offered Princess Isabel and her nation little to celebrate during the Christmas season of 1867. No end was in sight as the bitter conflict entered its fourth year.[1] The worst of the fighting continued to be borne by the Brazilians as revolutions in Argentina and Uruguay crippled the alliance.[2]

Twice Argentina's president abandoned the field to rush home to prevent his government from being overthrown.[3] Uruguay's president was less fortunate. His assassination ended Uruguay's active participation in the Triple Alliance.[4] Weary Brazilians fought on as criticism mounted against the emperor.

Discouraging war news, Gaston's restlessness, and Isabel's childlessness cast a melancholy pall over Brazil's royal family. As Carlota painfully discovered in Mexico, nineteenth century society held a woman responsible for her barrenness. Fertility and childbirth had a strong religious connotation. If a woman was not "blessed" with a child, many believed she was cursed. In Latin America's Roman Catholic Brazil, Isabel's situation was impossible to ignore. What had once been the subject of private family letters became the subject of public concern and gossip.

Aunt Francesca continued offering maternal advice in her letters, suggesting Isabel get more rest, give up horseback riding, and pursue both traditional and non-traditional medical advice. She repeatedly urged her niece to seek a cure at a mountain health spa specializing in helping woman overcome infertility. In one of her letters she delicately concluded, "May the waters have the desired expected results for the total happiness of your intimate life and for your position which is very much wished for by all of us."[5] The "position" she referred to was Isabel's role as the future empress. Between the lines could be read a growing worry shared by supporters of the constitutional monarchy.

Eventually Isabel and Gaston traveled to the mountain city of Caxambú, whose famous waters and hot springs were believed to be a cure for many ailments including infertiliy. Isabel took the "cure," promising to build a church there if her prayers were answered. The trip afforded the couple the opportunity to explore the large coffee plantations, sugar factories and mineral mines of the huge state of Minas Gerais. The richness of the countryside was magnificent, but the poverty and pain of the slavery supporting such wealth forced their minds from their own problems.

Gaston wrote his father, "It would be impossible to dream of a more beautiful country. There is really only one dark spot here, very dark. And that is the evil caused by the criminal nature of slavery. It is the basis of all opposition to positive change. The main challenge is how to destroy this evil, without destroying the country. How to end slavery without provoking a war that would turn the country into a barren desert? It is a problem that continually occupies us."[6]

During their travels enthusiastic crowds welcomed the royal couple, but the primary purpose of their journey was not successful. Aunt Francesca wrote, "Unfortunately the waters did not work their virtues, but we shall keep trying."[7]

When Isabel and Gaston returned to Rio de Janeiro, the war news did nothing to lift their spirits. The United States minister to Paraguay reported the horrifying experience of visiting a battlefield. "There were children of tender years who crawled back, dragging shattered limbs, or with ghastly bullet wounds in their little half naked bodies." Cholera, diarrhea, and smallpox claimed as many of the dead as bullets.[8]

Then in December the two-year siege of Paraguay's capital Asunción was broken in a blinding rainstorm. Three thousand Brazilians were wounded, including General Caxias, General Osório and the commander of Brazil's naval forces, but the Paraguayan defenders suffered the worst casualties and abandoned the city.[9] Caxias entered Asunción on December 30, 1868, only to discover his advance guard had looted everything of value, including the country's foreign legations. Weak from his wounds and drained by the sights, sounds and smell of death, Caxias collapsed during the victory celebrations. The senselessness and brutality of the war had brought him to despair. From his sickbed he wrote Pedro II, urging him to declare victory and bring the troops home. The emperor refused.

Paraguay's armies had suffered four years of military defeats, its capital had fallen and most of his country was at the mercy of vengeful foreign troops, but López continued to fight. The country's new provisional government denounced him as a "monster ... a blot on civilization ... the destroyer of his nation and an enemy of the human race." They publicly condemned him for bathing the country in blood, branded him an outlaw and proclaimed that he was "forever ejected from Paraguayan soil."[10]

The words did not appease Pedro II. If López remained free, the emperor believed there would be no peace. The United States minister Henry Blow agreed, writing, "If the contest is abandoned for any reason except the death or seizure of López and the troops are withdrawn from the capital, he will soon reappear at Asunción, welcomed by the people and without opposition from a provisional government."[11]

Brazil's emperor ordered Caxias to pursue, arrest or kill López, but the exhausted commander refused. Citing ill health he resigned his commission, turned his command over to his senior officer, and began the long journey back to Rio de Janeiro. Once he arrived in Rio de Janeiro Pedro II refused to see him, inquire about his health or express public or private appreciation to the man who had defeated his greatest enemy.[12]

In Paraguay Francisco López, his mistress Elisa Lynch and his remaining soldiers retreated to the deep interior of his country, waiting for Brazil's next move.[13] The war was at a stalemate. Unfounded rumors reached Rio de Janeiro that some Rio Grandense units were in open mutiny. The nation seemed to hold its breath.

Henry Blow noted "a deep gloom" over Brazil and reported, "As to the feeling in Rio, I think it can be safely asserted that all classes are becoming heartily tired, if not disgusted with a war resulting in ruin to Paraguay and without glory to Brazil, marked by a loss of life and property under circumstances without parallel, and which still imposes upon the allies the burden of justifying themselves before the civilized world."[14]

With the conflict entering its fifth year, observers believed time had run out for either Paraguay's dictator or Brazil's emperor. One or the other would not survive the year. Few shared the belief of the emperor that the war must continue, including his own generals. In order to finish López once and for all, Pedro II was forced to turn to the one officer still willing to fight. He announced that his twenty-seven-year-old son-in-law would become commander in chief of the allied forces.

The nomination sent shock waves through Brazil and the royal family. Princess Isabel had never before disagreed with her father over a political or military matter; but his action caused her to write him a letter filled with passion, stinging criticism and political insight:[15]

Petrópolis, 22 of February, 1869

My Dear Father,
   Gaston arrived three hours ago with the news that you wish him to go to war. How can that be my father, from you who so much loves the Constitution, yet wants to impose your will on the Ministers? Or are they so weak in character that one-day they say it is white and the next day it is black? Would they have all unanimously, and at the same time change their minds like my father?
   Why don't they invite Caxias to return? He is feeling better and the doctors have recommended the air of Montevideo. Why should Gaston go to war just because there have been rumors of dissidence [within the army]? And it is you who believes these rumors, when normally you refuse to believe the first thing they tell you?
   Dear father, I remember at the Tijuca Falls, three years ago, that you told me passion is blind. So, please don't let your passion for the affairs of war blind you! And on top of it all, you endanger the life of my Gaston!
   Dr. Feijó recommended Gaston not expose himself to too much sun, rain or drizzle; and how can he avoid these when at war? Caxias ... has some head problems that can be cured, and he could also stay at Montevideo where he does well; and why send my Gaston the one to catch any disease of the chest, which can

rarely be cured? Losing Gaston will be much worse to Brazil than losing Caxias! And now there is cholera in Montevideo! I will tell you that if Gaston goes to Asunción, I will be going there too.... I will go to the end of the world with my Gaston. Dear father, maybe you know what I am going through, so please forgive me if I say something harsh; burn this letter if you will but remember well what I tell you....

I need relief from my fears and pain and crying won't help. I surely hope in God that Gaston will not go. Maybe the war will be over.... Other things might happen. Dear God! Dear God! I really don't know how this decision was made, when now the only thing to do is to chase López into the jungle. To actually command from Asunción (you yourself told me that it would not do to have Caxias chase López) another person would suffice. The Rio Grandense are but a small part of the Army. Farewell father, please forgive me."[16]

Isabel gave her letter to Gaston to deliver to the emperor. He did so but added an attached note, sharing with his father-in-law his growing insight into his wife: "With this, your Majesty will also receive Isabel's lament. She was very anguished and I did not want to prevent her from opening her heart which helps better than tears. Concerning my health issue, I will repeat what I said yesterday: it would only be valid in case my life were in danger, which fortunately is not the case ... a change in the air and horseback riding do me good. As far as Isabel going to Asunción, needless to say I don't think it is convenient. At the most, she could go to Buenos Aires. But I did not want to make her suffer even more by starting a conversation which is not yet necessary."[17]

Gaston's appointment came at a time when Brazil's soldiers were desperate to return home. Most allied troops had been rotated back to their own countries years earlier. The war's entire naval operations were Brazilian, as were twenty-two thousand of the remaining twenty-six thousand coalition soldiers at the front.

There were many reasons to declare the war over, but none more important to the future of Brazil than the question of slavery. Henry Blow wrote, "I am the more anxious for this termination, because [I am] convinced that [with] this war once concluded, the public mind in Brazil will be turned to ... the emancipation of the slaves a powerful public sentiment being even now at work in favor of abolishing the institution entirely at variance with the civilization and humanity of this age."[18]

The stakes in the war may have never been greater. Abolitionists in Brazil were a small, but growing, minority who believed the royal family sympathetic to their cause. The nation's slaveholders continued supporting the monarchy, also believing it offered the best protection of their interests—including slavery.

Pedro II tried to position himself in the center of the growing national tensions. As the country grew more polarized, pro- and anti-slavery groups both saw him as their strongest possible ally, but the nation's political center was threatened by the war. Princess Isabel may have recognized the danger more than her father. Aside from fears for Gaston's health, she worried his appointment did not have the support of the emperor's own ministers.[19] If that was the case, damage to the monarchy and her husband's reputation might be irreversible.

Gaston must have heard Isabel's concerns. Prior to his departure for Paraguay, Gaston requested a meeting with Pedro II, seeking assurances his appointment as commander in chief had the full support of the government.[20] For three heated hours Gaston covered many of the difficult issues Isabel cited in her letter.[21]

The emperor was furious, but the confrontation forced him to meet with his ministers and return with the assurances Gaston sought. Isabel's fears and instincts may have precipitated the unpleasant altercation but they also served to protect the reputation and integrity of her husband, her father, and the constitutional monarchy. Isabel had taken a giant step toward finding a role for herself in the male world of power. She used her knowledge and insights into the Brazilian government to force her husband and father to address her concerns, and in doing so, legitimize them. In the future, it would become increasingly difficult for either of them to ignore or dismiss her thinking.

28

"The Never Ending War"

Princess Isabel continued to insist on accompanying Gaston to the front. Finally, the emperor acquiesced, writing her, "I will only tell your mother what I have just written you when you ask me to provide you with the transport, since this will tell me that you are determined to do what I myself could not, that is, to go to the war site. Farewell! Please accept the embrace of your father who cares for you so much."[1]

Gaston, however, convinced Isabel to remain at home. She did as her husband wished and he left for Paraguay alone. Following his departure news arrived from Austria that Poldie had delivered another healthy son. Aunt Francesca immediately wrote, urging Isabel to visit Europe as soon as possible to consult with medical experts there. She also wrote to Pedro II, "May God give to her what she and we all want so much. I hope and pray that she goes to see a doctor specialist and follows exactly the prescription he gives to her." Privately some in and out of government speculated Poldie and her family should be recalled to Brazil to prepare for a peaceful succession to the throne.[2]

Isabel seldom showed the tension and pressure she was under in public, but a glimpse of her inner turmoil was seen at the São Cristóvão Palace in May 1869. That month North America's greatest living pianist, the composer Louis Gottschalk, performed for the royal family. Isabel requested he play his beautiful but melancholy composition "Morte — She Is Dead." Guests were shocked when the princess imperial broke down and cried uncontrollably throughout the performance.[3]

Five months later, Gaston gave Princess Isabel, Brazilian abolitionists and Paraguay's slaves a reason to celebrate. Rather than wait for Paraguay's Law of Free Birth to take effect later, he requested its provisional government immediately free the country's remaining slaves.[4] His actions deprived López of one of his most powerful propaganda weapons, but also reverberated in Brazil. Gaston's proclamation on emancipation was the strongest public condemnation of slavery ever issued by a member of the royal family. In it he wrote, "If you grant the [slaves] freedom you will have solemnly broken with an institution which was unfortunately bequeathed to many of the peoples of free America by centuries of despotism and deplorable ignorance."[5]

Paraguay's provisional government quickly approved the request, raising the morale of Gaston's troops and further demoralizing López's dwindling supporters. Two of Brazil's leading conservative politicians visiting Asunción had dramatically different reactions to the emancipation decree. The Visconde Rio Branco, a life long supporter of slavery, began rethinking his position on abolition. The Baron Cotegipe reacted differently. As the acting secretary of state for foreign affairs, Cotegipe saw a streak of idealism and liberalism in Gaston's statement that frightened him.[6] He worried such thinking might politically influence the future empress. It never occurred to him that Isabel might have had a liberal effect on her husband's thinking.

In Cotegipe's world, slavery represented the very foundation of Brazil and the monarchy. To him the two were inseparable. No one, including a member of the royal family, should threaten either. Rio Branco came to the conclusion emancipation must be addressed at the end of the war, but no one knew when that would be. Rio's *Anglo-Brazilian Times* labeled the conflict "the never ending war."[7] Like other Brazilian and European newspapers, the paper held Pedro II responsible for its length.

In Paraguay Gaston found it easier to free the country's slaves than find his elusive enemy. Eventually, he divided his forces into pincers to search for López through some of the most forbidding jungles of South America. Insects and the weather assaulted them. Breaks in supply lines carrying food and medicine increased the number of sick Brazilians, who came to outnumber the healthy.[8]

By the middle of August, Gaston's army made contact with López's remaining forces and continuous fighting began. Two of Gaston's generals were wounded, another killed, a fourth retired to Asunción with his health broken and his mind clouded. Reports reached Rio de Janeiro the prince himself had suffered a nervous breakdown.[9] Gaston requested a temporary leave of absence, but the emperor refused. No one, including his son-in-law was coming home until López was eliminated.[10]

Isabel was beside herself with anger and worry. In the growing tensions between her husband and father, she sided with Gaston. Like many others, she insisted the war was over and Gaston and the troops should be called home.[11] Isabel confined her strong opinions within the walls of the palace, but the emperor paid no more attention to his daughter than he did to his other critics.

Gaston had no choice but to push on. He renewed the fight with such butchery that Paraguayans feared he had gone insane or was possessed by the devil. Captured Paraguayan soldiers revealed López's forces had been reduced to half-dead old men, maimed women and child soldiers as young as seven and eight. Gaston showed none of them mercy. An official report stated, "The roads are full of women and children hungry and exhausted. The number of corpses of these wretches, strewed on all sides, makes a horrible contrast with nature's green aspect."[12]

At one point, fighting became so intense Gaston charged ahead of his troops and was surrounding by Paraguayan soldiers. His adjutant saved his life by pulling him to safety, but Gaston ordered him arrested and quickly returned to combat. Some wondered if he were seeking death more than seeking López. [13]

On March 1, 1870, after nearly a full year of jungle warfare, López, Elisa Lynch, and his remaining soldiers became trapped. López fell fighting. The night before, he had signed his own mother's death warrant, but his death prevented the order from being executed.[14] Exhausted Brazilian and Paraguayan soldiers silently watched Elisa Lynch dig López's grave with her own hands. [15] The bloodiest war in South American history ended with his last breath.

Seven years of fighting cost Brazil one hundred thousand lives. Paraguayans lost three times that number. A postwar census found its prewar population of nearly one half million people reduced to 106,254 living women, 86,079 children, and 28,746 men. Paraguay's manhood was made up of the old, the crippled and Catholic priests.[16]

The United States minister in Brazil described the capital's reaction. "Immediately upon the reception of this news, the entire population of the two cities of Rio and Petrópolis turned out with demonstrations of great rejoicing, and a universal excitement prevailed. The Emperor's carriage was drawn by his enthusiastic subjects through the streets of the capital and the night following the Emperor, Empress and Princess walked through ... the two great streets of the city of Rio.... Music and marches, banners, torch lights and illuminations continued on the grandest scale for three successive days and nights and every manifestation indicated that there was but one feeling — a feeling of intense rejoicing over the capture and death of Marshal López and the consequent termination of a war which had destroyed Paraguay, and proved so prostrating to Brazil."[17]

Peace meant freedom for thousands of slaves who had volunteered to fight. With the war over, their wives were also freed. Supporters of slavery dreaded their homecoming, fearing former slaves hardened in battle and trained to fight. Proslavery elements voiced concerns Gaston's abolitionist statements would inspire the veterans to lead massive slave insurrections. Some politicians suggested the army be disbanded on the frontier rather than returned to the soldiers' home provinces. Others opposed parades or popular demonstrations, fearing such celebrations might politicize the army, inflating the freed slaves' sense of power and entitlement.

Isabel wrote Gaston of the political grumblings. He reacted in anger, threatening to resign his commission "with a crash" if his "companions in arms" failed to receive the respect they earned on the battlefields.[18] Gaston's sentiments became public knowledge, bringing a firestorm of criticism down on the royal family for involving themselves in politics. Some Brazilians were enraged a military officer, especially the son-in-law of the emperor, might question government policy. Others were furious over the treatment and lack of respect given the army.

In an attempt to deflect the controversy Pedro II and the General Assembly planned a formal victory parade to officially celebrate the victory. Eight thousand invitations were sent to leading citizens, but fewer than two hundred attended.[19] The humiliating rebuke dramatically and publicly trumpeted the unpopularity of the war. Pedro quietly ordered Gaston and a full division of his army to remain in Paraguay. With no other ceremonies planned, the rest of the soldiers were quietly brought home.

When Gaston finally returned to Rio de Janeiro, feelings had calmed down and Isabel's husband received the hero's welcome he believed should have gone to his troops. He wrote his father, "The reception was superb: a magnificent demonstration.... I doubt that in any other country ... one can find such unanimity in their demonstrations."[20]

The prince also proudly wrote his sister, "I arrived in Rio exactly on the 29th of April in the morning. It was really a beautiful day. You cannot imagine the excitement there was all over town. For four nights straight you could not find one house that was not illuminated."[21]

Gaston was the guest of honor at a brilliant reception hosted by the Baron of Itamaraty in Rio de Janeiro's most magnificent mansion. There General Manuel Luís Osório, a political liberal and one of the war's great heroes, toasted his victorious commander: "Cheers to the Count d'Eu. My companion in arms for his valued courage and for the justice with which he administered his soldiers. I propose a cheer to him because in Paraguay he always proved his love for Brazil, and he devoted his soul to his service like the proud Brazilians that served him."[22]

Only in a letter to his former teacher in England did Princess Isabel's husband share his innermost feelings. "And here I am now delivered from the hideous nightmare of the Paraguayan War. It was time for it to end. During the last months ... I indeed suffered both physically and morally.... if this war has left me with memories of sorrows and disappointments, I also have joys to remember and I can say that my efforts were not lost, not for Brazil, not for myself, and not for my family."[23] The war changed Brazil and its royal family. For Gaston the conflict took a double toll, first by being kept from the war, then by being thrust into its deepest abyss. He returned a public hero, but discovered a dark side within himself.

Physically his hearing had deteriorated to the point of near deafness, leaving him less confident, more nervous, withdrawn and circumspect. For the rest of their married lives, Gaston was forced to depend on Isabel to support him in his lengthening periods of self-doubt and depression.[24]

Pedro II was also transformed. He was by nature a peacemaker; but he had stubbornly, almost single handedly forced his nation through the longest war in its history. He and Brazil had been tested. As an emperor and as a man, he had never doubted the righteousness of his cause. His will had triumphed, his enemy was vanquished; but he had compromised his principles and strengthened the hands of his enemies.

The war also changed Princess Isabel. She had been forced to think for herself. The men in her life had achieved their goals but paid a terrible price in attaining them. Isabel saw perhaps for the first time how truly human her husband and father were. They too saw her differently. Slowly, perhaps without realizing it, they had begun to respect and rely on her in ways they might never be able to admit. Isabel's insights into their strengths and weaknesses increased her confidence in herself. She continued loving and respecting them; but she saw them in less idealistic, more human, terms. By war's end she had also gained a better sense of who she was, and who she could become.

29

"Flowers, Not Blood"

The long-postponed debates on abolition exploded across Brazil's political landscape. How the empire resolved its dependence on slavery would in all probability be its greatest legacy or its most damning indictment. History seemed to equate abolition movements with violence. Six years after slavery sparked civil war in the United States, military occupation, martial law, and racial lynching continued there.

Within days of Gaston's return from Paraguay, Pedro II privately wrote the president of the Council of Ministers, "I think that it would be a great mistake if the government did not say something on the question of emancipation in the Speech from the Throne.... [The question] seems to occupy everyone except the government."[1] The council opposed any direct mention of slavery, the same position it had taken prior to the war. A compromise was finally reached allowing Pedro to use the term "free labor" in his speech in a vague reference to the nation's agriculture.

The Baron of Cotegipe was alarmed at the direction the council discussions took. He privately confided, "When in this meeting it was said that the question of emancipation resembled a boulder tumbling down the mountainside and we should not start it rolling since we would be crushed, H[is] M[ajesty] replied that he did not hesitate to expose himself to the fall, even if he were crushed!"[2]

Unlike their emperor, his ministers were determined to avoid such an avalanche. Frustrated by their recalcitrance, Pedro attempted to encourage public dialogue through personal behavior. He announced he would personally pay for the education of any children whose fathers had been freed from slavery to fight in the war. Pedro II hoped others would join him. Few did.[3]

One fourth of Brazil's population continued to be held in bondage — nearly three million men, women and children. In the Chamber of Deputies Joaquim Nabuco and a new generation of political leaders began demanding an end to slavery.[4] Lawmakers, beholden to the slaveholders who had elected them, blocked debate on the issue. Economic fears about the growing national debt, ongoing labor shortages, and the declining production of sugar, cotton,

151

diamonds and gold were used to redirect the nation's attention away from emancipation.

The export of coffee saved the nation from financial ruin, causing one investor to declare, "Brazil is coffee, and coffee is the Negro."[5] The labor-intensive crop was harvested primarily on large family-owned plantations by slaves. Despite the emperor's active support of immigration, there were still not enough workers to cultivate the country's coffee. To Brazil's investors, abolition was unthinkable.

Emancipation divided the country. The emperor attempted to please one side, then the other, but as emotions escalated he found less and less room to maneuver. The political center was disappearing beneath him.

Pedro II spent much of his reign preparing his country for the end of slavery; but Brazil's powerful agricultural interests resisted even the suggestion of abolition. For years government commissions proposed alternatives to slave labor, but not one recommendation had ever been acted upon.

In an attempt to move the country forward, the emperor turned to an idea first advocated by his mother — the free birth of children born of slaves.[6] Spain had recently passed such a law for its colony in Cuba.[7] Ten years before the birth of Princess Isabel, Maria II proposed similar legislation for Portugal's colonies. Even dictatorial Paraguay had mandated a "free birth" law for its slave children. But to gain acceptance for the proposal in Brazil, Pedro had to create a political climate of compromise. He did it with equal parts of idealism, cynicism, and fear and by turning to two people he trusted most — his daughter Princess Isabel and veteran politician José Maria da Silva Paranhos, the Visconde of Rio Branco.

Pedro II announced that the health of the nation's beloved empress dictated an extended overseas trip for consultations and rest.[8] He would of course escort her. Princess Isabel and Gaston would be sent abroad first to make all necessary arrangements. Privately he may have hoped their trip would allow Isabel and Gaston to seek medical advice about their inability to conceive a child and Gaston's growing deafness.

The emperor knew his daughter and son-in-law would need to be healthy, rested and steadfast for the fight to come. He planned to appoint the twenty-four-year-old Isabel to serve as regent during his absence. She would be acting head of state as the law of free birth was presented, debated and came to a vote in parliament. Rio Branco as prime minister would steer the controversial legislation through the General Assembly.

Isabel's regency dramatically illustrated the confidence Pedro II placed in his daughter. But the gesture may have also been a cynical attempt to frighten the nation's politicians into considering a future without him. Brazil still needed the monarchy. Despite criticism during the war and the country's ongoing dependence on slavery, the Bragança monarchy represented to the world's investors and financial markets stability, continuity, and constitutional rule.

Rumors circulated that if the free birth proposal failed to become law, the emperor might abdicate and remain in Europe.[9] That fear had a chilling effect on the nation's politicians and the heated debates in parliament. The political climate of compromise Pedro II sought slowly came together. Calculated or collateral fears may have helped achieve his political goals, but they also created resentment, undermining confidence in the monarchy.

Near the end of September 1870, Princess Isabel and Gaston dutifully traveled to Europe, stopping first in England to visit the Duke of Nemours in his new home near Hampton Court. The outbreak of the Franco-Prussian war delayed further travels. Prussia swiftly routed the French armies, Napoleon III was captured, and Empress Eugenie and their son fled to England much as the Orleans family had done twenty-two years earlier. The French people, however, fought on, and Paris remained under the siege of German guns.

The widowed Condessa Barral and her French son were refugees staying in the nearby home of the Prince and Princess of Joinville.[10] All the condessa had saved from her life in France was a photograph of her late husband grabbed from her son's bedstand.[11] The reunion between the Countess and Princess Isabel was sad and painful.

Gaston's spirits lifted when he received a letter from England's Society for the Abolition of Slavery saluting him as the "French Emancipator" for his abolitionist efforts in Paraguay.[12] The society pressed him for information regarding Brazil's abolition movement. He tactfully replied that the emperor was committed to emancipation within the strict constitutional limits imposed on him.

Plans to visit Poldie in Vienna, where she was expecting her fourth child, were postponed first by the war and then by the worst winter of the century. In December, Isabel received news her sister had safely delivered another son she named for Gaston. In January a letter arrived informing her Poldie had been stricken with typhoid fever — the dreaded disease that had claimed so many of their family. Isabel and Gaston decided to leave England at once, traveling south by the Mediterranean Sea, then north to Italy and Austria in a nearly frantic effort to reach Poldie.

Despite repeated delays, they finally arrived in Vienna, but were not allowed to enter the sickroom until Poldie was near death. She died on February 7, 1871. A broken hearted Isabel accompanied her twenty-three-year-old sister's body to Coburg. There, like their grandmother Leopoldina, she was buried among strangers. The Condessa Barral wrote, "I can find no words of comfort.... Four little boys crying for their mother.... I plead to heaven for comfort."[13] Gaston wrote Poldie had been an "angel of goodness" blessing all of them through her brief time on earth.[14] And Francesca, Princess of Joinville, wrote Pedro "I confess that I am deeply discouraged and feel that I have already been in the world longer than the calendar says."[15]

Princess Isabel's days and nights were filled with tears and prayers. Like her father she feared her mother might not recover from the blow.[16] She begged them in a letter to remember they still had a daughter who needed and loved them. The trip allowed little time for rest or medical consultations. Isabel and Gaston returned to Brazil May 1st to the news that a massive slave revolt had been crushed in the state of Minas Gerais. Thirty ringleaders were arrested for plotting to unite hundreds of slaves from coffee plantations and gold mines in the hopes their uprising would spread across the nation.[17] The discovery inflamed the national debates on slavery.

The emperor's annual speech from the throne on the third of May presented the ministry's controversial plan for free birth. On the same day he secretly gave Isabel a memorandum confiding to her that the pro-slavery attitude of the nation "must be destroyed as soon as possible." He cautioned, however, that it must be done with great care.[18] Pedro was determined not to delay his trip longer and on May 15th Isabel took her formal oath as regent. Ten days later he and the empress sailed for Lisbon. Prior to the departure, Baron Cotegipe privately confessed, "I view with dread the Emperor's journey."[19] Pedro II displayed no qualms in leaving Brazil's eleven million people in the hand of his young daughter at one of the most critical points in its history. He would not be disappointed.

Although Isabel was ten years younger than the most youthful member of Rio Branco's cabinet, she proved to be an adept administrator, effectively executing her public duties while keeping her humility and sense of humor. In her first letter to her father, she wrote, "Yesterday I had my first [cabinet meeting]. But let me say that when Daddy left it seemed strange to me that from the bottom of my foot to the top of my head, I am suddenly a kind of emperor without having to change my skin, without a beard, and without *a very large belly*. Forgive me, that's naughty. Speaking of bellies let me tell you that Daddy beats out Valponto whom I have seen several times since you left."[20] After mocking herself, her father, and at least one minister, she then presented a comprehensive report on the cabinet meeting and ongoing events in the government. Her intelligence, moderation and common sense reminded many of her father.

Prior to his departure Pedro II had reconciled with his old friend, General Caxias. The retired war hero had recently been reelected to the General Assembly but not before Pedro elevated him to the highest rank of Brazilian nobility. The newly appointed duke had been persuaded by the Baron of Rio Branco to introduce the proposed law of free birth to the parliament. It was hoped his great popularity and prestige would defuse the controversial issue. It did not. The legislation met "determined opposition" from his own Conservative Party. They insisted, "The very existence of Brazilian society yet rests upon the labor of its 2,000,000 to 3,000,000 slaves." Opponents were especially resistant to any specific timeline that would restrict or limit slavery. For them, any timetable was too "hasty."[21]

Controversial parts of the legislation included implementation of a national census, an idea first proposed by Empress Leopoldina years earlier. Other sections included freeing all slaves held by monasteries, convents and other religious orders, all crown slaves working in the state owned mines of Minas Gerais, and all other slaves who built and maintained public roads, bridges, etc. The key provision of the legislation, however, was the legalization of a principle of free birth granting freedom to any child born of slaves once he or she reached adulthood.

The United States minister to Brazil wrote, "The influence of the slave-holders is very powerful, beyond a question, and there is naturally a nervous apprehension attending so radical a social revolution as that proposed by the government."[22] Acrimonious legislative debates raged for months. Name-calling and insults spilled from the galleries and echoed across the nation. No other order of government business was considered. Advocates and opponents of the legislation pointed to the cataclysmic civil war in the United States and its poisonous aftermath as an example of what was to come if their own position did not prevail.

Brazil's war over slavery, however, was fought with words, not guns. Princess Isabel met regularly with Rio Branco to discuss the progress of the bill. Not since the nation banned the slave trade two decades earlier had the full weight of the monarchy fought so strongly for a piece of slave legislation. And perhaps never before had so much pressure, money, or power been used to fight a government proposal.

In the midst of the legislative debates, Isabel and her doctors came to believe she was pregnant. On being informed of the news, Pedro II wrote that if the pregnancy came to full term, he would return for the baby's birth.[23] But after three months of high expectations it was determined Isabel was not pregnant.

The public responsibilities of her regency gave Isabel little time to deal with her sense of loss. She longed for time to grieve and wrote her father,[24] "In spite of the ministers' goodwill ... and of the interesting and, at time, even diverting side of the regency, what I would only give to be already free."[25] When the bill finally came to a vote in the General Assembly it passed by three votes. Princess Isabel promptly signed it into law. No one was completely satisfied with the final result, but everyone recognized it was a step toward abolition.

The heavily amended legislation was known in legal circles as the "Rio Branco Law." In addition to mandating a national census it freed slaves "belonging to the nation, those for the use of the crown, those abandoned by their masters, those to whom title through inheritance was vague, and all children born thereafter to slave mothers" at the age of twenty-one.[26] The last provision provided it with its popular name, the "Law of the Free Womb." The freeing of children born of slaves and the taking of a national census redeemed two of Empress Leopoldina's original dreams.[27]

A political leader of Bahia, one of the empire's strongest bastions of slavery, ruefully predicted, "Emancipation is inevitable." But Brazil's slaveholders

were far from defeated.[28] Demonstrations against the law were organized in
Rio de Janeiro, São Paulo and Minas Gerais. Pro-slavery forces began funding
newspapers to attack abolitionists and delay further attempts at abolition. Rio
Branco's bill granted slaveholders the option of immediate financial compensation *or* the temporary guardianship of slave children until the age of twenty-
one. Most slaveholders used the second option, giving them the laborers they
wanted and time to fight emancipation.

The law gave abolitionists hope. In parts of the country there were great
bonfires and celebrations among slaves. Some foreign diplomats such as the
minister from England expressed disappointment slavery was still protected by
law. Others like the United States minister were amazed such legislation could
be debated and passed without mobs or government resorting to violence. The
blood soaked history of his own country caused the U.S. minister to follow the
long and acrimonious debates with special interest. Following the final vote he
quietly descended to the senate chamber and picked up a few of the scattered
blossoms, explaining, "I shall send these flowers to my country to show them
how you achieved by law what cost there so much in blood."[29]

Princess Isabel immediately sent word to her father that the free birth legislation had become law. During the rest of his overseas travels, Brazil's emperor
received public acclamation for the events that had taken place during his
absence.[30] Like the American minister, Isabel collected several of the blossoms
from the celebrations. She sent them to her father to show him the freedom of
Brazil's slaves had been brought about "through flowers, not blood."[31]

In March 1872, after nearly a year abroad, Brazil's emperor and empress
returned to Rio de Janeiro. The American minister described the event: "The
whole population poured forth in its holiday-dress to greet them ... as their
Majesties came ashore, escorted by hundreds of steamers, vessels, and boats of
every size and description. The shouts of welcome, the music of the bands, the
military display, the thunder of the salutes from all the forts and gaily dressed
men-of-war echoed back from the mountains which surround this magnificent
bay, offered sights and sounds not to be forgotten."[32]

For Princess Isabel, the homecoming was bittersweet. Pedro II brought
with him Poldie's two oldest sons, six-year-old Pedro Augusto and five-year-
old Augusto Leopold. The emperor had reluctantly concluded that the monarchy must be safeguarded by preparing Poldie's oldest sons to be raised as
possible heirs to the Brazilian throne.[33]

~ 30 ~

"The Loss of All Our Hopes"

In September 1872, Brazil celebrated the fiftieth anniversary of national independence. It was also the golden anniversary of the founding of America's only hereditary monarchy. Much of the country's progress over the previous half-century was attributed to the progressive leadership of Pedro II, the only leader most Brazilians could remember. Outside of his own country, his reputation may have been even greater. In Europe and the United States he was compared to Rome's Marcus Aurelius and Peter the Great of Russia.[1] Many believed him the "most popular royal" in Europe.[2]

One newspaper wrote of the anniversary celebration, "Brazilians of all classes and colors proudly wore the green and yellow blade of independence, a long slender leaf peculiar to Brazil so called because it showed the colors of the national flag. In the evening the city's theatres were thronged, and when the national hymn written by Pedro I was sung, everyone joined in the chorus."[3]

A major highlight of the ceremonies was the unveiling of a large statue of José Bonifácio de Andrada e Silva in the heart of Rio de Janeiro. The entire royal family was in attendance honoring the "Patriarch of Brazilian Independence." To many the fact that he was a staunch supporter of the monarchy, the friend of Pedro II's parents, and tutor to the present emperor made the royal family his political heirs. Pedro presided with Empress Theresa, the princess imperial, the Conde d'Eu, Poldie's two young sons, and the "principal nobility and officers of the court and government."[4] Large crowds shared in the festivities. For Isabel and her family it was a time of pride and high hopes.

Princess Isabel again believed she was pregnant. Fears of a false pregnancy or an early miscarriage had passed. By the time of the fiftieth anniversary celebration it was publicly announced the princess imperial was carrying a child. Isabel was placed under the care of Brazil's best doctors, but shortly before her due date, she suffered a miscarriage. The loss sent Isabel into a deep depression.[5]

Isabel and Gaston decided to travel to Europe to consult medical experts about Gaston's hearing loss and Isabel's inability to safely deliver a child.[6] To deflect the press the government announced they would be officially representing Brazil at Vienna's Great International Exposition.[7] Their time in Europe

157

would also allow them to celebrate a family reunion on French soil. France's new republican government had lifted the ban exiling Gaston's family. For the first time since he was a small boy, Gaston, his father, sister, cousins, uncles and aunts would be allowed to return to France.[8] It was a good time to be away from Brazil. The country's small but vocal Republican Party had begun to focus much of their anti-monarchial criticism on Gaston, labeling him "the Third Sovereign" and "the Frenchman" for his imagined influence over his wife and father-in-law.[9] Newspapers speculated on the timing and motives behind the journey. Some wrote Gaston was plotting secret intrigues with royal relatives. Others reported Isabel was preparing to renounce her claims to the throne in favor of her young nephews. One journal declared the Conde d'Eu seriously ill.[10] The royal family offered no comment.

The Orleans family reunion in France was interrupted by nearly endless medical tests for Gaston's hearing and Isabel's infertility. The couple also took the waters at Bad-Gastein and other popular health spas as well as visiting the religious shrine at Lourdes.[11] Gaston's enemies mockingly claimed he was deaf to the Portuguese language. The multilingual prince actually spoke Portuguese well, but like many of his relatives he was plagued by a severe hearing loss. His uncle the Prince of Joinville, his aunt Princess Clementine and several of his royal Belgian cousins struggled with deafness. Despite consultations with the continent's finest doctors, none offered hope. Gaston accepted the diagnosis stoically, redirecting his time and energies to reacquainting himself with his family and homeland.

Princess Isabel also consulted medical experts. France had become the continent's center for women's health issues, and Aunt Francesca urged Isabel to place herself under the care of the country's most famous gynecologist, Dr. Jean Marie DePaul. DePaul recommended an experimental operation entailing some risks, but also the possibility her fertility problem could be resolved. Isabel agreed to the operation and the bed rest required afterward. Inactivity was always difficult for Isabel, but the ordeal proved to be worthwhile. A short time after her full recovery from the surgery, doctors confirmed she was pregnant. Initial happiness was soon clouded by political considerations. As Princess Imperial Isabel's marriage contract stated, the heir to the throne must be born in Brazil, but Dr. DePaul feared a sea voyage life threatening.[12]

Isabel had always struggled with seasickness. During her recent voyage to Europe, she had been unable to eat or sleep during most of the twenty-day crossing. The thought of being pregnant and undergoing the voyage was a nightmare. The Princess of Joinville wrote Pedro, "We are all full of hopes for our dear Isabel. We must take care. The travel to Brazil makes me afraid. Please think about that my dear brother. If it is possible, she should stay here until after everything is finished."[13]

As Isabel approached the sixth month of her pregnancy, Gaston sought additional medical advice. Queen Victoria's personal obstetrician and the princess's Brazilian doctor traveled to France. Both concurred on the dangers of a sea voyage.[14] Isabel appealed directly to her father: "If you think well about all the risks and dangers that we would take if we travel before the birth of our child, then I believe that you are not going to hesitate in allowing us to leave here after July. Our major wish would be that the birth take place in Brazil if we were not under such a risk of losing the reason for our happiness."[15] The conclusion of her letter revealed the depth of her fears. "Very dear Papa, think that besides your grandchild, you could lose your daughter because I could not survive the loss of all our hopes."[16]

Gaston, like Isabel, understood the decision went beyond personal considerations. He formally petitioned the emperor requesting the heir to the throne be allowed to be born outside of the country. In his request he included copies of the medical opinions and recommendations of the consulted physicians.[17]

The emperor decided to test public opinion in his annual speech from the throne. On May 5, 1874, he declared, "The last news I had from my beloved daughter, the Princess Imperial, Condessa d'Eu, brought me the grateful certainty of her pregnancy." He then added, "In ordinary circumstances she would return to Brazil, in fulfillment of ... [her] matrimonial contract, but perhaps she may find herself obliged to avoid so long a journey, in compliance with the opinion of medical authorities."[18]

The response of the public, the press, and the nation's politicians was overwhelmingly negative. A royal birth was a public event. To deprive the country access to the birth of their heir would not be tolerated. Isabel's father took the problem to the Council of State. He acknowledged the princess imperial's marriage contract mandated royal heirs be born in Brazil, but explained the risks involved. Pedro II took the unprecedented step of sharing his daughter's confidential medical records sent by Gaston with government ministers and counselors of state.[19] After long discussions the all-male leadership of the government voted unanimously that Isabel must return to Brazil at once to deliver her child.

Upon hearing the minister's decision, Isabel and Gaston agreed to depart immediately. The Princess of Joinville wrote Pedro about their reaction. "Isabel is naturally very afraid of putting into risk her child but the decision was made jointly with Gaston when they realized how unpleasant to all of Brazil the alternative was and the possible bad repercussions of not going to Rio."[20] Isabel shared her fears in a letter to her father about the possibility of having to make an emergency landing in West Africa. There was no place on the African coast where she could receive proper medical care. Her letter ended, "Daddy, Pray for we three."[21] In the centuries Portugal and other European nations had been in West Africa, no modern hospitals had been built offering local inhabitants or ill seafarers medical sanctuary.

The voyage was long and difficult, but the royal couple finally sailed into

Guanabara Bay on June 24, 1874.[22] The weak princess was eight months pregnant when she finally heard the traditional salute from the harbor forts announcing her return. The arrival coincided with Rio's celebrating the successful laying
of the Transatlantic Cable. Still all was not well.

The emperor's government was in the midst of its worst domestic crisis
since the passage of the law of the free womb. One of the nation's leading bishops had been jailed for treason and another was scheduled to go to trial within
days.[23] The very heart and soul of the empire seemed at war with itself. A popular Catholic priest had sparked the roots of the problem when he offered a
celebratory oration at a Masonic temple following passage of the Rio Branco
law.[24] Unlike in Europe and the United States, in Brazil many priests were active
Masons.[25] Pope Pius IX had earlier denounced masonry as anti–Catholic and
some of the nation's bishops used the priestly oration to demand Brazilian
priests sever Masonic ties.

Brazil's Masons were not anti–Catholic.[26] Many of the nation's most
influential Catholics were Masons, including Prime Minister Rio Branco, who
served as grand master of the country's highest Masonic order.[27] The priest
triggering the controversy refused to disaffiliate himself from the Masons and
was excommunicated, but the controversy did not end.

In the northern state of Pernambuco the twenty-eight-year-old bishop
threatened excommunication to *all* Masonic Catholics. He announced he recognized no civil authority in Brazil, including the constitution, and obeyed
only the laws of the Church and God.[28] The bishop of Pará joined him condemning all things liberal including free thought.[29] Families, congregations,
and entire communities divided over the issue. Two of the strongest pillars of
the monarchy — the powerful Masonic fraternities and the country's equally
powerful Catholic Church — squared off against each other.[30] Masonic lodges,
a Jesuit college, Catholic newspapers, and bishops' residences were attacked,
looted and burned by mobs.[31] Violence spread and government troops had to
restore order. The country seemed on the brink of a religious war.

On the same day he and the emperor marched together in the city's Cor-
pus Christi Day procession, Rio Branco gave a "spirited defense" of Masonry
in the General Assembly. "If the enemies of this society would take the trouble to inform themselves as to what Masonry is in Brazil, they would see that
enrolled among its Grand Master are the names of Dom Pedro I the founder
of our Empire, and José Bonifácio de Andrada e Silva, ... patriarchs of our independence. Our enemies have no reason for speaking so disdainfully and with
so much aversion, and if not aversion, with so much suspicion of freemasonry
in Brazil. It has been a pacific corporation from the beginning always respectful toward religion and very useful to society."[32]

Pedro II sought a compromise first by seeking the advice of his Council
of State then by sending his most trusted and experienced diplomat to negotiate directly with the Pope. As the negotiations proceeded, several bishops

continued attacking the legal jurisdiction of the government. Brazil's emperor and government viewed the "persistent and willful disobedience of the law" as an attack on the constitution and the pope's refusal to discipline the bishops a foreign intrusion into domestic affairs. Memories of the role the church played in the collapse of the Mexican Empire and the support the Masonic lodges offered the besieged Maximilian may have hardened Pedro's position.[33]

Two of the most vitriolic bishops were ordered arrested and charged with "declar[ing] formal war against the Imperial Government, the criminal Code and the political constitution of the Empire." Rio Branco's ministry declared, "The insubordination of the bishops was a brazen attempt, inspired by a foreign government, to usurp powers that incontestably belonged to the sovereign authority"[34] They were ordered to be tried separately before the Supreme Tribunal of Justice in the Empire, presided over by all fourteen judges of the Supreme Court. The bishop of Olinda was tried first and found unanimously guilty. This was the tense political standoff the exhausted and pregnant Princess Isabel found when she and Gaston returned home. Three days after their arrival in Rio, the trial of the bishop of Pará began.

It took just thirty minutes for the fourteen judges to issue a guilty verdict identical to the one issued earlier against the bishop of Olinda. Both men were found guilty of exceeding the legal lines of ecclesiastical jurisdiction. The court ruled they had instigated "notorious violence and oppression" against lawfully recognized Masonic brotherhoods and had "obstinately refused obedience ... to the order of the executive power."[35]

They were both sentenced to four years' imprisonment with hard labor. The United States minister reported. "All this gives great anxiety at the Palace. The Empress—who is very charitable and a most devout Catholic—looks at it, of course in but one way. The Emperor is much concerned. He is determined to vindicate the national supremacy, yet he is anxious not to offend."[36]

Within days of the second bishop's imprisonment, Isabel went into labor. Four Brazilian doctors were in attendance, as was a Parisian midwife. Gaston, the Condessa Barral, the emperor and empress, and selected government ministers served as witnesses. The birth did not go well. Following ten years of hopes and prayers, the event Isabel and Gaston had happily anticipated arrived without joy. Empress Theresa wrote in her diary, "After hours of horrible pain, [Isabel] gave birth to a baby girl, but the baby did not survive. [Isabel] behaved with incredible courage." Theresa wrote Queen Victoria, "God in his kindness permitted my dear Isabel to be spared and has only called to himself her poor little daughter. So beautiful that she seemed an angel. [Isabel's] sufferings were terrible—for fifty hours, but her convalescence is taking its natural course and everything makes us hope that she will quickly recover."[37] Gaston sadly wrote his father, "Our daughter was very beautiful. She had blond hair of which I am sending you a lock that was taken by the Condessa Barral so that you can show it to my sister. She had big blue eyes of my color and she measured fifty-one centimeters."[38]

The midwife baptized the perfectly formed baby, who had been alive until the last moments of labor. In the Catholic religious tradition, the christening allowed the baby to be immediately received into heaven. The Church her father was at war with provided Isabel comfort when she most needed it. If the baby had survived, the royal birth might have helped unite the badly divided country; but her death only added to the national uncertainty. Isabel's long awaited child was born and died one day short of her own twenty-eighth birthday.

By the age of twenty-eight, most Brazilian mothers had birthed several children and were nearing the end of their childbearing years. As a princess and daughter, wife and mother, Princess Isabel believed she had failed the three cornerstones of her life — God, family and country. She was nearly inconsolable.

꧁ 31 ꧂

"Just a Dream"

With his mind and heart elsewhere, the emperor offered Isabel little sympathy. His most cherished beliefs were being sorely tested by the church-state conflict: the constitution must be obeyed and everyone, from priest to emperor, must observe civil laws.[1] He had built his entire public life on such principles.

Pope Pius IX wrote Brazil's emperor, "Your Majesty! I beg you to reflect that we must all appear before the Tribunal of God and that the higher one has been, the more serious shall be the settling of accounts, for which reason while we, the living, journey through this world, we must do all in our power to prevent a severe judgment."[2] Pedro II rejected such appeals as spiritual blackmail. Princess Isabel found herself caught between the love she felt for her father and country, and her devotion to her religion and faith. She was not alone.

The recent unification of Italy had reduced the once powerful Papal States to the tiny grounds of Vatican City.[3] Following the church's loss of temporal power, the pope aggressively asserted his spiritual authority throughout Europe and South America.[4] In Great Britain the political reaction to his activities triggered the electoral defeat of every Catholic member of the House of Commons.[5] Queen Victoria wrote, "Religious questions are most unpleasant in any case; but one ought not to give in to the Catholics. Only it is very difficult, for they are fond of letting themselves be made martyrs of, which then brings people's sympathies over to their side.... The struggle seems impending everywhere."[6]

Victoria's predictions seemed to mirror the church-state struggle in Brazil. Supporters of the imprisoned bishops saw them as martyrs, while opponents viewed them as instigators of their own martyrdom. Pedro attempted to moderate passions by suspending the hard labor portion of their sentences and placing them under what was essentially house arrest.[7]

The United States minister described the jail of one of the bishops on an island in Guanabara Bay: "Instead of undergoing imprisonment, in any house of detention or jail ... the Bishop has been provided for by the Government in a sumptuous manner, by the seaside, in the house of the Commandant of the fort, which was expressly papered and painted for his sojourn, with a retinue of servants paid by the government, — whose officers await the Bishop's commands, whose Commandant in an Order of the Day requires the officers and garrison 'to pay the most reverent respect and attention to their illustrious guest'— and whose guards present arms to him, as he passes freely in and out."[8] Despite such gestures of conciliation, the controversy did not subside. In December, Pope Pius IX denounced the Brazilian government for failing to resolve the crisis.

A special session of the National Assembly failed to find a way out of the political impasse. Abdication rumors filled newspapers, reporting the weary emperor planned to step aside in favor of Princess Isabel, but the threats were no longer taken seriously. Isabel's depression and slow recovery following the death of her daughter caused her to avoid involvement in public events as much as possible. In a letter to her father she wrote, "Thank you for your letter and the Speech from the Throne. Obviously I read the letter at once, but the Speech I left for later on."[9]

The growing acrimony of the church-state crisis may have contributed to Isabel's withdrawal from public affairs. She and Gaston had been members of the Council of State since 1870 but seldom attended meetings. Whenever possible they retreated to a small house they purchased in Petrópolis that served as their private sanctuary. There, surrounded by her gardens, Isabel avoided involvement in the poisoned political climate of the country, but she could not escape her sense of personal failure.

Brazilian society believed women were "born to be mothers."[10] Males and females of the time viewed motherhood as the only acceptable gender role for women. Popular magazines such as A Mãe de Familia portrayed women and mothers as synonymous, while many Brazilian men bluntly proclaimed a woman's sole function was "to serve as a propagation machine."[11] Such pervasive attitudes must have been especially painful to the childless princess.

Opponents of the monarchy did not hesitate to use Isabel's infertility to their political advantage. Still, as the only living daughter of the much-loved emperor and empress, Isabel retained the affection of her nation, even as her husband lost much of the popularity he had earned in the Paraguayan War. Gaston's discomfort with strangers was attributed to French snobbishness rather than his natural shyness or worsening deafness. More than any other member of the royal family, he provided an easy target for critics.

Personal decisions and preferences compounded his difficulties. Gaston was one of the few prominent men in Brazilian public life who was not a Mason. Brazil's Masonic lodges provided its male elite a home base for social and intellectual activities. Gaston's desire for "a life of complete tranquility and isolation" kept him from developing important male friendships offered by the Masons. Such an attitude was impossible to maintain for a prince consort who needed to cultivate personal and political support.[12] Gaston's wish to avoid social situations denied him powerful alliances that might have protected him and the monarchy during the church-state crisis and in the future.

Gaston's solitary nature caused him to prefer to be alone or in the company of his wife rather than spending time with male contemporaries. And unlike his father, uncles, and even the emperor, he never took a mistress or engaged in extramarital affairs. Rather than discuss politics with others, he spoke of them only with his wife or in letters to his father. Gaston's behavior was personably admirable, but it distanced him from Brazilian men and the culture they dominated.

Privately he and Isabel agreed with their cousin Queen Victoria in one area of the church-state conflicts. It was a "dead end" for both sides with only "absurd consequences" for all concerned.[13] They believed both the church and government had mishandled the crisis. Citing the youth and inexperience of the bishops, Isabel believed Brazil's veteran politicians should have been able to prevent a crisis in which neither side could win. Once the two churchmen were found guilty and the laws of the nation upheld, she urged her father to declare victory, release the bishops, and put the crisis behind him. He steadfastly refused.

In the spring of 1875 Isabel discovered she was again pregnant and was ordered to undergo complete bed rest. For once she welcomed the opportunity for inactivity. Newspapers were filled with disturbing stories of deepening divisions within the country, foreign-born priests and Jesuits were being deported, and petitions flooded the government demanding the Church cease fostering anarchy and disturbing the peace.

An economic scandal finally helped break the stalemate between church and state. On May 15th Brazil's largest financial firm, owned by the Baron of Mauá, collapsed, leaving four million dollars in unpaid debts to the imperial government.[14] The resulting economic depression shook the nation politically and financially. Mauá's close ties to the prime minister forced Rio Branco to resign.[15]

Following Rio Branco's fall no one seemed able to restore national confidence. Twice Pedro II asked the elderly Duke of Caxias to form a new ministry, but citing age and poor health he declined. Aside from the emperor, no Brazilian commanded greater respect. With the nation divided and leaderless, Pedro seemed unable to find a way out of the crisis. When no one else stepped forward, Princess Isabel came to her father's aid. Ignoring the enforced bed rest order of her doctors, Isabel traveled to the home of General Caxias, pleading with him to reconsider her father's requests.[16] Her visit made a deep impression. Whether it was the personal risk to her health and unborn child or her powers of persuasion, Caxias agreed to form a new ministry. Isabel may have been the only person in Brazil able to persuade the "Iron Duke" to change his mind.[17]

In June of 1875 Caxias once again became prime minister. His fragile health, advanced age, and selection of "strait sect" conservative ministers signaled his would be a caretaker government. No one expected Caxias to do anything but provide a respite for the deeply polarized country, but he boldly moved to resolve the church-state conflict. The United States minister in Brazil wrote on July 16, 1875, "No new Ministry program has been put forth." But he added, "The only matter in which it seems likely at present that there will be a divergence from the late course, will be in the affair of the imprisoned martyrs—meaning the convicted Bishops—who, it is now feared by the Liberals and the liberal Conservatives—indeed, one may say, by the majority of the Enlightened of all parties save one — will be pardoned and allowed to leave their villas on the 29th of this month, being the anniversary of the birthday of the Princess Imperial."[18]

Like many, the United States minister attributed Caxias's actions to the growing influence of Princess Isabel. He explained: "Her very amiable and charitable disposition has been further incited of activity and great interest in her behalf by her condition and hopes (expecting to give birth to an heir in September)—and of course, her zeal, as well as the interest which Her Majesty and the Empress naturally takes in the affair has been inflamed by the incessant exertions of the 'friends of religion' as a certain party here modestly styles itself."[19]

In reality, Caxias had independently reached the same conclusion Isabel had earlier reached. The constitution had been enforced and Brazil's laws upheld. The bishops had been found guilty and were serving prison terms. Further imprisonment gained little for the government, but growing sympathy for the bishops. Caxias believed the time for compromise and amnesty had come, but Pedro II strongly disagreed.[20] Refusing to discuss the matter, he and the empress traveled to São Paulo, but Caxias and his conservative cabinet would not be put off. They continued urging the emperor to declare victory and release the bishops. The majority of the Council of State and even Baron Cotegipe felt amnesty necessary "to quiet the agitation of the country which might culminate in serious outbreaks during the coming election."[21]

Finally on the year and a half anniversary of their imprisonment, Pedro II announced amnesty for both bishops, setting off celebrations and outrage.[22] Anger focused not on Caxias or the emperor, but on the Princess Imperial, who newspapers painted as a puppet of the church and a religious zealot.[23] The amnesty was portrayed as a surrender to the pope and a frightening preface to Isabel's reign.

Caxias was both a Mason and a deeply religious Catholic. His own strong faith never became a public issue, but it did for Isabel. Opponents of the monarchy predicted that when Isabel became empress, Brazil would be ruled from Rome. *The New York Times*'s front-page headline trumpeted POPE RULE IN BRAZIL. The twenty-nine-year-old Isabel was described throughout the article as a "girl ... under Jesuitical influence."[24] The bishop's amnesty was presented as proof of Isabel's growing influence and her feminine ability to bend the government to her will.

The article reported,

> She utters vows that until the bishops are released she will make herself perpetu-
> ally miserable, and with an energy and industry worthy of a better motive she
> barefoot and unattended, proceeds to the sprinkling and sweeping, with ordinary
> corn broom all the churches in the neighborhood of her residence. It is pitiful! It
> produces an impression on the Emperor, Jesuitical senators work upon his paternal
> feelings, and at last he stretches the power invested in the imperial right and not
> only releases the bishops, but pardons their offences. Naturally Brazil feels humili-
> ated. The unofficial press of the country cries out in double headed editorials, and
> one, not an unusually mercurial journal asserts the Emperor has taken his first
> steps to his abdication.[25]

Reactionary forces in Brazil focused their fury on Isabel. Stories circulated
that Princess Isabel, not the emperor, had signed the unpopular amnesty document.[26] Rather than be credited for her political foresight, she was denounced
while the men responsible for the reversal of government policy went largely
unscathed.[27] Pedro II reacted with a rare public burst of anger. At a cabinet
meeting he declared, "A reading of today's newspapers obliges me to insist on
the need to declare what is the truth. My daughter in no way influenced my
mind nor did she try to have influence in the matter."[28]

In Petrópolis, Isabel remained under complete bed rest, unwilling or
unable to defend herself. She was struggling with another difficult pregnancy,
anxiety, fear and depression. Her due date was in October. At one point she
wrote Gaston, who was traveling, "God! How I would like for the month of
October to have come and gone! And gone *as we wish it to!* Pray to the Good
Lord and everyone in heaven for us!"[29]

Fearing complications, Isabel asked that Dr. DePaul travel to Brazil for the
delivery, but Gaston and the emperor resisted. They feared political opponents
would use the summoning of a foreign doctor to their advantage, but Isabel
insisted the decision was hers alone to make. Gaston reluctantly gave in to her
demands and the press savagely mocked the royal couple for insulting the country's medical establishment.[30]

The delivery date came and passed. A week and a half late, Isabel went
into labor. Assisting Dr. DePaul was a nurse midwife brought from Paris, the
Condessa Barral, the emperor and empress, government officials serving as witnesses and a nervous and profusely sweating Gaston. Isabel's fears regarding
the birth proved prophetic — the baby's position prevented delivery and what
should have been a routine procedure became life threatening.[31]

Isabel endured thirty-six hours of exhausting but fruitless labor. At one
point the hot melting wax of the emperor's candle scalded her, causing a moan-
ing, "Daddy, you're burning me!"[32] Later the emperor was injured when the
Condessa Barral spilled hot boiling water on him rushing into the room. Following a full day and night of labor everyone was tense from exhaustion and
fear. Still the baby did not come. Dr. DePaul finally resorted to forceps to save

Isabel and the infant. The baby arrived in the early hours of the morning — but was born apparently dead. Dr. DePaul's midwife attempted forcing air into its mouth and lungs, submerged the baby in cold water, and finally placed a feather in its tiny nose. Moments passed until the tickling feather was pushed away with the scream of life.[33] Tears shouts and prayers of the royal family joined the screams of Brazil's new prince. As a precaution he was immediately baptized.

On October 15, 1875, the eleventh anniversary of her wedding day, the baby of Isabel's dreams arrived. Dr. DePaul later wrote, "Nothing was more affecting than seeing the emotion, affection and concern of the Conde d'Eu. They are truly a close and loving couple."[34] The long-awaited birth was a cause of celebrations by supporters of the monarchy. Pealing church bells, booming cannons and dazzling fireworks announced the event. Isabel's son was given the title of the Prince of Grand Pará in compliance with the Brazilian constitution.

Newspapers, telegraphs, diplomatic dispatches and letters soon gave details of the birth. The U.S. minister to Brazil wrote to the secretary of state, "I have the honor to inform you that her Highness the Princess Imperial has safely delivered of a son and heir. Labor was severe and dangerous necessitating the use of surgical instruments and it was reported at first that the Prince had been injured to such an extent that one of his arms was useless; but I am very glad to say that Professor DePaul the Parisian physician in attendance informs me that both the Princess and her son are doing very well indeed and far better than he had ventured to hope for."[35]

Amidst his joyful report the minister added a cautious political observation. "There has been an illumination of three days; and the usual Masses and Te Deums. While everyone is rejoiced at the good success of the Princess who I believe is universally loved for her personal character, there are those whose fears alloy their pleasure, seeing in this another opportunity for the church to web its bonds on the people by contriving the birth of a Prince as a reward from Heaven for the release of the Bishops; a measure the Princess is believed to have had much at heart."[36]

Queen Victoria, President Grant, Emperor Franz Joseph of Austria, King Luís and Queen Maria Pia of Portugal and other heads of state sent happy congratulations. Hundreds of letters and telegrams poured in from well wishers. Gaston, remembering the daughter he and Isabel lost, wrote his former teacher, "I would have preferred a girl, but am very happy with a boy."[37] After returning to her own home Isabel wrote her parents. "I have to tell you that we are very happy with our little child. For so long it seemed to me just a dream. Now I believe it is a beautiful reality."[38]

In his annual year end report the United States minister to Brazil summarized the activities of the Brazilian royal family as 1875 drew to a close:

> The birthday of H.M. the Emperor was this year a special fete for not only did he on the 2nd of December complete his fiftieth year but on the same day took place the baptism of H.R.H. the Prince of Grand Pará and the opening of the greatest

National Exhibition of Brazil.... The ... Bishop Chief Chaplain ... administered with holy oils H.R.H. the Most Serene Senor Dom Pedro de Alcântara Luís Felipe Maria Gaston Miguel Gabriel Raphael Bragança Prince of Grand Pará born the fifteenth of October of this present year at four o'clock and fifty minutes in the morning. The Godfather was His Imperial Majesty the Senhor Dom Pedro II and the Godmother Her Imperial Majesty the Senora Dona Theresa Christina Maria.[39]

The United States minister also wrote, "On the evening of the fifth a ball was given by the Conde d'Eu and on the thirteenth a reception was held by their Highnesses the Conde d'Eu and the Imperial Princess, with an illumination of the city and a ball.... these [events] made up the festivities incident to the baptism."[40] Isabel and Gaston then returned to Petrópolis hopeful they would find relief from the harsh criticism and the glare of the nation's press. As new parents, the royal couple yearned for peace and time to enjoy their new child. They would have neither.

32

"Great and Good Friend"

After passage of the Rio Branco Law, the release of the imprisoned bishops and the safe birth of the princess imperial's son, a brief period of calm settled over Brazil. Once more using the health of the empress as an excuse, Pedro II seized the opportunity to travel abroad. Isabel would again serve as regent for the year and a half he and Theresa would be gone. Pedro instructed Isabel to "send me only the telegrams indispensable to the conduct of affairs."[1]

The length of his trip displayed a confidence in his daughter and Brazil's political system that stood in stark contrast to the strained relationships other monarchs had with their heirs. Never during their long reigns did England's Queen Victoria or Austria's Emperor Franz Joseph allow their designated heirs to serve as regents for a single day. Poldie's brother-in-law Ferdinand, the future tsar of Bulgaria, bitterly noted, "The majority of crown princes were tired out by waiting when they ascended the throne."[2] Pedro was determined such a fate not befall Isabel.

Pedro's extended itinerary included trips to the United States, Europe and Africa, but unlike most royals he traveled as a private citizen, paying his own expenses.[3] No formal state visits were planned and no part of the trip would be charged to the nation. His 1876 excursion coincided with the one hundredth anniversary celebration of the United States' declaration of independence. England's Prince of Wales was expected to be the centennial's most important foreign visitor; but when he declined the invitation, Brazil's emperor became the exposition's great media event. Coffee had become increasingly popular in the United States, and the press quickly lionized the leader of America's own coffee producing neighbor while castigating Europe's tea drinking prince.[4] The trip was good for Brazil's booming coffee industry, whose growers only complaint continued to be a shortage of laborers.

Immigration was essential to Brazil if it hoped to end slavery in the next generation, but by 1876 it had actually declined. England, Germany and Italy banned citizens from moving to Brazil because of the harsh experiences of earlier settlers.[5] Following his tour of the United States, Pedro planned to visit each of those countries, hoping his trip might ease restrictive immigration policies

170

and facilitate additional foreign loans. His confidence in Princess Isabel's sovereign ability allowed him time to visit not only those nations, but others that satisfied his intellectual curiosity.[6]

Despite its reliance on slavery and being a hereditary monarchy in a continent of republics, Brazil was viewed favorably by the United States. In diplomatic circles the emperor and princess imperial were viewed as strict constitutionalists personally friendly toward abolition. Compared to their neighbors, the huge nation they ruled seemed an island of stability in a continent wracked by revolutions and "military" dictatorships.

The American minister wrote at the time, "The condition of things in Brazil is infinitely better than in certain other Republics in South America where the Supreme Government is subject to constant change, and in fear of being overturned at any moment by a mob instigated and led by adventurers who are not even military except in name. That is the condition in Mexico and Colombia, in Central America, Bolivia, Venezuela, in Ecuador and Peru and lately in Montevideo and even Buenos Aires."[7]

Brazil wanted to use the Philadelphia Centennial Exhibition to promote its best image to the world. Gaston, president of Brazil's own recent National Exposition, chose all the exhibits sent to the United States with one exception. Pedro II selected the gems and stones representing his country's enormous mineral wealth from the great national collection begun by his mother. Princess Isabel donated two gifts for Brazil's pavilion. The first was an embroidered pair of Brazilian silk and lace pillowcases she herself had sewn. Delicate needlework at the time was popularly admired as an example of how ladies of high social standing, including royalty, made productive use of their leisure time. England's exhibition included several embroidered creations by Queen Victoria. To represent its rich agricultural products Isabel also created a large rainbow pattern of foodstuffs using the widest assortment of Brazil's grains, cereals, and other farm products. She had learned about Brazilian agriculture as a child and used that knowledge to publicize her nation's rich farming potential. Both of Isabel's creations were awarded Centennial Exhibition medals.[8]

It was a crucial time for Brazil to present itself well. The nation was suffering its worst economic depression since independence while struggling under huge budget deficits from the Paraguayan war. The country longed for peace. After granting amnesty to the bishops, Prime Minister Caxias reverted to the role expected of him, a transitional caretaker. In the twilight of his career, he had no intention of taking his country in new directions.[9]

Even with the country's economic crisis Princess Isabel approached her second regency with confidence. Prior to their travels the emperor and empress vacationed with Isabel and Gaston north of Petrópolis in Nova Friburg, a town founded by German immigrants with the support of Empress Leopoldina. The royal family did not discuss politics or any government business on their holiday. Pedro II had faith his daughter would know what to do when the time came.

Due to an outbreak of yellow fever in Rio de Janeiro, Pedro asked diplomats to remain in Petrópolis rather than see him off in the capital. Isabel, however, insisted on accompanying her parents to their launch at the city's waterfront. Even the fear of the epidemic did not prevent a large crowd from gathering to wish them a safe journey. After a long tearful embrace her parents departed and the princess imperial returned to the São Cristóvão Palace, where she would live during their absence. When they stepped ashore in New York City in April 1876, Pedro II and Theresa Christina became the first emperor and empress to ever visit the United States.[10] The visit created a sensation among the nation's newspapers.

Pedro II was impressed with the size and energy of the city, but its newspapers showed another side of the great republic. Banner headlines and articles reported race riots in the American heartland and of a black man being murdered for attempting to vote in Indiana. *The New York Times* carried a front-page story titled "The Lost Cause Not Dead," quoting a North Carolina Memorial Day speaker who insisted the south was "vanquished but not cowed." Ten years after the civil war he continued proclaiming slavery "a divine institution."[11] Newspapers also reported on the growing women's suffrage movement.[12] Susan B. Anthony, Elizabeth Cady Stanton, Lucretia Mott and their supporters were attending their ninth annual National Suffrage Convention at New York City's Masonic Hall. One speaker declared, "The men of this nation are political monarchs, with their wives, their sisters, and their daughters as subjects.... Women of this nation have greater cause for discontent, rebellion, and revolution than our fathers of 1776."[13]

At that very moment the twenty-nine-year-old daughter of Brazil's own constitutional monarch was leading a nation larger in size than the United States. Pedro II kept his political opinions about women's suffrage and other social and political issues to himself. As he traveled across the country his letters to Isabel instead focused on the buffaloes and Indians he saw on the Great Plains and on how poorly San Francisco's bay compared to Rio de Janeiro's. His observations might have been those of any foreign tourist in the late nineteenth century. But privately he was shocked at the racial segregation he found everywhere and the lack of people of color in positions of authority. Brazil's respected Prime Minister Caxias and Minister of Finance Cotegipe were both products of the nation's blended racial heritage. It disturbed him that a nation that nearly destroyed itself ending slavery was doing so little to foster racial harmony.[14]

While Pedro II was visiting the United States a North American visitor to Brazil found that country equally amazing. He wrote, "There is black blood everywhere stirred in compounded over and over again like an apothecary's preparation. African blood runs freely through the marble halls, as well as in the lowest gutters, and the Indian blood swells the general current. There is no distinction between white and black, or any intermediate colors, which can act as a bar to social intercourse or political achievement."[15]

Throughout his travels Pedro continued refusing to answer political questions, referring all inquiries to the Constitutional Emperor and Perpetual Defender in Brazil—meaning her Serene Highness, Princess Regent Isabel. Pedro's grand tour became a public relations triumph for himself and his country. In the nation that gave birth to the republican form of government, a San Francisco newspaperman wrote the royal visitor had "given respectability to the trade of kings."[16]

At a reception for the Diplomatic Corps, Isabel proudly acknowledged the prestige her father was bringing to Brazil. Their personal and political partnership was unique in the corridors of monarchial power, where rivalries and ambitions often poisoned family relationships. Back in the United States Pedro II and Theresa visited the White House. On May 10, 1876, as the private guests of President and Mrs. Grant, they officially opened the United States Centennial Exposition in Philadelphia.

The opening ceremonies reached a spectacular climax when the president and his two Brazilian guests pulled levers starting the huge rotating wheels of the Corliss Engine, a gargantuan machine created to showcase the industrial age in which they lived.[17] Thirteen acres of ear shattering machinery joined the cheering crowds to announce to the world the great celebration had begun. Informed of the great number of revolutions per minute the massive Corliss Engine produced, Pedro dryly responded that that many revolutions per minute even "beats our South American Republics."[18] His joke was repeated endlessly across the United States; but its pointed humor effectively contrasted the stability of Brazil's constitutional monarchy to its chaotic neighbors.

The Fourth of July, 1876, found Brazil's most famous private tourist back in Philadelphia with President Grant to celebrate the actual birthday of American independence. In the midst of the carefully orchestrated speeches, patriotic hymns, and rousing marches, Susan B. Anthony, the country's most famous suffragette, made an unscheduled appearance on the speakers' rostrum. To the surprise of the president, the emperor, and watching crowds she took the occasion to announce a new declaration of independence for American women. After her short speech she scattered copies of her proclamation to the crowd before being forcefully escorted from the stage.[19]

The day of Susan B. Anthony's declaration Princess Isabel, acting as Brazil's head of state, sent a telegram to President Grant. In it she officially congratulated the American president and his nation on "the occasion of the centenary of the Independence of those States, for whose prosperity she offers sincere prayers." Grant's response reflected the warm feelings existing between the two nations. It read, "Great and Good Friend: I received by telegram the congratulations which your Imperial Highness was pleased to address to me on the occasion of the centennial anniversary of the Independence of the United States. The good wishes which you kindly offer for our continued prosperity are cordially reciprocated.... I pray God to have your Imperial Highness in His safe and holy keeping. Your good friend, U. S. Grant.[20]

That same week Princess Isabel wrote her parents, encouraging them to include France on their travel itinerary. During their earlier European travels Gaston's homeland had been devastated in the Franco-Prussian War. Now five years later Paris was once again the "center of the world in science, literature and art." She urged them to visit the city she had come to love.[21]

Pedro surprised the homesick empress by announcing the inclusion of the French capital on their list of must-see cities. The travel-hungry emperor was confident his daughter would handle any emergencies in his absence. Princess Isabel's enemies were delighted at the news.

33

"The Best Virtues of Having Power"

Princess Isabel, like the emperor and prime minister, hoped her regency would remain peaceful and uneventful. Others wished the exact opposite. Enemies of the constitutional monarchy viewed Isabel's regency as an opportunity to advance their own political agenda through division and polarization. Their poisonous tactics had become a major concern of Isabel's father.

After over thirty tumultuous years in power, the common ground Pedro II depended on continued to be chipped away. Called to the throne when he was only five, he had shouldered the full responsibilities of governing Brazil since he was fourteen. During his thirty-year reign eleven different men had been presidents of the United States, most serving a single four-year term. Only one, Ulysses S. Grant, held power for a full eight years; but he was not considered an effective president. Three of Grant's predecessors died in office, one by assassination and two through illness. A fourth was impeached. A fifth died from exhaustion months after leaving the presidency. Brazil's Latin American neighbors disposed of even more leaders during that time span, few of them peacefully.

Despite the emperor's solid accomplishments, slavery remained. Pedro II hoped the Law of the Free Womb would give his nation's agricultural interests time to prepare for emancipation, but most refused to consider life without slavery. The country was in an economic malaise. The wealthiest, most influential Brazilians stubbornly clung to the past, refusing to invest in areas not directly related to agriculture. Diplomats feared the nation seemed adrift.[1]

Brazil's slaves began to stir. It had been years since the nation's last major slave revolt but its slaves continued resisting bondage sometimes passively, other times actively. Rumors of emancipation encouraged hope among slaves and fear among slaveholders.[2] A newspaper in Rio de Janeiro reported, "All planters and their families dread attacks at any moment. In view of the attitude of the slaves, their existence and personal security run great risk."[3] Such headlines did little to reassure nervous slavocrats.

175

During Isabel's first regency, Rio Branco firmly held the reins of government at the peak of his political skills. But Prime Minister Caxias, elderly and in poor health, was determined more than ever to avoid controversy. The pacific nature of the princess and the caretaker desires of the prime minister tempted political adventurers to look for a crisis to turn to their advantage. The Baron of Cotegipe explained the challenge of the government's position:

> After H[is] M[ajesty] left ... and the Princess Imperial became Regent, the ministry's position became more delicate, if not precisely difficult. It had to maintain peace abroad and political order at home, and to this end it could not provoke or respond to controversies; it did not embark on reforms which would excite passions, even less could it appear to abuse the credulity or experience of the Regent.
> The scruple was the more significant because of the powers of governance entrusted to the Regent, whereas in every other constitutional monarchy they are limited during the incapacity of the ruler. So that no one will construe my words against my intent it is my duty to declare that H[er] H[ighness] was in the conduct of her constitutional duties what Queen Victoria is said to be in England.[4]

Complicating Princess Isabel's position was that shortly after assuming the regency she discovered she was again pregnant. That September she suffered another miscarriage, leaving her physically drained and emotionally vulnerable.[5] The men in her life were unable or unwilling to offer support. Pedro II had no intention of returning home or allowing Empress Theresa to do so without him, and Gaston was afflicted with "his usual ailments; liver, dizzy spells in his head, some fever at times, dyspepsia."[6]

The health of Isabel's husband kept him away from public responsibilities but did not prevent him from traveling to avoid them. Immediately after Isabel's miscarriage, he took a two-week vacation alone.[7] He wrote his former teacher, "This nervous state is aggravated by any kind of stress and cannot be otherwise at this moment due to the excess of worry that the Emperor's absence causes."[8]

At the time she most needed her husband and father, Princess Isabel was forced to draw on her own resources. She wrote Gaston, who was in Minas Gerais, "I must complain to you, my poor darling, about the drudgery of these evenings. During more than an hour I have done nothing but open and dispose of letters, papers and dispatch boxes.... I have still not had time to read even one line in the newspapers or to be present at darling Baby's supper! I hear him now talking and tapping in his bedroom."[9] Isabel's sense of duty offered her no respite or rest while her husband and father both managed to care for themselves.

Isabel had to depend on her own judgment and learn to trust it. Her daily letters to her father were usually filled with personal rather than political content. In part she was protecting him from political burdens, but she also discovered she enjoyed exercising some royal prerogatives. One letter included the following comments: "I pardoned six accused criminals and commuted two death sentences. It is one of the best virtues of having power. I would like to push forward the development projects in the country, railroads, colonization, etc. etc., but the cart is very heavy and I don't know whether I will have the strength to help in the way that I wish. God grant it!"[10] Although Isabel remained self-effacing without personal or political ambitions, she began to have her own vision and ambitions for Brazil.

As the length and pace of his trip accelerated Pedro wrote Isabel less and less. His lack of correspondence troubled her. Isabel wrote him, "Why don't you write to me anymore? Believe me that I spent a good part of last night meditating on this and I tell you, even in tears, thinking that perhaps Papa may be angry with me."[11] Even as she became more independent and able to think for herself in her public role, she continued seeking her father's attention and approval as his daughter.

Isabel understood her father more as an emperor than as a parent. Pedro II refused to share power with almost anyone, the exception being Isabel, whose devotion and loyalty were unquestioned. Politically he was secure knowing she understood his thinking, and had the strength to see that it prevailed in his absence. Still, as she became more of her own public person, his letters decreased. He had always been emotionally distant, and become more so the longer his daughter ruled in his place.

As regent Isabel initially exercised her constitutional duties by carefully following her father's daily and weekly schedules. Most days were spent reading and responding to government correspondence as well as making public appearances, chairing meetings, and listening to petitioners. Shortly after returning to Rio de Janeiro from Minas Gerais, Gaston reported to the Condessa Barral a drastic change in that schedule: "We have completely given up visits to public establishments, lectures, and institutes that depress us so much. We experience sufficient pain and suffering from diplomatic receptions, audiences for the poor and other nuisances in the household that never end."[12] The withdrawal from public duties clearly met the emotional needs of Isabel's husband, but not his more extroverted wife. It also deprived the princess imperial of opportunities to cultivate political and public support she would need in the future.

Limiting public appearances did not remove Isabel from her responsibilities as regent. Petitions from the nation's rich agricultural basin in the northeast soon alerted her to impending disaster there. A spreading drought threatened the region and the country's already strained economy. Even with large numbers of slaves, there were not enough laborers to save damaged crops. Food prices were rising and agricultural exports sharply in decline. Living conditions, especially for recent immigrants, were deteriorating. The earlier collapse of Brazil's largest investment firm made money for loans scarce and private charity nearly impossible to secure.[13]

Princess Isabel encouraged the government to provide immediate assistance but her requests were firmly but respectfully rebuffed by Minister of Finance Cotegipe. Described as "an angel with gown and sword to guard the national treasury," the strict fiscal conservative refused to make additional expenditures at a time the government struggled with huge deficits.[14] The fear and desperation of petitioners failed to move Cotegipe to loosen government purse strings.

He told Isabel local funds allocated for relief had already been spent and emergency supplementary funds exhausted. When Isabel persisted in her requests, she was reminded that local authorities, not the national government, had the constitutional responsibility to maintain their economic affairs. Any deviation from policies of the past, Cotegipe assured her, set dangerous precedents.[15] Isabel resorted to organizing charity concerts and auctions to raise money for drought victims. The Princess of Joinville in Paris, the queen mother in Portugal, and the Viscount of Rio Branco in Brazil all worked to raise funds. Donations arrived from Argentina, Bolivia, Portugal and Italy. Even Gaston, never known for his generosity, made a personal donation as did thousands of private citizens.[16] Charity provided "the mainstay of relief operations" but the enormity of the crisis quickly exhausted such efforts.[17]

Months passed with no rainfall in northeastern Brazil. Daily petitions told of desperate water shortages and fears of starvation. Cotegipe insisted most stories were manufactured by alarmists and political enemies trying to embarrass the government. His suspicions focused on local officials he labeled corrupt, but who were also known to be his longtime political opponents. Politics aside, he assured the princess regent without firm government data, he had no choice but to dismiss the reports as unsubstantiated rumors.[18]

Princess Isabel continued pressing for action, basing her position on the legal principle that "public relief was guaranteed to every Brazilian citizen by the constitution of 1824."[19] Isabel's arguments finally prevailed. Cotegipe's ministry agreed to send food and water to the northeast but only if all aid was centralized and distributed exclusively from Rio de Janeiro.[20] Delays were inevitable, but he believed necessary in order to safeguard government funds from being mismanaged or stolen.

Princess Isabel's frustration was compounded by the realization that some of the worst effects of the drought might have been prevented if planters had invested in modern farming technology rather than contining their dependence on Brazil's rich soil and slaves. Now planters, slaves, and newly arrived immigrants all faced disaster. It became increasingly clear to her that the politics and solutions of the past did not always work. Local governments, even supplemented by private charity, could not solve such a monumental crisis. Using the full powers of the regency she pressured banks to provide low interest loans for struggling farmers while continuing to press private charities to provide additional relief.[21] She also accepted a proposal from the Auxiliary Society for National Industry for "a twelve point program for the development of industry and manufacturing that included 'fair protection by means of a custom tariff.'" Although her father strongly opposed tariffs, Isabel did not. After the tariff bill passed the General Assembly, she signed it into law.[22] Such efforts raised the eyebrows of traditional money interests but were praised by Brazil's small but growing manufacturing industries and even by Pernambuco's Agricultural Society.[23]

Foreign developments also demanded Isabel's time. Leaders in Argentina and Uruguay masked their own political and economic problems by falsely portraying Brazil as a military threat. The United States minister to Brazil noted, "Those menaces are used for electioneering purposes because it has been found to be a popular thing to threaten to put an end to alleged Brazilian influence.... Here in Brazil there is no desire for any war. The people have learned that even a successful war would be a disaster financially for the empire."[24] Princess Isabel, Caxias and Cotegipe worked together to lessen international tensions. After prolonged and sometime intense negotiations, peace was maintained.

During Isabel's second regency the country scheduled a national election, the long delayed peace treaty with Paraguay was finalized and Brazilian diplomats negotiated a financial settlement between the United States and England over war damages dating back to the American Civil War.

Critics of the constitutional monarchy continued to remain active. Abolitionists denounced Isabel for not doing more to advance the cause of emancipation, and Republicans condemned Isabel's French husband for his imagined influence on the regent and her government. As a political party, Republicans remained officially neutral on the issue of slavery. Still one of Isabel's fiercest critics was a Republican abolitionist who singled her out as a favorite target for his propaganda.[25]

Despite his party's silence on the issue José Patrocínio became known as the John the Baptist of the abolition movement for his early crusade against slavery.[26] Patrocínio was a brilliant journalist and charismatic orator who delighted in regularly attacking Princess Isabel in writings and speeches. In a long epic poem published in 1876 he used the literary style of Brazil's most popular poet, Castro Alves, to cast Isabel's regency as the logical descendant of the ill fated monarchy of Marie Antoinette.[27]

One of the guiding principles Princess Isabel had learned from her father was to ignore critics. She was determined nothing would deter her from leading the nation on a moderate path. The success of Isabel's regency infuriated enemies of the constitutional monarchy who continued looking for an issue to turn against her. They soon found one.

34

"The Politics of Horror"

Pope Pius IX took the opportunity of Isabel's second regency to send an envoy to Brazil to negotiate a final settlement of the Masonic crisis. The United States minister reported,

> We have news ... from Rome, that Monsignor Roncetti will be sent here as Internuncio, for the purpose of arranging the still unsettled "ecclesiastical question" by insisting on the exclusion of the Masonic order from the religious brotherhoods; and with intention, also, of making a Concordant upon this and other points involved in that question. This announcement has aroused the press and the political pamphleteers; and a series of articles have been published by Counselor Saldana Marina speaking in very plain language, and declaring that if during this [the Princess's] Regency the present government yield at all to the pretensions and exactions of the Roman Curia, the Brazilian people will know how to resist any such surrender of their liberties and sovereignty, and will themselves do the work that is necessary to remedy the evil already done and prevent in future all priestly influence, through females, for the subverting of the Constitution. In short, it is plainly said, and by men who mean what they say — that any repetition of what has been done in this matter, and any sign of further yielding will be met by revolution.[1]

The words left little doubt about the raw nerve the religious question still engendered. The announcement and the reaction it provoked provided Isabel's enemies the wedge issue they sought. Critics quickly used the pope's decision to cast suspicions on Isabel's loyalty. References to the "evil already done" and the need to "prevent ... all priestly influence, through females, for the subverting to the constitution" were aimed directly at her imagined role in granting the imprisoned bishops amnesty.[2]

The United States minister placed responsibility for rising tensions squarely on the shoulders of the Masonic brotherhoods for attempting to gain a political advantage through the issue. He wrote, "The [Catholic] Ultramontane party has been very quiet and awaits the negotiations by Monsignor Roncetti, the new Papal Internuncio who has not yet been formally received by the Regent. The anti-ecclesiastical party, on the contrary, has been very active and even noisy. Inflammatory articles have appeared.... There are so many elements of discontent just now, in the depressed condition of trade, in the yearly deficits in receipts in the imperial treasury, as well as in each of the provinces and in the wide spread want of confidence in financial matters, that this ministry must exercise the greatest caution and forbearance."[3]

Princess Isabel refused to receive the papal envoy formally or informally, but her actions failed to dampen rising emotions. Opportunists seemed determined to provoke a crisis. As the bishop of Rio de Janeiro prepared to preach his Sunday sermon he was attacked in his own cathedral by rock-throwing demonstrators. In the pandemonium that followed, bishop and congregation were driven from the church and a riot ensued. The United States minister reported,

> So very unusual an outrage, in a country like this especially was of course the theme of conversation everywhere, and of newspaper comment. By the Ultramontanes it was declared to be proof of the impious wickedness and designs of the radical and atheistical Republicans....[4]
> By the ultra-liberals it was declared to be "a trick of the Jesuits" gotten up by them to bring discredit on the liberal cause. The police are still said to be investigating the matter but the probability is that we shall never know the truth. Either party is capable of either committing or getting up the affair which is another proof of the condition of this question and the temper and feeling on either side.[5]

Scheduled national elections were held and the pro–Masonic Conservatives were heavily returned to office. Electioneering violence and charges of voter fraud seemed near the same levels as when Pedro II resided in the country. But with the emperor away, Isabel became the target of dissenters.[6] In Rio's annual Carnival the colorful masks, music, dances, and parades heavily satirized the religious parties. One of the floats mockingly portrayed the emperor as Isabel's puppet. Feelings ran so high against the Church that police had to be called to protect priests after partygoers attacked them with garbage and rotting vegetables.[7]

Princess Isabel continued to refuse to meet with the papal envoy, but when a popular native born priest was made a bishop she visited his residence to offer personal congratulations. The widely respected clergyman was a religious moderate known for avoiding all things political, but that did not prevent Isabel's enemies from using the event to their advantage. The visit became front-page news in Rio de Janeiro's newspapers. The private call between the princess regent and the newly appointed bishop was portrayed as a state visit during which the regent secretly pledged political and religious allegiance to the Vatican. News stories elaborated in great detail descriptions of a solid gold cross inlaid with emeralds and other precious stones Isabel supposedly presented to the prelate sealing the clandestine accord. In a further bid to inflame public opinion the articles reported that the costly gift had been purchased with state funds.

Isabel was stung with embarrassment. The controversy sold many newspapers, but the princess regent remained silent. During her brief stop at the small parish rectory no gift had been given, no pledge made, but the story was kept alive for weeks. Gaston wrote his father, "The Princess is accused everyday of sacrificing the national dignity at the expense of religious sentiments. This even though she avoids the subject at all times and in all conversations and only goes to mass on Sundays. She doesn't even have a chaplain or court confessor yet she is accused of being under his influence. It is terrible that these rantings seem to be almost unanimous. There doesn't seem to be a public journal that doesn't give illustrations of these terrible insults or repeat these abuses and lies. It seems that few people if any defend us. This anti-religious propaganda escalates and infects all classes of society. This is very worrisome and a terrible thing to endure."[8]

Press accounts further inflamed public opinion by reporting Isabel was ignoring telegrams and instructions from the emperor. The stories caused such an intense reaction Prime Minister Caxias issued an unprecedented public denial. He asserted the princess regent had never undertaken policies or made decisions without consultations with her ministers. After his unusually strong statement the controversy died down.[9]

In the midst of the political storm Princess Isabel realized she was once again pregnant. To avoid another miscarriage doctors ordered complete bed rest and Isabel retired to her home to await the birth.[10] Gaston was relieved the pregnancy allowed them to escape what he referred to as "the politics of horror."[11] He gloomily wrote his father, "As far as us, we only stay to render service to God and are grateful to have survived this duty without worse injuries. The only really difficult problems had to do with the hatred stirred up again by the religious question."[12]

Isabel herself was more hopeful. She wrote at the time, "I am never prone to view things entirely in black. It may be a good or bad habit, but it is never the less a fortunate one for me, and it will always be a part of me."[13] As her second regency drew to a close she could review it with a sense of accomplishment. At her insistence the government had finally accepted responsibility to offer help to local communities when natural disasters struck.[14] Despite the continuing drought, relief efforts were working better than at any time since the crisis had begun. Tensions with Brazil's neighboring countries had decreased, and diplomatic and economic treaties with the United States and European nations had been successfully concluded. A protective tariff had passed and the empire's economy was beginning to show improvement. Brazil was in the strongest position it had been in years to negotiate foreign loans and resolve its immigration problems.

The United States minister in his annual report to the State Department concluded, "It may be said that the past year had been to Brazil one of uninterrupted peace. The credit of the Empire, in the money markets of the world, has been surprisingly good; the demand for Brazil's staples has been constant; and the competition among foreign nations for her trade has been keen and well sustained, and the outward signs for the nation's prosperity and good standing have been uniformly favorable."[15]

Princess Isabel understood and respected the public life her husband detested. More then her beloved Gaston ever could, Isabel began to recognize the positives her position offered. Her knowledge and understanding of the constitution had forced Baron Cotegipe to bend the state bureaucracy to her will. She had learned to make her position "bear fruit" politically, but also recognized the power her public role afforded her to soothe, comfort, and elevate those in need sometimes by nothing more than a mere smile, a small act, or a carefully chosen gesture.[16]

The "politics of horror" were real; yet the very religious faith her enemies attacked provided her a private sanctuary and comforting perspective. Her public life was challenging, in many ways frustrating and difficult, but it afforded her in her own words opportunities "to do good as cannot be found in any other situation." Isabel took the words to heart. By the end of her second regency they had become the private creed she would use to guide the rest of her public life.[17]

35

"A Cordial Democracy"

The first night the emperor and empress returned to Brazil they stayed at the Isabel Palace, where the bedridden princess, her husband, and their child were living. Many interpreted the gesture as a way of showing public support for the princess regent. Others saw it as a dramatic example of the changing power relationship between the princess imperial and the emperor. The reality was more complicated.

Pedro II met the following day with his ministers and immersed himself in reading government reports and documents. What he did not do when visiting Isabel was discuss her year and a half regency with her. Gaston wrote his father, "He has never spoken with either of us, Isabel and I, either before or after the regency about politics or affairs of State. We don't complain, because we hold politics in horror. But it is all the same odd that he is not informed as to what happened on specific matters during his absence."[1] Gaston as usual assumed to speak for his wife. The Conde and Condessa of d'Eu, as they preferred to be called, shared a distaste for politics. But to Gaston his public responsibilities were a sacrifice and a burden. Isabel, however, had grown to appreciate the positive opportunities her position afforded. That recognition appealed to the very core of her deepening religious faith.

After twice serving as regent, she better understood what motivated her painfully shy and weary father to continue holding power after so many years on the throne. His love for Brazil and his commitment to constitutional government gave him the strength to carry his burden on. More than once he admitted if the choice were his alone, he would have preferred the life of a teacher to that of an emperor. But Isabel's empathy for her father was one sided. Pedro loved his daughter, but never gained an insight into her thinking or personal sacrifices. Despite her struggles to conceive and safely deliver a child he could never understand her desire to select her own doctor. Isabel's insistence on having the French gynecologist who saved the life of her first child, deliver her second, infuriated him. He refused to even discuss the matter with her.[2]

Although Isabel prevailed in choosing her doctor, it was not because her father appreciated or understood her needs or fears. That he was never able to do. Even after depending on her abilities during two regencies, he was unable to privately admit his gratitude. His sense of entitlement as a male, as a father or perhaps as the emperor always asserted itself. Throughout his life he was unable to be beholden to anyone, including the one person he trusted above all others—his daughter.[3] Still a few days after returning to Brazil, he issued an unusual public statement. "I want it to be known that throughout my entire journey of eighteen months I did not send to H.H., the Regent or to any of the ministers a single telegram on the country's affairs."[4] It was a remarkable admission. Not only had he placed the nation's welfare completely in the hands of the princess regent and prime minister, but at no time during his year and a half abroad did he feel the need to advise or supervise his heir. The statement was a stinging rebuke to critics who claimed Isabel ignored his telegrammed directives.

Gaston in his usual pessimistic manner missed the remarkable confidence implied by the statement. He and the opposition press interpreted the emperor's statement as an attempt "to distance him self from everything that was done." The point missed was that Isabel's regency had been a remarkable success.[5] The emperor embraced all of Isabel's decisions, including, much to the consternation of Minister of Finance Cotegipe, relief efforts to the drought stricken northeast. Describing the spreading drought as a "massive disaster," Pedro pressed the government for even more involvement in the crisis—not less.[6]

As he had done with Isabel, Cotegipe reported no government funds available to "succor" the devastated areas.[7] The emperor firmly rejected his arguments. Rumors circulated that he had instructed the crown jewels be sold if no other funds could be found. Cotegipe soon reversed his opposition. Like the earlier amnesty controversy, Isabel received no credit for her correct thinking on a difficult political issue. But the emperor's behavior caused some to grumble that his daughter had become the real power behind the throne. Pedro would have laughed at the suggestion; but throughout his reign his actions always conveyed more than his words. Increasingly it was becoming difficult to know where the emperor's thinking ended and the princess imperial's began.

Isabel's direct political influence was debatable. But her regencies demonstrated an uncommon ability to rule, a talent for untraditional problem solving, and a resiliency to survive the "politics of horror." For centuries such qualities had been nearly synonymous with her Bragança ancestors. Isabel's regencies provided her a vision of leadership, and a sense of how to make that vision a reality. The question many asked was whether she would have the opportunity to exercise that leadership as empress.

A North American visitor, observing the reactionary response triggered by Isabel's latest regency, wrote that her opponents saw her as a genuine threat to the status quo. Pedro II was slowing down, but his energetic heir seemed more than ready to put his idealistic thinking into political action. That realization caused some to whisper a revolution might be necessary to prevent

Isabel from succeeding to the throne. The same observer wrote, "If they play this game they must be prompt in their operations for should that young lady once get established there, her enemies will regret their temerity or delay."[8]

Opponents of Princess Isabel seized upon her preference for a "foreign" doctor over Brazil's best physicians as one more opportunity to undermine her popularity. Ignoring her medical history, they portrayed her choice as a personal affront to Brazil. Their attacks continued even a month past her due date and another life threatening delivery. Although Isabel's "foreign" doctor once again saved her life and the life of her child, her complicated breech birth was dismissed as a non-event. The real story according to critics was that the princess imperial placed her confidence in a French rather than Brazilian doctor. A relieved Gaston wrote his family, "Without the help and energy of Dr. DePaul our new son would have died. For the second time we experienced birth problems and dread that this would ever happen again."[9] Reluctantly he and Isabel decided they would risk no more pregnancies.

Gaston had prayed for a girl to replace the daughter they had lost four years earlier, intending to name her Marie Amélia Luísa Victorie Marguerite in honor of his grandmother, aunt, mother, and sister.[10] Instead the prince was christened Dom Luís-Felipe Pedro de Alcântara Gaston Miguel Rafael Gonzaga de Orleans e Bragança. Gaston's father and sister served as godparents.

The following May the royal family were driven through the streets of Rio de Janeiro for the opening of parliament. The imperial coaches, many dating back to the celebrations welcoming Empress Theresa to Brazil, had grown old and faded. Pedro had long ceased trying to impress anyone through the golden trappings of monarchy. Despite earning a salary five times greater that the president of the United States, his charitable gifts kept the emperor of Brazil in almost genteel poverty.

Riding before the emperor and empress were Isabel and Gaston in their official capacity as princess imperial and royal consort. Except for the matched diamonds accenting her blond hair, Isabel dressed in simple elegance; but Gaston was resplendent in his full military uniform.[11] During his annual speech from the throne Pedro II thanked Isabel for her successful regency, publicly verbalizing as emperor what he found impossible to say as a father. His actions, more than his words, spoke volumes. The princess imperial and her husband were included in all public events, ceremonies, and celebrations as personal extensions of himself and his monarchy.[12] At official state functions they sat on thrones directly by his side. No other monarch on earth displayed such a unique solidarity with his or her heir.

Still, Princess Isabel's position was a delicate one. Her husband's abhorrence of the public spotlight made her role even more challenging. But Isabel had learned from her father the power of actions in signaling her thoughts and feelings, especially in social situations. The delicate health of the empress allowed Isabel to serve as hostess at the few regular social events sponsored by the monarchy. On one such occasion André Rebouças, the young Afro-Brazilian civil engineer and war veteran, was abandoned on the dance floor as a musical quadrille began to play. White female dancers scattered or seized the arms of white partners dancing away from him. Princess Isabel quickly crossed the ballroom and asked Rebouças to dance.[13] By the next quadrille everyone had a partner regardless of race, color, or social position. Princess Isabel's dance became the talk of Rio de Janeiro. Like her father, she understood the power of actions over words.

Isabel's home in a fashionable Rio de Janeiro neighborhood became a symbol for the kind of diverse society she and Gaston hoped to foster in Brazil. Like the butterflies and large hummingbirds attracted to her colorful gardens, it became filled with gifted Brazilians regardless of social background or skin color. As the future empress, Isabel used the prestige and status of her social gatherings to model an equalitarian society representing the best her nation had to offer. Such actions earned her few friends among those judging others by family origins, social standing, or race, but it gave others a new respect and appreciation for the monarchy.

Despite his initial republican political leanings, André Rebouças became a frequent visitor and recorded a typical evening in his diary. "After being invited earlier by the Conde, we arrived at the Isabel Palace in the evening. One hundred people were invited and everyone listened and danced to the orchestra music the entire night. At eight o'clock sharp the Emperor and Empress arrived. The Emperor conversed with me about my current projects and promised that he would visit them soon. I then danced three cotillions.... The party continued until 1:00 A.M."[14] He also described the atmosphere he found there. "Simplicity is the law in the rooms of the Condessa d'Eu's home.... There the spine and soul will not suffer the tortures of uncomfortable furniture or ponderous bores. In the frank and expansive physiognomies of the Conde d'Eu and his wife (dressed modestly and unpretentiously) shine a cordial democracy. One can comfortably be entertained in pleasure, as if in the rooms of a fine and well educated bourgeois."[15]

Socially conscious traditionalists were disturbed by the modern thinking of the princess imperial and her prince consort. One story in a popular publication reported, "The future Empress of Brazil and her noble husband, Prince Luís Felipe Marie Ferdinand Gaston d'Eu, are conveyed in full dress and glittering uniform, from their palatial residence in the suburbs to the Imperial Theatre of Dom Pedro Segundo, on occasions of the Italian opera, in one of [the open air public] streetcars."[16]

Princess Isabel represented to many a future where the roles and status of what had gone before offered no guarantee for the future. It seemed a strange contradiction coming from the heir of a hereditary monarch. Those relying on the past to frame the future began looking for clues to her private thinking in the protégés she promoted. Few men were more scrutinized than André

Rebouças, who became Brazil's leading engineer. In 1877 his pronouncement that the ongoing drought crisis presented the nation "a magnificent opportunity to display the power of modern engineering" raised more than a few eyebrows. Rebouças's suggestion that a series of national forums be held to discuss how best to deal with the crisis was quickly embraced.[17]

The Conde d'Eu moderated three days of meetings on the drought at the Polytechnic Institute where Rebouças taught, and former prime minister Rio Branco presided over a similar meeting at the Society for Aid to National Industry.[18] Their final reports concluded much of the natural disaster in the north was man made, caused in part by the ongoing destruction of the rain forest and over-planting by plantation owners. Participants put forth a radical national reform agenda, sending shock waves through the traditionalist establishment. Suggestions were made that the government pass legal restrictions on lumbering the rain forests and use the military to distribute massive relief efforts. They also advocated reforesting large tracts of land to stop additional erosion and the creation of massive public works projects such as reservoirs to deal with future droughts.[19] Modernizing the methods of raising livestock, improving the construction of wells, drainage, irrigation and transportation infrastructure were also proposed. The reports concluded that the "blind following of traditional practice ... [was] ... the bane of all Brazilian agriculture" and must be actively fought with "foresight, perseverance and good sense."[20]

The proposals were greeted with chilled hostility. Rebouças's vision of government, military and science working together to improve the nation's general welfare was not the future imagined by most of the country's power holders. Brazil's planter aristocracy reacted by calling their own forums, not to discuss soil conservation or ecological disaster but to forestall emancipation and combat the rising expectations of slaves. "Agricultural" congresses called for new laws to control, intimidate and punish slaves. One proposal mandated up to fifteen years in prison — the first five years in solitary confinement — if a slave violently resisted the orders of an overseer or master.[21] The harshness of the proposed laws created an angry backlash.

André Rebouças was not the only professor stirring Brazil's political cauldron. Jeronymo Sodré, a young medical professor from the north, set off a "political explosion" by publicly stating what others only whispered: "Everyone knows it. Brazilian society is sitting on a volcano. Let us not delude ourselves."[22] His solution to the fears of slave violence was immediate emancipation. He demanded any government agenda not immediately addressing slavery be discarded until abolition become a reality. "You are asking for educational reforms? You are asking the government to guarantee the rights of non–Catholics? You are asking for liberation of the citizen through direct elections? You want all these things while conserving the cancer that deteriorates all and corrupts all!"[23]

His outburst catapulted slavery to the forefront of the nation's political agenda. It would not be eclipsed until the emancipation question was resolved.[24] A new generation of political leaders enlisted in the abolitionist crusade, but Princess Isabel was not among them. Forbidden by the constitution from involvement in political debates, she decided to travel to Europe to seek medical attention for her oldest son, whose arm and hand had been damaged during birth.

European specialists tried many treatments including electro-shock therapy, but none proved successful. Still, Isabel remained grateful for both her sons and mindful of the daughter she had lost. She and Gaston made a special pilgrimage to the Catholic shrine of Lourdes, leaving behind an engraved marble plaque with the intertwined Bragança and Orleans coat of arms. Included on it were three dates: 28 July 1874, 15 October 1875, and 26 January 1878. The first was the day their daughter had been born, baptized, and died; the others marked the birthdays of their sons.[25]

Isabel had not forgotten her promise to build a church at Caxambú if she and Gaston were blessed with a child. As debates on slavery shook Brazil, she busied herself in Europe working on architectural plans for a mountain church to be built in Minas Gerais, dedicated to her ancestor Saint Elisabeth of Hungary. With her thoughts and energy distracted from the growing slavery crisis she experienced a sense of freedom she had never known at home. Once they were in Europe, as long as his participation was not required, Gaston encouraged Isabel to engage in the social activities he detested. While he traveled, she was left with time for her music, to be with her sons and other family and friends and run the household as she wished in his absence.[26]

During their time in Europe Isabel discovered she was once again pregnant, her sixth risky pregnancy in seven years.[27] Since two sons had been born in Brazil, with the permission of the emperor, the prime minister, and government, she and Gaston were allowed to extend their stay and deliver the baby in Paris. The Brazilian press loudly protested despite assurances the Princess Imperial would follow all established protocol including the mandated presence at the birth of Brazil's ambassador and diplomatic corps. Isabel's Aunt Francesca and the Condessa Barral joined her to wait for the delivery. Early on the warm morning of August 7th, 1879, diplomats and family were called to Princess Isabel's bedroom in the Paris home of her father-in-law. Dr. DePaul and the appointed witnesses waited thirty hours in the rising heat until Isabel's prolonged contractions were mercifully brought to an end by a caesarian operation. The result was the birth of a healthy prince.

The trauma of such a delivery might have killed a woman of less strength and courage. For someone as private and modest as Isabel the nightmarish events must have seemed unreal. She was so weak at the moment of birth she later recalled the cheers from the attending observers seemed from another world. A local parish priest baptized Brazil's newest prince Dom Antônio Gaston Felipe Francisco de Assisi Maria Gabriel Rafael Gonzaga de Orleans e

Bragança. His first name honored Gaston's mother Victorie Antoinette. Serving as godparents were Gaston's uncle, the Duke of Montpensier, and the
Princess of Joinville.

Isabel's recovery was slow and painful, and political dispatches from Brazil
did nothing to lift the princess's severe postnatal depression. Two of the monarchy's strongest supporters, former Prime Ministers Caxias and Rio Branco, died
months apart. Isabel must have joined others in wondering who would replace
such men in Brazil's withering political climate as the slavery crisis grew. Even
on his deathbed Rio Branco begged the emperor not to interfere with "the slave
problem."[28]

On December 10, 1881, Princess Isabel and her family returned home to a
nation astir with the abolition debates.[29] More than anything else, Isabel wanted
to devote herself to her young family. She had dreamed, prayed and sacrificed
her own health to give her children life, but the emancipation question confronted all Brazilians, including the princess imperial. As a woman, a wife, and
a mother Isabel longed for time with her family. Yet as heir to the throne, she
could not ignore the crisis threatening Brazil. Whatever role she would play
was clouded by an awkward reality. Princess Isabel was the highly visible heir
to the throne of a country where women were expected to be nearly invisible.

36

"The Place Which Is Rightfully Hers"

Just sixteen years earlier Pedro II had invited Harvard University's famous professor-scientist Louis Agassiz to do field research in Brazil. His assistant was his wife Elizabeth Cary Agassiz, a respected educator in her own right. The emperor then encouraged Agassiz to present a series of scientific lectures open to the public. When the series was announced, Mrs. Agassiz mentioned how much she looked forward to attending them. Her statement was met by stunned silence. She was respectfully informed, "Certainly no ladies would appear."[1]

Professor and Mrs. Agassiz insisted ladies be admitted. The event's organizer explained that only the emperor could approve such an unusual request. Agassiz sought an audience with Pedro, who explained he had no personal objection to women attending, but doubted any would understand or comprehend a scientific lecture. After much discussion a compromise was reached allowing females to appear if accompanied by a father, a husband, or a brother.[2]

When the lectures took place, a number of Brazilian ladies attended. An American observer noted, "The royal family were always present and partook in the highest degree of the general interest. Their eyes were never diverted from the lecturer or his blackboard. The expression on the face of Princess Isabel was intense. It is far from being pretty ... but if physiognomy tells anything it speaks of intelligence, energy and such firmness as can be dispensed with in conjugal relations, but is invaluable in affairs of state. It is Elizabethan!"[3]

The initial reaction of Isabel's own highly educated father indicated the mindset confronting Brazilian women. Hers was a patriarchal culture handed down for centuries as a birthright to males. Words, deeds and tradition taught Brazilian women they were inferior to men. Wives, daughters, and sisters deferred to males in much the same way slaves deferred to masters.[4] A "woman's captivity" was less severe in cities, but it was still a reality.[5] In the countryside, conditions were worse. A local school teacher described the "status of a free plantation woman" in 1873. "She still bears on her wrists the marks of chains; she has not yet taken the place which is rightfully hers as a powerful agent of social progress."[6]

191

No Brazilian woman was seen as a "powerful agent of social progress" more than the princess imperial. Her gender, deep Catholic faith, and imagined domination by her French husband were effectively used against her. But the real source of much suspicion and hostility against Isabel was the fear that she would embrace the future over the past. The strongest supporters of the reactionary Queen Carlota Joaquina had been staunch traditionalists. They overcame their gender bias, abhorrence of powerful women, prejudice against her Spanish background, and apprehension over her genuine religious zealotry because she represented a conservative alternative to her more forward-thinking husband. If Isabel had embraced the reactionary attitudes of her racist great-grandmother, many of her fiercest critics might have been her greatest supporters.

Princess Isabel never publicly uttered a feminist or pro-suffragist position, but her private correspondence revealed she supported many of their aspirations.[7] When her father traveled to Europe, she sharply rebuked him for meeting with the "pioneer feminist" George Sand, not because of Sand's radical political positions, but because she exhibited public behavior Isabel would have also condemned in a man. Isabel wrote him, "I am going to begin with a reprimand. Not even a short line for me, yet you find time to visit George Sand, a woman of much talent, it is true, but also so immoral! ... However much you try to preserve your incognito, everyone always knows who D. Pedro d'Alcântara is, and shouldn't he be above all else a good Catholic and keep away from anything that is immoral?"[8] As always she immediately apologized for speaking her mind, but not before making her point.

Isabel's father was a man of many contradictions, strongly attracted to relationships with independent, well-educated woman. One of the few royals with whom he became friends was the liberal Crown Princess Victoria of Germany, married to the like-minded Crown Prince Freidrich, heir to the German imperial throne. Victoria had been the princess royal of England and was Queen Victoria's first and favorite child. In 1872 she and Freidrich asked Pedro and Theresa to serve as godparents to their youngest and last-born child, Princess Margarete.[9]

For years the emperor jostled verbally and in writing with the Condessa Barral over politics, religion, and even abolition. Their disagreements never threatened or damaged their friendship and may at times have influenced his thinking. Four years prior to his own support of the Law of Free Birth, Barral began freeing the children born of her slaves.[10] Despite encouraging Isabel to surrender to her father and husband, the condessa regularly disagreed with Pedro II as an intellectual equal. Few subjects were off limits in their letters or conversations. To most Brazilian men such exchanges would have been unthinkable, but Pedro seemed to need and enjoy them. Still, he would have never tolerated such independence or dissent from his wife.[11] In his own household, the husband ruled. The thinking and needs of Theresa were not a consideration. After their daughters wed, despite repeated requests, she was never allowed to visit either of them without him in attendance.[12]

Pedro saw himself as ruler of his family and country. He clearly believed Brazil a family heritage and intended to pass the monarchy and government on to his daughter.[13] Yet he shared most of the same prejudices against females as his contemporaries. He trusted Isabel in areas where he would have trusted no one else, but never questioned his dominance over her.[14] She would rule Brazil, but he would rule her.[15]

Gaston, the other man in Princess Isabel's life, subscribed to similar gender prejudices. Following his nervous breakdown in Paraguay, his emotional fragility allowed her more independence than his patriarchal thinking would normally have tolerated. He recognized his wife's genuine goodness and appreciated that they lived well through her position but was emotionally unfit for public life. After Paraguay he depended more and more on her for emotional support.[16] Isabel loved Gaston, who gave her the structure, security, and sanctuary of family life, but as prince consort he was a political liability.

When they returned to Brazil in late 1881 Isabel maintained a low public profile, quietly lending her time and support to charities such as the Association for Neglected Children, and the Commission of Ladies for Public Education.[17] But she continued avoiding the weekly meetings of the Council of State that had degenerated into bitter diatribes against emancipation. Her father believed Brazilian politics poisoned by a "lack of patriotism and good judgment." He privately noted, "Politics in our country are more unpleasant to understand than ever before ... [hobbled by] rivalries and more rivalries."[18]

The anger and angst of traditionalists was further aggravated by the fact that Brazilian women were beginning to threaten male bastions in their patriarchal culture. The country's first woman doctor had recently returned from studies abroad, her education financed in part by the emperor himself.[19] An 1879 law allowed female students and faculty into the nation's colleges and universities. Prior to that time the institutions of higher education had been reserved for and controlled exclusively by males.[20] For the first time in Brazil's history, newspapers and magazines written, published, and edited by women were also appearing.[21] Princess Isabel and Pedro II both subscribed to *The Feminine Sex*, a self described journal dedicated to "the education, instruction, and emancipation of women."[22]

The abolitionist movement Cotegipe and his conservative supporters fought so hard to stop had become a two headed monster, energizing and attracting women into politics. More and more Brazilian women from all races and classes became politicized as they fought alongside men to free the nation's slaves. Well dressed gentlemen *and* ladies could be found in packed theatres and lecture halls listening to speakers, dramatic readings, and musical presentations on emancipation. Within a short time mixed-gender abolitionist clubs appeared. Unescorted women were seen at the entrances to lecture halls, cemeteries, and churches taking up collections and selling flowers and handicrafts to purchase the freedom of slaves.[23] They soon took to the platforms themselves.

Princess Isabel was not among them. When not working with her public charities she spent time with her sons or retreated to her music and gardens of Petrópolis. She also took up the study of photography and visited her parents when they were available. Every day she could be seen driving her carriage to the train depot to pick up the current newspapers and journals but was never heard to publicly comment on what she read.

As an anniversary gift to Isabel, Gaston brought a magnificent four-story greenhouse from France that became known as the Crystal Palace, to use for horticultural shows in Petrópolis.[24] Within its striking glass walls Isabel showcased year-round orchids and perennially blooming flowers enclosing a large open space reserved for entertaining. There she and Gaston began hosting biweekly evening soirees for friends, diplomats, artists, and Brazilians from business, finance, the arts and Isabel's charities. Politicians were notable by their absence.[25] At night, surrounded by music and flowers, candled chandeliers reflecting on its glass walls created a dreamlike sanctuary that was shattered when Isabel quietly stepped into the growing emancipation debate.

The princess imperial announced she would sponsor a charity flower show. The event had no trouble attracting publicity, participants, or controversy. Gardening and charity events were appropriate outlets for women of a certain social class. But when it was announced monies raised would be used to purchase the freedom of slaves, slavocrats accused Isabel of involving herself in politics. Defenders pointed out that the event was a private affair. The princess had always been known for her love of flowers, and the government itself had set up the emancipation fund to buy and free slaves. Still, critics protested it gave the appearance that Isabel was taking sides on the issue. The controversy was soon dubbed the war of the flowers.[26]

It was becoming increasingly difficult for any Brazilian, including the royal family, to remain completely neutral in the political storm shaking Brazil. Pedro II tried, but his attempts seemed to please no one. Even his friend Joaquim Nabuco, president of the Brazilian Society against Slavery, condemned him, accusing the emperor of being "strictly accountable for the existence of slavery, illegal and criminal." He pointed out, "After a reign of almost half a century, Brazil squandered more than 600,000 contos [330 million dollars] in a politically disastrous war but ... spent only 9,000 contos [five million dollars] to liberate her slaves."[27]

Despite a personal abhorrence of slavery and rising attacks, Pedro II maintained his constitutional duty to remain impartial on the politically explosive issue. He ordered his government to ignore the abolitionist conflict unless laws were broken, angering pro-monarchy abolitionists like Joaquim Nabuco, anti-monarchial Republicans like José Patrocínio, and all of the powerful proslavery forces and their allies.[28] Slavocrats condemned Pedro II for not using the full power of the government to smash the anti-slavery crusade. Isabel's charity flower show, the emperor's private donations to purchase the freedom of slaves, and his practice of granting titles of nobility to slaveholders emancipating slaves infuriated them. Many believed the hidden hands of the emperor and princess imperial were manipulating the emancipation crusade.

By 1884 the political dynamics of the nation, slavery, and the monarchy shifted dramatically. In the drought-plagued northeast, plantations, towns, and entire tracts of land had begun to be abandoned. The social fabric of the provinces was unraveling in the very regions where Baron Cotegipe denied a crisis existed. So few people remained in some areas that local governments threatened to pass laws outlawing transporting slaves out of the depopulated provinces. Slaveholders rushed to sell slaves to the coffee growing regions of the south, but public demonstrations stopped them. Men and women ran to the docks shouting, "No more slaves will leave the port of Ceará." Black raftsmen and sailors refused to transport slaves to waiting ships. Survivors of a decade of natural disasters refused to allow one more soul to leave the province. Frightened politicians passed laws to legally enforce what the people had mandated. The northern provinces of Ceará and Amazonas became the first in Brazil to legally ban slavery.[29] The abolition fears of Baron Cotegipe and his political allies were coming to pass, caused in part by their own reactionary policies.

The country's previous two prime ministers had been conservative allies of Baron Cotegipe, but both failed to stem the rising tide of abolition. Recognizing the shift in public opinion, Pedro II selected the Liberal Party leader Manuel Pinto de Souza Dantas to serve as prime minister. Slavocrats reacted with anger and hostility to the appointment.[30] Gaston wrote his father he feared the monarchy would not survive the coming abolitionist struggle. Princess Isabel disagreed. Privately she had come to believe slavery, not the constitutional monarchy, was doomed. Only the monarchy had the prestige, power and popular support to peacefully bring about emancipation. Most Brazilians continued supporting the monarchy. Its major opponent, the Republican Party, was small, disorganized and deeply split over the slavery question.

Prime Minister Dantas announced he would present to the General Assembly legislation mandating freeing all slaves over sixty years of age, a tax increase to purchase the freedom of additional slaves, and the granting of immediate emancipation to any slave not properly registered with the government. Many legislators found something in the proposal to support, but few endorsed the entire package. Fearing any concession a threat to their way of life, supporters of slavery brought the government to a standstill.[31] A Dantas supporter angrily predicted, "Every battle on the slave issue that the liberals lose in the political arena, every reverse that you inflict by crushing with your votes the Cabinet that personified this proposed enactment, shall constitute no advantage whatever to the vested interests concerned but rather a step toward unconditional emancipation."[32]

The stalemate dragged on for months. Elected representatives insulted, harangued and verbally attacked each other, but the emancipation legislation was never brought to a vote. A letter in the newspaper *O Paíz* declared, "Rejection of the Dantas project would be a calamity.... Fortunately, until now abolitionist propaganda has been maintained on legal terrain with extreme moderation."[33] Still, threats of physical violence hung over the debates, stiffening the resolve of both sides. The General Assembly adjourned without passing any part of the proposed law, making the upcoming elections a national referendum on abolition. The campaign promised to be angrier than the legislative session.

As 1884 drew to a close and elections loomed, Princess Isabel took a giant step back into the public spotlight. Civic leaders in São Paulo asked the princess imperial to visit the historic site where her grandfather had declared Brazilian independence. They wanted her to review the plans for a great monument to be built there. Isabel's tour was presented as non-political in nature, but in reality had a strong political agenda. The trip would provide her an opportunity to measure the public's attitudes toward emancipation, calm heated passions, and rally supporters of the monarchy. The itinerary was extended again and again until the trip was to last five months through four of the nation's southernmost provinces. The primary destination, however, remained São Paulo, Brazil's second largest city, birthplace of its Republican Party, and a stronghold of support for slavery.[34]

If the monarchy were to guide the ship of state successfully through the approaching struggle, Princess Isabel would be needed. Even the reclusive Gaston believed times demanded they "get away from this Petrópolis routine."[35] Not since Isabel's second regency would she assume so high a public profile.

Gaston and her children would accompany her, but the princess imperial would be the focus of the journey. Isabel understood the importance of the tour for herself and the monarchy. She would be traveling into an area José Patrocínio labeled a "fortress of heinous slavism" just as the emancipation question was being debated in the national election. Passions would be running high. Every step she took would be carefully watched, but Isabel had no intension of stumbling.

37

"Walking Toward an Abyss"

Princess Isabel's schedule was carefully planned allowing her to see and be seen while touring regions and industries forming the backbone of the national economy. Many of the individuals and groups visited were important allies of the monarchy, friends who would be needed in the difficult times ahead.

The excursion began early on the morning of November 5, 1884. Isabel and her family left Rio de Janeiro by train, traveling until mid-afternoon. Smoke and coal from the engine burned their eyes, hair and clothing, making for an exhausting, uncomfortable ride.[1] Like a modern whistle stop campaign tour, frequent stops slowed their journey. Speeches were given, flowers accepted, and extended sojourns made to the homes of important monarchist such as the Viscount Moreira Lima, who arranged a two-hour meal followed by a concert and reception. Friendly crowds greeted the princess imperial as she toured local churches, landmarks and factories. Gardens and parks farms and plantations were showcased. Isabel arrived in São Paulo late in the evening. Despite a pounding rainstorm the largest crowd of the day welcomed them. The princess imperial managed to squeeze in a number of public receptions before going to bed well after midnight.[2]

Isabel's private diary of the journey revealed her critical eye and ear for detail. Her notations critiqued architecture, music performances, the productivity of farms, the cleanliness of hospitals, the pedagogical methods of schools and more. She especially noted the size, friendliness and composition of crowds. In the midst of her busy itinerary, Isabel set aside time to be with her children. After the grueling first day of her tour, the next morning she returned to the role she most enjoyed — mother to her three sons. She was up early to take them fishing.[3]

By noon, Brazil's princess imperial returned to her public appearances, visiting publishing houses, markets, factories, warehouses and the city's new Grand Hotel. She also toured the city hall, the provincial assembly, and other public buildings, climbing to the roof and balconies of each to view the cityscape. Wherever she traveled reporters from the local and national press followed her every step.

On a visit to the university she observed students taking part of their oral exams, confiding in her diary, "What an examination. Oh my God and there was more for them to take?! I worried that they might not pass, but when it was over they seemed confident and relaxed. I myself have passed even worse exams, but more than ever I am disappointed in such an exam system. After that I assisted in giving the exam to several other boys ... another disillusion. I was told this was one of the better-furnished schoolrooms and that they are better equipped than they have been in the past!" She added, "All of this was followed by my own examinations by the reporters following me everywhere always outside every door we entered, hovering and waiting. They have been here more than anywhere. They can't wait to ambush me at every turn."[4] Isabel jokingly asked one her hosts if there was a secret way out of their building. But she admitted, "There is no avoiding them."[5]

Isabel took time to write her impressions of São Paulo to her father. "This is a great city, with a magnificent location, well proportioned and positioned to become even greater. There are some beautiful buildings here, but in general, no distinctive architecture and unfortunately no master plan for growth."[6] She ended her letter, "We have seen many people that we know and who know you. They always ask about my good parents and embrace us with great affection. Everyone is in good health here. This letter is for both of you. Your daughter who loves you. Isabel."[7]

If it was possible, the frenetic pace of Isabel's schedule intensified. The ninth of November she wrote,

> Mass at the convent nearest the house.... Visited the new hospital of Santa Casa de Misericórdia with Pedro and Luís. Very modern and new. It has nursing sisters for one hundred and fifty patients with plans to expand. It is built along the lines of a modern hospital. Very beautiful. The Sisters of St. Joseph are the nurses. Everything was very clean and neat. The sisters have taken in many poor girls who work for their room and board. They were also taken in at the old convent. As soon as they saw us they ... serenaded us with songs and gifts of flowers....[8]
> Visited the church of the House of God. This was an ugly somber church.... Then Pedro and Luís and I visited the Museum of Colonel Sertorio (a local republican). He wasn't there because he was away on business. His excuses are very original! ... visited the Episcopal seminary with nearly 200 boys. Due to the high enrollment it was very crowded and we were packed tight. The boys were preparing to celebrate the anniversary of the founder of the school and were very happy....[9]
> The last visit was to a big park which was very beautiful.... Then after dinner, visits as usual. We went to the theatre of San José and saw the students from local schools and clubs perform.... It was very good. They represented themselves and their city well. We left after two acts and a lecture with warm welcomes and much applause. We were very tired and our legs ached.[10]

Despite the long day of events and late evening, the next morning Isabel and her entire family attended a special mass at 7:00 A.M. marking the twenty-eighth anniversary of the death of Gaston's mother, Antônio's namesake Princess Victorie Antoinette of Saxe-Coburg. Then the public part of the day began by touring steel mills and schools, both of them a disappointment. She noted that the cost of manufacturing Brazilian steel was three times higher than imports from Europe and that the mills were undercapitalized and handicapped by inadequate transportation. The co-educational schools Isabel visited lacked books and were staffed by a number of ineffective teachers. She and her father continued disagreeing on the need for a protective tariff, but both agreed on the necessity of improved roads and schools.[11]

Isabel continued her hectic tour, filling her days with visits to mines and manufacturing plants, schools and colleges, churches and hospitals, sugar and textile mills, city halls, fish hatcheries and coffee plantations. She carefully noted which foreign nations had invested in which industries, and the efficiency, safety, cleanliness, productivity and profitability of each commercial venture visited.

Every stop elicited a brief observation. "Better than some but still not clean enough" was a succinct comment written between visits to a slaughterhouse and a large public luncheon. In another town she watched the installation of municipal gaslights. She noted, "Four hundred in place since 1875 but 10,000 needed. Just not enough money to go around."[12]

Her schedule was slowed but not stopped by rain clogging the roads and streets with thick nearly impassible mud. Even with weather delays, time was made for stops with local friends and supporters. Each visit was recorded with a brief comment such as "funny stories and good local food."[13] Whenever possible she found activities to enjoy alone with her children and husband.

One of the highpoints of Isabel's tour was a stop at a city hall where the emperor had purchased the freedom of fourteen local slaves in 1846, the year of her birth. The event was still celebrated thirty-eight years later with a public display prominently featuring his signed letters of freedom. Princess Isabel was asked to pass out the latest fourteen letters of freedom paid for by the National Emancipation Fund. She wrote her father, "The slave holders seemed more happy than the freed themselves."[14] The date of the ceremony held special significance for her. It was November 15th, the name day of her grandmother Leopoldina and the anniversary of her own baptism and entrance into public life.

Princess Isabel also visited the home of Dona Veridiana da Silva Prado, matriarch of the most prominent political family in southern Brazil. Over the past two centuries the Prado family had risen to the pinnacle of Brazilian society, investing first in sugar, then in slaves, and eventually in banking. They had been strong friends and supporters of José Bonifácio and Pedro I. The night Isabel's grandfather declared Brazilian independence, he slept as a guest in the Prado home.[15]

Next to Isabel herself, Veridiana may have been Brazil's most controversial woman. She had once been the traditional "chief slave of the home," producing children and spending her days "embroidering, arranging flowers, and playing music." Following her arranged marriage at thirteen to an older uncle she delivered seven children in the first eight years of marriage.[16] Her last son was twenty years younger than her first. Unlike most Brazilian girls Veridiana was taught as a child by an exceptional teacher who provided her the same education he gave to her brothers.[17] As a mother she insisted on regularly checking her children's lessons. By doing so, she serendipitously continued her education.

Veridiana separated from her husband in 1877 after insisting their daughter be allowed to choose her own marriage partner.[18] Divorce was not an option, but from that day forward they lived independent lives. Such an arrangement was scandalous in 19th century Brazil. She kept the family home, purchased property under her own name, and in time became the publisher of a popular monarchist newspaper. Her independence was duplicated in her family. One of her sons championed the monarchy; another was one of the few Republicans elected to the nation's General Assembly.[19]

Prado turned her home into a social and intellectual center for Brazilians from all races and backgrounds.[20] Many resented a woman who "fought with her husband, traveled alone, raised her children as she wanted, brought artists into her home, and had no fear of the tongues that cut her life to pieces." Traditionalists saw her as "the germ of the bourgeoisie's dissolution, a scratch on the Christian face of the sacred family."[21] She was the one woman Princess Isabel made a point of publicly visiting during her busy tour. Although different in many ways, they shared many of the same values — and enemies. Following her visit Isabel wrote, "I left there enchanted."[22]

On November 23, 1884, the princess and her family visited the site where the great Independence Day monument was to be built. The hillside, five kilometers from the center of São Paulo, was to be crowned with a magnificent museum. The elevated location and the striking Italian architectural design promised to transform the surrounding area. The plans were a source of great regional and national pride. Isabel was pleased that the monument would be the center of an improved transportation system for the city. The site was to be connected by wide boulevards and roads, providing both an economic stimulus and esthetic focal point for the entire region.

A local politician told Isabel he could hear the footsteps of those who once stood there and glimpse their ghostly figures. Locals believed the spirits of her grandfather and his comrades lingered on the hillside. Year later the site became the final resting place for the remains of Emperor Pedro I and Empress Leopoldina.[23] To Isabel the location connected her with Brazil's past, present, and future. She took long deep breaths and surveyed the surrounding countryside. Her statement that the monument was worthy of a great people and a great nation pleased her hosts and the applauding crowds. Princess Isabel reported the visit in great detail to her parents before returning to a frenzied travel schedule that would have depleted most, but seemed to invigorate her.

The trip was considered a success for the monarchy and a personal triumph for Isabel. She enjoyed meeting people in ways her husband and equally introverted father-in-law could never understand. In the guarded language she had learned to use with the men in her life, she wrote the Duke of Nemours, "As you know, it cost me a lot to leave my dear parents, my tranquil home, several friends whom I left in Rio, and my dear music, but I am very pleased to have decided to come. I am at the present happy with everything I have seen, and the warm receptions given to us everywhere."[24]

By the time Isabel returned to Rio de Janeiro, the contrast between her friendly reception in the south and the heated political rhetoric in the capital was disconcerting. For the first time in his reign Pedro was publicly denounced in the General Assembly as "the conspirator prince," his reign labeled as "forty years of lies and betrayals."[25] Parliamentary elections had increased passions and hardened viewpoints. Following the seating of the new legislators, the Dantas ministry lost a key confidence vote, forcing him to resign as prime minister to be replaced by José Saraiva, a highly respected moderate within his own party. Prior to submitting his own emancipation law, Saraiva freed his seventy slaves then proposed a complicated, but watered-down version of the Dantas legislation, managing to confuse both supporters and opponents of abolition.

Through the use of convoluted language, innumerable loopholes and confusing amendments, he hobbled together a coalition of legislators who agreed in principle to vote for a bill none of them completely understood. Saraiva's political maneuverings and seeming willingness to compromise allowed each side to believe it had triumphed over the other.[26] After presenting his proposed bill, he abruptly resigned, throwing the debates and his own political party into turmoil.[27]

The stunned Liberal Party was unable to form a new ministry. After gaining agreement from the Conservatives to support Saraiva's legislation, Pedro asked its leader, Isabel's old nemesis Baron Cotegipe, to form a new government. The *Rio News* wrote, "When we see a genuine abolition measure originating from Baron Cotegipe we shall believe that an omelet can be made from bad eggs."[28] Cotegipe immediately went to work to further weaken the legislation. He pushed back the proposed emancipation of slaves from sixty to sixty-five years of age, provided slaveholders more legal control over existing slaves, and expanded their powers to capture and punish fugitive slaves.[29] In its details and fine points, the Saraiva-Cotegipe Law provided slaveholders the additional legal rights and protections they had sought after passage of the Law of the Free Womb. It cynically gave slaves their freedom at the close of their life when they were least able to care for themselves or their families.

Abolitionist reacted with anger, bitter resignation, and despair. José Patrocínio denounced the law as a complete "capitulation to the slavocrats."[30] Joaquim Nabuco wrote it signaled the "eclipse of abolitionism." And a leading anti-slavery newspaper sadly editorialized, "Abolitionism Is Dead."[31] Still even proslavery forces understood the emotional issue would not disappear. One of them publicly exclaimed, "We are walking toward an abyss. We do not have work hands and in the meantime the solution to a terrible problem presses upon us— the slavery question. It is the shadow of Banquo at the banquet of Macbeth."[32]

Racist slurs and rhetoric became a part of the political debates. A prominent senator responded to pleas from abolitionists by shouting, "I love the country more than the Negro," and an opponent of Joaquim Nabuco accused him of wishing "to sacrifice the population of the empire for a half dozen brutal and savage Africans."[33] Hecklers harassed José Patrocínio's speeches, screaming, "Shut up Negro!" But he evoked cheers by taunting back, "God gave me the color of Othello so that I would be the envy of my country."[34]

Princess Isabel was discouraged by her father's actions, the failure of the Liberals to curtail slavery, and the blind stubbornness of the Conservatives to cling to the past. With Baron Cotegipe as prime minister she feared the life of slavery could be indefinitely extended. She was not alone. A former envoy from the United States wrote he was confident Brazilian slavery would extend well into the next century.[35] Despite their setback, abolitionists fought on. Joaquim Nabuco won reelection as a Liberal abolitionist deputy to the General Assembly and used his column in the Republican newspaper *O Paíz* to rail against the abuses of slavery.

On July 29, 1886, he dedicated to Princess Isabel his column which told a story about a jury sentencing four slaves to three hundred lashes across their backs. Two of the four died as a result. Nabuco ended his column by linking the fate of the dead slaves to the living heir to the throne: "It must be sad for the Imperial Princess to have to read this news on her birthday, and I am profoundly sorry to have to publish it today. However, that picture will enable the future empress to recognize the condition of our slaves and to understand the mission of the abolitionists in her father's kingdom."[36]

The article caused an uproar. Senator Dantas demanded an investigation into what *O País* called "a disguised death penalty." Within weeks, the Chamber of Deputies and the Senate legally outlawed the whipping of slaves. The day prior to the vote, Nabuco acknowledged in parliament, "Our campaign, which began on the birthday of the Imperial Princess, will be finished tomorrow on the birthday of her son, with the approval of the law we demanded."[37] It was a surprising setback for Cotegipe's ministry.

Cotegipe received another blow from Queen Regent Christina Habsburg-Bourbon, the young widow of the Spanish King Alphonso XII, who signed a decree abolishing slavery in Cuba. Years of unrest, revolutions and slave uprisings there convinced Princess Isabel's cousin to end three centuries of Cuban slavery. The action of the queen regent politically isolated Brazil, making it the only country in North or South America still legally protecting slavery.[38] Brazilian slaves quickly learned of the events in Cuba, encouraging them to renew their struggle for freedom.

That year on her sixty-fourth birthday, Empress Theresa presented one hundred and seventy-six slaves their manumission papers purchased by funds privately raised by the Rio de Janeiro Municipal Council. The council then asked the princess imperial to serve as patron of their next emancipation drive, but Cotegipe's ministry flatly refused to allow it. They had had enough of royal women involving themselves in emancipation. Cotegipe announced that the Municipal Council had exceeded its elected mandate by involving itself in private fund raising. Isabel was told, "The cabinet does not recommend that Her Highness the Princess Imperial lend it the great prestige of her position and of her virtues. Rather it respectfully requests, for the good of the State's service, that in a question of this nature Her Imperial Highness maintains the neutrality that is in every respect required of individuals in exalted positions."[39]

The stinging rebuke effectively removed Isabel from the abolitionist struggle. What the Cotegipe ministry could not say to the emperor or empress, they said bluntly to Isabel. Gaston, always ready to escape public life, suggested the time right for an overseas holiday. On January 1887, with the emperor's approval and the blessings of the Cotegipe government, Isabel, Gaston and children sailed for Europe. One newspaper noted the size and enthusiasm of crowds sending them off. "Everyone tried to touch the princess's hand that someday is going to guide the empire." But a Republican newspaper mocked the Conde's "nervous pacing ... [his] red and sweating face," and even the blond hair of the royal children.[40] Enemies of the princess imperial celebrated Cotegipe's victory in removing her from the political scene. They could not imagine in a few short months she would be returning to fight Prime Minister Cotegipe for the heart, soul, and future of Brazil.

38

"The Unfathomable Designs of Providence"

After a short family visit in wintry Seville and Paris, Isabel, Gaston and their sons traveled south, seeking the warmth of the Mediterranean. Shortly after they arrived in Nice, they were awakened by an early morning earthquake. No one was injured, but less then two weeks later their lives were forever changed by a political earthquake.[1] A telegram arrived from Prime Minister Cotegipe informing them the emperor was seriously ill.

Several years earlier Isabel's father had been diagnosed with diabetes, but only recently had fatigue and sleeplessness begun to affect his lifestyle. Shortly after they departed for Europe, blinding headaches, high fevers and vomiting incapacitated him. Doctors were unable to diagnose the cause. Although he rallied several times, by April his ability to speak and his short-term memory had become impaired. Cotegipe called Princess Isabel back to Brazil as rumors swept the capital that the monarchy might not survive the death of the emperor.[2]

Isabel and her family rushed home assaulted by fears. The archconservative Cotegipe was no friend of Isabel's, but he was a staunch supporter of the monarchy. He had tried not to alarm her or the public, but it was clear he would not have recalled her unless the threat to Pedro and the monarchy was real.[3] Princess Isabel was not only concerned for her father but for also for her country and its constitutional government. She was convinced abolition, peaceful abolition, was essential but could only be accomplished under the monarchy. But emancipating the country's slaves would alienate the strongest supporters of the monarchy, those men who dominated the economic and political affairs of the nation.

She and her father both believed at some point in the future Brazil might become a republic; but a republican government could only succeed if it were built on the stability and legal foundations of a constitutional past. The reform, renewal and political realignment necessary to reach that point needed time. And time was what Isabel and the ill emperor seemed not to have. Princess Isabel was in a race not only for the life of the monarchy, but also for the future of Brazil. The choices facing her were daunting. If her father failed to recover, she might have only a small window of opportunity for the monarchy to preserve and strengthen Brazil's legal and economic foundations. But the only way to buy time for that option was to extend the life of slavery. The alternative was to swiftly and legally end slavery; but abolition would in all probability doom the constitutional monarchy before the nation was ready for republican self-rule. Time might run out for either option. Hanging over her was the painful realization of her father's failing health. Grief, fear, dread and uncertainty must have crowded Isabel's thoughts as she raced back to Brazil.

Once she arrived home Isabel was confronted with her father's deteriorating health. The *Rio Times* reported, "The unpleasant truth is that he is very much broken in body and spirit."[4] Pedro's doctors, the empress, and the Council of State all believed an extended rest in Europe might be the only hope of saving his life, but the emperor stubbornly refused to consider it.

Isabel understood her strong willed father better than anyone else understood him. With a careful eye on the political landscape and another on her father's ego, she excused herself from involvement in the debate. Gaston wrote, "We have refused and with reason to take the responsibility for this initiative."[5] Finally the emperor begrudgingly agreed to his doctor's orders, perhaps because travel still appealed to his weary soul. For the third time in sixteen years, the General Assembly appointed Isabel as regent. The emperor, the empress, and Poldie's oldest son, Pedro Augusto, departed Rio de Janeiro on June 30, 1887. Crowds of concerned Brazilians bid them farewell.[6]

That day the *Journal of Commerce* wrote, "The Emperor embodies the supreme direction of the destinies of the nation which cannot but feel itself profoundly disturbed by the uncertainties of the future. Put out of mind the speculations which hold the Emperor's health to be irretrievably lost: we find no justification for thus distressing the sovereign's spirit, discussing outcomes still in the unfathomable designs of Providence. Depart in peace our sovereign. God protect him and return him to us. All Brazilians unite their voices to that of the Church in a fervent prayer: 'Lord save the Emperor.'"[7] Their sentiments were not universally shared. A Republican journalist mockingly referred to the ship carrying Pedro to Europe as the "coffin of the monarchy."[8]

Isabel moved into the São Cristóvão Palace, writing her parents, "Our installation here is very convenient, and even the solitude ... [made happy by the children] is good especially during these first days."[9] One of the first challenges she confronted was cleaning and organizing her father's famously cluttered study. So much facing Isabel was beyond her immediate control that she might have found refuge in a task with a clear beginning, middle and end. She and Gaston sorted the chaotic collection of papers, letters diaries and correspondence her father had accumulated in his nearly a half century as emperor. The empress had always feared "the danger of the purloining of private correspondence now strewn in every corner."[10] Gaston wrote the Condessa Barral of their task and asked her "not to talk to the Emperor about these activities which might annoy him."[11]

Isabel's housecleaning must have caused her thoughts to race between the cluttered past and the uncertainty of the future. One way or another affairs had to be put in order. If the emperor was no longer able to finish all he had begun, she would do it for him. As she sorted through the messy mementos of a lifetime, her father's health, the difficult choices she would soon have to make, and the pressure of time must at times have seemed overwhelming. During her second regency Isabel had teasingly offered advice to her father about working with his ministers: "Don't judge yourself so infallible, show more confidence in them, and don't intervene so much in matters which are entirely within their mandate."[12] She ended her lecture by saying that if he followed her suggestions, he would have more time to spend with her! She then apologized for her boldness, but as usual, had made her point.

Now as Princess Regent, Isabel was once again dealing with her father's ministers, but with the added pressure and uncertainty of time. The Bragança's were not known for living long lives. Princess Isabel had already outlived both her brothers and her sister. Three of her first cousins in Portugal died young. The revolution in France that brought down Gaston's Orleans dynasty had been triggered in part by the accidental death of its popular young heir to the throne.

In Germany after the conservative ninety-one-year-old Emperor Wilhelm I died, his liberal son Crown Prince Friedrich finally came to the throne. Friedrich and his like-minded wife Vicky had waited for years to steer Germany away from its militaristic leanings. But after three months as emperor, throat cancer ended Friedrich's life and his reform agenda.[13] Wilhelm II, his reactionary son, embraced the policies of German Chancellor Bismarck, who believed the great issues of the day were settled by blood and iron, not by the will of the majority. Friedrich's brief reign took place entirely during Isabel's third regency — perhaps giving her own hopes for the future added urgency.

Time for Isabel was both a gift and an enemy. She had waited ten long years before delivering, then losing, her first child. Fifteen fearful months later, she held her own living child in her arms. The impatient princess had learned to be patient, to take nothing for granted. After rushing back to Brazil, she was beset by her father's uncertain health and political malaise. There was little she could do but wait. Tradition required Cotegipe's ministry hand in their resignations but also demanded she not accept them. The moment was not right, but she must have prayed it would come soon.

In 1887 Princess Isabel was forty-one years old, in many ways a dramatically different person than she had been in her previous regencies. She had traveled extensively, lived abroad and observed her nation from a foreign perspective most Brazilians could never imagine. Outwardly as she would do her entire life, Isabel remained the respectful wife and deferential daughter. She had learned to keep her own counsel, to trust herself with little if any encouragement from those closest to her. The Condessa Barral wrote, "I will not congratulate you on the regency you will have to exercise, but trusting in your good sense and your husband's good advice, I hope with God's help all goes well during this absence."[14]

Isabel's distaste for politics never left her, but like many of the royal women and men in her family she had the natural instincts of an astute politician. With her father's strength fading, she needed all the political skills she could muster to deal with the unfinished business of his reign — especially slavery. But unlike her father, who had her as his surrogate, she stood alone. Slavery remained the darkest stain on the Bragança family heritage. Yet once Isabel returned to Brazil, there was little she could do but play the Bragança waiting game. Her father had spent nearly his entire public life, almost half a century, waiting for the right moment to deal slavery a deathblow. That moment never seemed to come. Now she too waited.

Caution and timing had always been a hallmark of the Braganças. They had often rescued their fortunes and that of the nation they ruled by recognizing the exact moment to place themselves at the forefront of public opinion. More than once they had forestalled revolutions by leading them. It was a dangerous game. But in the unsettled political climate of late 19th century Brazil, Isabel had few other options. With the Conservative Party and its reactionary ministers firmly in control of the government, the growing abolition movement became increasingly radicalized. Gaston wrote the Condessa Barral Isabel's sessions with her ministers were "infrequent and short."[15] As regent she put as much distance between herself and her controversial prime minister as possible. In order to crush the rising abolitionist tide, Cotegipe needed the strong support of the crown. Isabel respectfully withheld it.

By July 1887, one month after she assumed the regency, cracks appeared in the foundations of the nation's social order.[16] An editorial in *O Paíz* predicted abolition to be only the first step to reforming Brazil from top to bottom. They called for a major realignment of the country's political parties in order to take the next natural step, a redistribution of the nation's land holdings, ending the nation's land monopoly, the *latifundia*, enjoyed for centuries by a small group of privileged planters. André Rebouças and others demanded Brazil be remade into a true rural democracy by breaking up the large estates owned by a few wealthy families and redistributing the land to the poor, former slaves and immigrants. It was not a new idea. Joaquim Nabuco and others had made similar proposals years earlier. But now, the momentum caused by the abolition movement gave people hopes for even wider reforms.

Planters accused the abolitionists of declaring class warfare and promoting "class hatred." They charged that anti-slavery forces sought the "destruction of the old order ... to build upon these ruins a new one."[17] Frustrated and angry abolitionists found themselves agreeing with the accusation. By September and October of 1887, growing numbers of slaves refused to work the land

and fled to Brazilian cities. Planters were stunned that some of their most trusted slaves were among the first to disappear.[18]

In Santos, trains carrying provincial police to capture runaway slaves were met by mobs of women who refused to let them disembark. Sympathetic railroad conductors began allowing escaped slaves free passage to cities where they could not be traced. And for the first time in Brazil's judiciary history individual courts and judges ruled in favor of lawyers who argued that "owners" had no legal rights to reclaim escaped slaves. Even some members of the conservative Catholic clergy began cautiously questioning slavery from the pulpit and in pastoral letters.[19] Public opinion and active and passive slave resistance made it difficult for local authorities to continue maintaining slavery. Still planters, and the Cotegipe ministry they controlled, refused to discuss emancipation.[20]

Five separate attempts over four years to set a gradual timetable for abolition had been defeated in the General Assembly.[21] Brazil's aristocratic planters and their elected representative clung to slavery, but abolitionists believed the tide of public opinion had turned in their favor. The *Gazeta da Tarde* prophesized, "Remember that our century has at times demonstrated that the power is not with the legislature, nor with the ministers, but with the people, who once in a while impress upon the pseudo-masters that slavery only persists while the slaves tolerate it."[22]

In October 1887 one hundred and fifty enslaved men, women and children armed with "firearms, knives, and machetes" fled a plantation near São Paulo. Police attempting to capture them were beaten in a pitched battle, stripped of their weapons, and forced to flee. The fugitives were "hunted like wild beast" and "shot without mercy."[23] Thirty of the escaped slaves reaching Santos were welcomed as heroes.[24] Just three years earlier Princess Isabel had granted letters of freedom to fourteen slaves in the area. Now hundreds were freeing themselves.

As the year drew to a close, outbreaks of bloodshed with fleeing slaves caused local authorities to plead for military help to restore order.[25] Joaquim Nabuco and other abolitionist leaders demanded the army not be used as "bloodhounds" to recapture Brazil's fleeing slaves. With civil obedience mounting, General Manuel Deodoro da Fonseca, a strong monarchist, abolitionist and veteran of the Paraguayan War, announced he would present an anti-slavery petition to Princess Isabel on behalf of a group of officers asking in the name of "humanity, Christian charity, and civilization" that the military not "be in charge of capturing poor Negroes fleeing slavery."[26]

The general at various times had been a protégé of the emperor, Gaston and Cotegipe, but had recently split with the prime minister over the politicization of the army. His petition allowed Deodoro da Fonseca to embarrass Cotegipe while tapping into abolitionist sentiment in the armed forces.[27] He was not the only former ally abandoning the embattled prime minister. In May, Antônio Prado, from São Paulo's powerful Prado family, resigned as minister of agriculture, declaring Cotegipe's defense of slavery undercut his efforts to increase European immigration. By September Prado publicly demanded the government stop using force to maintain slavery.[28]

Despite setbacks Cotegipe used his oratory skills, fear, and the power of incumbency to defeat opponents in upcoming elections. Enemies were accused of promoting a "propaganda of anarchy," threatening both the country's labor force and its economy.[29] Following a particularly violent riot during an election campaign he officially reported, "No harmless persons sabered," but Senator Dantas shared contradictory reports with Princess Isabel.[30] Widespread intimidation of voters could not save the General Assembly seat of one of Cotegipe's own cabinet ministers defeated by abolitionist firebrand Joaquim Nabuco.[31] A newspaper noted, "Though constantly defeated, Cotegipe never resigns."[32] Despite public humiliations and the loss of key supporters, Cotegipe maintained a voting majority in the General Assembly. Conservatives still saw him as their best hope in stopping the abolitionists.

Princess Isabel summoned the politically weakened prime minister to São Cristóvão Palace in an attempt to persuade her old enemy to alter his course. Pointing to the electoral defeats of several of his strongest allies, she warned him that unless he softened his opposition on abolition, his ministry could not survive.[33] Perhaps no other politician was in a better position to find common ground for the monarchy, the planters, and the abolitionists, but Cotegipe rebuffed Isabel's overture.

With public opposition against slavery continuing to grow, Isabel called Cotegipe to another meeting in early January 1888. At its conclusion Cotegipe wrote that he had never heard Isabel express herself so directly. She pointedly criticized his campaign against the abolitionists, especially in São Paulo, as ineffective and dangerous. Passive resistance and violence were rising. The princess regent informed the prime minister that she feared "the government was losing the respect of the people."[34] Gaston also attended the meeting and told Cotegipe he believed São Paulo's planters eager to find a solution to the crisis. He urged the prime minister to call a conference of planters, asking for their help in resolving the deteriorating situation.[35]

The uncharacteristic directness of the imperial couple prompted Cotegipe to be equally blunt. He reminded them it was his constitutional responsibility to execute Brazil's laws and their constitutional responsibility not to interfere. A verbal duel ensued as Isabel reminded him it was her constitutional duty to defend the nation. If Cotegipe's ministry was unable to find a peaceful resolution to the spreading violence, she assured him she would appoint someone who could.[36]

The heated exchange between regent and prime minister quickly became the talk of Rio de Janeiro. Princess Isabel's enemies focused their criticism on Gaston as the source of the widening split within the government. Not even Isabel's enemies could imagine her strong words were her own. One newspaper wrote, "Without doubt the Fatherland is threatened by future tyranny, by the loss of its dearest liberties; because the regime runs the risk of losing its liberty to a foreign prince, who was expelled from his own home- land, and now wants to plant the tree of oppression in ours— the Conde d'Eu."[37]

Cotegipe wrote of his meeting: "It seems to me that H[er] H[ighness] ... has been influenced, since never before has she spoken so clearly and emphat- ically. She has previously expressed a desire for some kind of action, but she has never before put in question the ministry's continuance as she did now."[38] As rumors of their disagreement reverberated throughout Brazil, Princess Isabel invited Cotegipe to be her guest at a Petrópolis charity concert raising funds for emancipation. As regent, Isabel publicly initiated a series of subscriptions and charity events dedicated to making Petrópolis a slave free city.[39] Cotegipe had forbidden the princess imperial from undertaking just such a sponsorship; but the uncomfortable prime minister had little choice but to accept the invi- tation of the princess regent.[40]

That same February Isabel's love of flowers revealed a glimpse into the direction her thinking was taking. She began wearing camelias, the flower of liberty, cultivated in the deepest parts of the Brazilian forests by runaway slaves. The flower had become the symbol for their aspirations for freedom.[41] Isabel continued raising funds to free Petrópolis's slaves by organizing an abolition- ist parade there. With her husband and three sons at her side she wore camelias to the event, igniting nearly hysterical denunciations from slavocrats and Republicans.

Antônio da Silva Jardim sarcastically mocked the "innocent" coincidence of the regent appearing in public wearing camelias. He angrily denounced Isabel for flaunting social conventions and public morals because Brazilian culture and tradition dictated well-bred Brazilian women not take positions on social or political issues.[42] To Jardim and other men of a certain mindset her behavior was not only scandalous, but threatening. José Patrocínio commented in his newspaper that everyone seemed to be talking about the latest battle in the war of the flowers.[43] André Rebouças noted in his diary it was the first unmistak- ably clear public manifestation of the abolitionist leanings of Isabel I.[44] Slaves also recognized the significance. Many began referring to the princess regent as a saint and their mother. Isabel's picture began appearing in their homes, often surrounded by camelias.[45]

At the very time Brazil's cities had become sanctuaries for runaway slaves and abolitionist disorder spread across the country, Isabel was aligning the monarchy with the emancipation movement. One prominent São Paulo planter wrote, "During the month of February we endured hours of bitterness and ter- ror ... witnessing the most complete disorganization of labor imaginable. The whole body of workers deserted the plantations, which were almost all aban- doned! I do not exaggerate when I say that 80 out of every 100 ... deserted."[46]

Cotegipe redoubled his efforts to gain control over the situation. Some feared the country was sliding toward civil war, revolution or worse.[47] Republican journalist José Patrocínio continued to focus his own vitriolic attacks on the monarchy for not curtailing Cotegipe's dictatorial powers.[48] Others began urging the government to prepare for the inevitable. Liberal Party leaders, including former Prime Minister Dantas and Senator Afonso Censo, proposed small farming communities be established along rivers and railroads to accommodate former slaves and future immigrants.[49]

The *Rio News* wrote, "Up to the present moment we have not seen one serious discussion or plan in regard to the future status of freemen in Brazil."[50] It urged "the establishment of the freedmen on the soil, in homes of their own, and with all the protection which the law and the generous sentiment of the public can accord them."[51] In early February, its editor singled out the group posing the greatest impediment to Brazilian progress: "Until the exaggerated plantations are divided among working men, until these can have a voice in the election of the legislators, there is not the slightest chance that any appeals from them will be considered."[52]

Princess Isabel called a meeting of the Cotegipe cabinet to repeat to all of them what she had privately told her recalcitrant prime minister. Their response was courteous silence.[53] As February drew to a close, a discouraged Isabel wrote the Condessa Barral, "Abolition in the near future ... seems to be on everyone's mind, save on that of the stubborn who must be woken up. Either they will wake up or they will be swept away. May God protect us, and may this revolution or evolution of ours occur as peacefully as possible."[54] By March 1, 1888, Isabel had firmly decided she would not surrender Brazil's future to those wanting to hold back the clock. As the one-year anniversary of her being called back to Brazil approached, Princess Isabel searched for the right moment to act on her decision.

39

"The Hour of Reason"

Opportunity presented itself within days. The severe police beating of a navy officer in Rio de Janeiro sparked civilian and military riots. The chief of police, a hated target of abolitionists and a close political ally of Prime Minister Cotegipe, became the focus of angry demonstrations. Escalating violence revealed that the police had lost control in large sections of the city. Cotegipe and his police chief continued denying the seriousness of the situation, but after days of fighting Isabel ordered the chief dismissed. Rather than lose one of his most trusted lieutenants, the prime minister offered his own resignation. To his shock, Isabel accepted.

After months of cautious waiting, no one had expected the princess regent to make such a bold move or for Cotegipe to make such an uncharacteristic blunder. One newspaper reported, "Having withstood repeated criticism, adverse votes in the senate, and a decisive defeat on the military question ... it became a general impression that the Baron Cotegipe was determined to remain in power. The Cabinet meeting of the 7th however developed an opposing force which the astute premier could not put aside, nor ignore, nor overcome with a vote of confidence in the Chamber." The opposing force that caught everyone, including Cotegipe by surprise, was Princess Isabel.[1]

The *Rio News* speculated the prime minister had "probably overrated his own strength."[2] In addition to being the leading spokesman for the slavocracy, Cotegipe was also the country's leading monarchist politician. No one questioned his loyalty or devotion to the monarchy. But Cotegipe believed the monarchy could not survive without the support of its planters; and its planters could not survive without their slaves. Princess Isabel believed he was mistaken. Even if he were not, she decided that despite the monarchy's unfinished business, abolition must be undertaken at once. She later wrote, "Each day that passed convinced me that [Cotegipe] would do nothing.... [As] the abolitionist cause advanced; its ideas every day gained ground with me."[3]

Isabel wrote her father, "The most recent confrontations very much saddened me. For some time my ideas diverged from those of the ministry. I felt that the government had lost a great deal of moral standing. I had said something to this effect a good many weeks ago and did so now with considerable firmness and in writing, at the same time blaming the police in large part for what happened — the police or rather the attitude adopted by the police authorities.... My observation about the loss of moral standing and the fact that I insisted on the dismissal of the chief of police caused the ministry's fall. I do not regret what I did. Sooner or later I would have done it. I confess that a blind irritation took command of me, and in conscience I could not continue with a ministry when I felt for my part and was convinced that it did not meet the country's aspirations in the existing situation. God help me, and may the question of emancipation soon reach the final stage that I so much want to arrive. A great deal needs doing, but this most of all."[4]

Isabel's timing could not have been better for the abolitionists or herself. The change of ministries came during a parliamentary recess, allowing her time to select a new prime minister who could hopefully build support for a successful abolition plan. The timing also maximized her own role and influence in writing the legislation.[5]

Cotegipe's departure as prime minister troubled many loyal monarchists, but another pillar of the monarchy provided much-needed support. That same month, after meeting with Brazilian abolitionist leader Joaquim Nabuco, Pope Leo XIII issued a powerful statement denouncing slavery. "Slavery is condemned by the Church and should have ended a long time ago. A man cannot be a slave of another man. All are equally sons of God, des infants de Dieu."[6] The pope's pronouncement placed the church solidly behind the abolitionist cause. Ten years earlier Leo XIII had been elected pope and had steadily tried to lead the Church away from many of the reactionary policies of his immediate predecessor. He donated 300,000 francs to the anti-slavery movement and canonized Pedro Claver, a priest who had dedicated his religious life to ministering to Latin America's slaves.[7] He also sent a letter to Brazil's bishops quoting scripture and verse from the Bible interspersed with statements from past popes condemning slavery.[8]

Princess Isabel and abolitionists welcomed the pope's assistance, but the news she most hoped to hear from Europe did not come. The emperor's health was not improving, in large part because he refused to follow his doctor's advice. When it was clear her father would not soon be returning to Brazil, Isabel searched for her own prime minister to create a coalition supporting emancipation. She rejected Liberal Party leaders and longtime abolitionists as being too divisive. Instead she sought a moderate politician able to work with the traditionalists controlling the General Assembly. She wanted someone with strong conservative credentials, able to rally support without splitting the majority Conservative Party.

Her first choice was Dona Verdiana da Silva Prado's influential son Antônio. Despite his Republican brother, Antônio remained a strong monarchist. He was a lifelong supporter of slavery but had recently advocated emancipating all slaves in three years. A longer delay would be "to attempt the impossible ... it would be as if one wished to control a swelling river by means of a dam!"[9] By March 1888, he had shortened his abolition timetable to two years, pleading with his fellow politicians to work with the government to prevent abolition from coming about through "popular revolution."[10]

But as the month drew to a close Isabel decided further delays might prove disastrous and turned to one of Prado's closest political allies. João Alfredo Correia de Oliveira was a past president of the pivotal province of São Paulo and a longtime friend of Baron Cotegipe.[11] He had been a fierce defender of slavery, but recent events convinced him that immediate emancipation was necessary to maintain peace. Within the past year he had freed his own slaves, and devoted much of his time to forming political alliances with planters sharing his views. Correia de Oliveira fit the profile Princess Isabel sought. He was a respected Conservative, a realist and a coalition builder. Following a series of interviews, she believed she had found a prime minister able to lead Brazil toward peaceful emancipation.

Princess Isabel's appointment surprised and reassured both friends and foes. Despite fears and dire predictions, Correia de Oliveira formed a new Conservative ministry without splitting the party. The *Rio News* admiringly noted, "This was a task of no slight difficulty as the transfer of power from one section to another of the same party, where no rupture has yet occurred would be sure to arouse violent jealousies and perhaps open opposition. The task was accomplished successfully."[12]

Like many prominent Brazilians, Correia de Oliveira was of a blended racial heritage. That life perspective may have afforded him the expertise he used to create a diverse cabinet that included both loyal monarchists like Antônio Prado and vitriolic critics of the imperial family like Antônio Ferreira Vianna.[13] The thread binding them together was a shared belief that the time for abolition had come. The *Rio News* predicted, "If [this cabinet] fails there is little hope for the future."[14]

André Rebouças and others realized that despite the Conservative majority in the Chamber of Deputies, votes of Liberal Party deputies would be needed to pass any emancipation legislation. Working behind the scenes, Rebouças wrote a version of a bill that Liberal deputies could support. By March 30th his finished draft was ready. It called for immediate and unconditional abolition.[15]

On Easter Sunday, April 1, 1888, Princess Isabel presided over a celebration granting freedom to one hundred and twenty-seven slaves at Petrópolis's Crystal Palace.[16] She had hoped the event would cleanse the city of all slaves, but three slave holders refused to sell or free their slaves. At the close of the ceremony fifty runaway slaves suddenly appeared, electrifying the audience by publicly appealing to the Princess Imperial for protection. She instantly asked the committee sponsoring the event to safeguard their freedom.[17] Cheering crowd embraced the refugees.

Two of Brazil's leading abolitionists, André Rebouças and José Patrocínio, witnessed the emotionally charged event. Rebouças for years had been a close friend and protégé of the royal family; Patrocínio, the tiger of the abolition movement, was a fierce republican. The sincerity, charisma and leadership of the princess deeply affected both men. Rebouças's own commitment to the monarchy was re-enforced; but Patrocínio experienced an epiphany. Princess Isabel's majestic behavior seemed to elevate and validate the righteousness of the abolitionist crusade in the twinkling of an eye. If Patrocínio had not seen the incident, he could never have imagined it. The experience convinced him that the social revolution he had sought his entire life might be best led by his longtime enemy — the princess imperial. Within days Patrocínio began using his newspaper to rally support for the regency and to attack the hypocrisy of his own Republican Party.[18] His stinging articles criticized the "neutral" Republicans for claiming to represent the masses, ignoring the abolitionist cause, and courting the planter elite. He documented cynical Republican election strategies that ran its few abolitionist candidates only in races they were certain to lose.[19] Republicans were furious. Isabel had succeeded in converting one of her most powerful opponents to her cause.

By April the breakdown of the slave system could be seen throughout the country.[20] Hundreds, then thousands, of slaves freed themselves from bondage by quietly walking away from the fazendas of their birth.[21] Others wreaked revenge on property, masters, mistresses and overseers.[22] Planters and mobs violently fought back. Fears of a race war rocked the nation as slavocrats demanded the government save them from the chaos they had sown.

On May 3, 1888, when the General Assembly convened in Rio de Janeiro, expectations were high the new ministry would move quickly against slavery. The *Rio News* reported, "The Princess Regent was received with the wildest applause and her carriage was literally covered with flowers. Such a demonstration at the opening of parliament has not been witnessed for many years."[23]

Isabel's speech from the throne was unusually long. She began it with an optimistic but wishful report on the improved condition of her parent's health. She then presented a litany of legislative initiatives proposed by the new ministry, including a call for increased immigration, greater utilization of public lands, additional financial credit for agriculture, improvement of the education system, and a brief review of foreign relations. She then addressed the issue on everyone's mind. In a firm clear voice she declared, "The extinction of the servile element, through the influence of the national sentiment and of the private liberality ... had peacefully advanced so that it is today the proclaimed hope of all classes, with admirable examples of self sacrifice on the part of the owners. When private interest itself comes spontaneously to assist in relieving Brazil of the unhappy inheritance which agricultural needs have maintained; I trust that you will not hesitate to remove from the national law the only exception in it to the Christian and liberal spirit of our institutions."[24]

It was a remarkably understated, moderate speech. The princess regent assigned no blame to individuals, groups or institutions for the nation's "unhappy inheritance." Rather she appealed for recognition of a change in public opinion and encouraged Brazilians to do what was right as citizens and Christians. Nowhere did she mention the word slavery, or abolition, or compensation to the owners for their slaves. The speech ended with the words, "I have confidence that you will respond to that which Brazil expects of you." It was a last appeal to the conservative legislators to recognize and respond positively to "the drift of public opinion."[25]

Princess Isabel was acutely aware of the importance of the speech and might have asked any current or former member of the government to help write it. She chose as her principal ghostwriter and collaborator Antônio Vianna, the leading critic of the monarchy in the Conservative cabinet. It was Vianna who years earlier had labeled her father "the conspirator prince," denouncing his reign as "forty years of lies and betrayals."[26] Isabel was determined to create a base of support by reaching out to friends and enemies. In doing so, she continued recruiting converts to her cause. Vianna was soon proposing public toasts to the health of the princess imperial and the entire royal family.[27]

To the end of Vianna's life, he remained a dedicated monarchist in part because Isabel's leadership had convinced him that monarchy was the best system to promote what he came to call the "cult of the constitution."[28] Princess Isabel continued confounding and exasperating her opponents.

Despite her positive public report about the health of her parents, rumors spread that the emperor had taken a turn for the worse. Newspapers reported Empress Theresa had asked the nation for prayers, and reports predicted the death of Pedro II was "momentarily expected."[29] The stories "had the effect of arousing feelings of keen expectations and profound sympathy," adding another emotional layer to Princess Isabel's already powerful speech.[30]

On the seventh of May, the new ministry announced it would present an abolition proposal to the General Assembly the following day.[31] The newspaper *Novidades* angrily responded. "There is no one who does not see that the Princess Isabel is the one who is decreeing abolition; there is no one who does not perceive the large part she is playing in this.... At this moment it is almost impossible to point out all the consequences of this dictatorial act of the excellent heiress to the throne.... The hour of reason has not yet arrived."[32]

Princess Isabel believed the hour of reason had arrived. But to avoid the confusion caused by the typical convoluted language of most laws, she insisted the emancipation bill be short, to the point, and free all slaves immediately.[33] She rejected its first draft, demanding it be rewritten and simplified. At her insistence all confusing legalized language was edited out. No loopholes or delays of any kind would delay abolition. Her Aunt Maria da Glória once wrote "words must be like stars," clear and easy to follow.[34] Isabel's embrace of her aunt's dictum is evident in the final draft of the legislation, making it one of the shortest, most straightforward, but far-reaching laws ever proposed in a democratic legislative body. The final bill contained just seventeen words:

Article One: From the date of this Law slavery is declared abolished in Brazil.

Article Two: All contrary provisions are revoked.

When she shared the final draft with Gaston he begged her not to sign it. Despite his own abolitionist sentiments he warned her it would mean the end of the monarchy.[35] Years later, Isabel could still recall nearly word for word their heated exchange. She assured him she recognized the danger in signing the abolition bill, but believed it the only way to stop the violence threatening the country. Powerful men begged her to seize the moment, people trusted her to do the right thing, and the slaves had waited too long. Finally she reminded him they might never again have the chance if they did not act immediately. On that point the pessimistic prince could not disagree.

Once the proposal was presented in the Chamber of Deputies, the Liberal Party legislator Joaquim Nabuco appealed for members of all parties to support the legislation. "This is not the moment for party controversy, for we are approaching what is incomparably the most solemn hour of our history. The present generation had never before experienced such depths of emotion and to find a parallel we must turn back to the exultation felt by our fathers on the proclamation of independence. For us Brazilians the year 1888 is a landmark in our history even greater than 1789 was for France. It is literally a new nation that is born."[36]

At one point, Nabuco left the legislative chamber and made his way to a window looking out on a huge crowd of expectant Brazilians. José Patrocínio described the scene in his newspaper: "Erect, motionless, immovable as a statue, he stood there, grand and solemn.... After a long pause ... he saw the people, with their heads uncovered as if before an idol, and he led a bravo to the Imperial Princess."[37]

The next day "amid tremendous enthusiasm" and in record time the Chamber of Deputies voted eight-three to nine in favor of the bill. It was then sent to the Senate, where Baron Cotegipe waited.[38] The brilliant former prime minister gave the greatest speech of his career in an attempt to stop emancipation. He eloquently used humor, sarcasm, reason, theatrics, economics, history, and fear to save slavery.[39] A newspaper reporter wrote, "His speech was undoubtedly a powerful effort and it seems a pity it was lost on so bad a cause."[40]

When word of Cotegipe's speech reached Petrópolis, Princess Isabel immediately arranged for a special train to return her to the capital to rally support for the abolitionists. Frenzied crowds greeted her on her arrival with waving flags and bouquets of flowers. Her arrival at the nearby City Palace was keenly felt and heard in the legislative chambers. A vehement opponent of abolition abruptly concluded his vitriolic attack on the legislation by admitting he "bowed to the storm." He ended his speech by saying he would be remiss in his duties as a gentleman if he kept waiting "a lady of such exulted rank."[41] Forty-three

LA AVISPA

PRECIO
15
CÉNTIMOS

AÑO V   NÚM. 196.

MADRID 30 DE MAYO DE 1888

PRECIO
15
CÉNTIMOS

HOMENAJE

Á. S. A. I. la Regente del Brasil, por
su decreto de abolicion de la esclavitud, felicitan
sincera y respetuosamente,

Los pueblos civilizados.

Reproducção da 1ª pagina do jornal de Madrid, "La Avispa", com-
memorando a Lei de 13 de Maio.

senators voted in favor of unconditional emancipation. Cotegipe and five others voted "against the proposal of the Princess Regent."[42]

Witnesses recalled, "Even the stones ... trembled" as ten thousand people of every age and color squeezed into the City Plaza chanting "Vivas" to Princess Isabel. At 3:30 P.M. the princess imperial regent signed her signature to the legislation in the name of "His Majesty Emperor Dom Pedro II." In doing so Isabel legally freed all the remaining slaves in Brazil, peacefully ending what her royal ancestors had violently begun over three hundred and fifty years earlier.

The date, May 13, 1888, was the anniversary of the birth of her great grandfather who under the banner of his mother Maria I first brought the Braganças to America, and the wedding anniversary of Isabel's grandparents, Brazil's first emperor and empress. They, and their ancestors, all played a role in the rise and fall of Brazilian slavery. Perhaps most significantly it was also the anniversary her grandfather was given the title, "Constitutional Emperor and Perpetual Defender of Brazil." To Millions of voiceless Brazilians, more than any of her royal ancestors, Isabel fulfilled the promise of that title.

News of abolition spread across the city with an "explosion of joy in the streets."[43] People cheered the princess regent, the nation's legislators, and other heroes of abolition.[44] Time and again Princess Isabel was called to the City Palace balcony to be saluted by singing, dancing crowds.

Inside the crush of the palace José Patrocínio tried to read a speech of gratitude to Princess Isabel. Overcome by emotion he broke down and wept. Falling to his knees he kissed his onetime enemy. It was a time for reconciliation, and Princess Isabel sought out Baron Cotegipe, who kissed her hand. She drew him to her side, gently asking if he did not regret opposing a law that had brought so much joy to Brazil. Without bitterness he sadly replied, "You have freed a race, Your Majesty, but lost a throne."[45]

Passage of what its supporters came to call "the Golden Law" ignited waves of spontaneous celebrations as the word spread from person to person across Brazil.[46] Urban areas were taken over by "processions, and torchlight parades, and bands of music ... speeches from windows, student demonstrations, balls, and popular amusements."[47] On May 17th an open air mass was held for twenty thousand celebrants on the grounds of the São Cristóvão Palace. Princess Isabel and her entire family joined with other Brazilians in thanking God for the final extinction of slavery in the Americas. Joaquim Nabuco exclaimed, "It was as if an enemy of occupation had suddenly evacuated, leaving us free and independent, in possession of our fatherland."[48]

Even if the nation's slaveholders had wished to ignore the role Princess

Opposite: Isabel was hailed as the woman of the century and the Abraham Lincoln of Brazil at the time she signed the document legally abolishing slavery in Brazil. Here she is celebrated on the cover of a popular magazine published in Madrid, Spain, in 1888. Courtesy the Catholic University of America, Oliveira Lima Library, Washington, D.C.

Isabel played in abolition, it was impossible. Former slaves took to singing freedom songs with the chorus, "I stepped on the stone, the stone tottered. The world was twisted, the queen straightened it out."[49] Isabel had been the "queen" to the poor ever since she led relief efforts during the great drought. To former slaves, she was their once and future queen.

France and the United States scheduled a day to publicly celebrate the emancipation of Brazil's slaves.[50] Queen Victoria's England and other countries from around the world sent warm congratulations. And the United States minister to Brazil, a Confederate veteran of the late Civil War, wrote, "My country laid waste thousands of dead to preserve slavery; many of our wealthiest citizens went bankrupt. My congratulations to the imperial family and the people of Brazil on the grand work accomplished by law on the 13th of May."[51]

In neighboring Argentina, "thirty thousand persons paraded before the Brazilian Legation" to celebrate the end of American slavery. The Argentine minister to Brazil publicly saluted Princess Isabel as the woman of the century.[52] Amidst the happy chaos, the princess regent seemed at peace. She was certain she had done the right thing at the right time for the right reasons serving her conscience, Brazil's constitution, her God and her country.

Isabel took time while the events were still fresh in her mind to write her sons a letter explaining her thoughts and feelings about her role in the day's historic events. "My children, should you read this later, please realize that if your mother acted thus in the great question of abolition, it was out of conviction that it would be best for the nation, which she had a duty to watch over, and for you all, to whom she would leave her reputation as mother and the throne free of any blemish of egotism or of weakness. God aided me, my children, in acting entirely in accord with my conscience."[53]

In the moment of her greatest triumph, Isabel's thoughts also traveled far from Brazil. On May 13th she wrote, "Today would be one of the most beautiful in my life if I did not know my father to be so ill."[54] That same day Isabel sent a telegram to Italy with the news her father had waited a lifetime to hear. Her message began, "My good beloved parents. I don't know where to begin ... with Mummy who has suffered so much in recent days, or Daddy; because of the occasion."[55] A return telegram read, "I congratulate you on the great success of this campaign entrusted to your care." It was sent under the emperor's signature, but was composed by the empress. Theresa decided to keep the news from Pedro II, fearing he was too weak to survive it. She rationalized she would tell him when he felt stronger.

As celebrations continued throughout Brazil, the emperor's health took a turn for the worse. On May 22, he lost consciousness; vital signs indicating he was dying. Doctors injected caffeine, ether and other stimulants into his failing system, shocking him into consciousness. The archbishop of Milan heard his confession and gave him the last rites of the Catholic Church.[56] Only when she feared her husband might die without knowing of emancipation, did Theresa tell him of Isabel's telegram.

The emperor was still weak, but asked in a whisper if it were true there were no more slaves in Brazil. When the empress confirmed Isabel's signature had legally freed the slaves, he wept. Thanking God, he asked that a telegram be sent saluting Isabel as the redeemer of the slaves, bestowing blessings and congratulations on his daughter and nation. Almost immediately he began an uneven, but nearly miraculous recovery.[57]

In England, the *London Daily Mail* wrote, "Dom Pedro II, Emperor of Brazil is reported out of danger. If a man has in fact had his hand upon the helm for 50 years and has all things in working order, perhaps the wisest use he can make of his declining years is in this very system of affording the opportunity of the training of his successor. Dom Pedro's daughter governed Brazil with apparently as happy a hand as her father; and if the maladies that came upon him in Italy had proven fatal, her office as Regent might have been merged into that as Empress without the perception of a change."[58]

When the exhausted princess returned to Petrópolis several days later, she and Gaston held an abolitionist ball for friends in the Crystal Palace. There in the midst of candlelight, music, and her beloved flowers Isabel allowed herself to dance and celebrate. For one brief night she allowed herself not to worry about what would come next to her family — and country.

"Sheer fatigue" ended the celebrations.[59] Most former slaves returned to work on neighboring plantations if not on those of their birth.[60] Many planters replaced disbelief with anger. Their refusal to consider the possibility of emancipation kept them from negotiating compensation for their slaves prior to abolition. Baron Cotegipe and conservative legislators moved to rectify the situation.[61] Proposals were hurriedly brought forward to compensate planters for lost slaves. Hard-line Conservatives were joined in the quest by the small but vocal Republican Party, but it was too late. The slaveless planters refused to surrender on the issue, but public opinion refused to tolerate it.[62]

40

"Turning Point"

Novidades, a conservative newspaper, wrote on May 26, "The law of 13 May only gives liberty to the slaves: it behooves us to complete it, decreeing indemnification for the masters."[1] Its editorial ended with a thinly disguised threat: "Either the government indemnifies and in that case defers abolition to an ordinary case of expropriation for public utility; or it does not indemnify and in that case puts abolition in the category of a revolutionary act, whose consequences will not be long in coming."[2] The journal *Revista Illustrada* presented the viewpoint shared by most Brazilians. Under a caricature of Princess Isabel it wrote, "I am amazed that people want to be rewarded for something in which they should be punished."[3] The words were not Isabel's, but the sentiments reflected popular thinking.

As early as March Princess Isabel had decided to oppose indemnification. In a letter to her sons she explained her thinking. "Despite never having stated my opinion on this idea prior to the proposal being made, I could not grant it as being either advisable or just.... First the country could have compensated only in an illusory fashion, since it would have to be provided by taxes that would have fallen on those who had no connection with the question. The emancipation fund, financed by taxes, the only one applicable for this purpose, would have been less than sufficient. And whom would it aid? Those who had not voluntarily freed their slaves? It would only be to pay off over due debts with no benefit to agriculture, and it would be better spent on projects that would serve the general good of farming, which would be most just. Beside this, as I have already noted, the idea of the injustice of slavery and the excessive time that owners had exploited their slaves could not fail to influence my spirit."[4]

Indemnification was one of the points Gaston tried and failed to get Isabel to consider at the time the abolition bill was written. He also worried exploitive Republicans would recruit the nation's planters to their cause. For some planters, that campaign began in earnest on May 14th.[5]

The newspaper *O Paíz* carried stories that a number of the agricultural clubs organized to oppose abolition had transformed themselves into Republican clubs.[6] By July, the *Rio News* reported that "enthusiastic Republican meetings have been held in various cities and towns of the Paraíba Valley.[7] In the senate, Baron Cotegipe expressed alarm at the growing success Republicans were having in recruiting the disenchanted. Debt ridden planters from the provinces of Rio de Janeiro, Minas Gerais, and São Paulo were especially irate at the monarchy because their lack of capital made it difficult for them to hire free laborers.[8]

Still, the thinking of the more progressive planters mirrored Isabel's.[9] Planters who had freed their slaves prior to the thirteenth of May, those who had already hired "colonists" and other immigrant laborers to till their fields, and those modernizing and streamlining their agricultural methods were the least hurt by abolition. As individuals and as a group they opposed indemnification.

One abolitionist planter in São Paulo wrote a friend, "You should tell your fellow provincials ... that they are laboring under serious error when they imagine that they will suffer great damage through the loss of slave property ... free labor is not as expensive as it seemed at first. This was my greatest surprise.... As I told you with my ex-slaves I have the same contract that I had with my colonists."[10]

The fear of economic collapse and predicted financial chaos that held slavery in place never materialized. Antônio Prado reported in the Chamber of Deputies, "The freedmen, with only a few exceptions, were working effectively to harvest the coffee crop.[11] Other observers noted, "The Law of the 13th of May [had gone into effect] without any perturbation in the country, without any revolution ... as predicted ... without the slightest disturbance of public disorder and even without diminution of coffee shipments to the market of Rio de Janeiro."[12]

The pacific effect abolition had on the economy did not surprise the United States minister to Brazil. He reported to his government, "Every indication of public sentiment is in hearty accord with this action of the General Assembly, and I may add that this sentiment has been well prepared for the changes to take place.... I therefore do not share in the fears expressed by some as to its immediate effect on various industries.... In my view, the country has been so well prepared for this action that its present effect will not be deleterious."[13]

Everyone seemed "prepared" for abolition except planters who lost their chance for indemnification by blindly fighting emancipation to the bitter end. After May 13th public opinion united against them. Still, indemnification was debated in the General Assembly throughout 1888. One opponent pointed out, "If anyone ought to be indemnified, it should be the slaves."[14] Aside from the angry feelings the debates precipitated, no one, including supporters of compensation, offered suggestions on how to pay for it.[15] The same hard-line planters demanding indemnification strongly opposed raising taxes.

Princess Isabel continued opposing indemnification, but supported attempts to secure overseas loans to help those in temporary financial distress.

She believed a combination of free labor, competition, and a strong market economy could secure the nation's financial future.[16] Time would prove her correct, but after the parliamentary euphoria of May 13th all government business was blocked by the indemnification debates. The Conservatives, the Ultra-Conservatives and the Liberals fought the issue to a paralyzing standstill.

Those who owned large tracts of land in Brazil were few in number, but their influence was disproportionate to their size. Prior to emancipation, they had never known political defeat. The events culminating on May 13th provided them a dramatic wakeup call that their influence and wealth no longer automatically guaranteed them the entitlement they expected.

Brazil's largest landowners led the fight against abolition. Following years of absolute power, they and the government they thought they controlled failed to hold back the tidal wave of abolition or provide them the indemnification they demanded. Change was clearly in the air. The *Rio News* wrote, "We have repeatedly called attention to the facts that the planters [already] pay no taxes, railroads are built for their accommodation, immigrants are imported at public expense to labor for them, and finally the treasury lends them money, at reduced interest, to pay these imported and other laborers."[17]

The newspaper editorialized. If with all the help the government afforded planters over the years they were still unable to make their land productive, they should forfeit it to those who could.[18] José Patrocínio publicly stated that "eight million landless workers" would be happy to farm such "unprofitable" land.[19] Baron Cotegipe and his supporters denounced such rhetoric as the words of anarchists, socialists, and communists.[20] But name-calling and the guilt by association labeling of enemies no longer seemed enough to stop their opponents.

With indemnification doomed, many large land owners demanded legal restraints on the newly freed slaves. The minister of justice declared in parliament, "What do the noble deputies propose? To re-enslave those declared free?... The government cannot lend itself to [efforts] to reduce them to a kind of serf, tied to the soil or to their ex-masters. If anyone has this illusion, he is mistaken.... If they want exceptional laws, laws of repression, they cannot count on the support of the present government, which through so much effort promoted and consummated the law of 13 May."[21]

"Laws of repression" were exactly what many recalcitrant former slaveholders wanted. The most reactionary planters had no intention of gracefully accepting defeat, surrendering their influence, or changing their way of life. The "politics of horror" swept away in the euphoria of the "Golden Law" returned with renewed vengeance; much of it focused on Princess Isabel. *Novidades* accused the princess regent of betraying the common past they once shared, and believed they understood why. "Personal power, despotic power, seigniorial power is, yes, exercised at this moment by the Regent. The third reign announces itself by the bastardization, by the corruption, of our system of government, that begins by compromising the political parties and will finish by compromising the crown itself."[22]

Others viewed Isabel's dramatic break from the past differently. Joaquim Nabuco, popularly acclaimed as "the most charismatic politician of the empire,"[23] declared the princess regent had "forever changed the nature of monarchy, making it a popular institution, loyal to the people and opposed to the oppressing classes."[24] Abolition transformed Princess Isabel into the most loved, and most hated, woman in Brazil. Whether she was seen as a hero or a villain depended much on the race, social position, and political viewpoint of those passing judgment. Afro-Brazilians had always been strong supporters of the monarchy. After abolition their support grew stronger.[25]

Many former slaves idolized Isabel as a near goddess.[26] To them she represented all that was good in those who held authority.[27] One newspaper reported former slaves refusing to work on "plantations whose owners had joined the Republican Party.... They would not serve persons rebelling against the Princess Regent who had freed them."[28] *Novidades* scornfully noted, "There are crowds of slaves scattered through the plantations harvesting coffee and grain, work which is interrupted by clamorous cheers for the Serene Princess Isabel and José Patrocínio."[29]

Longtime leaders of the abolitionist crusade championed her role in freeing the nation's slaves. André Rebouças wrote Joaquim Nabuco, "My dear Nabuco! You well know the whole truth. It was She who accomplished abolition, She alone!"[30] To social reformers, Princess Isabel represented their best opportunity for a just and equitable future. Patrocínio and other activists believed emancipation the first of many steps in making that dream a reality. They warmly embraced Isabel as their leader, the living embodiment of their hopes. To them, the events of May 13th represented "the democratic dawn of the third reign."[31]

Nabuco wrote, "Isabel is now the last person to harbor runaways: her throne has become a runaway settlement.... The monarchy is more popular than ever."[32] To Nabuco and others, Isabel's leadership "idealized" the monarchy, reframed and renewed its popularity by "separate[ing it] off from its actual institutional function ... [making it] more and more popular."[33] By guiding the ship of state peacefully through abolition, Princess Isabel earned the respect and support of most Brazilians, but Brazil had never been a country where the majority ruled, or even mattered.

William Graham Sumner, a respected sociologist and political economist in the United States, wrote, "All history is only one long story to this effect: men had struggled for power over their fellow men in order that they might win the joys of earth at the expense of others, and might shift the burdens of life from their own shoulders, to others." He might have been speaking of Brazil's embittered planters determined to revenge their defeat over abolition. On one point slavocrats found common agreement with André Rebouças. Like

Anno 15   Rio de Janeiro. 1888.   N.º 507

Revista Illustrada

CORTE	PUBLICADA POR ANGELO AGOSTINI.	PROVINCIAS
Anno 16$000 Semestre 9$000 Trimestre 5$000	A correspondencia e reclamações devem ser dirigidas Á Rua de Gonçalves Dias, N.º 50, Sobrado	Anno 20$000 Semestre 11$000 Avulso 1$000

29 de Julho de 1888.

Princess Isabel enjoyed broad popular support "primarily from ... 'outsiders' traditionally 'denied political rights ... economically deprived' and of African descent." Here former slaves pay homage to her picture with flowers on the cover of *Revista Illustrada*, a popular Brazilian magazine published in Rio de Janeiro in July 1888. Courtesy the Catholic University of America, Oliveira Lima Library, Washington, D.C.

him, they held Isabel responsible for abolition. The *Rio News* pointed out the regent enjoyed broad popular support, but it came primarily from "the lowest of the people."[34] Isabel's newest supporters were "outsiders" traditionally "denied political rights ... economically deprived," and of African descent.[35]

Brazil's heir to the throne alienated many who traditionally viewed the monarchy as a personal representative and protector. These former monarchists now saw Isabel as a traitor to their class.[36] For centuries, governments in times of crisis from Russia to Japan, Prussia to England cynically granted "personal but not political rights" to the masses.[37] Such illusionary reforms were not meant to effect real changes, but to prevent them.[38] Brazil's slavocrats might have accepted a surface change in the status of slaves if economic exploitation and control remained. But Isabel sincerely embraced abolition, seeing it as the first of many badly needed reforms needed to remake Brazil.

Unable to judge her by any standards but their own, opponents saw her behavior as a brazen attempt to retain and gain power at their expense.[39] *Novidades* publicly articulated what some conservatives feared: Princess Isabel was leading a "revolution from above."[40] The events of May 13th led one critic to bluntly state, "It is not a time for despair, it is a time for reaction."[41]

Bitter planters and ambitious Republicans were soon joined by a dissident group of military officers brought together by a common enemy — the princess who freed the slaves. Isabel had always been supportive of the military, especially in recent conflicts with Prime Minister Cotegipe. Her lack of popular support within its ranks could be traced to the feelings of many young officers toward Gaston. They disliked and distrusted her husband despite his love for all things military. Since the stinging criticism he received for championing veterans at the close of the Paraguayan war, he had carefully avoided even the appearance of support for military adventuring into politics.

Throughout Latin America, the army played an important, even a dominant role in many nations' political affairs. That had never been the case in Brazil. After the Paraguayan War, elements of the military grew increasingly frustrated by the government's unwillingness to promote their special status in society. Government policies and budget constraints checkmated their political aspirations. Following the war Gaston headed a government reform commission to modernize and reorganize the army. That commission recommended improvements in equipment, pay, and military pensions; but decided against increasing the size of the army or its officer corps.[42] Pedro II and both major political parties agreed with the commission's conclusions, believing Brazil had better uses for its money than to increase the size and influence of its military.

Gaston's final report on modernizing the army made advancement through the ranks slow and difficult. It saved money but alienated the next generation of army officers. Gaston became the human face behind every delayed promotion. Since the prince marshal, the emperor, and both major political parties offered no alternative to the existing government policy, a growing number of junior officers embraced the Republican cause. A radical change in government seemed their only hope to achieve their ambitions.

Older military officers such as the late Duke of Caxias and General Deodoro da Fonseca scorned the Republicans. Deodoro urged his nephew, a cadet at the military academy, to avoid Republicans, who he described as "fools and crackpots," predicting "a real calamity" for Brazil if they ever gained power.[43] But even he and some of his fellow officers were frustrated by the army's lowly status and the government's indifference to their ambitions. The constitutional principles of Pedro II provided protection for his fiercest critics in and out of the military, and he refused to allow authorities to purge revolutionary thinking instructors in schools, including military academies. Princess Isabel continued her father's open-minded policies despite escalating attacks against her, the monarchy, and the constitution.

In the weeks of popular euphoria following abolition, the explosive mix of politics and religion returned with a vengeance to fight Isabel. One of the proposed pieces of legislation languishing in the stalemated General Assembly concerned the freedom of public worship. Protestants had always freely worshiped in Brazil, but legal restrictions had been placed on the outward appearances of Protestant churches. A proposed piece of legislation retained the Roman Catholic faith as the official state religion, but allowed the outside architecture of Protestant churches to reflect their status as houses of worship.

Several Catholic bishops used their pulpits to encourage the faithful, especially Catholic women, to oppose the stalled legislation. Petitions rained down on the Chamber of Deputies, one signed by 14,000 Brazilian women.[44] The combination of bishops, women, politics, and religion provoked a strong backlash in the patriarchal country. One Brazilian newspaper editorialized, "If a man be master of his own house he might and should have prevented any such document, visibly organized by priests, being signed by his family."[45]

The controversy stirred up bitter memories of the earlier church-state conflicts and Isabel's perceived role in them. Despite the fact that the regent had not signed the petitions, had no direct or indirect connection to them, and that no legislation since the abolition bill including the Freedom of Worship act had been passed in the deadlocked session, Isabel's enemies worked tirelessly to link her to the latest church-state storm.

By July, an exhausted Isabel was too ill to attend the public celebrations for her forty-third birthday, but the *Rio News* reported the day was greeted by "enthusiastic demonstrations throughout the whole empire."[46] Popular support for the princess only caused her enemies to further press their attacks. Friends and allies rallied to her defense. Powerful voices from abroad joined many voiceless Brazilians in supporting the embattled princess. Austria-Hungary awarded her the Starred Cross for her political leadership during the abolition crisis, and Portugal appointed her to the Order of Saint Isabel in recognition of her position as a Christian role model.

In Italy, Antônio Carlos Gomes, Latin America's most famous composer, dedicated his latest opera to her. His dedication read in part, "Your Highness, with gentle and patriotic spirit, had the glory of changing slavery into the eternal joy of freedom. Thus the word slave in Brazil belongs only in the legend of the past. Therefore, it is as a token of the deep gratitude and homage that, as a Brazilian artist, I have the great honor of dedicating this work of mine to the Serene Princess in whom Brazil venerates the same high spirit, the same greatness of soul of Dom Pedro II.... Today, the 29th of July, the day in which Brazil salutes the birthday of the August Regent, I bring to the feet of Your Highness this 'Escravo'— perhaps as poor as the thousands of others who bless Your Highness with the same effusion of gratitude with which I am, of your Imperial Highness, Faithful, and Reverent Subject."[47]

Pope Leo XIII also announced he would honor Isabel. On September 28, 1888, the 17th anniversary of the passage of the Law of the Free Womb, she was presented the Golden Rose, a decoration given Christian women whose public service represented the highest ideals of their faith. Forty-six years earlier Isabel's Aunt, Maria II of Portugal, had received the Golden Rose, but no Christian woman in North or South America had ever before been so honored.

The prestige such awards brought to Brazil temporally muted Isabel's critics; but enemies used even her honors against her. Rumors were spread the Golden Rose had been awarded the princess for promising to surrender Brazil's sovereignty to the pope. The prime minister and the minister of foreign affairs denounced the allegations, denying "the Princess Imperial had taken any oath of allegiance to the Pope before, during or after the ceremonies."[48] No lie seemed too outrageous to use against her.

On August 22, 1888, the emperor and empress returned to Brazil. The ghostly appearance of Pedro II caused many to believe he had come home to die. The sixty-two-year-old emperor was aged beyond his years.[49] Despite concerns over his health the minister of empire warmly welcomed him home "to a land free from slavery." Pedro was heard to cryptically mutter, "Yes, yes, but if I had been here, what was done would not have been done."[50]

His reception by the citizens of Rio de Janeiro was less cryptic. The United States minister wrote, "Thousands upon thousands crowded the piers or went out in ships to meet him, not knowing whether he could be seen at all.... It was under these circumstances that he made his appearance [and received] a heart felt ovation."[51] Gaston wrote, "The avidity and the enthusiasm of the public for the Emperor have been very great, even more marked, it appears to me, than on his previous arrivals."[52] Cadets from the military academy climbed the steep cliffs of Sugar Loaf Mountain to unfurl a huge banner welcoming him home.[53]

No one, including his family, knew whether Pedro's health would allow him to resume his responsibilities. There were times his mind was clear and alert, but he was unable to sustain his attention for extended periods of time. It quickly became clear to those nearest him that he would never again be the complete master of his surroundings. The president of the Council of Ministers and his doctor urged Princess Isabel to remain as regent, but she refused to even broach the subject with her father.[54] The president assumed the awkward task. When he proposed the idea, the emperor snapped into focus, refusing to be treated as "an invalid, occupying only an honorary post."[55]

Princess Isabel immediately supported her father's decision. The prime minister later remembered she raised her hands and declared with "fierce sincerity," "I Thank God that my father feels that he has the strength to govern and remove this great responsibility from me." In loyally supporting her fragile father, Isabel surrendered the fate of Brazil's constitutional monarchy to an invalid.[56] As she had done throughout most of her life, she also surrendered her own fate to others.

At the end of the parliamentary session in October, prolonged periods of rest and a carefully regulated diet allowed Pedro II to give the closing speech from the throne. He read in part, "My context in appearing in this chamber is the more intense because of my fortune in being enabled to return to the country to continue to serve it." It was an emotional moment for all who heard the emperor's words. He continued, "At the same time I was gladdened by the sight of the satisfactory condition of the Empire, for the third time delivered through the regency of my much loved daughter, the Princess Imperial.... Order and tranquility have been maintained, the guarantee of individual liberty respected.... We may flatter ourselves upon the pacific manner in which the transformation of labor was secured by virtue of the Law of May 13th, the decreeing of which ... consoled me in my homesickness alleviating my physical sufferings."[57]

On the emperor's birthday in December a reporter wrote, "The sixty-third birthday of His Majesty was celebrated ... by the subjects and friends with a tenderness and solicitousness good will which falls only on those resting from the burdens of years and broken health."[58] As the year drew to a close, Princess Isabel and supporters of the monarchy privately feared for the emperor and their country. They were not alone.

The *Rio News* reported, "The year 1888 will probably figure as one of the most eventful, if not the most eventful in Brazil's history. If wise counsel, prudence and industry prevail, it will mark the turning point in the life of the nation, the opening of a new era of prosperity and enlightenment. If these counsels do not prevail, however, if reactionary ideas, inertia, petty intrigues and prejudice dominate the course of events, then the worse may still be feared."[59]

41

"Fight for the Princess"

Brazil was at a crossroads. Republicans and reactionary conservatives dismissed Pedro II as if he were already dead. Their attacks against the constitutional monarchy were directed against the princess imperial and her consort. Isabel was labeled a religious zealot manipulating the weakened emperor to advance a radical religious and political agenda. Gaston was caricatured as a malevolent foreigner pulling his wife's strings so that through her, he could rule Brazil. Enemies used the nation's deepest fears and prejudices against them.

Princess Isabel, however, proved to be a formidable opponent. During the abolition crisis she preserved the peace and unity of Brazil, claimed the loyalties of what should have been the natural constituency of the Republican Party, and positioned the constitutional monarchy at the forefront of a powerful progressive movement.[1] As regent and acting head of state she broadened support for the monarchy, ushering in the nation's greatest economic boom in half a century. Despite decades of threats that abolition would bring financial disaster, it brought unparalleled prosperity. And all her accomplishments had been done under the strict guidelines of constitutional government.

With slavery abolished, immigrants rushed to Brazil in record numbers and overseas investors were more willing than ever before to invest in a slave-free country. Still, reactionary anger against Isabel and the monarchy grew, in part because almost no one believed abolition to be the end of the revolution shaking Brazil. Following her father's homecoming, Isabel gracefully surrendered the reins of government to him. Her devotion to her father and the constitution guided her, but monarchists were concerned. If Brazil was to be saved from the forces of reaction, the emperor needed to act firmly and decisively; but Pedro II could do neither.

Isabel's tireless work behind the scenes to help restore her father's health left little time to defend herself or the government. Supporters and opponents of the monarchy recognized the outcome of the escalating conflict would probably determine the future direction of Brazil. Unable to act on her own, others stepped forward to do the job for her. Joaquim Nabuco framed the context of the struggle. "I must fight for the Princess, who is our Lincoln, as I fought for abolition.... All of my efforts are bent toward making the monarchy the creator and the protector of the only democracy that we can have in Brazil, that of the people themselves."[2]

He was not alone. On December 15, 1888, the *Rio News* reported, "The premier Senator João Alfredo Correia de Oliveira celebrated his birthday on the 12th and was visited by many friends and admirers. Among the visitors was an association of freemen who have adopted the very far from euphonious name of the Black Guard."[3] The guard was one of many groups rallying to support the princess imperial. Like many free blacks, the guard felt a special loyalty toward Isabel, and a strong fear of Republicans and their planter allies.[4] They feared both groups wanted to legally or economically re-enslave them.[5] The one public individual they trusted to protect them, and they felt drawn to protect, was Princess Isabel.

José Patrocínio's newspaper *A Cidade do Rio*, covering the birthday of the prime minister, wrote, "Senator João Alfredo responded agreeably to the spontaneous demonstration, wishing the Black Guard hundredfold growth in order to honor the virtues of the reigning sovereign and Her Imperial Highness, who is the angel of Brazil."[6]

Police loyal to the monarchy ignored the Black Guard's anti–Republican activities. Guard members were well trained, highly organized, and Masonic in their rituals and ceremonies. Part of their initiation included the following oath: "By the blood in my veins, by the happiness of my children, by the honor of my mother and the purity of my sisters, and above all by Christ who lives for centuries, I swear to defend the throne of Isabel, the Redeemer."[7]

The antipathy many felt against the guard was caused in part by their belief that blacks were incapable of orchestrating an effective political opposition movement. *Novidades* reported that the prime minister and princess imperial had secretly organized the Black Guard "to replace the planter class as the main support of the monarchy during the third reign."[8] Patrocínio angrily responded, "This affirmation ... is false, very false. Actually, in the capital, there is a group of men that have sworn to defend the Princess, even if it costs them their blood, so that all those who rise behind Republican barricades might beware. This defensive society was not created by the government, but by the heart."[9]

Verbal fireworks escalated as the Republican's alliance with recalcitrant slavocrats grew. One Republican newspaper dismissed the disaffected socioeconomic groups they once claimed to represent: "The corrupting monarchy always finds, in the uncultured classes of society, the docile instruments for the realization for its caprices."[10] Poisoned rhetoric and political tensions spilled into the streets as the Black Guard monitored and harassed Republican meetings, especially those attended exclusively by whites.[11] In December a black man was beaten for attempting to enter a Republican meeting in Rio de Janeiro. A riot ensued.[12] Police on the scene passively watched as shots were fired, a number of people were wounded, and one Republican was killed.

Violence threatened to spread as the emperor's involvement in the government alternated between periods of lucidity and foggy detachment. Princess Isabel and Correia de Oliveira hid the seriousness of his infirmities from Pedro II and the public.[13] Isabel worked to keep her father mentally involved, without burdening him with the venomous propaganda of their enemies.

Support for the monarchy, the emperor, and Princess Isabel remained strong despite the fact that no member of the royal family was able to rally or build upon their natural constituency. The emperor's doctor and the prime minister discouraged Isabel from leaving her father or the capital. Empress Theresa remained in poor health, and Pedro continued forbidding his wife to travel without him. Poldie's younger son was away in the navy, and her oldest son increasingly showed signs of the mental instability that would eventually institutionalize him for the rest of his life.

With no one else able to publicly represent the royal family, Gaston reluctantly stepped forward. He wrote his father, "The situation is embarrassing, but it is essential to maintain support for the sainted emperor. Journalist and others spread the most terrible lies about Isabel, things that only a stranger could say against her."[14] In March Gaston undertook a medical relief mission to Santos, where a yellow fever epidemic was raging. When he was not visiting hospitals, consulting with doctors, and distributing needed medical supplies, he tried to gauge public opinion in areas the Republicans claimed as their own.

Posters appeared throughout the city accusing Gaston of "laughing at the misery of the people" and proclaiming that the "third reign" was building itself upon the sufferings of the sick and dying. One Republican broadside proclaimed, "Let the people die without the menace of the monarchy that is worse than the pestilence."[15] Despite attempts to discredit the visit, to the surprise of many Gaston was well received.

The trip proved to be a humanitarian and political success.[16] Gaston wrote his father, "An effort was made by some ill bred persons to create hostile manifestations, but their efforts happily failed."[17] The editor of the *Journal of Commerce* wrote, "It was fortunate that the Conde d'Eu decided to go there, showing interest in the people.... I wish that the Princess too had shown the same respect."[18]

Isabel's low public profile failed to curtail the hostility of her enemies or the enthusiasm of her supporters. Many of her followers began calling themselves "Isabelists." The *Rio News* analyzed part of their intense allegiance: "She has attached to herself many a subject upon whose loyalty she could never have relied, and she has made her name a household word in places among the lowliest of her people where before it was rarely heard."[19] As the anniversary of the Golden Law approached, "Isabelists" viewed the princess imperial as a living symbol of emancipation, the protector of their hopes and dreams.[20]

Privately Isabel also came to see herself as an agent for change. Like the abolitionists, she believed additional reforms necessary if Brazil were to ever reach its full potential.[21] The emperor and prime minister arrived at the same conclusion. In his speech from the throne on May 3, 1889, a stronger Pedro II seemed to embrace at least some of the land reform proposals advocated by Rebouças, Nabuco, Prado and other social activists. The pronouncement gave hope to supporters of the third reign, but further angered opponents.

Pedro II declared, "In order to increase immigration and agricultural labor, it is important that the proposal to regularize landed property and facilitate the acquisition and cultivation of public lands be passed into law according to your best judgment. On that occasion, you should consider the convenience of conceding to the government the right to expropriate uncultivated lands along railroad to serve as nuclei of colonization."[22]

The speech caused a virtual firestorm in and out of parliament. *Novidades* thundered, "After the slave, the land: There we have it, toward the end of the Speech from the Throne, leaving no room for doubt in anyone's mind. The government understands that it has the right to attempt a criminal act against landed property, to divide it, to decimate it, to distribute it to whomever it pleases."[23] The *Gazeta da Tarde* called the government proposal a simple act of socialism. And in Minas Gerais a newspaper promised that this "bold and monstrous attack ... against the planter class ... will inevitably bring a general conflagration to the country."[24]

A tempestuous parliamentary session followed. The renewed prosperity of the country, the increase in public revenues beyond all budget projections, and the arrival of 200,000 immigrants in the year following abolition were dismissed or ignored.[25] Within weeks Prime Minister Correia de Oliveira lost his working majority in the General Assembly. All efforts of reconciliation and compromise failed. The ministry that had peacefully brought abolition to Brazil resigned.[26]

Conservatives were unable to find a leader able to mend the split within their party, and Pedro II turned to former prime minister Saraiva to form a new Liberal ministry. Saraiva, citing ill health and age, declined. But during their discussions he was asked if a third reign, Princess Isabel's, would be possible. Saraiva replied that in Brazil's politically poisoned climate he feared not, gently confiding, "The kingdom of Her Highness is not of this world."[27]

The pessimistic words may have spurred the emperor to turn to the charismatic Liberal Party leader Afonso Celso, the Visconde Ouro Preto, who had only recently been elevated to the nobility by Princess Isabel.[28] He believed the third reign not only possible, but an absolute necessity in order to preserve Brazil's constitutional government. The respected resourceful leader quickly and enthusiastically agreed to form a new ministry.

Ouro Preto selected a cabinet composed of strong reformers, most of whom were recognized supporters of the princess imperial. The position of minister of empire, the "patronage rich" post controlling the nation's all important "electoral machinery," was given to the Baron of Loreto. Amandinha, his wife, was Isabel's closest childhood friend. Such appointments caused one opposition newspaper to report the cabinet "was definitely organized not in the palace of the Emperor, but in the palace of the heir to the throne."[29]

Gaston nevertheless was privately disappointed. He wrote the Condessa Barral, "I would have much preferred the acceptance of the most radical elements in order to satisfy the longings for reform and to compete with the Republicans. If the new ministry is going to appear, as did its predecessor, as the vehicle for the Princess's desires, nothing will have been truly gained."[30]

As the first anniversary of the Golden Law approached, the *Gazeta da Tarda* predicted bloodshed:

> The Princess is responsible for all that is about to occur, and consequently, her natural counselor the Conde d'Eu because one word from him to his wife and from her to her minister would impede this profound anarchy into which it is designed to cast Brazilian society by the establishment of a war of the races. Therefore it is necessary that the people should hold the Princess, her husband, and her minister responsible for the smallest drop of blood which is shed on the 13th, and whoever on this day loses a father, husband, son or brother, should in the interest of personal preservation make good use of dynamite against those persons who take the responsibility of so abominable an occasion doing against the Princess, the Conde d'Eu, and her minister and against the Princess's "Black Guard."

Even as the *Gazeta* railed against the violence it claimed to fear, it encouraged violence against Isabel, her family and supporters: "The Imperial family of Brazil is the only reigning family against which there has never been a criminal attempt, but it merits this since it publicly promotes a society of assassins.... Should there be blood spilled, the Princess Imperial is responsible."[31] The Golden Law's anniversary passed with no reports of violence anywhere in Brazil. The only recorded explosion was a verbal one. In Petrópolis, the emperor was quoted in newspapers as again confirming he and Princess Isabel were fully committed to continuing the reforms begun the previous May.[32]

Anger and frustration buffeted opponents of the monarchy. They felt their way of life threatened, their politicians outmaneuvered, and neglect and isolation from the center of power they had always believed was theirs alone. The Chamber of Deputies handed them their latest defeat, rejecting Republican demands for an inquiry into the state of the emperor's health.[33] The vote was a lopsided ninety-four to four. That same week newspapers reported that the size of the army, already small by Latin American standards, was below authorized troop strength. The report infuriated supporters of the military. The government had recently outlawed, then disbanded, press gangs, the only recruitment tool available to fill the army's dwindling ranks.[34]

Republican newspapers fanned military anger by identifying the imagined villain behind such affronts. "Who does not know that, in the nominations and promotions in the army, nothing is resolved without pleasing the Marshal Conde d'Eu?... The entire career of our officer corps is in the hands of the prince-consort.... The [position of] perpetual lord of our armed forces ... is assumed by the husband of the presumptive heiress."[35] Gaston, "tired of being used as a scapegoat," requested permission from the government to make an extended tour of the Northern provinces.[36] He hoped his absence would make it difficult for his enemies to blame him for meddling in political and military affairs.[37] The ministry soon announced the prince marshal would visit the "drought stricken districts" of the northeast. Privately Gaston hoped to use his travels to "learn the real feelings of the people regarding the succession of the Princess Imperial."[38] Prime Minister Ouro Preto and Pedro II believed Isabel should also accompany Gaston, but the court doctor vetoed her participation. He feared if the emperor died suddenly and Isabel did not immediately assume power, their enemies would overthrow the constitutional monarchy.[39]

Gaston's four-month tour was a personal triumph, convincing him and others the monarchy retained broad popular support.[40] Silva Jardim, the firebrand radical republican, shadowed Gaston's early itinerary in an attempt to steal headlines and disrupt his trip. He failed miserably. Jardim's poorly attended speeches were violently attacked by pro-monarchist mobs. Within weeks he fled home, lucky to escape with his life.

The Conde d'Eu prided himself on being politically astute, but compared to his wife and even the ailing emperor, his instincts were perpetually clouded by a blind pessimism. In the midst of his wildly successful tour, he confounded an admiring crowd in Recife by volunteering the monarchy would never fight to hold onto power. He then added if elections indicated the people preferred a republic to the monarchy, the imperial family would willingly go into exile. His speech stunned his audience into silence, and gave renewed hope to the monarchy's enemies.

Princess Isabel was deeply upset when she read her husband's remarks. Gaston's words discouraged their supporters and damaged the monarchist cause. The editor of Rio de Janeiro's *Journal of Commerce* wrote in an ironic understatement, "The Conde d'Eu made in Pernambuco a speech that was politically of small prudence."[41] Rather than address the political implications of his words, Isabel wrote Gaston her personal reaction. "I well understand that, should there be another form of government, we would perhaps be obliged to withdraw, but I don't like saying that. I am attached to the country, I was born here, and everything in it reminds me of my 43 years of happiness!"[42] Upon reflection, Isabel decided not to send Gaston the letter but saved it in her personal papers. Princess Isabel found her future dependent on a husband willing to accept a fate that would destroy everything she had prepared her entire public life to do.

Isabel may have drawn comfort that the charismatic Ouro Preto seemed able to restore the emperor to some of his former vitality. The new prime minister counseled Pedro II, "Your Majesty has noticed that in some of the provinces there is agitated and active propaganda for a change in the form of government.... In my humble opinion, it is important not to underestimate this torrent of false and imprudent ideas, but instead to weaken and incapacitate it.... The way to achieve this is not through violence and repression, but rather by demonstrating practically that the present system of government has sufficient elasticity to recognize the most progressive principles, satisfy all demands of enlightened public opinion, consolidate liberty, and realize the prosperity and greatness of our nation, without disturbing the internal peace.... We will reach this goal, Sir, by initiating, with strength and courage, wide political, social, and economic reforms, inspired by democratic ideals. These reforms should not be postponed.... That which today is enough, may perhaps be too little by tomorrow."[43]

Ouro Preto's words appealed to the very roots of the emperor's best values and principles. The need for meaningful and progressive reforms and a plan to make them a reality seemed to energize the emperor. He endorsed far-reaching economic and political programs including the Jeffersonian ideals of a rural democracy advocated by André Rebouças. Pedro II may have believed an aggressive effort necessary to weaken the Republican threat and prepare the way for Isabel's peaceful ascension to the throne.[44]

The agenda was radical in its design and implications, abolishing the life term of senators, reducing the power of the Council of State, granting more administrative and electoral power to provinces, and publicly allowing freedom of religion for all faiths. It promised to reform education, to reduce export duties, to improve infrastructure and transportation, the amortization of foreign debt, universal suffrage for all males, and the enactment of major land reforms to allow more Brazilians to own their land.[45] In the past Pedro II had opposed many of the reforms he now supported.

When the Liberal legislative program was presented in the General Assembly, a Conservative deputy became so incensed he declared himself a Republican, ending his harangue, "Down with the monarchy! Long live the Republic!"[46] Ouro Preto responded, "No! No! And, again No! For it is under the monarchy that we have obtained the liberty which other nations envy.... Viva the monarchy! — the only form of government to which the immense majority of the people are attached, and the only one that can make for its happiness and greatness!"[47] His remarks were met by long and enthusiastic applause. But opponents denounced reforms they once advocated when their own party was in power.

The energetic prime minister moved quickly to divide his enemies, appealing directly to the presidents of the provinces for support.[48] Since the government's finances had never been in a stronger position, he guaranteed new low interest bank loans to planters while encouraging foreign investment in agriculture, business, commerce and industry. He granted titles of nobility to those he wished to court, including some of his enemies. With parliamentary elections scheduled at the end of August, he intended to use the same tactics his

Conservative predecessors used to achieve majorities necessary to pass his reform program.[49] Ouro Preto was confident the constitutional monarchy would survive by promoting social, political, and economic opportunities built on a foundation of dramatically expanding land ownership.[50]

As his health continued to stabilize, the emperor was seen more frequently in public. On July 15th, he, the empress and Princess Isabel attended the Santa Anna Theatre in Rio de Janeiro. As they left the theatre, a man shouting "Long live the Republican Party" fired a shot at their carriage. Despite the shock, no one was injured, and the emperor and princess imperial reacted with great coolness. The Republican assailant was quickly apprehended but insisted he would not miss the next time.[51] It was apparent politics in Brazil had taken a dangerous turn. The assassination attempt temporally caused the propaganda assault against the monarchy to subside. The Condessa Barral wrote the emperor, "The earth is trembling."[52]

When Gaston returned from his northern tour in September he seemed unusually refreshed and optimistic. He had been "received everywhere with manifestations of good will." Even conservative planters assured him of their unshaken loyalty to the monarchy.[53] Gaston's feelings seemed validated by the recent overwhelming victory of the Liberal Party, helped by the government's full support and perhaps by the emotional backlash of the assassination attempt. Many planters, city dwellers, bankers, investors and merchants enthusiastically endorsed Ouro Preto's reform agenda.[54]

Despite vigorous campaigning, large expenditures of legal and illegal funds, and fear generating rhetoric, a badly divided Republican Party elected only one candidate to the General Assembly.[55] The demoralized Conservatives retained only a handful of their former seats.[56] Defeated candidates claimed the election was stolen, but opposition members in the legislature had few options but to pledge to work with the Liberal majority. The sheer size of the victory reassured the emperor and Princess Isabel the throne retained the wide support of the people.[57]

That August Isabel took the opportunity to secretly write a letter to her close friend the Visconde de Santa Vitória. In her letter she shared her innermost thoughts and hopes for the future. She had been quietly working with a group of landowners to donate lands so former slaves would be able to make a living through farming and raising livestock. But she did not stop there, writing, "I now want to dedicate myself to freeing women from the fetters of domestic captivity. This will be possible through feminine suffrage. If women can reign, they can also vote."[58] The letter revealed Isabel's vision for a Brazil where economic, racial, and gender opportunities would not be bound by the prejudices and traditions of the past.[59]

Princess Isabel looked to the future with great hope and confidence. *O Paíz*, the influential Republican newspaper, wrote in resignation, "The monarchy has never seemed so secure on its pedestal, so sure of its rights.... By the

"The earth is trembling," Isabel's former governess wrote following an unsuccessful assassination attempt on the royal family in 1889. Here the family gathers that same year on the steps of the Isabel Palace in Petrópolis. From left to right: seated, Empress Theresa; seated at her feet, Isabel's youngest son Antônio; standing, Princess Isabel holding onto Emperor Pedro II; seated, her second son, Luís; standing, Isabel's nephew Pedro Augusto; husband Gaston; and oldest son Pedro. Courtesy of Imperial Museum / Iphan / Ministry of Culture, Petrópolis, Brazil.

exclusion of the Republicans from the Chamber and by the formal or informal league of Conservatives and Liberals, it seems that the monarchy is firm."[60]

A month after Isabel wrote her letter to the Visconde de Santa Vitória, General Deodoro da Fonseca returned to Rio de Janeiro after a tour of duty on the Mato Grosso frontier. Since an earlier defeat for a senate seat, the popular monarchist had become increasingly outspoken in his demands for an expanded political role for the military.[61] Like many junior officers, he found it difficult to accept the election results. The Liberal Party viewed the political ambitions of the military even less favorably than did the Conservatives.[62] That week the liberal *Rio News* editorialized, "It does not appear to be ordinary common sense to fill a class with exaggerated opinions of its weight in the nation while it is really dangerous in the case of the army."[63] Deodoro da Fonseca was flattered to find himself courted by a group of military officers and Republicans he had only recently scorned, but who saw in him a leader and possible ally they might use against the monarchy.

Brazilians not discussing politics found something else to talk about. A brilliant meteorite was seen streaking across the night skies before crashing to the earth. For centuries the superstitious believed such heavenly displays foretold the death of kings, natural disasters, or other impending calamities. Some held their breath, others prayed, a few decided to act.

42

"Conspiracy"

That July, as in every year since she was born, Princess Isabel's birthday was celebrated as a national holiday. All government buildings were closed. A celebration was held at the City Palace attended by the entire diplomatic corps, Prime Minister Ouro Preto, his cabinet, and Brazilians from all levels of society. Despite the surface calm, Ouro Preto refused to rest until the constitutional monarchy was safe from its enemies.

Since his appointment he had worked feverishly toward that goal. His political reforms and the country's booming economy isolated and undermined the appeal of the frustrated Republicans. Following the Liberal electoral landslide, only scattered Republicans in the provinces of São Paulo, Minas Gerais, and Rio de Janeiro continued their shrill campaign against the government. Joaquim Nabuco dealt the Republicans a further blow by discontinuing his popular column for the Republican newspaper *O País* but not before denouncing the party for preaching democracy "while courting the oligarchy."[1] He wrote, "My conscience tells me that I am with the people in defending the monarchy, because the republic has no room for the illiterate, for the little guy, for the poor."[2] Nabuco warned of another growing threat: "The army has, in fact, become the focus of the republican conspiracy in this country."[3]

He was not alone in recognizing that electoral defeats and repeated political setbacks strengthened a growing alliance between the Republicans and disgruntled military men. To further inflame their allies, Republican propaganda accused Ouro Preto of seeking the "total destruction of the military class."[4] One Republican newspaper predicted, "The noble Prime Minister will destroy the army at its roots, annulling it organically, substantially, irremediably."[5]

With Republican attacks focused on Ouro Preto, Princess Isabel and Gaston were able to peacefully celebrate their twenty-fifth wedding anniversary. On October 15th, they received a steady stream of friendly visitors to their home. The Black Guard also celebrated, peacefully marching through the streets of Rio de Janeiro in strength to honor their princess.[6] A few newspapers wrote alarming accounts of the guard's marches and the threat of anarchy they represented. Rumors of the impending abdication of Pedro II also filled the news.[7]

241

Still, for the most part, the day belonged to monarchists and supporters of the princess imperial. Gaston wrote his father, "The greater part of the press ... showed a friendliness to which we are not accustomed and the dissenters confined themselves to silence."[8]

On the ninth of November 1889, Prime Minister Ouro Preto hosted the most elaborate imperial ball in decades.[9] To many, the celebration signaled the rebirth of the monarchy. The occasion was precipitated by a good will tour of Chilean war ships and was held in the glittering new neo–Gothic customhouse on an island in Guanabara Bay. Its location allowed the ships of both nations and the entire city to share in the celebration. A holiday was declared, and people danced to Latin rhythms in the large plaza in front of the City Palace.

When night fell, revelers rushed to the beaches to marvel at "the basket of lights in the middle of the darkness of the sea."[10] Three Chilean battle cruisers and ships from the Brazilian navy were "a blaze of light." Music and champagne flowed, and thousands of candles and gaslights lit the castle-like customhouse. The brilliant illuminations against the sky and reflections on Guanabara Bay were long remembered by the 4000 invited guests and the thousands watching from shore and on ships.[11]

Two events stood out in people's minds long after the glorious lights faded. The first focused on the emperor. At exactly 10:00 P.M. the royal barge arrived at the island carrying Pedro II, Theresa, Isabel and Gaston. Their arrival was greeted by spontaneous salutes and thunderous applause, but as the emperor stepped onto a large granite step he seemed to lose his balance and trip.[12] Guests rushed to his assistance, but he caught himself, joking, "The monarchy stumbles, but does not fall."[13]

The second memorable part of the evening was the conspicuous absence of nearly the entire officer corps of the Brazilian army. All had been invited, but few attended. Earlier in the day as Pedro II, Empress Theresa, Princess Isabel and Gaston dedicated a new hospital, one hundred and fifty army officers met in secret to finalize plans for a military coup d'etat. Days earlier the newspaper O Paíz had printed a story about an imagined plot "to secure the throne for the Imperial Princess [by] scattering the army over the empire."[14] Fears the army would be dispersed and replaced by National Guard and Black Guard, regiments were used by dissident army officers to justify overthrowing the constitutional government.

The planted story convinced wavering conspirators to act before Ouro Preto's newly elected parliament could convene on November 20th. Most were junior level officers, recent recruits to the Republican Party protected by high-ranking officers sympathetic to their goals. They joined with frustrated Republican activists determined to seize by force what they had failed to capture through the ballot box. Following their meeting, one of its leaders was badgered by his adolescent daughters into renting a boat so they could observe the imperial ball. As he and his daughters watched from their launch, he gave no indication they were watching the last magnificent hours of Brazil's constitutional monarchy.[15]

Rumors of a possible coup had been circulating for weeks, causing Ouro Preto to place the police force on high alert. He also requested the president of the province to dispatch additional troops to the capital. The minister of war, the adjutant general and other high ranking military officers assured Ouro Preto they too had heard the rumors, but the government could depend on the loyalty of their soldiers.

As midnight approached on the evening of November 14th the prime minister heard by telephone that a coup attempt had begun. He immediately ordered the adjutant general to move against the rebellious troops. During the night, Ouro Preto continued receiving information confirming that two isolated cavalry units and a battalion of artillery stationed near São Cristóvão Palace led the mutiny. At 4:00 A.M. he sent a telegram to Pedro II in Petrópolis informing him of the revolt, that the city's remaining troops remained loyal and he was confident the situation under control.

The minister of war urged Ouro Preto and his ministers to move to the fortified army headquarters where they would be safe and their presence would help rally loyal troops. Ouro Preto agreed. At seven that morning, a small detachment of mutineers approached army headquarters led by General Deodoro da Fonseca. Ouro Preto ordered his minister of war and adjutant general to immediately move against them, but they refused. As Ouro Preto argued with the two men, the gates of the army headquarters were opened.

General da Fonseca greeted Ouro Preto with the traditional salute of "Long Live the Emperor," but followed it with a bitter personal denunciation of the prime minister and his liberal government. The general informed Ouro Preto his ministry had been dismissed to be replaced by one more favorable to the military.[16] In the midst of the confrontation the loyal minister of the marine arrived. An altercation broke out and he was wounded and arrested. Surrounded, isolated, and outnumbered, Ouro Preto muttered, "We have been miserably betrayed."[17]

Princess Isabel and Gaston awakened at their usual time at the Isabel Palace knowing nothing of the army mutiny taking place. The date was November 15, 1889, forty-three years to the day Isabel had begun her public life with her baptism. Gaston and their three sons went for their usual horseback ride in the country as Isabel planned a reception for the Chilean navy officers at the Isabel Palace. Shortly before ten, two senior military officers arrived to inform her that part of the army was in revolt.[18]

Conflicting information followed. Word reached them Ouro Preto and his ministry was under arrest and the minister of the marine had been shot by insurgents, but telephone calls to the army and navy arsenals reported nothing amiss. Within minutes a dispatch arrived telling them "peace had been restored," but the army had forced the ministry to resign. When Gaston was notified General da Fonseca was at army headquarters with leaders of the Republican Party, he told Isabel the end of the monarchy was at hand. She refused to believe it. Gaston urged them to retreat to Petrópolis to join the emperor, but Isabel again rejected his words. Later she remembered, "I was concerned that if things were not as stated, I might later be accused of fear, of which ... I have never given a sign."[19]

Only when Isabel discovered the telegraph office had been taken over by mutineers did she agree to send her sons to Petrópolis, where her father could be notified of the unsettling events.[20] Shortly following her children's departure, she received word that her parents had left Petrópolis and would soon arrive at the City Palace. She and Gaston quickly went to join them. Upon their arrival and throughout the day, Pedro II refused to believe the situation serious. He repeatedly rejected arguments that he contact army insurgents or rally military or civilian authorities.

As disturbing news continued to arrive, the emperor became more and more detached from the events swirling around him. When told of Ouro Preto's resignation, he announced it would not be accepted. Only when Ouro Preto himself traveled to the palace was he personally able to convince the emperor a new cabinet must be formed at once; but when he discovered his first choice for prime minister was traveling at sea he refused to consider anyone else.

Gaston alternated between periods of gloomy resignation and agitated calls for action. The empress was frightened and distraught. Pedro II retreated into denial and lethargy. Isabel pleaded with her father to call a meeting of the Council of State, but he ignored her. By evening, Isabel summoned the council in her own name. They responded at once, but her father did not join them until shortly before midnight. During the tense meeting that followed, the council agreed with Isabel that a new prime minister must be appointed at once. The distracted emperor finally agreed to ask former prime minister Saraiva to form a new ministry. By the time Saraiva was sent for, the day and the empire had been lost.[21]

Saraiva arrived at 1:30 in the morning. After consulting with the emperor, he reluctantly agreed to serve as prime minister and sent a letter to General da Fonseca requesting a meeting. The emperor retired for the night, but Princess Isabel and Gaston anxiously waited for the reply. When the messenger returned, he told them, "The republic was definitely established."[22] For the first time since the mutiny began, shots were fired outside the City Palace. Marines loyal to the emperor were forcibly removed.[23]

By morning, infantry and cavalry units sent by the coup leaders surrounded the palace, sealing all public entrances and exits. Pedro Augusto, Poldie's oldest son, had joined them, but his younger brother was overseas with the navy. Except for Isabel's sons in Petrópolis, the entire royal family had become prisoners. An escape plan was presented urging the emperor to leave the palace by a hidden passage and seek refuge on one of the Chilean warships.

A similar escape had once allowed his grandfather to save his Portuguese throne. Despite Isabel's pleas, he refused to consider it.

The following afternoon, Pedro II was presented a manifesto from the coup leaders justifying their actions and informing the royal family they were to leave Brazil within twenty-four hours. Isabel later wrote, "It is impossible to recount what we felt in our hearts! The idea of leaving friends, the country that I love ... that recalls a thousand happinesses ... made me break into sobs."[24]

Princess Isabel could not take a stand against the mutineers without her father's support, and he refused to give it. Gaston had already accepted the death of the monarchy and Empress Theresa had been overcome with grief. Imprisoned and isolated in the City Palace, separated from her children in Petrópolis, Isabel had few options but to acquiesce. She sent for her children and with the rest of the royal family quietly began to put her affairs in order. Messages were sent to her home and to the São Cristóvão Palace to pack whatever belongings time allowed. Then Princess Isabel, the emperor, and Gaston each wrote farewell letters to the nation.

Shortly after midnight, their captors awakened the royal family to tell them it was no longer safe for them to remain in Brazil. They were told they must leave the City Palace at once. Alarm, confusion, and fear seemed everywhere. In reality, the mutineers feared a popular uprising to save the constitutional government, but the anxiety of the captors added to the uncertainty of moment.

The royal family had planned to attend mass the following morning in the nearby Carmo Convent, the former Brazilian home of Maria I. There they hoped to wait for Isabel's children, but those plans were dashed. Isabel informed her captors she would not leave without her children. Only when she was repeatedly promised their reunion would soon take place on board a waiting ship did she consent to depart. Her oldest friend the Baroness of Loreto had joined Isabel in the City Palace and would follow her into exile.

Then as if coming out of a deep fog, Pedro II angrily protested. He insisted he not be treated like a fugitive slave, demanding to know by whose authority he was being expelled in the middle of the night. Guards informed him the decision had been made by the head of the provisional government, General Deodoro da Fonseca. The emperor muttered, "They have all lost their senses."[25] Only when he was assured the departure had been timed to prevent the shedding of Brazilian blood did Pedro II quietly acquiescence and prepare to leave the City Palace for the last time.

He and the empress, slowed by age and poor health, slowly walked down the steep steps to a waiting carriage to be driven the short distance to the boat launch. Despite the darkness of the night and a drizzling rain, Princess Isabel and Gaston slowly walked arm in arm from the palace to the water's edge. The plaza and surrounding streets, so often filled with cheers and blazing fireworks in their honor, were empty and deathly quiet. Flickering gaslights lit their way.

The entire area had been cleared so that no Brazilians could bid the imperial family farewell.[26]

Princess Isabel had a bittersweet reunion with her three children on a ship anchored far away from the Brazilian shore. Her sons were accompanied by André Rebouças, who had chosen to share the royal family's exile. Gaston left behind a lengthy farewell letter to Brazil. Of the three testimonies to the nation written by the royal family, his was the longest. It was as if he had been preparing to write it his entire life.[27] The letter of Pedro II was simple and straightforward. It read in part, "I have decided to yield to the force of circumstances and leave with my entire family.... I with all members of my family, will cherish for Brazil, the deepest, most yearning remembrances, while praying earnestly for its greatness and prosperity."[28]

Isabel's statement was the shortest: "With a broken heart I part from my friends, from the whole people of Brazil, and from my country which I have so loved and still do love, toward whose happiness I have done my best to contribute, and for which I shall ever entertain the most ardent good wishes."[29]

Empress Theresa wrote no letter. Her farewell was not in words, but a gesture. In sight of the place where Carlota Joaquina had thrown her shoes in Guanabara Bay to keep from carrying a speck of Brazilian dirt back to Europe with her, Theresa stopped and slowly bent over until kneeling on both knees. During her last moments in her adopted country she leaned forward and kissed the cobblestones goodbye. It was nearly the same spot where forty-six years earlier she had first stepped as a bride.[30]

43

Exiles Under the Southern Cross

Princess Isabel's family left Brazil as they had come — as exiles. Pedro II found comfort that his nation was at peace. As the sights of Rio de Janeiro faded in the distance, he quietly recited to André Rebouças the words from the Song of Simeon, "Now let us thy servants depart in peace."[1]

Gaston also seemed at peace. He was the only member of the royal family to mention their "voyage of exile" in his farewell letter. The words seemed to come easier to him than the rest of the family. Empress Theresa was inconsolable. Through her tears she asked over and over what they had done to be expelled from the country they had served for so long. No one could answer her question, including the soldiers who seemed embarrassed to be guarding the beloved empress. Once their ship sailed, she admitted she had been unable to erase the tragic fate of Emperor Maximilian and Empress Carlotta from her mind.[2] Isabel's mother remained ill throughout the voyage as did Poldie's oldest son. Pedro Augusto seemed to suffer a nervous breakdown. Family members kept a suicide watch, fearing he would throw himself overboard.

Princess Isabel, like her mother, gave way to her tears. But unlike the rest of her family she remained defiant. She confided to the Baroness of Loreto, "If abolition is the cause for this, I don't regret it; I consider it worth losing the throne for."[3] Isabel consigned her grief to her diary: "One cannot be entirely happy in this world! My truly good times are already over! May God let me keep, at least my loved ones! The country of my truest affections is at this very moment receding from sight! God protect it! The memory of happy hours both upholds and saddens me!"[4]

Princess Isabel's last night in Brazil was under an overcast sky. In one of the many letters Isabel wrote her father during her first regency she noted, "I have only looked where the Southern Cross should be and the sky is full of clouds."[5] As she departed from the public stage, all that was familiar to her, including the Brazilian heavens and the future, was hidden from her. Like the constellation of the Southern Cross, Isabel too would soon become invisible.

247

The previous May, Brazil's National History and Geographical Society had asked Princess Isabel's permission to erect a statue commemorating her role in ending slavery. She refused. The society then issued the following proclamation. "One day, far into the future, when the passion of the moment is cooled, when the voices of spite are muted, and the pure truth is re-established, stern and just posterity, with the impartial pen of history, will write the golden page of the glorious seven days in May.... Undoubtedly all the Catholic peoples, when reading 'The Life and Deeds of Princess Isabel' ... will ask that she ... be sanctified as the consoler of the afflicted, as the mirror of justice, the cause of our joy, and in the calendar of saints, we will one day read the name of St. Isabel of Brazil, Condessa d'Eu — Redeemer of the Slaves."[6]

The society was wrong.[7] The army mutineers and rebels who overthrew Brazil's constitutional monarchy believed it "necessary to erase the memory of the Empire."[8] They selected the scribes and historians who interpreted "The Life and Deeds of Princess Isabel." Official reports and subsequent histories of Brazil were written or approved by men with the best reasons to discredit the woman they most feared. In initial newspaper accounts of the revolution, no hero of the abolition crusade was interviewed about the princess who freed the slaves. None of the elected legislators who were denied their seats in the Chamber of Deputies, no former slaves, no members of the Black Guard, and no females were asked their opinion of Isabel.[9]

Brazilians, stunned by the suddenness of the revolution, greeted the birth of the republic in silence. The collapse of the constitutional monarchy was like a death in the family. The cheers that greeted the coming and going of the royal family were not repeated for those who exiled them. For Joaquim Nabuco, José Patrocínio and other social reformers, their dreams for social and economic equity in Brazil ended with the exile of the princess imperial.[10]

Newspapers in the United States quickly embraced the official interpretation presented by the army mutineers. The *Washington Star* of November 16, 1889, headlined: "REVOLUTION— Brazil Suddenly Becomes a Republic — Princess Isabel the Cause ... A Dreaded Woman — Dissatisfaction with Princess Isabel causes the revolt ... Isabel is universally detested both by the masses and the classes."[11] The *New York Times* headlined: "The Cause of Discontent — The Unpopularity of Dom Pedro's daughter and husband."[12] A front page article reported, "The Crown Princess is openly denounced by all hands because of her apparent determination to make the Empire of Brazil a mere tributary to the Pope's revenues. She has expressed herself in this regard in many ways and at many times. She is opposed by the liberals who declare that she will never succeed her father."[13] Princess Isabel's devotion to constitutional principles, her passion for social and economic justice, her concern for "the poor and lowly" and their loyalty to her was unreported.[14]

A few North American newspapers viewed the coup d'etat differently. The *New Orleans State Democrat* wrote, "A liberal imperialism has given place to a nondescript military despotism."[15] And the *Philadelphia Ledger* called the leaders of the revolt "selfish and grasping military adventurers."[16] In Brazil Joaquim Nabuco's daughter Caroline sadly wrote that it was a "revolution ... carried out in the classic South American style by a group of officers who were unfaithful to their trust."[17] The president of Venezuela lamented that with the fall of the Brazilian monarchy, the continent had lost its only true republic.[18]

Brazil's new rulers moved quickly to reshape the country into their own image. Although the nation was at peace with no external threats or enemies, their first order of business was to double the size of the army.[19] Freedom of the press was immediately curtailed, and strict government censorship instituted. Within a short period of time Brazilian bank notes lost two-thirds of their value and the national debt doubled. A female Brazilian journalist noted, "The violence of the government was equaled only by its vigilance."[20]

Within a year of seizing power, General da Fonseca dismissed the parliament his government had installed, declared martial law, and was deposed by another general who had been his vice president. Legal slavery was replaced on plantations by "a form of peonage." Brazil was soon indistinguishable from its neighboring military dictatorships.[21]

Princess Isabel and her family retraced the original voyage of exile her ancestors had taken eighty-two years earlier. Their first sighting of Portugal was the nation's jagged southeastern coast, unchanged since long before the days of Prince Henry the Navigator. It had been the last sight her ancestors had seen on their way to America and was still referred to by sailors as the end of the world.

The family landed in Belém, Portugal, without money or a home. King Carlos I, who had succeeded to the throne of his late father just weeks earlier, welcomed his cousins with full royal honors. It was a gesture Pedro II had never offered any of his own family when they were exiled. The emperor and the Conde d'Eu were eagerly interviewed by waiting reporters. Princess Isabel was ignored. Within weeks, death claimed Empress Theresa. Queen Victoria wrote, "The revolution doubtless killed her. It is too sad."[22] Theresa's last words were, "Poor Brazil."[23]

Following the death of the empress, the family moved to France, where the restless emperor struggled with the changing seasons and homesickness. He moved frequently from hotel to hotel, seeking refuge in his books and family. Isabel and Gaston lived in a rented villa paid for from a monthly allowance granted them by the Duke of Nemours. To Gaston's surprise, after living a quarter of a century in Brazil, his sense of being an exile followed him to the land of his birth.[24]

On the anniversary of the Golden Law, Joaquim Nabuco wrote a letter to Princess Isabel in the name of his nation's abolitionists. It read in part, "Only for your Imperial Highness will this day retain the same shining brightness. For those who up until November 15th thought only of revenge, the day now recalls only the disillusionment of vengeance. For the slaves it has become a day of mourning, and for all abolitionists a day of expiation. The slaves feel a wound in their freedom and the abolitionists a flaw in their gratitude."[25] Isabel spent the anniversary quietly with her father and the son of the Visconde Rio Branco. Rio Branco's father had successfully guided the Law of the Free Womb through parliament. Like his late father, the son remained a friend to the monarchy and its royal family until the end of his own life.[26]

Two Decembers later, Pedro II died in a Paris hotel room where he had been living. It had been his last wish to die on Brazilian soil, and in a way he did. Under his pillow Princess Isabel found a small container of soil he carried with him from Brazil. France accorded Pedro II a full state funeral befitting a head of state. He was buried in the Royal Bragança Mausoleum atop a Lisbon hill at São Vicente Monastery. There he joined his father, sister, grandparents and most of the Braganças who had ruled Portugal since 1640.

The death of the Duke of Nemours provided Isabel and Gaston an inheritance that, with the sale of their properties in Brazil, allowed them to pay off their debts. They used the money to purchase a home in the suburbs of Paris and the fire damaged country estate of Louis Philippe in Eu, where they quietly raised their children and later enjoyed their grandchildren.

Although Princess Isabel was now the head of the imperial dynasty, she continued referring to herself only as the Condessa d'Eu. All family matters were deferred to Gaston, but when it came to Brazil, no one was allowed to speak for her or to use her name in any cause but a peaceful one. An 1893 issue of *Harper's Weekly* magazine reported, "Brazil has not been absolutely at peace since the dethronement of Dom Pedro."[27] Repressive tactics of Brazil's military dictatorship had resulted in resistance in both the military and civilian population. The leaders of an 1892 navy revolt petitioned Isabel for support, but she refused, explaining in a letter, "I would regret anything that arms brother against brother.... I do not consider it to be the role of the royal prerogative to be involved in such a struggle."[28]

Privately she wrote Correia de Oliveira, prime minister during her third regency, "In no way do I wish to encourage such a war.... When will politicians stop resorting to means that diminish the moral stature of people and individuals?... How preferable it would be if moral persuasion alone enabled us to return."[29] Since the overthrow of the constitutional monarchy, moral persuasion seemed not to matter in Brazil. Isabel longed to return to her homeland, but would not use force to achieve her dream. Years later her granddaughter remembered her as "charming, intelligent, and assertive," a strong woman who knew how to express her authority. Still, her grandmother never spoke of Brazil without tears filling her eyes.[30]

For Princess Isabel, life in French exile was devoted to her family, her music, her beloved gardens, and her church. She seldom spoke on public affairs, but in 1905 she granted a female journalist an interview in which she was asked about the abolition of slavery in Brazil. Isabel told her, "That was a glorious moment indeed and I have tasted its sweetness ever since.... I have lived to achieve that deed.... Would not any Christian worthy of the name give up every spark of human happiness to live the overwhelming beauty of that hour.... Even now I hear through my dreams the voices that were raised in exuberance and blessing.... To me the word freedom is one full of import. In that word I have put the aim of my every effort. Now I work to free slaves again, but of course on a smaller scale."[31]

Isabel confined her comments on current events to speaking out against the slavery that continued to exist in Africa and for the cause of world peace. But even in exile, war and violence found her. Her cousin King Carlos I of Portugal and his heir Luís Felipe were assassinated in Lisbon in 1908. Two years later revolution drove her surviving Portuguese cousins into English exile. The assassination of another cousin, Austrian archduke Franz Ferdinand, sparked the First World War in 1914.

Years earlier her cousin Maximilian had tried to arrange a marriage between Poldie and his younger brother, the man who became Franz Ferdinand's father. Poldie's youngest son Gaston, named for Isabel's husband, fought for Austria and the Triple Entente in the conflict. Isabel's two youngest sons resigned commissions in the Austrian army to fight for the allies against their Austrian and German cousins.[32]

The mother of the last empress of Austria-Hungary was a Bragança and Poldie's youngest brother-in-law was tsar of Bulgaria, an ally of Germany and Austria. The Kaiser's sister, godchild of Isabel's parents, lost her firstborn son fighting for Germany. By the 1918 armistice, most of Princess Isabel's relatives on both sides of the trenches had lost their thrones, but more painful losses were closer to home. Within weeks of the armistice, her two youngest sons died of war related injuries. Princess Isabel's faith, the faith her enemies had so often maligned, sustained and comforted her.

In 1920, as the centennial of Brazil's independence approached, the law of exile banishing the royal family was finally lifted. The Republican government asked that the remains of Emperor Pedro I, Emperor Pedro II, and Empress Theresa Christina be returned to Brazil. Gaston and Princess Isabel were also formally invited to return, but at seventy-five years of age, Isabel could no longer walk and was too ill to travel. She died the next year on November 14, 1921, and was buried in the mausoleum of the French royal family in Druex. Death claimed her one day before the thirty-second anniversary of the Brazilian revolution. In 1922 Gaston was invited by Brazil's Republican government to be their guest during the nation's centennial celebration. He died on the ship taking him from Europe to South America, dying as he had lived, between two worlds.

On the 150th anniversary of Brazilian independence in 1971, the body of Princess Isabel finally returned to America. For two weeks her coffin rested not in Rio de Janeiro's cathedral, but in a small church named for Saint Benedict

Princess Isabel returns to the Isabel Palace for the last time in 1971. From the steps of her palace may be seen the cathedral where she would be buried with her husband beside the emperor and empress. Courtesy of Imperial Museum / Iphan / Ministry of Culture, Petrópolis, Brazil.

the Moor — one of the few Catholic saints who was black. The church was chosen because it had once been the religious center for black abolitionists fighting for emancipation.

In its annex was the Museum of the Negro, chronicling the history of Brazilian slavery. An allegorical sketch in the museum of a black slave woman with blue eyes, "her face muzzled by a face mask," sparked speculation among black pilgrims that the silenced woman had been Isabel's wet nurse. So powerful was Princess Isabel's appeal to the underclass, the mythical figure was popularly declared a saint. Today she is worshipped by millions of poor Brazilians despite the Catholic Church's condemnation of the legend as a "noxious superstition" and an investigation that officially concluded the woman never existed.[33]

As a former head of state Princess Isabel was given a state funeral before being laid to rest in Petrópolis. There she was buried in the Catholic cathedral a short walk from her former home and the Crystal Palace, where she danced in celebration after legally ending Brazilian slavery.

Gaston rests by her side. They are buried behind the more impressive tombs of her parents in the cool shadows of the large Gothic church. Isabel's tomb is ignored by most busy tourists; but it is regularly visited by streams of nameless Brazilians bringing flowers to the princess they continue to claim as their own.

Appendix A:
Monarchs of Portugal, 1321–1853

João I	(1385–1433)	and Philippa of Lancaster, founders of the Avis Dynasty and monarchs during the first Portuguese invasion of Africa. Philippa encouraged her sons to invade Africa. One of them, Prince Henry the Navigator, began Portugal's African slave trade.
Duarte I	(1433–1438)	and Leonora of Aragon, monarchs during the second Portuguese invasion of Africa. Leonora's alliance with Prince Henry allowed the African slave trade to continue.
Afonso V	(1438–1481)	Philippa's grandson and Leonora's son becomes known as Afonso the African for his interest in all things African — including its slave trade.
João II	(1481–1495)	During his reign the Portuguese reached the Congo and João which added the "Lord of Guinea" to his title as monarch.
Manuel I	(1495–1521)	During his reign the Portuguese crown became allies of the kings of the Congo, spreading Christianity and slavery. Portugal reached the peak of its wealth and power.
João III	(1521–1557)	and Catherine of Austria led the colonization of Brazil after its European discovery in 1500. Catherine's diplomatic machinations allowed Portugal to transport African slaves to America for Spain and Portugal. Their grandson Sebastião became king after their son's death.
Sebastião	(1557–1578)	Catherine's grandson and heir to the throne was killed in an invasion of Africa. The Avis Dynasty ended with the death of Sebastião's elderly unmarried childless uncle two years later.

Phillip I   (1581–1598)   Spanish monarch seized the throne of Portugal, con-
                                 tinuing the slave trade.

Phillip II   (1598–1621)   Spanish monarch of Portugal.

Phillip III   (1621–1640)   Spanish monarch of Portugal.

João IV   (1640–1658)   and Luísa of Bragança declared Portuguese inde-
                                 pendence from Spain and reclaimed the throne as
                                 the first Bragança monarchs of Portugal. Luísa
                                 expanded the slave trade.

Afonso VI   (1643–1683)   and Maria Francisca of Savoy. Portugal regained its
                                 independence and continued its African slave trade.

Pedro II   (1683–1706)   and Maria Francisca of Savoy continued the slave
                                 trade.

João V   (1706–1750)   African slave trade continues.

José I   (1750–1777)   Slavery abolished in Portugal — slave trade contin-
                                 ued in Brazil.

Maria I   (1777–1816)   Queen of Portugal under whose royal standard Por-
                                 tugal's government in exile sailed to Brazil in 1807–
                                 1808. Maria was Princess Isabel's great-great-grand-
                                 mother. During her reign African slave trade with
                                 Brazil reached an all time high.

João VI 1767   (1816–1826)   Isabel's great-grandfather attempted to end the
                                 African slave trade north of the equator.

Pedro IV 1798   (1826)   Isabel's grandfather declared Brazil's independence
                                 from Portugal and attempted to end the African
                                 slave trade south of the equator.

Maria II 1819   (1834–1853)   Princess Isabel's aunt was the queen of Portugal who
                                 attempted to end Portugal's centuries-long involve-
                                 ment with the slave trade.

Appendix B:
The Monarchy in Brazil,
1808–1889

Maria I	1777–1816	/	1808–1816 in Brazil
João VI	1767–1826	/	1808–1821 in Brazil
Carlota Joaquina	1775–1830	/	1808–1821 in Brazil
Pedro I	1798–1834	/	1808–1831 in Brazil
Leopoldina	1797–1826	/	1817–1826 in Brazil
Pedro II	1825–1891	/	1825–1889 in Brazil
Theresa Christina	1822–1889	/	1843–1889 in Brazil
Isabel I	1846–1921	/	1846–1889 in Brazil
Gaston of Orleans	1842–1922	/	1864–1889 in Brazil

1846	Princess Isabel born
1847–1850	Death of brothers makes Isabel heir to the throne of Brazil
1860	Isabel takes public oath to constitution
1864	Marriage to Gaston of Orleans
1871–1872	First Regency — Princess Isabel signs the Law of Free Birth
1875–1877	Second Regency — Emperor travels to USA, Europe and Africa
1884	War of the Flowers — Isabel's involvement in abolition crusade
1887–1888	Third Regency — Princess Isabel legally ends slavery in Brazil

Chapter Notes

Preface

1. James McMurtry Longo, *An Example of the Hidden Curriculum: The Neglected Role of Women in the Rise and Fall of Brazilian Slavery,* Harvard Graduate School of Education, 1999, Student Research Conference and International Forum, Cambridge, MA, February 26, 1999, 1.

2. James McMurtry Longo, *Isabel of Brazil: The Woman That Ended Slavery in the Americas,* Issues in Third World History, Twenty-first Annual Great Lakes History Conference — The Individual in Society, Grand Rapids, MI, October 4, 1996, 2.

3. Longo, *Hidden Curriculum,* 4.

4. Ibid., 2.

5. Ibid.

6. Ibid.

7. Ibid.

8. Ibid.

9. Ibid.

10. Anna Luísa Orleans-Bragança, interview with author, São Paulo, Brazil, July 29, 1995.

11. Luís Felipe Orleans-Bragança, interview with author, Boston, MA, January 20–21, 1996.

12. Lilian Rixley, *Bamie: Theodore Roosevelt's Remarkable Sister* (New York: David McKay, 1963), vi.

13. Charles Edmund Akers and L.C. Elliott, *A History of South America* (New York: E.P. Dutton, 1930).

14. James McMurtry Longo, *Shadow of Power: Five Generations of Brazilian Women — The Role of the Royal Bragança Women in Brazilian History,* National Association of Hispanic and Latino Studies, International Conference, History and Civil Rights Monograph Series, Houston, TX, February 26, 2000, 16.

15. James McMurtry Longo, *Princess Isabel and the Emperor Pedro II: Imperial Power in the Hands of the Abolitionist Regent of Brazil, 1888,* Latin American Studies Association International Conference, Washington, DC, September 8, 2001, 93.

16. Longo, *Hidden Curriculum,* 2.

17. Longo, *Princess Isabel,* 92

18. Thomas Ewbank, *Life in Brazil* (New York: Harper and Brothers, 1856), 395.

19. Ibid.

20. Ibid.

21. Ibid.

22. Longo, *Shadow of Power,* 16.

23. Ibid., 1.

Chapter 1

1. Bertita Harding, *Amazon Throne: The Story of the Braganças of Brazil* (New York: Bobbs-Merrill, 1941), 28.

2. Neill Macaulay, *Dom Pedro: The Struggle for Liberty in Brazil and Portugal 1798–1834* (Durham, NC: Duke University Press, 1986), 19.

3. Henry H. Keith and S.F. Edwards, *Conflict and Continuity in Brazilian Society* (Columbia: University of South Carolina Press, 1969), 177.

4. Kenneth Light, *The Journal of the Royal Family to Brazil 1807–1808,* 1993, http:// www.fcsh.unl. pt/congressoceap/k-light.doc.

5. Light, 1.

6. Light, 4.

7. Harding, 25.

8. Keith and Edwards, 155.

9. Keith and Edwards, 174.

10. Light, 2.

11. Keith and Edwards, 153.

12. Ibid., 153.

13. Ibid., 156.

14. Ibid., 158.

15. Hugh Thomas, *The Slave Trade: The Story of the Atlantic Save Trade 1440–1870* (New York: Simon and Schuster, 1997), 86, 105.

16. Joseph A. Page, *The Brazilians* (New York: Addison-Wesley, 1995), 28.

17. John Hemming, *Red Gold: The Conquest of the Brazilian Indians 1500–1790* (Cambridge, MA: Harvard University Press, 1978), 146, 151.

18. Luciana Savelli, *Lisbon and Surroundings* (Florence: Bonechi, 1954), 112.

Chapter 2

1. Gonçalo Ribeiro Telles, ed., *A Monarquia Portuguesa* (Lisbon: Reader's Digest, 1993), 298–9.

2. H. V. Livermore, *A History of Portugal* (Cambridge, UK: Cambridge University Press, 1947), 241.

3. Ibid., 179.

4. Peter Russell, *Prince Henry "The Navigator": A Life* (New Haven, CT: Yale University Press, 2000), 23.

5. Rose Macaulay, *They Went to Portugal* (London: Jonathan Cape, 1946), 42.

6. Ibid., 43.

7. Russell, 120.

8. J. P. Olivera Martins, *The Golden Age of Prince Henry the Navigator* (London: Chapman and Hall, 1914), 169.

9. Russell, 146, 162–63.

10. H. V. Livermore, *A New History of Portugal* (Cambridge, UK: Cambridge University Press, 1966), 112.

11. Martins, 235.

12. Russell, 168.

13. Ibid., 168.

14. Martins, 178.

15. Ibid., 172–80.

16. Charles R. Boxer, *The Portuguese Seaborne Empire: 1415–1825* (New York: Alfred A. Knopf, 1969), 26.

17. Russell, 191.

18. Ibid., 134.

19. Manuel De Sousa, *Reis e Rainhas de Portugal* (Lisbon: SporPress, 2000).

20. Livermore, *New History of Portugal*, 113–14.

21. De Sousa, 70.

22. Russell, 192.

23. Ibid., 194.

24. T. F Earle and K. J. P. Lowe, *Black African in Renaissance Europe* (Cambridge, UK: Cambridge University Press, 2006), 169.

25. Thomas, *The Slave Trade*, 14.

26. Henry Kaman, *Empire: How Spain Became a World Power 1492–1763* (New York: HarperCollins, 2003), 124.

27. Charles A. Coulombe, *Vicars of Christ: A History of the Popes* (New York: Citadel Press Books, 2003), 343.

28. Rodney Stark, "The Truth About the Catholic Church and Slavery," *Christianity Today*, 18 August 2003, http://www.christianity today.com/ct/2003/128/53.0.html, 2–3.

29. Hugh Thomas, *Rivers of Gold: The Rise of the Spanish Empire* (London: Weidenfeld and Nicolson, 2003), 353–4, 380–81.

30. Kaman, 17.

31. Thomas, *Rivers of Gold*, 65.

32. Ibid., 83.

33. Ibid., 34.

34. Earle and Lowe, 281.

35. Thomas, *The Slave Trade*, 65–74.

36. Ibid., 106.

37. Kaman, 403.

38. Katia M. DeQueiros Mattoso, *To Be a Slave in Brazil 1550–1888* (New Brunswick, NJ: Rutgers University Press, 1986), 41.

39. Livermore, *New History of Portugal*, 158.

40. Boxer, *Portuguese Seaborne Empire*, 107.

41. Livermore, *History of Portugal*, 279.

42. Ibid.

43. Rose Macaulay, *They Went to Portugal*, 80.

44. Boxer, *Portuguese Seaborne Empire*, 109–110.

45. Edmund B. D'Auvergne, *The Bride of Two Kings* (London: Hutchinson, 1910), 4.

46. Ibid., 4.

47. Martin Gostelow, *Discover Portugal* (Oxford, UK: Berlitz, 1996), 53.

48. Stephen Wise, *Though the Heavens May Fall: The Landmark Trial That Led to the End of Human Slavery* (Cambridge, MA: Perseus, 2005), 16–17.

49. Ibid., 17.

50. Boxer, *Portuguese Seaborne Empire*, 113–114.

51. Thomas, *The Slave Trade*.

52. Ibid., 113.

53. Hemming, *Red Gold*, 318.

54. Ibid., 343.

55. Thomas, *The Slave Trade*, 115.

56. Robert Edgar Conrad, *Children of God's Fire* (Princeton, NJ: Princeton University Press, 1984), 164.

57. Thomas, *The Slave Trade*, 417–421.

58. Ibid., 26.

59. Charles Boxer, *Race Relations in the Colonial Portuguese Empire, 1415–1825* (Oxford, UK: Oxford University Press, 1963), 28.

60. Ibid. 62.

61. D'Auvergne, 36.

62. Ibid., 36.

63. Ibid., 81–82.

64. Ibid., 57–58.

65. Ibid., 57.

66. Ibid., 231, 235, 245.

67. José Custodio Vieira da Silva, *National Palace, Sintra* (London: Scala, 2002), 93.

Chapter 3

1. Neill Macaulay, *Dom Pedro*, 27.

2. Jane Elizabeth Adams, "The Abolition of the Brazilian Slave Trade," *The Journal of Negro History* 4 (Oct. 1925): 606.

3. Earle and Lowe, 9.

4. Thomas, *The Slave Trade*, 552.

5. Ibid., 552.

6. Livermore, *History of Portugal*, 223.

7. Marcus Cheke, *The Life of the Marquis of Pombal* (London: Sidgwick and Jackson, 1938), 7.

8. Livermore, *History of Portugal*, 375.

9. Ibid., 376.

10. Ibid., 377.

11. Ibid., 375.

12. Ibid., 376.

13. Rose Macaulay, *They Went to Portugal*, 100.

14. Ibid.

15. Livermore, *History of Portugal*, 379–380.

16. David Francis, *Portugal 1715–1808* (London: Tamesis, 1985), 193.

17. Ibid.

18. Luíz Edmundo da Costa, *Rio in the Time of*

the Viceroys (Rio de Janeiro: Athena Editora, 1935), 12.

19. Maria Inês Ferro, *Queluz: The Palace and Gardens* (London: Scala, 1997), 33.

20. Ibid., 36–7.

21. Ibid., 37–8.

22. Teresa Saldanha, *Reis de Portugal Seculo VVII a o Seculo XX* (Lisbon: Instituto é Português do Património Arquitectónico, Ministério da Cultura, 2005), 8.

23. Kenneth Maxwell, *Pombal: Paradox of the Enlightenment* (Cambridge: Cambridge University Press, 1995), 164.

24. Ribeiro, 141.

25. L.E. Da Costa, 155.

26. William Beckford, *Italy with Sketches of Spain and Portugal* (London: Richard Bentley, 1834), 257.

27. Francis, 208.

28. Ibid., 187.

29. Boxer, *Race Relations*, 193.

30. Beckford, *Italy*, 276.

31. Boxer, *Portuguese Seaborne Empire*, 257.

32. Boxer, *Race Relations*, 118.

33. Kirsten Schultz, *Tropical Versailles Empire, Monarchy, and the Portuguese Royal Court in Rio de Janeiro, 1808–1821* (New York: Routledge, 2001), 49.

34. Livermore, *History of Portugal*, 382–384.

35. Ibid., 385.

36. Ibid., 382.

37. Ibid., 386.

38. Michael Walzer, *Regicide and Revolution: Speeches at the Trial of Louis XVI* (New York: Columbia University Press, 1993), 64.

39. Livermore, *New History of Portugal*, 243.

40. Carlos Rocquette, interview with author, 29 May 2006.

41. Neill Macaulay, *Dom Pedro*, 48.

42. Ibid., 17.

43. Francis, 281.

44. Harding, 23.

45. Ibid., 22.

46. Light, 9.

47. Neill Macaulay, *Dom Pedro*, 28.

48. L.E. Da Costa, 16.

49. Schultz, 121.

50. Neill Macaulay, *Dom Pedro*, 45.

Chapter 4

1. L.E. Da Costa, 212–13.

2. A.J.R. Russell-Wood, *Society and Government in Colonial Brazil 1500–1822* (Aldershot, Great Britain: Variorum, 1992), 1.

3. Neill Macaulay, *Dom Pedro*, 8–9.

4. Ferro, 38.

5. Ibid., 41.

6. Rose Macaulay, *They Went to Portugal*, 109.

7. John D. Bergamini, *The Spanish Bourbons: This History of a Tenacious Dynasty* (New York: Putnam, 1974), 118.

8. Ibid., 113–14.

9. Ibid., 102.

10. Ibid., 124.

11. Ibid., 135.

12. Ibid., 104.

13. Ibid., 187.

14. Ibid.

15. Ferro, 41.

16. Marcus Cheke, *Carlota Joaquina: Queen of Portugal* (London: Sidgwick and Jackson, 1947), 5.

17. Ibid., 14.

18. Eul-Soo Pang, *In Pursuit of Honor and Power: Noblemen of the Southern Cross in Nineteenth Century Brazil* (Tuscaloosa: University of Alabama Press, 1988), 28.

19. Cheke, *Carlota Joaquina*, 7.

20. Ibid., 9.

21. Ibid., 5.

22. Pang, 28.

23. Ibid., 6.

24. Ibid., 6.

25. Neill Macaulay, *Dom Pedro*, 7.

26. Ibid., 6.

27. Pang, 27.

28. William Beckford, *Recollections of an Excursion to the Monasteries of Alcobaca and Batalha* (London: Richard Bentley, 1835), 219–220.

29. Cheke, *Carlota Joaquina*, 7.

30. Ibid., 6.

31. Bergamini, 127.

32. Ibid., 127.

33. W. Koebel, *British Exploits in South America: A History of British Activities and Exploration* (New York: Century, 1917), 65.

34. Ibid., 19.

35. Stanley G. Payne, *A History of Spain and Portugal* (Madison: University of Wisconsin Press, 1973), 429.

Chapter 5

1. Sydney Greenbie, *The Fertile Land, Brazil* (New York: Row, Peterson, 1943), 35.

2. Pang, 28.

3. Jane Elizabeth Adams, "The Abolition of the Brazilian Slave Trade," *Journal of Negro History* (Oct. 1925): 614–15.

4. Harding, 38.

5. HRH Princess Michael of Kent, *Crowned in a Far Country: Portraits of Eight Royal Brides* (New York: Weidenfeld and Nicolson, 1986), 87.

6. Koebel, 69.

7. Michael of Kent, 86–87.

8. Cheke, *Carlota Joaquina*, 43.

9. Koebel, 121.

10. Ibid., 125.

11. Ibid., 120, 129.

12. Beckford, *Recollections*, 215.

13. William R. Manning, *Diplomatic Correspondence of the United States Inter-American Affairs 1831–1860*, vol. 2 (Washington: Carnegie Endowment for International Peace, 1932), 525, 616.

14. Ibid., 616–17.

15. John A. Crow, *The Epic of Latin America,* 4th ed. (Los Angeles: University of California Press, 1992), 92.
16. Cheke, *Carlota Joaquina,* 40.
17. Crow, 525.
18. Neill Macaulay, *Dom Pedro,* 69.
19. Ibid., 47.
20. Ibid., 314.
21. Ibid., 47–48, 314.
22. James D. Henderson and Linda Roddy Henderson, *Ten Notable Women of Latin America* (Chicago: Nelson-Hall, 1978), 128.
23. Michael of Kent, 82.
23. Macaulay, *Dom Pedro,* 314.
24. Ibid., 47-48, 314.
25. Gloria Kaiser, *Dona Leopoldina: The Habsburg Empress of Brazil* (Riverside, CA: Ariadne Press, 1998), 376-377.
26. Henderson and Henderson, 128.

Chapter 6

1. Andre Castelot, *King of Rome: A Biography of Napoleon's Tragic Son,* Robert Baldick, trans. (New York: Harper and Brothers, 1960), 211.
2. Michael of Kent, 84.
3. Ibid., 85.
4. Maria Dundas Graham (Lady Maria Calcott), *Journal of a Voyage to Brazil and Residence There, During Part of Three Years 1821, 1822, 1823* (New York: Frederick A. Praeger, 1824), 159.
5. Gloria Kaiser, *Dona Leopoldina: The Habsburg Empress of Brazil* (Riverside, CA: Ariadne Press, 1998), 79.
6. Ibid., 48.
7. Edward Crankshaw, *The Habsburgs: Portrait of a Dynasty* (New York: Viking Press, 1971), 10.
8. Kaiser, *Dona Leopoldina,* 292.
9. Neill Macaulay, *Dom Pedro.*
10. Kaiser interview, 1998.
11. Ibid.
12. Michael of Kent, 89.
13. Kaiser, *Dona Leopoldina,* 68.
14. Michael of Kent, 97.
15. Emmi Baum, "Empress Leopoldina: Her Role in the Development of Brazil, 1817–1826," dissertation, New York University, June 1965, 74.
16. Kaiser, *Dona Leopoldina,* 157.
17. Baum, 75.
18. Michael of Kent, 90.
19. Jane Elizabeth Adams, "The Aboliton of the Brazilian Slave Trade," *Journal of Negro History* (4 October 1926): 620.
20. Ibid. 623.
21. Thomas, *The Slave Trade,* 125, 413, 419-421, 457.
22. Kaiser, *Dona Leopoldina,* 55.
23. Baum, 76.
24. Ibid.
25. Michael of Kent, 83.
26. Henderson and Henderson, 132.
27. Maccauley, *Dom Pedro,* 176.

28. Ibid. 70.
29. Ibid.
30. Henderson and Henderson,132.
31. Michael of Kent, 94.

Chapter 7

1. Jerome Adams, *Notable Latin American Women: Twenty-Nine Leaders, Rebels, Poets, Battlers and Spies, 1500–1900* (Jefferson, NC: McFarland, 1995), 144–145.
2. Jerome Adams, *Liberators and Patriots of Latin America: Biographies of 23 Leaders* (Jefferson, NC: McFarland, 1991), 112.
3. Cheke, *Carlota Joaquina,* 82.
4. Harding, 87.
5. Ibid., 89.
6. Livermore, *History of Portugal,* 409–412.
7. Neill Macaulay, *Dom Pedro,* 85.
8. Ibid., 124–125.
9. Cheke, *Carlota Joaquina,* 90.
10. Ibid., 92–93.
11. Ibid., 92.
12. Payne, *History of Spain and Portugal,* 518–519.
13. Ibid., 518.
14. Ibid.
15. Cheke, *Carlota Joaquina,* 107.
16. John Armitage, *The History of Brazil from the Period of the Arrival of the Bragança Family in 1808 to the Abdication of Dom Pedro I in 1831* (London: Smith Elder, 1836), 357–358.
17. Cheke, *Carlota Joaquina,* 110–113.
18. Ibid.

Chapter 8

1. Kaiser, *Dona Leopoldina,* 77.
2. Baum, 135.
3. Neill Macaulay, *Dom Pedro,* 87.
4. Henderson and Henderson, 138.
5. Kaiser interview, 1997.
6. Livermore, *History of Portugal,* 412.
7. Kaiser interview, 1997.
8. Graham, *Journal of a Voyage,* 177.
9. Henderson and Henderson, 136.
10. Baum, 136.
11. Graham, *Journal of a Voyage,* 180–182.
12. Ibid., 186.
13. Neill Macaulay, *Dom Pedro,* 12.
14. Ibid., 112.
15. W. Stevens, "Dom Pedro II, Emperor of Brazil," *Blackwood's Magazine,* London, 1873, 553.
16. Neill Macaulay, *Dom Pedro,* 102–106.
17. Kaiser, *Dona Leopoldina,* 132.
18. Baum, 146.
19. Ibid., 131.
20. Adams, *Liberators and Patriots,* 113.
21. Baum, 141.
22. Kaiser, *Dona Leopoldina,* 372
23. Kaiser interview, 1997.

Chapter 9

1. Kaiser, *Dona Leopoldina*, 217.
2. Baum, 123.
3. Henderson and Henderson, 137.
4. Ibid.
5. Kaiser, *Dona Leopoldina*, 235.
6. Adams, *Liberators and Patriots*, 116.
7. Rollie Peppino, *Brazil, the Land and People* (New York: Oxford University Press, 1968), 183.
8. Michael of Kent, 96.
9. Ibid., 96.
10. Ibid.
11. Harding, 150.
12. Michael of Kent, 97.
13. Baum, 141.
14. Cheke, *Carlota Joaquina*, 40.
15. Brian Vale, *Independence or Death: British Sailors and Brazilian Independence* (London: Tauris Publishers, 1822–1825; 1996), 43.
16. Donald Pierson, *Negroes in Brazil: A Study of Race Contact at Bahia* (Carbondale: Southern Illinois University Press, 1942), 83.
17. Ibid., 83.
18. Baum, 128.
19. Ibid., 206.
20. Adams, *Notable Latin American Women*, 145.
21. Baum, 147.
22. Ibid., 150.
23. Ibid., 150.
24. Ibid., 150.
25. Ibid., 150.
26. Adams, *Notable Latin American Women*, 146.
27. Adams, *Liberators and Patriots*, 114.

Chapter 10

1. Adams, *Liberators and Patriots*, 114.
2. Lilia Moritz Schwarcz, *The Emperor's Beard: Dom Pedro II and the Tropical Empire of Brazil* (New York: Hill and Wang, 2004), 193.
3. Kaiser, *Dona Leopoldina*, 15.
4. Ibid., 19.
5. W.H. Koebel, *British Exploits in South America: A History of British Activities and Exploration* (New York: Century, 1917), 159.
6. Ibid., 298.
7. Ibid., 366.
8. Kaiser, *Dona Leopoldina*, 59.
9. Ibid., 39.
10. Neill Macaulay, *Dom Pedro*, 215.
11. Kaiser, *Thomas Ender Brasilien-Expedition 1817*, 25.
12. Neill Macaulay, *Dom Pedro*, 215.
13. Ibid., 147–148.
14. Ibid.
15. Koebel, 305.
16. Kaiser, *Dona Leopoldina*, 282.
17. Baum, 173.
18. Ibid., 174.
19. Kaiser, *Dona Leopoldina*, 317.
20. Baum, 177.
21. Neill Macaulay, *Dom Pedro*, 214.

22. Kaiser interview, 1997.
23. Roderick J. Barman, *Brazil: The Forging of a Nation* (Stanford, CA: Stanford University Press, 1988), 136.
24. Kaiser, *Dona Leopoldina*, 210.
25. Barman, *Brazil*, 136.
26. Percy A. Martin, *Argentina, Brazil and Chile Since Independence*, A. Curtis Wilgus, ed. (New York: Russell and Russell, 1963), 175–177.
27. Graham, *Journal of a Voyage*, 106.
28. Greenbie, 39.
29. Ibid., 41.
30. Carlos Rocquette, interview with author, 29 May 2006.
31. Neill Macaulay, *Dom Pedro*, 251.
32. J.E. Adams, "Abolition of the Brazilian Slave Trade," 617.
33. Adams, 617.

Chapter 11

1. J.E. Adams, "Abolition of the Brazilian Slave Trade," 618–619.
2. Ibid., 622–623.
3. Robert Edgar Conrad, *Children of God's Fire* (Princeton, NJ: Princeton University Press, 1984), 418–419.
4. Joaquim Nabuco, *Abolitionism: The Brazilian Antislavery Struggle*, Robert Conrad, trans., ed. (Urbana: University of Illinois Press, 1977), 37.
5. Harding, 131.
6. Kaiser, *Dona Leopoldina*, 307.
7. Robert Harvey, *Liberators: Latin America's Struggle for Independence* (Woodstock, NY: Overlook Press, 2000), 474.
8. Baum, 242.
9. Ibid., 187.
10. Ibid., 242.
11. Kaiser, *Dona Leopoldina*, 298.
12. Michael of Kent, 98–99.
13. Baum, 233.
14. Ibid., 243.
15. Ibid., 425.
16. Kaiser, *Dona Leopoldina*, 300.
17. Ibid., 353–354.
18. Henderson and Henderson, 145.
19. Kaiser interview, 1998.
20. Baum, 251.
21. Ibid., 256.
22. Ibid., 257.
23. Ibid.
24. Ibid.
25. Ibid., 238.
26. Ibid.
27. Sergio Correa da Costa, *Every Inch a King: A Biography of Dom Pedro I Emperor of Brazil* (New York: Macmillan, 1950, 1997), 43.

Chapter 12

1. Mary Wilhelmine Williams, *Dom Pedro the Magnanimous* (Chapel Hill: University of North Carolina Press, 1937), 222.

2. Kaiser, correspondence with author, September 29, 1997.

3. Armitage, 232.

4. Agnes de Stoeckl, *King of the French: A Portrait of Louis Philippe 1773–1850* (New York: G. P. Putnam's Sons, 1958), 167.

5. Kaiser, *Dona Leopoldina*, 372.

6. Hubert Herring, *A History of Latin America from the Beginnings to the Present,* 3rd ed. (New York: Alfred A. Knopf, 1968), 789.

7. Kaiser interview, 1997.

8. Ibid.

9. Guy Stair Sainty, "The Order of Our Lady of the Conception of Vila Vicosa: To the Royal House of Portugal," http://www.chivalricorders.org/orders/portual/vilavic.htm, 3.

10. Cheke, *Carlota Joaquina*, 166–169.

11. Ibid., 166.

12. Rose Macaulay, *They Went to Portugal*, 135.

13. Ibid., 410.

14. Ibid., 292.

15. Ibid.

16. Armitage, 90.

17. Harvey, 493.

18. Neill Macaulay, *Dom Pedro*, 252.

19. Ibid.

20. Martin, 177.

21. Williams, 23.

22. Ibid., 24.

23. Macaulay, 252.

24. Harding, 190–192.

25. Williams, *Dom Pedro the Magnanimous*, 23.

26. Koebel, 353.

Chapter 13

1. Harding, 215.

2. Williams, *Dom Pedro the Magnanimous*, 27.

3. Ibid., 34.

4. Cheke, *Carlota Joaquina*, 196.

5. Ibid., 197.

6. Kaiser interview, 1998.

7. Williams, *Dom Pedro the Magnanimous*, 26.

8. Schwarcz, 38.

9. Roderick J. Barman, *Citizen Emperor, Pedro II and the Making of Brazil, 1825–91* (Stanford, CA: Stanford University Press, 1999), 82.

10. William R. Manning, *Diplomatic Correspondence of the United States Inter-American Affairs 1831–1860*, vol. 2 (Washington: Carnegie Endowment for International Peace, 1932), 513.

11. Barman, *Citizen Emperor*, 116.

12. Ibid., 93.

13. Ibid., 66.

14. *Homenagem do Instituto Histórico e Geografica Brasileiro*, 1894, 687–690.

15. Rose Macaulay, *They Went to Portugal*, 39.

16. Payne, *A History of Spain and Portugal*, 524.

17. Neill Macaulay, *Dom Pedro*, 299.

18. Ibid., 257.

Chapter 14

1. Harding, 215.

2. Amiral Jacques Guillon, *François d'Orleáns Prince de Joinville 1818–1900* (Paris: Editions France-Empire, 1894), 64.

3. Williams, *Dom Pedro the Magnanimous*, 50.

4. Barman, *Citizen Emperor*, 73.

5. Williams, 54.

6. Barman, *Citizen Emperor*, 438.

7. Williams, 58.

8. Guillon, 50.

9. Ibid., 116.

10. Ibid., 124.

11. Ibid.

12. Ibid., 129.

13. Daniel Noble Johnson, *The Journals of Daniel Noble Johnson (1822–1863) United States Navy* (Washington, DC: Smithsonian Institution Press, 1959), 144.

14. Ibid., 145.

15. Ibid., 144.

16. Barman, *Citizen Emperor*, 73.

17. De Stoeckl, 237.

18. Ibid., 223–224.

19. Barman, *Citizen Emperor*, 87.

20. Gloria Kaiser, *Pedro II of Brazil, Son of the Habsburg Empress,* Lowell A. Bangerter, trans. (Riverside, CA: Ariadne Press, 2000), 219.

Chapter 15

1. Schwarcz, 65.

2. Daniel Noble Johnson, 179–180.

3. Ibid., 178–179.

4. Anna Luísa Orleans-Bragança, interview with author, 29 July 1995.

5. Ibid.

6. Harding, 246.

7. Barman, *Citizen Emperor*, 97.

8. Kaiser interview, 1998.

9. Daniel Noble Johnson, 183.

10. Ibid.

11. Ibid.

12. Ibid., 186.

13. Ibid.

14. Barman, *Citizen Emperor*, 99.

15. Kaiser, *Pedro II of Brazil*, 250.

16. Williams, *Dom Pedro the Magnanimous*, 88.

17. Hermes Vieira, *Princesa Isabel — Uma Vida de Luzes e Sombras,* 3rd ed. (São Paulo: Nova Ensalos Brasileiras, 1990), 21.

Chapter 16

1. Vieira, 17.

2. Ibid., 17.

3. Heloisa Buarque de Hollanda, Alfonzo Carlos Marquês dos Santos, Augusta Ivan de Freitas Pinheiro, Iole de Freitas, *Paço Imperial* (Rio de Janeiro: Sextante Artes, 1999), 84–85.

4. Vieira, 18–19.

5. Ibid.

6. Ibid.

7. Ibid., 21.

8. Ibid.

9. Eric Wood, *The Boy's Book of the Sea* (New York: Funk and Wagnall, 1915), 224–225.

10. Ibid.

11. J.E. Adams, "Abolition of the Brazilian Slave Trade," 607.

12. Roderick J. Barman, *Princess Isabel of Brazil: Gender and Power in the Nineteenth Century* (Wilmington, DE: Scholarly Resources, 2002), 25.

13. Williams, *Dom Pedro the Magnanimous*, 90.

14. Vieira, 21.

15. Ibid., 21–22.

16. Richard Graham, *Britain and the Onset of Modernization in Brazil 1850–1914* (Cambridge, UK: Cambridge University Press, 1968), 27.

17. Barman, *Citizen Emperor*, 123–125.

18. Payne, *A History of Spain and Portugal*, 52.

19. Graham, *Britain and the Onset of Modernization in Brazil*, 166.

20. Dale T. Graden, "An Act 'Even of Public Security': Slave Resistance, Social Tensions, and the End of the International Slave Trade to Brazil, 1835–1836," *Hispanic American Historic Review* 76.2 (May 1996): 249.

21. Graham, *Britain and the Onset of Modernization in Brazil*, 166.

Chapter 17

1. Barman, *Princess Isabel*, 25.

2. Ibid., 145.

3. Ibid.

4. Ibid., 136.

5. Ibid., 136–137.

6. Lourenço Luiz Lacombe, *Isabel: A Princesa Redentora* (Petrópolis: Instituto Histórico de Petrópolis, 1989), 31–32.

7. Ibid.

8. Kaiser, *Pedro II of Brazil*, 114.

9. Barman, *Princess Isabel*, 275.

10. Kaiser, *Pedro II of Brazil*, 116.

11. Ibid., 116–117.

12. Lacombe, *Isabel: A Princesa Redentora*, 35–39.

13. Kaiser interview, 1998.

14. Ibid.

15. Barman, *Citizen Emperor*, 441.

16. Ibid., 77.

17. Barman, *Princess Isabel*, 32.

Chapter 18

1. Barman, *Citizen Emperor*, 100.

2. Kaiser interview, 1998.

3. Barman, *Citizen Emperor*, 144.

4. Graham, *Journal of a Voyage*, 246.

5. Barman, *Citizen Emperor*, 441.

6. Ibid., 114–115.

7. Barman, *Princess Isabel*, 28.

8. Barman, *Citizen Emperor*, 150.

9. Barman, *Princess Isabel*, 28.

10. Ibid., 46.

11. Ibid., 46–48.

12. Ibid., 32.

13. Vieira, 31.

14. Ibid.

15. Ibid., 31–32.

16. Ibid., 33.

Chapter 19

1. Barman, *Citizen Emperor*, 108.

2. Ibid.

3. Roger Fulford, ed., *Dearest Child: Letters Between Queen Victoria and the Princess Royal 1858–1861* (London: Evans Bros., 1964), 286.

4. Ghislain Diesbach, *Secrets of the Gotha* (New York: Meredith Books, 1967), 254.

5. Vincenzo delle Donne, ed., *Naples* (Singapore: APA Publications, 1992), 42.

6. Kaiser interview, 1997.

7. Neill Macaulay, *Dom Pedro*, 241.

8. Francis H. Gribble, *The Royal House of Portugal* (Port Washington, NY: Kennikat Press, 1915), 208.

9. Ibid., 208.

10. Ibid., 214.

11. Guy Stair Sainty, 3–4

12. Guillon, 62.

13. Gribble, 215.

14. Ibid., 257.

15. Ibid., 207.

16. Conde da Carnota, *Memoirs of Field Marshal the Duke de Saldanha with Selections from His Correspondence*, vol. 2 (London: John Murray, 1880), 103.

17. H. V. Livermore *A New History of Portugal* (Cambridge, UK: Cambridge University Press, 1966), 301.

18. José Manuel Martins Carneiro and Louis Filipe Marquês da Cama, *Palacio Nacional da Pena* (Lisbon: Publicidade Artes Gráficas, 1994), 6–16.

19. Daphne Bennett, *King Without a Crown* (New York: Lippincott, 1977), 64.

20. Elizabeth Longford, *Queen Victoria: Born to Succeed* (New York: Harper and Row, 1969), 184.

21. Gribble, 224.

22. Charles E. Nowell, *Portugal* (Englewood Cliffs, NJ: Prentice-Hall, 1973), 105.

23. Gloria Kaiser, *Saudade: The Life and Death of Queen Maria Gloria of Lusitania*, trans. Lowell A. Bangerter (Riverside, CA: Ariadne Press, 2003), 323.

24. Da Carnota, 224.

25. Ibid., 315.

26. Gribble, 231.

27. Nowell, 108, 198.

28. Ibid., 107.

29. Gribble, 234.

30. Nowell, 106.

31. United States diplomatic correspondence

from Portugal, Benjamin Moran to Hamilton Fish, July 19, 1875.

32. United States diplomatic correspondence from Portugal, Benjamin Moran to Hamilton Fish, July 3–19, 1875.

Chapter 20

1. Hector Bolitho, ed., *Letters of Queen Victoria from the Archives of the House of Brandenburg-Prussia* (New Haven: Yale University Press, 1938), 236.

2. Longford, 179, 208, 240, 248, 266.

3. Joan Haslip, *Imperial Adventurer Emperor Maximilian of Mexico* (London: Weidenfeld and Nicolson, 1971), 53.

4. Prince Michael of Greece, *The Empress of Farewells: The Story of Charlotte, Empress of Mexico* (New York: Atlantic Monthly Press, 1998), 32.

5. Ibid., 36.

6. Ibid., 87.

7. Ibid., 91.

8. Richard Bentley, ed., *Recollections of My Life: Maximilian Emperor of Mexico*, vol. 3 (London, 1868), 116–119.

9. Ibid.

10. Ibid.

11. Ibid.

12. Ibid.

13. Richard O'Connor, *Cactus Throne: The Tragedy of Maximilian and Charlotte* (New York: J. P. Putnam's Sons, 1971), 95–96.

14. Ibid., 153.

15. Ibid., 361.

16. Brian Loveman, *The Constitution of Tyranny: Regimes of Exception in Spanish America* (Pittsburgh and London: University of Pittsburgh Press, 1993), 370.

17. N. Andrew Cleven, "Some Plans for Colonizing Liberated Negro Slaves in Hispanic America," *The Journal of Negro History*, vol. 11, Carter G. Woodson, ed. (Lancaster, PA, and Washington, DC: Association for the Study of Negro Life and History, January 1926), 47.

18. Stephen Sears, *George McClellan: The Young Napoleon* (New York: Ticknor and Fields, 1988), 115.

19. United States Senate, *Index to the Senate Executive Documents or the Third Session of the Fortieth Congress of the United States of America, 1868–69* (Washington, DC: Government Printing Office, 1869), 32.

20. Michael of Greece, 117.

21. Ibid., 103.

22. Henry Lion Young, *Eliza Lynch, Regent of Paraguay* (Great Britain: Anthony Blond, 1966), 81.

23. Sian Rees, *The Shadows of Elisa Lynch: How a Nineteenth-Century Irish Courtesan Became the Most Powerful Woman in Paraguay* (London: Review, 2003), 103.

24. Kaiser interview, 1998.

25. Ibid.

26. Ibid.

27. Luís da Camara Cascudo, *Conde D'Eu* (São Paulo: Companhia Editora Nacional, 1933), 56.

Chapter 21

1. Barman, *Citizen Emperor*, 153.

2. Ibid., 152–153.

3. Kaiser, 1997 interview, 230.

4. Barman, *Citizen Emperor*, 153.

5. Ibid., 153–155.

6. Ibid., 154.

7. Ibid., 155.

8. Alberto Rangel, *Gastão de Orleáns (O Ultimo Conde D'Eu)* (São Paulo: Companhia Editora Nacional, 1935), 91–92.

9. Pedro Calmon, *A Princesa Isabel "A Redentora"* (São Paulo: Companhia Editora Nacional, 1941), 43.

10. Ibid., 43.

11. Rangel, 92.

12. Ibid., 93.

13. Ibid.

14. Ibid., 94.

15. Cleven, "Some Plans for Colonizing," 44–45.

16. Rangel, 95.

17. Emma Toussaint, *A Parisian in Brazil*, Mme. Toussaint Samson, trans. (Boston: James H. Earle, 1891), 128.

Chapter 22

1. Pierson, 167–168.

2. Rangel, 95.

3. Ibid.

4. Vieira, 38–39.

5. Ibid., 40.

6. Ibid., 39.

7. Ibid., 40.

8. Ibid., 41.

9. Ibid., 40–41.

10. Ibid., 41.

11. Lourenço Luiz Lacombe, *Isabel: A Princesa Redentora* (Petrópolis: Instituto Histórico de Petrópolis, 1989), 109.

12. Barman, *Princess Isabel*, 61.

13. Ibid., 59.

14. Vieira, 41.

15. Barman, *Princess Isabel*, 59.

16. Ibid.

17. Calmon, 44.

18. Lacombe, *Isabel: A Princesa Redentora*, 77.

19. Barman, *Citizen Emperor*, 156.

20. Lacombe, *Isabel: A Princesa Redentora*, 77–78.

Chapter 23

1. Vieira, 47–48.

2. Ibid., 48.

3. Lacombe, *Isabel: A Princesa Redentora*, 82.

4. Ibid., 83.

5. Ibid.
6. Ibid.
7. Ibid.
8. Barman, *Princess Isabel*, 158.
9. De Stoeckl, 284–290.
10. Ibid.
11. Ibid., 292.
12. Sidney Lee, *Queen Victoria: A Biography* (London: Smith, Elder, 1908), 150.
13. G. H. De Schubert, *Memoir of the Duchess of Orléans by the Marquess de H----* (New York: Charles Scribner, 1860), 377–378.
14. Lee, 254.
15. Ibid., 277.
16. Ibid., 254.
17. De LaMartine, *History of the French Revolution*, vol. 1 (Boston: Phillips, Sampson, 1849), 80.
18. Guizot and Guizot De Witt, 282.
19. De Stoeckl, 235.
20. Guizot and Guizot De Witt, 382.
21. Lee, 185.
22. Philip De Ronde, *Paraguay: A Gallant Little Nation* (New York: G.P. Putnam's Sons, 1935), 49.
23. William Barrett, *Woman on Horseback: The Biography of Francisco López and Eliza Lynch* (London: Peter Davies, 1938), 29.
24. Rees, 185.

Chapter 24

1. Priscilla Leal, "O Lado Rebelde da Princesa Isabel," *Nossa Historia* (May 2006): 68–74.
2. Carolly Erickson, *Her Little Majesty: The Life of Queen Victoria* (New York: Simon and Schuster, 1997), 147.
3. Barman, *Citizen Emperor*, 65.
4. Ibid., 66.
5. Ibid., 147.
6. Gribble, 193.
7. Lacombe, *Isabel: A Princesa Redentora*, 96.
8. Ibid., 101.
9. Marco Houston, ed., "House of Windsor Has Black Ancestors," *Royalty* 16.1 (1999): 18.
10. Pamela Clark, letter to the author, 14 April 2000.
11. Lacombe, *Isabel: A Princesa Redentora*, 103.
12. Ibid., 101.
13. Barman, *Princess Isabel*, 8.
14. Barrett, 140.
15. Anna Luísa Orleans-Bragança interview, 1995.
16. Lacombe, *Isabel: A Princesa Redentora*, 104.
17. Ibid.
18. Ibid., 102.
19. Ibid., 105.
20. Anna Luísa Orleans-Bragança interview, 1995.

Chapter 25

1. Calmon, 51
2. Barman, *Princess Isabel*, 77.

3. John Hoyt Williams, *The Rise and Fall of the Paraguayan Republic, 1800–1870* (Austin: University of Texas Press, 1979), 133.
4. Pelham Horton Box, *The Origins of the Paraguayan War* (New York: Russell and Russell, 1873), 298.
5. Ibid., 52.
6. Crow, 165.
7. Barman, *Citizen Emperor*, 204–205.
8. Kaiser interview, 1998.
9. Barman, *Citizen Emperor*, 203.
10. Charles Edmond Akers and L.E. Elliott, *A History of South America* (New York: E.P. Hutton, 1930), 156.
11. Ibid., 155.
12. Kaiser interview, 2005.
13. Ibid.
14. Ibid.
15. John Codman, *Ten Months in Brazil with Notes on the Paraguayan War,* 2nd ed. (New York: James Miller, 1872), 158.
16. Eduardo Silva, *Prince of the People: The Life and Times of a Brazilian Free Man of Colour,* Moyra Ashford, trans. (London and New York: Verso, 1993), 98.
17. Ibid., 99.
18. Barman, *Princess Isabel*, 77–78.
19. Barman, *Citizen Emperor*, 204.
20. Williams, *Rise and Fall*.
21. Calmon, 54.
22. Ibid.
23. Bruce Levine, *Confederate Emancipation: Southern Plans to Free and Arm Slaves During the Civil War* (Oxford: Oxford University Press, 2006), 33, 36, 44.
24. Barman, *Citizen Emperor*, 211.
25. Robert M. Levine and John J. Croc, eds. (Peter M. Beattie), *The Brazil Reader* (Durham, NC: Duke University Press, 1999), 88.
26. Williams, *Rise and Fall*, 266.
27. Ibid., 267.
28. Ibid., 268.
29. Barman, *Princess Isabel*, 125.
30. Lacombe, *Isabel: A Princesa Redentora*, 179.
31. Kaiser interview, 1998.
32. Barman, *Princess Isabel*, 125.
33. Barman, *Citizen Emperor*, 202, 211.
34. Calmon, 72.
35. Rangel, 200.
36. Barman, *Citizen Emperor*, 222.
37. Box, 222.
38. Barman, *Citizen Emperor*, 225.

Chapter 26

1. O'Connor, 99–100.
2. Rangel, 27.
3. Haslip, 215.
4. Ibid.
5. Prince Michael of Greece, 122.
6. Kaiser, Pedro II of Brazil, 295.
7. Guy Thomson, "Popular Aspects of Liberal-

ism in Mexico, 1848–1888," *Journal of Latin American Research* 3 (1991): 53.

8. Prince Michael of Greece, 215.
9. Ibid.
10. Ibid.
11. Haslip, 328.
12. Crow, 45–65, 664.
13. Ibid., 65.
14. Ibid.
15. Ibid., 67.
16. Ibid.
17. Haslip, 358, 397.
18. Ibid., 330.
19. O'Connor, 234–235.
20. Ibid., 235.
21. Harding, 327.
22. Kaiser, *Pedro II of Brazil*, 295.

Chapter 27

1. Charles J. Kolinski, *Independence or Death! The Story of the Paraguayan War* (Gainesville: University of Florida Press, 1965), 142–145.
2. Ibid., 142–145.
3. Akers and Elliott, 169.
4. Ibid., 173.
5. Lacombe, *Isabel: A Princesa Redentora*, 180.
6. Ibid., 179–180.
7. Ibid., 181.
8. Williams, *Dom Pedro the Magnanimous*, 223.
9. Akers and Elliott, 178.
10. United States Senate, *Index to the Executive Documents, 1870–71* (Washington, DC: Government Printing Office), 7.
11. Ibid., 15.
12. Barman, *Citizen Emperor*, 225.
13. Ibid., 224.
14. United States Senate, *Index to the Executive Documents, 1870–71*, 12.
15. Calmon, 80.
16. Ibid.
17. Vieira, 86.
18. United States Senate, *Index to the Executive Documents, 1870–71*, 16.
19. Rangel, 210–212.
20. Calmon, 80.
21. Barman, *Citizen Emperor*, 227.

Chapter 28

1. Rangel, 222.
2. Lacombe, *Isabel: A Princesa Redentora*, 181.
3. Louis Moreau Gottschalk, *Notes of a Pianist,* Clara Gottschalk, ed., Robert Peterson, M.D., trans. (Philadelphia: J.B. Lippincott, 1881), 72.
4. Joaquim Nabuco, *Abolitionism: The Brazilian Antislavery Struggle,* Robert Conrad, trans., ed. (Urbana: University of Illinois Press, 1977), 47.
5. United States Senate, *Index to the Senate Executive Documents..., 1868–69*, 7.
6. George F. Masterman, *Seven Eventful Years in Paraguay: A Narrative of Personal Experience Amongst the Paraguayans,* 2nd ed. (London: Sampson Low, Son, and Marston, 1870), 310–312.
7. United States Senate, *Index to the Senate Executive Documents..., 1868–69*, 7.
8. Masterman, 310–311.
9. Barman, *Citizen Emperor*, 264.
10. Ibid., 229.
11. Barman, *Princess Isabel*, 105.
12. United States Senate, *Index to the Senate Executive Documents..., 1868–69*, 5.
13. United States Senate, *Index to the Executive Documents, 1870–71*, 9.
14. Rees, 289.
15. Ibid., 291.
16. Harris G. Warren, *Paraguay and the Triple Alliance: The Postwar Decade, 1869–1878* (Austin: University of Texas at Austin, 1978), 16–17.
17. Ibid., 243.
18. Calmon, 93.
19. Levine and Croc, *Brazil Reader*, 87–89.
20. Rangel, 302.
21. Barman, *Citizen Emperor*, 230.
22. Da Camara Cascudo, 7.
23. Rangel, 302.
24. Barman, *Citizen Emperor*, 108.

Chapter 29

1. Barman, *Citizen Emperor*, 231.
2. Ibid., 232.
3. Kaiser interview, 1998.
4. Caroline Nabuco, *The Life of Joaquim Nabuco* (Stanford, CA: Stanford University Press, 1950), xii–xiii.
5. Anthony Wild, *Coffee: A Dark History* (New York: W.W. Norton, 2004), 173.
6. Kaiser interview, 1998.
7. Jeff Simons, *Cuba: From Conquistador to Castro* (New York: St. Martin's Press, 1996), 145–146.
8. Williams, *Dom Pedro the Magnanimous*, 149.
9. Barman, *Citizen Emperor*, 111.
10. Kaiser, *Pedro II of Brazil*, 259.
11. Ibid.
12. Rangel, 307.
13. Kaiser, *Pedro II of Brazil*, 330–331.
14. Rangel, 307.
15. Kaiser, *Pedro II of Brazil*, 331.
16. Barman, *Princess Isabel*, 110.
17. *New York Times*, "Slaves Plot for Liberty," March 21, 1871.
18. Ruy Vieira da Cunha, preface and ed., *D. Pedro II Conselhos a Princesa Isabel de Como Melhor Governar* (São Paulo: Edições GRD, 1985), 31.
19. Barman, *Citizen Emperor*, 111.
20. Barman, *Princess Isabel*, 260.
21. *New York Times*, 14 June 1871.
22. United States Senate, *Index to the Executive Documents, 1870–71*.
23. Barman, *Princess Isabel*, 123–124.
24. Barman, *Citizen Emperor*, 267.

25. Ibid.
26. E. Bradford Burns, *A Documentary History of Brazil* (New York: Alfred A. Knopf, 1966), 257–263.
27. Kaiser interview, 1997.
28. Harry Bernstein, *D. Pedro II* (New York: Twayne, 1973), 129.
29. Germán Arciniegas, *Latin America: A Cultural History* (Knopf: New York, 1967), 421–422.
30. Williams, 162-163.
31. Kaiser interview, 2002.
32. United States House of Representatives, *Executive Documents 1872–1873* (Washington, DC: Government Printing Office, 1873).
33. Barman, *Princess Isabel*, 124.

Chapter 30

1. *New York Times*, 23 September 1875.
2. Williams, *Dom Pedro the Magnanimous*, 158–159.
3. *New York Times*, 25 October 1873.
4. United States Diplomatic Correspondence, Charles Hale to Hamilton Fish, 24 September 1872.
5. Barman, *Princess Isabel*, 124.
6. Ibid., 126.
7. Ibid., 127.
8. Ibid.
9. Lecombe, 144–145.
10. "Imperial Tourists," *New York Times*, 31 May 1873.
11. Lecombe, 127.
12. Ibid., 128–129.
13. Ibid., 179–183.
14. Calmon, 114.
15. Lecombe, 180–183.
16. Ibid.
17. Barman, *Citizen Emperor*, 267.
18. United States Diplomatic Correspondence, Partridge to Fish, 20 May 1874, no. 60.
19. Lecombe, 181.
20. Ibid.
21. Lecombe, 182.
22. *New York Times*, 21 July 1874.
23. C.H. Haring, *Empire in Brazil: A New Experiment in Monarchy* (Cambridge, MA: Harvard University Press, 1958), 119–120.
24. Williams, *Dom Pedro the Magnanimous*, 174.
25. Mary Criscentia Thornton, *The Church and Freemasonry in Brazil, 1972–1875: A Study in Regalism,* dissertation (Washington, DC: Catholic University of America Press, 1948), 49.
26. Percy A. Martin, "Causes of the Collapse of the Brazilian Empire," *Hispanic American Historical Review* 13 (May 1933): 11–13.
27. Ibid.
28. Ibid.
29. Percy Alvin Martin, *A History of Brazil* (Chapel Hill: University of North Carolina Press, 1939), 238.
30. Ibid., 238–243.
31. Williams, *Dom Pedro the Magnanimous*, 176, 183.

32. "The Romish Church and Freemasonry," *New York Times*, 10 August 1873.
33. Wilfrid Hardy Callcott, *Liberalism in Mexico, 1857–1929* (Stanford, CA: Stanford University Press, 1931).
34. Harding, 123.
35. "Notes from Rio de Janeiro," *New York Times*, 20 August 1874.
36. Thornton, 186.
37. Barman, *Citizen Emperor*, 267–268.
38. Rangel, 315.

Chapter 31

1. Williams, *Dom Pedro the Magnanimous*, 182, 192.
2. Thornton, 244.
3. Ibid., 185.
4. Harding, 117.
5. *New York Times*, 24 November 1874.
6. Bolitho, 198.
7. Williams, *Dom Pedro the Magnanimous*, 180.
8. Thornton, 184.
9. Barman, *Princess Isabel*, 132.
10. Sandra Lauderdale Graham, *House and Street: The Domestic World of Servants and Masters in Nineteenth-Century Rio de Janeiro* (Austin: University of Texas Press, 1992), 125.
11. June E. Hahner, "Feminism, Women's Rights, and the Suffrage Movement in Brazil, 1850–1932," *Latin American Research Review* 15 (1980): 71.
12. Barman, *Princess Isabel*, 108.
13. Calmon, 115.
14. United States Diplomatic Correspondence, 24 June 1875, Partridge to Fish, no. 266.
15. Ibid.
16. Lourenço Lacombe, "Princesa Isabel 1846–1921," *Grandes Personagens da Nossa Historia*, vol. 3, Victor Civita, ed. (São Paulo: Abril SA Cultural e Industrial, 1970), 633.
17. Luís Felipe Orleans-Bragança interview, 1996.
18. United States Diplomatic Correspondence, 10 July 1875, Partridge to Fish, no. 268.
19. Ibid.
20. Haring, 124.
21. Thornton, 199.
22. Ibid., 183.
23. Vieira, 124.
24. *New York Times*, 9 November 1875, 1.
25. Ibid., 1.
26. Thornton, 197.
27. Ibid., 198.
28. Barman, *Princess Isabel*, 135.
29. Ibid., 136.
30. *New York Times*, 16 May 1873.
31. Barman, *Princess Isabel*, 139.
32. Lacombe, "Princesa Isabel 1846–1921," 187.
33. Barman, *Princess Isabel*, 139.
34. Lacombe, "Princesa Isabel 1846–1921," 186–187.

35. United States Diplomatic Correspondence, Purrington, W.H., State Department Document, #291, 20 October 1875.
36. Ibid.
37. Rangel, 321.
38. Lacombe, "Princesa Isabel 1846–1921," 188.
39. United States Diplomatic Correspondence, 300, 6 December 1875, James Partridge to Hamilton Fish.
40. Ibid.

Chapter 32

1. Barman, *Citizen Emperor*, 275.
2. Stephen Constant, *Foxy Ferdinand: Tsar of Bulgaria* (New York: Franklin Watts, 1980), 106.
3. Rose Brown, *American Emperor: Dom Pedro II of Brazil* (New York: Viking Press, 1945), 221.
4. Ibid., 226.
5. United States Diplomatic Correspondence, Partridge to Fish, 22 January 1876, no. 308.
6. United States Diplomatic Correspondence, 10 October 1875.
7. United States Diplomatic Correspondence, 24 July 1875.
8. Rose Brown, *American Emperor*, 232–233.
9. United States Diplomatic Correspondence, 29 September 1876, 47.
10. Dee Brown, *The Year of the Century: 1876* (New York: Charles Scribner's Sons, 1966), 121.
11. *New York Times*, vol. 25, no. 7692, 11 May 1876, 1.
12. Dee Brown, *Year of the Century*, 138.
13. Ibid., 144–145.
14. Rose Brown, *American Emperor*, 235.
15. John Codman, "Brazil and Her Emperor," *Galaxy Magazine* 21 (June 1876): 826.
16. Williams, *Dom Pedro the Magnanimous*, 195.
17. John Y. Simon, ed., *The Personal Memoirs of Julia Dent Grant* (New York: G.P. Putnam's Sons, 1975), 188.
18. Dee Brown, *Year of the Century*, 197.
19. Ibid., 167.
20. United States Diplomatic Correspondence, no. 25.
21. Mildred Criss, *Dom Pedro of Brazil* (New York: Dodd, Mead, 1945), 227.

Chapter 33

1. Barman, *Citizen Emperor*, 149.
2. Stanley Stein, *Vassouras: A Brazilian Coffee County, 1850–1900* (Cambridge: Harvard University Press, 1957), 146.
3. Ibid., 146.
4. Barman, *Citizen Emperor*, 481.
5. Barman, *Princess Isabel of Brazil*, 145.
6. Ibid.
7. Ibid., 146.
8. Ibid., 145.
9. Ibid., 143.

10. Ibid., 262.
11. Barman, *Citizen Emperor*, 285.
12. Barman, *Princess Isabel*, 146.
13. *New York Times*, 24 June 1875.
14. Roger Cuniff, *The Great Drought: Northeast Brazil, 1877–1880*, dissertation (Austin: University of Texas at Austin, 1970; University Microfilms, 1971), 148.
15. Ibid.
16. Cuniff, 144.
17. Ibid., 145.
18. United States House of Representatives, *Executive Documents 1878–1879*, 191.
19. Cuniff, 132.
20. Ibid., 148.
21. Eugene Ridings, *Business Interest Groups in Nineteenth Century Brazil* (Cambridge, UK: Cambridge University Press, 1994), 141.
22. Ibid., 79, 215.
23. Ibid., 141.
24. United States Diplomatic Correspondence, Partridge to Fish, 21 March 1875, no. 244.
25. Osvaldo Orico, *Patrocínio* (Rio De Janeiro: Irmaso Pongettim Editores, 1934), 147.
26. Percy A. Martin, "Slavery and Abolition in Brazil," *Hispanic American Historical Review* 4 (1921): 183.
27. Thiers Martins Moreira, "José do Patrocínio 1853–1905," in *Grand Personagens da Nossa História*, vol. 3, ed. Victor Civita (São Paulo: Abril Cultural, 1970), 593.

Chapter 34

1. Thornton, 201.
2. United States Diplomatic Correspondence, 31 August 1876, Partridge to Fish.
3. Ibid.
4. United States Diplomatic Correspondence, 31 October 1876, Partridge to Fish, no. 349.
5. Ibid.
6. Barman, *Citizen Emperor*, 285.
7. Rangel, 324.
8. Barman, *Princess Isabel*, 144–145.
9. Barman, *Citizen Emperor*, 285.
10. Calmon, 135.
11. Rangel, 330.
12. Barman, *Princess Isabel*, 34.
13. Linda Lewin, *Politics and Parentela in Paraíba: A Case Study of Family-Based Oligarchy in Brazil* (Princeton, NJ: Princeton University Press, 1987), 52.
14. United States House of Representatives, *Executive Documents 1878–1879*.
15. Helene Vacaresco, "Pedro II, Emperor of Brazil," *Contemporary Review* 86 (November 1904): 735.
16. Ibid.

Chapter 35

1. Barman, *Princess Isabel*, 154.
2. Ibid., 153.

3. Bernstein, 15.
4. Barman, *Citizen Emperor*, 287.
5. Barman, *Princess Isabel*, 132.
6. Cuniff, 201, 270.
7. Williams, *Dom Pedro the Magnanimous*, 230.
8. Codman, "Brazil and Her Emperor," 824.
9. Rangel, 334–335
10. Ibid., 335.
11. Williams, *Dom Pedro the Magnanimous*, 265.
12. Lacombe, "Princesa Isabel 1846–1921," 632.
13. Robert Toplin, "The Abolition of Slavery in Brazil," *Studies in American Negro Life*, August Meyer, ed. (New York: Athenaeum, 1975), 155.
14. Lacombe, "Princesa Isabel 1846–1921," 630.
15. Ibid.
16. Frank Carpenter, *Roundabout Rio* (Chicago: Jansen, McClurg, 1884), 88.
17. Cuniff, 191.
18. Ibid., 185.
19. Ibid., 186.
20. Gerald M. Greenfield, "The Great Drought and Elite Discourse in Imperial Brazil," *Hispanic American Historical Review* 72.3 (1992): 382–384.
21. Toplin, *Abolition of Slavery*, 60.
22. Ibid., 61.
23. Ibid.
24. Ibid.
25. Barman, *Princess Isabel*, 207.
26. Ibid., 157.
27. Barman, *Princess Isabel*, 158.
28. Stefan Zweig, *Brazil, Land of the Future* (New York: Viking Press, 1941), 75.
29. Rangel, 338.

Chapter 36

1. Williams, *Dom Pedro the Magnanimous*, 223–224.
2. Ibid.
3. Codman, *Ten Months in Brazil*, 159.
4. Ibid., 157–152.
5. C.C. Andrews, *Brazil: Its Condition and Prospects* (New York: Appleton, 1887), 35.
6. Stein, 152.
7. Leal, 71.
8. Barman, *Princess Isabel*, 126.
9. Ibid., 281, 479.
10. Pierson, 54.
11. Barman, *Citizen Emperor*, 121.
12. Ibid., 144.
13. Monica Salem de Zayas, interview with author, Museolga Arquivo Grao Pará, Petrópolis, 1 June 2006.
14. Bernstein, 152.
15. Ibid.
16. Barman, *Princess Isabel*, 164.
17. Ibid., 168.
18. Barman, *Citizen Emperor*, 290.
19. Barman, *Princess Isabel*, 162.
20. Ibid., 161.
21. June E. Hahner, "Feminism, Women's Rights, and the Suffrage Movement in Brazil, 1850–1932," *Latin American Research Review* 15 (1980): 77, 79.
22. Ibid., 75, 86.
23. Ruth Judice, *Palácio Cristal* (Petrópolis: Editora Crayon Noir, 1998), 56.
24. Barman, *Princess Isabel*, 170.
25. Eduardo Silva, *As Camélias do Leblon e a Abolição da Escravatura* (Editora Schwarcz, 2003), 31.
26. Nabuco, *Abolitionism*, 138.
27. Williams, *Dom Pedro the Magnanimous*, 275.
28. Toplin, *Abolition of Slavery*, 66, 88, 97–98.
29. Ibid., 97.
30. Ibid., 99–100.
31. Ibid., 102–103.
32. Emilia Viotti Da Costa, *The Brazilian Empire Myths and Histories* (Chapel Hill: University of North Carolina Press, 2000), 214.
33. Barman, *Citizen Emperor*, 328.

Chapter 37

1. Ricardo Gumbleton Daunt, *Diario da Princesa Isabel* (São Paulo: Editora Anhembi, 1957), 1, 27.
2. Ibid., 27–28.
3. Ibid., 29.
4. Ibid., 28.
5. Ibid.
6. Ibid., 29.
7. Ibid.
8. Ibid.
9. Ibid.
10. Ibid., 30.
11. Ibid., 31.
12. Ibid., 32.
13. Ibid.
14. Barman, *Princess Isabel*, 173.
15. Daunt, 27–28.
16. Levi, 7, 25.
17. Ibid., 37.
18. Ibid., 38.
19. Ibid.
20. Ibid., 45.
21. Ibid., 63–64.
22. Daunt, 37.
23. Gloria Kaiser, *Thomas Ender Brasilien-Expedition 1817* (Washington, DC: Library of Congress, 1993).
24. Barman, *Princess Isabel*, 173.
25. Barman, *Citizen Emperor*, 318.
26. Toplin, *Abolition of Slavery*, 107.
27. Ibid., 108.
28. *Rio News*, 5 February 1886.
29. Toplin, *Abolition of Slavery*, 108–109.
30. Ibid., 109.
31. Ibid., 110.
32. Ibid., 147.
33. Ibid., 155.
34. Ibid.
35. Andrews, 329.
36. Caroline Nabuco, *The Life of Joaquim Nabuco*, 149.

37. Ibid., 150.
38. *New York Times*, 6 October 1886.
39. Barman, *Princess Isabel*, 175.
40. *Rio News*, 24 December 1886, 4; 5 January 1887, 4.

Chapter 38

1. Barman, *Princess Isabel*, 176.
2. Barman, *Citizen Emperor*, 332–333.
3. Ibid., 333.
4. *Rio News*, 24 June 1887.
5. Barman, *Citizen Emperor*, 333.
6. Ibid.
7. Ibid., 332.
8. Ibid., 334.
9. Ibid., 335.
10. Ibid.
11. Ibid.
12. Barman, *Princess Isabel*, 118.
13. "Kaiser Friedrich III (1831–1888), Biographie, Lebenslauf in Bildern," http://www.deutsche-schutzgebiete.de/kaiser_friedrich.htm.
14. Schwarcz, 313.
15. Barman, *Princess Isabel*, 178.
16. Barman, *Citizen Emperor*, 337.
17. Richard Graham, "Causes for the Abolition of Negro Slavery in Brazil: An Interpretive Essay," *Hispanic American Historical Review* 2 (May 1966): 52.
18. Toplin, *Abolition of Slavery*, 207.
19. Ibid., 234.
20. Robert B. Toplin, "Upheaval, Violence, and the Abolition of Slavery in Brazil: The Case of São Paulo," *Hispanic American Historical Review* 49 (1969): 644.
21. Toplin, *Abolition of Slavery*, 38.
22. Toplin, "Upheaval," 642.
23. Conrad, 186.
24. Ibid., 186.
25. Toplin, "Upheaval," 645.
26. Ibid., 651.
27. Barman, *Citizen Emperor*, 354.
28. Rebecca Bergstresser, *The Movement for the Abolition of Slavery in Rio de Janeiro, Brazil, 1880–1889*, dissertation (Stanford, CA: Stanford University, 1973), 130.
29. Toplin, *Abolition of Slavery*, 219.
30. *Rio News*, 6 September, 1887.
31. Toplin, *Abolition of Slavery*, 235.
32. *Rio News*, 15 September 1887, 2.
33. Toplin, *Abolition of Slavery*, 236.
34. Michael R. Trochim, *Retreat from Reform: The Fall of the Brazilian Empire, 1888–1889*, dissertation (Chicago: University of Illinois at Chicago, 1983; UMI Dissertation Services, 1983), 126.
35. Ibid.
36. Ibid.
37. Ibid.
38. Barman, *Princess Isabel*, 180.
39. Caroline Nabuco, *The Life of Joaquim Nabuco*, 163.
40. Trochim, 41.

41. Silva, *As Camelias do Lebon*, 7.
42. Ibid., 38.
43. Ibid., 36.
44. Ibid.
45. Ibid.
46. Toplin, "Upheaval," 206, 237.
47. Ibid., 224.
48. Ibid., 97, 254.
49. Trochim, 97.
50. Ibid.
51. Ibid.
52. Ibid., 98
53. Barman, *Princess Isabel*, 180.
54. Ibid., 181.

Chapter 39

1. *Rio News*, 15 March 1888, 2.
2. Ibid., 2.
3. Barman, *Princess Isabel*, 178–179.
4. Ibid., 181.
5. Caroline Nabuco, *The Life of Joaquim Nabuco*, 164.
6. Toplin, "Upheaval," 240.
7. Coulombe, 403–406.
8. Caroline Nabuco, *The Life of Joaquim Nabuco*, 163.
9. Toplin, "Upheaval," 231.
10. Ibid., 233.
11. Trochim, 126.
12. *Rio News*, 15 March 1888, 2.
13. Gilberto Freyre, *The Mansions and the Shanties: The Making of Modern Brazil*, Harriet de Onis, trans. (New York: Alfred Knopf, 1968), 136.
14. *Rio News*, 15 March 1888, 2.
15. Conrad, 202.
16. Judice, 76.
17. *Rio News*, 15 April 1888, 1.
18. Orico, 146–150.
19. Trochim, 63.
20. Toplin, "Upheaval," 223.
21. Ibid., 220.
22. Ibid.
23. *Rio News*, 5 May 1888, 2.
24. Williams, *Dom Pedro the Magnanimous*, 283.
25. *Rio News*, 5 February 1888, 2.
26. Barman, *Citizen Emperor*, 318.
27. *Rio News*, 24 April 1888, 2.
28. Barman, *Citizen Emperor*, 403.
29. Williams, *Dom Pedro the Magnanimous*, 285.
30. *Rio News*, 5 May 1888, 2.
31. Caroline Nabuco, *The Life of Joaquim Nabuco*, 164.
32. Trochim, 128.
33. Conrad, 203.
34. Kaiser, *Saudade*, 27.
35. Hermes Vieira, *Princesa Isabel — Uma Vida de Luzes e Sombras*, 3rd ed. (São Paulo: Edições GRD, 1990), 168.
36. Percy A. Martin, "Slavery and Abolition in Brazil," *Hispanic American Historical Review* 4 (1921): 193.

37. Caroline Nabuco, *The Life of Joaquim Nabuco*, 168.
38. Martin, "Slavery and Abolition in Brazil," 192.
39. *Rio News*, 12 May 1888, 2.
40. Ibid.
41. Stein, 255.
42. Schwarcz, 315.
43. Williams, *Dom Pedro the Magnanimous*, 284.
44. Toplin, *Abolition of Slavery*, 256.
45. Martin, *History of Brazil*, 259.
46. Toplin, "Upheaval," 244.
47. Caroline Nabuco, *The Life of Joaquim Nabuco*, 169.
48. Ibid.
49. Gilberto Freyre, *The Masters and Slaves* (New York: Alfred A. Knopf, 1946), 158–159.
50. Pierre Denis, *Brazil,* South American Series, vol. 5 (New York: Charles Scribner's Sons, 1911), 69.
51. *Rio News*, 13 June 1888, 1.
52. Caroline Nabuco, *The Life of Joaquim Nabuco*, 169.
53. Barman, *Princess Isabel*, 183–184.
54. Barman, *Citizen Emperor*, 341.
55. Ibid., 315.
56. Williams, *Dom Pedro the Magnanimous*, 295.
57. Ibid., 286.
58. *Rio News*, 13 June 1888, 1.
59. Conrad, 205.
60. Toplin, "Upheaval," 260.
61. Ibid., 252.
62. Barman, *Princess Isabel*, 188.

Chapter 40

1. Trochim, 129.
2. Ibid., 130.
3. Angelo Agostini, *Revista Illustrada*, Ano 13, #496, 1.
4. Barman, *Princess Isabel*, 183.
5. Trochim, 164.
6. Ibid., 164.
7. Ibid., 165.
8. Ibid., 129.
9. Ibid., 131.
10. Conrad, 478–479.
11. Trochim, 131.
12. Ibid., 131.
13. United States House of Representatives, *Papers Relating to the Foreign Relations of the United States, Transmitted to Congress, with the Annual Message of the President, December 3, 1888* (Washington, DC: Government Printing Office, 1889), 72–73.
14. Toplin, "Upheaval," 253.
15. Ibid., 252.
16. Ibid.
17. Trochim, 138.
18. Ibid.
19. Ibid.
20. Ibid., 149.
21. Ibid., 142.
22. Ibid., 151.
23. Schwarcz, 355.
24. Trochim, 146.
25. John Burdick, *Blessed Anastacia: Women, Race, and Popular Christianity in Brazil* (New York: Routledge, 1998), 220.
26. Gilberto Freyre, *Order and Progress: Brazil from Monarchy to Republic*, Rod W. Horton, ed., trans. (New York: Alfred A. Knopf, 1970), 8, 404–405.
27. Luís Felipe Orleans-Bragança interview, 1996.
28. Freyre, *Order and Progress*, 8.
29. Trochim, 178.
30. Caroline Nabuco, *Life of Joaquim Nabuco*, 72.
31. Trochim, 151.
32. Schwarcz, 313.
33. Ibid.
34. *Rio News*, 4 August 1888, 1.
35. Ibid.
36. Barman, *Citizen Emperor*, 346.
37. Levine, *Confederate Emancipation*, 103–107.
38. Ibid.
39. Trochim, 137.
40. Ibid., 150.
41. Ibid., 150–151.
42. Andrews, 214–215.
43. June E. Hahner, *Officers and Civilians in Brazil, 1889–1898*, dissertation (Ithaca, NY: Cornell University, 1966), 37.
44. *Rio News*, 24 November 1888, 2.
45. *Rio News*, 5 September 1888, 4.
46. *Rio News*, 5 August 1888, 1.
47. Cyrene Paparotti, "An Analysis of Ilara's Recitative and Aria: Alba dorata ... O Ciel di parahyba." http://westnet.com/~ngcpc/acg/parahyba.html.
48. *Rio News*, 15 October 1988, 3.
49. Vieira, 169.
50. Williams, *Dom Pedro the Magnanimous*, 286.
51. United States Diplomatic Correspondence, 145, no. 62.
52. Barman, *Citizen Emperor*, 343.
53. Williams, *Dom Pedro the Magnanimous*, 321.
54. Barman, *Citizen Emperor*, 343.
55. Ibid., 343.
56. Barman, *Princess Isabel*, 185.
57. *Rio News*, 24 November 1888, 3.
58. *Rio News*, 5 December 1888, 2
59. *Rio News*, 7 January, 1889, 2.

Chapter 41

1. Barman, *Princess Isabel*, 189.
2. Caroline Nabuco, *Life of Joaquim Nabuco*, 182.
3. Trochim, 176.
4. Ibid., 178.
5. Ibid., 179.
6. Ibid., 181.

7. Ibid., 180.
8. Ibid., 185.
9. Ibid., 181.
10. Ibid.
11. Ibid., 183.
12. Ibid., 182.
13. Barman, *Princess Isabel*, 86.
14. Rangel, 375.
15. Ibid., 6, 375.
16. *Rio News*, 1 April 1889, 3.
17. Barman, *Princess Isabel*, 191.
18. Trochim, 178.
19. Ibid.
20. Ibid.
21. Luís Felipe Orleans-Bragança interview, 1996.
22. Trochim, 189.
23. Ibid., 218.
24. Ibid.
25. *Rio News*, 28 October 1889, 2.
26. Barman, *Citizen Emperor*, 349.
27. Williams, *Dom Pedro the Magnanimous*, 302.
28. Trochim, 198.
29. Ibid., 207.
30. Barman, *Citizen Emperor*, 350.
31. Conrad 115.
32. *Rio News*, 17 May 1889, 2.
33. *Rio News*, 13 May 1889, 4; 10 June 1889, 4.
34. Trochim, 205.
35. Barman, *Princess Isabel*, 191.
36. Vieira, 171.
37. *Rio News*, 3 June 1889, 5.
38. Barman, *Princess Isabel*, 191.
39. Ibid., 193.
40. Ibid.
41. Ibid.
42. Emilia Viotti da Costa, *The Brazilian Empire: Myths and Histories*, revised ed. (Chapel Hill: University of North Carolina Press, 1985), 230–231.
43. Trochim, 197.
44. Ibid., 211.
45. Williams, *Dom Pedro the Magnanimous*, 303–304.
46. Ibid.
47. Ibid.
48. Barman, *Citizen Emperor*, 351.
49. Trochim, 198–199.
50. *Rio News*, 22 July 1889, 1.
51. Kaiser, *Pedro II of Brazil*, 23.
52. Lewin, 227.
53. Trochim, 199.
54. Williams, *Dom Pedro the Magnanimous*, 307.
55. Trochim, 225.
56. Ibid.
57. Leal, 70–71.
58. Ibid.
59. Trochim, 244.
60. William S. Dudley, "Professionalism and Politicization as Motivational Factors in the Brazilian Army Coup of 15 November, 1889," *Journal of Latin American Studies* 8.1 (May 1976): 121.
61. Trochim, 292.
62. *Rio News*, 23 September 1889, 4.

Chapter 42

1. Trochim, 255.
2. Ibid.
3. Ibid., 288.
4. Ibid., 297.
5. Ibid.
6. Schwarcz, 322.
7. Ibid.
8. Barman, *Princess Isabel*, 195.
9. Schwarcz, 81.
10. Ibid., 325.
11. Errol Lincoln Uys, *Brazil* (New York: Simon and Shuster, 1986), 883.
12. Ibid., 884.
13. Williams, *Dom Pedro the Magnanimous*, 325.
14. *Rio News*, 11 November 1889, 4.
15. Hendrick Kray, "Os Militaes e a Republica: um estudo sobre cultura e acao politica," *Hispanic American Historic Review* (February 1998): 155–156.
16. Barman, *Citizen Emperor*, 358.
17. David E. Worcester, *Brazil: From Colony to World Power* (New York: Scribner's Sons, 1973).
18. Barman, *Princess Isabel*, 196.
19. Ibid., 201.
20. Ibid., 196.
21. Barman, *Citizen Emperor*, 350.
22. Ibid., 361.
23. Williams, *Dom Pedro the Magnanimous*, 399.
24. Barman, *Princess Isabel*, 197.
25. Williams, *Dom Pedro the Magnanimous*, 348.
26. *(The) Nation*, 6 February 1890, 107.
27. *Rio News*, 17 November 1889, 3.
28. Williams, *Dom Pedro the Magnanimous*, 345.
29. *New York Times*, 9 December 1889, 1.
30. Kaiser interview, 2005.

Chapter 43

1. Caroline Nabuco, *Life of Joaquim Nabuco*, 192.
2. Williams, *Dom Pedro the Magnanimous*, 335.
3. Barman, *Princess Isabel*, 249.
4. Ibid., 202.
5. Ibid., 116.
6. *Homenagem no Instituto Histórico e Geográfico Brasileiro a Memoria de Sua Magestade o Senhor D. Pedro II* (Rio De Janeiro: Companhia Typografia do Brasil, 1894), LVI.
7. Longo, *Shadow of Power*, 93.
8. De Hollanda et al., 104.
9. Longo, *Hidden Curriculum*, 1–2.
10. Caroline Nabuco, *Life of Joaquim Nabuco*, 197.
11. *New York Times*, 17 November 1889, 1.
12. Ibid.
13. Ibid.
14. Langworthy Marchant, "Dona Isabel of Bragança and Orleáns, Ex Princess-Imperial of Brazil," *Pan American Union Bulletin*, no. 3 (March 1922): 233, 243.
15. *Public Opinions* 8.12 (28 December 1889): 279.

16. Ibid., 280.

17. Caroline Nabuco, *Life of Joaquim Nabuco*, 197.

18. Herbert F. Johnson, *Braziliana* (Ithaca, NY: Cornell University Press, 1959), 137.

19. Charles Skidmore, *Brazil: Five Centuries of Change* (New York: Oxford University Press, 1999), 73.

20. Caroline Nabuco, *Life of Joaquim Nabuco*, 202.

21. Rose Brown, *The Land and People of Brazil* (New York: Lippincott, 1972), 57.

22. Barman, *Citizen Emperor*, 372.

23. *Homenagem no Instituto Histórico e Geográfico Brasileiro*, 742.

24. Vacaresco, 733.

25. Caroline Nabuco, *Life of Joaquim Nabuco*, 191.

26. Barman, *Princess Isabel*, 214.

27. *Harper's Weekly* 37 (7 October 1893): 955.

28. Barman, *Princess Isabel*, 281.

29. Ibid.

30. Ibid., 220, 228.

31. Vacaresco, 734–735.

32. Kaiser interview, 1998.

33. Burdick, 67–68, 71, 74.

Bibliography

Adams, Jane Elizabeth. "The Abolition of the Brazilian Slave Trade." *The Journal of Negro History* 4 (Oct. 1925): 606.

Adams, Jerome. *Liberators and Patriots of Latin America: Biographies of 23 Leaders.* Jefferson, NC: McFarland, 1991.

_____. *Notable Latin American Women: Twenty-Nine Leaders, Rebels, Poets, Battlers and Spies, 1500–1900.* Jefferson, NC: McFarland, 1995.

Agostini, Angelo. *Revista Illustrada.* Rio de Janeiro: Ano 13, #496.

Akers, Charles Edmond, and L.E. Elliott. *A History of South America.* New York: E.P. Dutton, 1930.

Andrews, C.C. *Brazil: Its Condition and Prospects.* New York: Appleton, 1887.

Armitage, John. *The History of Brazil from the Period of the Arrival of the Bragança Family in 1808 to the Abdication of Dom Pedro I in 1831.* London: Smith Elder, 1836.

Barman, Roderick J. *Brazil: The Forging of a Nation.* Stanford: Stanford University Press, 1988.

_____. *Citizen Emperor: Pedro II and the Making of Brazil, 1825–91.* Stanford: Stanford University Press, 1999.

_____. *Princess Isabel of Brazil: Gender and Power in the Nineteenth Century.* Wilmington, DE: Scholarly Resources, 2002.

Barrett, William E. *Woman on Horseback: The Biography of Francisco López and Eliza Lynch.* London: Peter Davies, 1938.

Baum, Emmi. *Empress Leopoldina: Her Role in the Development of Brazil, 1817–1826.* Dissertation, New York University, June 1965.

Beckford, William. *Italy with Sketches of Spain and Portugal.* London: Richard Bentley, 1834.

_____. *Recollections of an Excursion to the Monasteries of Alcobaca and Batalha.* London: Richard Bentley, 1835.

Bennett, Daphne. *King Without a Crown.* New York: Lippincott, 1977.

Bentley, Richard, ed. *Recollections of My Life: Maximilian Emperor of Mexico.* Vol. 3. London, 1868.

Bergamini, John D. The *Spanish Bourbons: The History of a Tenacious Dynasty.* New York: G.P. Putnam's Sons, 1974.

Bergstresser, Rebecca. "The Movement for the Abolition of Slavery in Rio de Janeiro, Brazil, 1880–1889." Dissertation, Stanford University, 1973.

Bernstein, Harry. *Dom Pedro II.* New York: Twayne, 1973.

Bolitho, Hector, ed. *Letters of Queen Victoria from the Archives of the House of Brandenburg-Prussia.* New Haven: Yale University Press, 1938.

Box, Pelham H. *The Origins of the Paraguayan War.* New York: Russell and Russell, 1873.

Boxer, Charles. *The Portuguese Seaborne Empire: 1415–1825.* New York: Alfred A. Knopf, 1969.

_____. *Race Relations in the Colonial Portuguese Empire, 1415–1825.* London: Oxford University Press, 1963.

"Brazil Notes." *New York Times,* 25 October 1873.

Burdick, John. *Blessed Anastacia: Women, Race, and Popular Christianity in Brazil.* New York: Routledge, 1998.

Brown, Dee. *The Year of the Century: 1876.* New York: Charles Scribner's Sons, 1966.

Brown, Rose. *American Emperor: Dom Pedro II of Brazil.* New York: Viking Press, 1945.

_____. *The Land and People of Brazil.* New York: Lippincott, 1972.

Burns, E. Bradford. *A Documentary History of Brazil.* New York: Alfred A. Knopf, 1966.

Callcott, Wilfrid Hardy. *Liberalism in Mexico, 1857–1929.* Stanford: Stanford University Press, 1931.

Calmon, Pedro. *A Princesa Isabel "A Redentora."* São Paulo, Rio, Porto-Alegre: Companhia Editora Nacional, 1941.

Calogeras, João Pandia. *A History of Brazil.* Percy Alvin Martin, ed. and trans. Chapel Hill: University of North Carolina Press, 1939.

Carpenter, Frank. *Roundabout Rio.* Chicago: Jansen, McClurg, 1884.

Castelot, Andre. *King of Rome: A Biography of Napoleon's Tragic Son.* Robert Baldick, trans. New York: Harper and Brothers, 1960.

Cheke, Marcus. *Carlota Joaquina: Queen of Portugal.* London: Sidgwick and Jackson, 1947.

_____. *The Life of the Marquis of Pombal.* London: Sidgwick and Jackson, 1938.

Clark, Pamela. Letter to the author. 14 April 2000.

"Clergy and Masons." *New York Times,* 16 May 1873.

Cleven, N. Andrew. "Some Plans for Colonizing Liberated Negro Slaves in Hispanic America." *The Journal of Negro History* 10. Lancaster, PA, and Washington, DC: Association for the Study of Negro Life and History, 1926.

Codman, John. "Brazil and Her Emperor." *Galaxy Magazine* 21 (June 1876).

_____. *Ten Months in Brazil with Notes on the Paraguayan War.* 2nd ed. New York: James Miller, 1872.

"Conflict Between Priests and Masons." *New York Times,* 21 July 1874.

Conrad, Robert Edgar. *Children of God's Fire.* Princeton, NJ: Princeton University Press, 1984.

Constant, Stephen. *Foxy Ferdinand: Tsar of Bulgaria.* New York, London, Toronto, Sydney: Franklin Watts, 1980.

Coulombe, Charles A. *Vicars of Christ: A History of the Popes.* New York: Citadel Press, 2003.

Crankshaw, Edward. *The Habsburgs: Portrait of a Dynasty.* New York: Viking, 1971.

Criss, Mildred. *Dom Pedro of Brazil.* New York: Dodd, Mead, 1945.

Cronin, Vincent. *Louis and Antoinette.* New York: William Morrow, 1975.

Crow, John A. *The Epic of Latin America.* 4th ed. Los Angeles: University of California Press, 1992.

Cuniff, Roger. *The Great Drought: Northeast Brazil, 1877–1880.* Dissertation, University of Texas at Austin, 1970. University Microfilms, 1971.

Da Camara Cascudo, Luís. *Conde D'Eu.* São Paulo: Companhia Editora Nacional, 1933.

Da Carnota, Conde. *Memoirs of Field Marshal The Duke de Saldanha with Selections from His Correspondence.* Vol. 2. London: John Murray, 1880.

Da Conceição, Maria José. *The Revelation of God in the Black Resistance.* São Paulo: Nossa Senhora da Assunção Theology College, 1995.

Da Costa, Luíz Edmundo. *Rio in the Time of the Viceroys.* Rio de Janeiro: Athena Editora, 1935.

Da Costa, Sergio Correa. *Every Inch a King: A Biography of Dom Pedro I First Emperor of Brazil.* New York: Macmillan, 1950.

Daunt, Ricardo Gumbleton. *Diario da Princesa Isabel.* São Paulo: Editora Anhembi, 1957.

D'Auvergne, Edmund B. *The Bride of Two Kings.* London: Hutchinson, 1910.

De Hollanda, Heloisa Buarque; Afonso Carlos Marquês dos Santos, Augusta Ivan de Freitas Pinheiro, and Iole de Freitas. *Paço Imperial.* Rio de Janeiro: Sextante Artes, 1999.

De LaMartine. *History of the French Revolution.* Vol 1. Boston: Phillips, Sampson, 1849.

Delle Donne, Vincenzo, ed. *Naples.* Singapore: APA Publications, 1992.

Denis, Pierre. *Brazil.* New York: Charles Scribner's Sons, 1911.

DeQueiros Mattoso, Katia M. *To Be a Slave in Brazil 1550–1888.* New Brunswick, NJ: Rutgers University Press, 1986.

De Ronde, Philip. *A Gallant Little Nation.* New York: G.P. Putnam's Sons, 1935.

De Schubert, G.H. *Memoir of the Duchess of Orleans by the Marquess de H----.* New York: Charles Scribner, 1860.

DeSousa, Manuel. *Reis e Rainhas de Portugal.* Lisbon: SporPress, 2000.

De Stoeckl, Agnes. *King of the French: A Portrait of Louis Philippe 1773–1850.* New York: G.P. Putnam's Sons, 1958.

Diesbach, Ghislain. *Secrets of the Gotha.* New York: Meredith Books, 1967.

Dudley, William S. "Professionalism and the Politicization as Motivational Factors in the Brazilian Army Coup of 15 November, 1889." *Journal of Latin American Studies* 8.1 (May 1976): 121.

Earle, T.F, and K.J.P. Lowe. *Black African in Renaissance Europe.* Cambridge: Cambridge University Press, 2006.

"Emancipation Program." *New York Times,* 14 June 1871.

Erickson, Carolly. *Her Little Majesty: The Life of Queen Victoria.* New York: Simon and Schuster, 1997.

Ewbank, Thomas. *Life in Brazil; or Journal of a Visit to the land of the Cocoa and the Palm.* New York: Harper and Brothers, 1856.

Ferro, Maria Ines. *Queluz: The Palace and Gardens.* London: Scala, 1997.

Francis, David. *Portugal 1715–1808.* London: Tamesis, 1985.

Freyre, Gilberto. *The Mansions and the Shanties: The Making of Modern Brazil.* Harriet de Onis, trans. New York: Alfred A. Knopf, 1968.

_____. *The Masters and Slaves.* New York: Alfred A. Knopf, 1946.

_____. *Order and Progress: Brazil from Monarchy to Republic.* Rod W. Horton, ed., trans. New York: Alfred A. Knopf, 1970.

Fulford, Roger, ed. *Dearest Child: Letters Between Queen Victoria and the Princess Royal 1858–1861.* London: Evans Bros., 1964.

Gostelow, Martin. *Discover Portugal.* Oxford, UK: Berlitz, 1996.

Gottschalk, Louis Moreau. *Notes of a Pianist.* Clara Gottschalk, ed., Robert Peterson, M.D., trans. Philadelphia: J.B. Lippincott, 1881.

Graden, Dale, T. "An Act 'Even of Public Security': Slave Resistance, Social Tensions, and the End of the International Slave Trade to Brazil, 1835–1836." *Hispanic American Historic Review* 76.2 (May 1996).

Graham, Maria Dundas. *Journal of a Voyage to Brazil and Residence There, During Part of the Years 1821, 1822, 1823.* Originally published 1824. New York: Frederick A. Praeger, 1969 (reprint).

Graham, Richard. *Britain and the Onset of Modernization in Brazil 1850–1914.* Cambridge, UK: Cambridge University Press, 1968.

_____. "Causes for the Abolition of Negro Slavery in Brazil: An Interpretive Essay." *Hispanic American Historical Review,* no. 2 (May 1966).

Graham, Sandra Lauderdale. *House and Street: The Domestic World of Servants and Masters in Nineteenth-Century Rio de Janeiro.* Austin: University of Texas Press, 1992.

Greenbie, Sydney. *The Fertile Land, Brazil.* New York: Row, Peterson, 1943.

Greenfield, Gerald M. "The Great Drought and Elite Discourse in Imperial Brazil." *Hispanic American Historical Review* 72:3. Durham: Duke University Press, 1992.

Gribble, Francis H. *The Royal House of Portugal.* Port Washington, NY: Kennikat Press, 1915.

Guillon, Jacques, Amiral. *François d'Orleans Prince de Joinville 1818–1900.* Paris: Editions France-Empire, 1894.

Guizot, M., and Madame Guizot de Witt. *France.* Vol. 8. New York: Peter Fenelon Collier, 1869.

Hahner, June E. "Feminism, Women's Rights, and the Suffrage Movement in Brazil, 1850–1932." *Latin American Research Review* 15 (1980).

_____. *Officers and Civilians in Brazil, 1889–1898.* Dissertation, Cornell University, 1966.

Harding, Bertita. *Amazon Throne: The Story of the Braganças of Brazil.* New York: Bobbs-Merrill, 1941.

Haring, C.H. *Empire in Brazil: A New World Experiment with Monarchy.* Cambridge, MA: Harvard University Press, 1958.

Harper's Weekly 37 (7 October 1893): 955.

Harvey, Robert. *Liberators: Latin America's Struggle for Independence.* Woodstock, NY: Overlook Press, 2000.

Haslip, Joan. *Imperial Adventurer Emperor Maximilian of Mexico.* London: Weidenfeld and Nicolson, 1971.

Hemming, John. *Red Gold: The Conquest of the Brazilian Indians 1500–1790.* Cambridge, MA: Harvard University Press, 1978.

Henderson, James D., and Linda Roddy Henderson. *Ten Notable Women of Latin America.* Chicago: Nelson-Hall, 1978.

Herring, Hubert. *A History of Latin America from the Beginnings to the Present.* 3rd ed. New York: Alfred A. Knopf, 1968.

Homenagem no Instituto Histórico e Geográfico Brasileiro a Memoria de Sua Magestade o Senhor D. Pedro II. Rio De Janeiro: Companhia Typográfia do Brasil, 1894.

Houston, Marco, ed. "The House of Windsor Has Black Ancestors." *Royalty* 16.1 (1999).

"Imperial Tourists." *New York Times,* 31 May 1873.

"An Imperial Visitor." *New York Times,* 23 September 1875.

Johnson, Herbert F. *Braziliana.* Ithaca, NY: Cornell University Press, 1959.

Judice, Ruth. *Palacio Crystal 1884.* Petrópolis: Editora Crayon Noir, 1998.

Kaiser, Gloria. Correspondence with the author. 29 September 1997.

_____. *Dona Leopoldina: The Habsburg Empress of Brazil.* Riverside, CA: Ariadne Press, 1998.

_____. Interviews with the author. Library of Congress, Washington, DC, 18 March 1997; 19 October 1998; Library of Congress and Austrian Embassy, 18–19 September 2005.

_____. *Pedro II of Brazil, Son of the Habsburg Empress.* Lowell A. Bangerter, trans. Riverside, CA: Ariadne Press. 2000.

_____. *Saudade: The Life and Death of Queen Maria Gloria of Lusitania.* Lowell A. Bangerter, trans. Riverside, CA: Ariadne Press, 2003.

_____. *Thomas Ender Brasilien-Expedition 1817.* Washington, DC: Library of Congress, 1993.

"Kaiser Friedrich III. (1831–1888), Biographie, Lebenslauf in Bildern." http://www.deutsche-schutzgebiete.de/kaiser_friedrich.htm.

Kaman, Henry. *Empire: How Spain Became a World Power 1492–1763.* New York: Harper Collins, 2003.

Keith, Henry H., and S.F. Edwards. *Conflict and Continuity in Brazilian Society.* Columbia: University of South Carolina Press, 1969.

Koebel, W. *British Exploits in South America: A History of British Activities and Exploration.* New York: Century, 1917.

Kolinski, Charles J. *Independence or Death! The Story of the Paraguayan War.* Gainesville: University of Florida Press, 1965.

Lacombe, Lourenço Luíz. *Isabelle: A Princess Redentora.* Petrópolis: Institute Historico de Petrópolis, 1989.

_____. "Princesa Isabel 1846–1921." *Grandes Personagens da Nossa Historia.* Vol. 3. Victor Civita, ed. São Paulo: Abril Cultural, 1973.

Lee, Sidney. *Queen Victoria: A Biography.* London: Smith, Elder, 1908.

Leal, Priscilla. "O Lado Rebelde da Princesa Isabel." *Nossa Historia,* May 2006.

Levi, Darrell E. *The Prados of São Paulo Brazil: An Elite Family and Social Change, 1840–1930.* Athens and London: University of Georgia Press, 1987.

Levine, Bruce. *Confederate Emancipation: Southern Plans to Free and Arm Slaves During the Civil War.* Oxford and New York: Oxford University Press, 2006.

Levine, Robert M., and John J. Croc, eds. (Beattie, Peter M.). *The Brazil Reader.* Durham, NC: Duke University Press, 1999.

Lewin, Linda. *Politics and Parentela in Paraíba: A Case Study of Family-Based Oligarchy in Brazil.* Princeton, NJ: Princeton University Press, 1987.

Light, Kenneth. *The Journal of the Royal Family to Brazil 1807–1808.* http://www:fcsh.unl.pt/congressoceap/k-light.doc.

Livermore, H.V. *A History of Portugal.* Cambridge, UK: Cambridge University Press, 1947.

_____. *A New History of Portugal.* Cambridge, UK: Cambridge University Press, 1966.

Longford, Elizabeth. *Queen Victoria: Born to Succeed.* New York: Harper and Row, 1969.

Longo, James McMurtry. "An Example of the Hidden Curriculum: The Neglected Role of Women in the Rise and Fall of Brazilian Slavery." Harvard University Graduate School of Education 1999 Student Research Conference and International Forum, Cambridge, Massachusetts, 26 February 1999.

_____. "Princess Isabel and the Emperor Pedro II: Imperial Power in the Hands of the Abolitionist Regent of Brazil 1888." Latin American Studies Association International Conference, Washington, DC: 8 September 2001.

_____. "Shadow of Power Five Generations of Brazilian Women: The Role of the Royal Bragança Women in Brazilian History." National Association of Hispanic and Latino Studies International Conference, Houston, Texas, 26 February 2000.

_____. "The Woman Who Ended Slavery in the Americas." Issues in Third World History. The 21st Annual Great Lakes History Conference: The Individual and Society in History, Grand Valley State University, Grand Rapids, Michigan, 4 October 1996.

Loveman, Brian. *The Constitution of Tyranny: Regimes of Exception in Spanish America.* Pittsburgh: University of Pittsburgh Press, 1993.

Macaulay, Neill. *Dom Pedro: The Struggle for Liberty in Brazil and Portugal 1798–1834.* Durham, NC: Duke University Press, 1986.

Macaulay, Rose. *They Went to Portugal.* London: Jonathan Cape, 1946.

Manning, William R. *Diplomatic Correspondence of the United States Inter-American Affairs 1831–1860.* Vol. 2. Washington: Carnegie Endowment for International Peace, 1932.

Marchant, Langworthy. "Dona Isabel of Bragança and Orleans, Ex Princess-Imperial of Brazil." *Pan American Union Bulletin* 3 (March 1922).

Masterman, George F. *Seven Eventful Years in Paraguay: A Narrative of Personal Experience Amongst the Paraguayans.* 2nd ed. London: Sampson, Low, Son, and Marston, 1870.

Martin, Percy A. "Causes of the Collapse of the Brazilian Empire." *Hispanic American Historical Review* 13 (May 1933).

_____. "Slavery and Abolition in Brazil." *Hispanic American Historical Review* 4 (1921).

_____, and Isaac J. Cox. *Argentina, Brazil and Chile Since Independence.* A. Curtis Wilgus, ed. New York: Russell and Russell, 1963.

Martins, J.P. Olivera. *The Golden Age of Prince Henry the Navigator.* London: Chapman and Hall, 1914.

Martins Carneiro, José Manuel, and Louis Filipe Marquês da Cama. *Palacio Nacional da Pena.* Lisbon: Publicidade Artes Gráficas, 1994.

Martins Moreira, Thiers. "José do Patrocínio 1853–1905." Victor Civita, ed. *Grandes Personagens da Nossa Historia.* Vol. 3. São Paulo: Abril Cultural, 1973.

Maxwell, Kenneth. *Pombal: Paradox of the Enlightenment.* Cambridge, UK: Cambridge University Press, 1995.

Michael of Greece, Prince. *The Empress of Farewells: The Story of Charlotte, Empress of Mexico.* New York: Atlantic Monthly Press, 1998.

Michael of Kent, HRH Princess. *Crowned in a Far Country: Portraits of Eight Royal Brides.* New York: Weidenfeld and Nicolson, 1986.

"Ministry of Viscount Rio Branco." *New York Times,* 24 June 1875.

Nabuco, Caroline. *The Life of Joaquim Nabuco.* Stanford, CA: Stanford University Press, 1950.

Nabuco, Joaquim. *Abolitionism: The Brazilian Antislavery Struggle.* Robert Conrad, trans., ed. Urbana: University of Illinois Press, 1977.

"(The) Nation." Magazine article. 6 February 1890, 107.

New York Times, 17 November 1889.

New York Times, 24 November 1874.

New York Times, 6 October 1886.

New York Times, 9 December 1889.

Noble Johnson, Daniel. *The Journals of Daniel Noble Johnson, (1822–1863) United States Navy.* Washington, DC: Smithsonian Institution Press, 1959.

"Notes from Rio de Janeiro." *New York Times,* 20 August 1874.

Nowell, Charles E. *Portugal.* Englewood Cliffs, NJ: Prentice-Hall, 1973.

O'Connor, Richard. *Cactus Throne: The Tragedy of Maximilian and Charlotte.* New York: G.P. Putnam's Sons, 1971.

Orico, Osvaldo. *Patrocínio.* Rio de Janeiro: Irmaso Pongettim Editores, 1934.

Orleans-Bragança, Anna Luísa. Interview with the author. São Paulo, Brazil, 28 July 1995.

Orleans-Bragança, Luís Felipe. Interviews with the author. Boston, MA, 21–22 January 1996.

Page, Joseph A. *The Brazilians.* New York: Addison-Welsey, 1995.

Pang, Eul-Soo. *In Pursuit of Honor and Power: Noblemen of the Southern Cross in Nineteenth Century Brazil.* Tuscaloosa: University of Alabama Press, 1988.

Paparotti, Cyrene. "An Analysis of Ilara's Recitative and Aria: Alba dorata ... O Ciel di parahyba." http://westnet.com/~ngcpc/acg/parahyba.html.

Payne, Stanley G. *A History of Spain and Portugal.* Madison: University of Wisconsin Press, 1973.

Peppino, Rollie. *Brazil: The Land and People.* Oxford and New York: Oxford University Press, 1968.

Pierson, Donald. *Negros in Brazil: A Study of Race Contact at Bahia.* Carbondale: Southern Illinois University Press, 1942.

Public Opinions 8.12 (28 Dec. 1889).

Rangel, Alberto. *Gastão de Orleans (O Ultimo Conde D'Eu).* São Paulo: Companhia Editora Nacional, 1935.

Rees, Sian. *The Shadows of Elisa Lynch: How a Nineteenth-Century Irish Courtesan Became the Most Powerful Woman in Paraguay.* London: Review, 2003.

Revista Illustrada, Ano 13, #496.

Ribeiro Telles, Gonçalo, ed. *A Monarquia Portuguesa.* Lisbon: Reader's Digest, 1993.

Ridings, Eugene. *Business Interest Groups in Nineteenth Century Brazil.* Cambridge, UK: University Press, 1994.

Rio News, February 5, 1886. December 24, 1886. January 5, 1887. June 24, 1887. September 6, 1887. September 15, 1887. February 5, 1888. March 15, 1888. April 15, 1888. April 24, 1888. May 5, 1888. May 12, 1888. June 13, 1888. August 4, 1888. August 5, 1888. September 5, 1888. October 15, 1888. November 24, 1888. November 24, 1888. December 5, 1888. January 7, 1889. April 1, 1889. May 13, 1889. May 17, 1889. June 3, 1889. June 10, 1889. July 22, 1889. September 23, 1889. October 28, 1889. November 11, 1889. November 17, 1889.

Rixley, Lilian. *Bamie: Theodore Roosevelt's Remarkable Sister.* New York: David McKay, 1963.

Rocquette, Carlos. Interview with the author. Rio de Janeiro, 29 May 2006.

"The Romish Church and Freemasonry." *New York Times,* 10 August 1873.

Russell, Peter. *Prince Henry "The Navigator": A Life.* New Haven, CT: Yale University Press, 2000.

Russell-Wood, A.J.R. *Society and Government in Colonial Brazil 1500–1822.* Aldershot, Great Britain: Variorum, 1992.

Sainty, Guy Stair. *The Order of Our Lady of the Conception: To the Royal House of Portugal.* http://www.chivalricorders.org/orders/portugal/vilavic.htm.

Saldanha, Teresa. *Reis de Portugal Seculo VVII a o Seculo XX.* Lisbon: Instituto Português do Património Arquitectónico, Ministério da Cultura, 2005.

Schultz, Kirsten. *Tropical Versailles: Empire, Monarchy, and the Portuguese Royal Court in Rio de Janeiro, 1808–1821.* New York: Routledge, 2001.

Schwarcz, Lilia Moritz. *The Emperor's Beard: Dom Pedro II and the Tropical Empire of Brazil.* New York: Hill and Wang, 2004.

Sears, Stephen. *George McClellan: The Young Napoleon.* New York: Ticknor and Fields, 1988.

Silva, Eduardo. *As Camelias do Leblon e a Abolição da Escravatura.* São Paulo: Editora Schwarcz, 2003.

_____. *Prince of the People: The Life and Times of a Brazilian Free Man of Colour.* Moyra Ashford, trans. London and New York: Verso, 1993.

Simon, John Y., ed. *The Personal Memoirs of Julia Dent Grant.* New York: G.P. Putnam's Sons, 1975.

Simons, Jeff. *Cuba: From Conquistador to Castro.* New York: St. Martin's Press, 1996.

Skidmore, Charles. *Brazil: Five Centuries of Change.* Oxford and New York: Oxford University Press, 1999.

"Slaves Plot for Liberty." *New York Times,* 21 March 1871.

Stark, Rodney. "The Truth About the Catholic Church and Slavery." *Christianity Today,* 18 August 2003. http://www.christianity today.com/ct/2003/128/53.0.html.

Stein, Stanley. *Vassouras: A Brazilian Coffee County, 1850–1900.* Cambridge: Harvard University Press, 1957.

Stevens, W. "Dom Pedro II, Emperor of Brazil." *Blackwood's Magazine* (London), 1873.

Thomas, Hugh. *Rivers of Gold: The Rise of the Spanish Empire.* London: Weidenfeld and Nicolson, 2003.

_____. *The Slave Trade: The Story of the Atlantic Save Trade 1440–1870.* New York: Simon and Schuster, 1997.

Thomson, Guy. "Popular Aspects of Liberalism in Mexico, 1848–1888." *Journal of Latin American Research* 3 (1991).

Thornton, Mary Criscentia. *The Church and Freemasonry in Brazil, 1972–1875: A Study in Regalism.* Dissertation, Catholic University of America Press, 1948.

Toplin, Robert. *The Abolition of Slavery in Brazil.* Studies in American Negro Life, August Meyer, ed. New York: Athenaeum, 1975.

Toplin, Robert B. "Upheaval, Violence, and the Abolition of Slavery in Brazil: The Case of São Paulo." *Hispanic American Historical Review* 49 (1969).

Toussaint, Emma. *A Parisian in Brazil: Mme. Toussaint Samson.* Boston: James H. Earle Publishers, 1891.

Trochim, Michael R. *Retreat from Reform: The Fall of the Brazilian Empire, 1888–1889.* Dissertation, University of Illinois at Chicago, 1983. UMI Dissertation Services, 1983.

"Ultramonism and Freemasonry." *New York Times,* 16 July 1873.

United States Diplomatic Correspondence. United States Department of State. Charles Hale to Hamilton Fish, 25 September 1872, no. 55.

_____. James Partridge to Hamilton Fish, 20 May 1874, no. 60; 24 June 1875, no. 266; 24 July 1875; no. 25; 21 March 1875, no. 244; 6 December 1875, no. 300; 22 January 1876, no. 308; 29 September 1876.

_____. Correspondence from Portugal, Benjamin Moran to Hamilton Fish, July 3, 1875, and July 19, 1875.

_____. Purrington, 10 October 1875, no. 291.

_____. August 31, 1876.

_____. nos. 62, 145.

United States House of Representatives. *Executive Documents 1872–1873.* Washington, DC: Government Printing Office, 1873.

_____. *Executive Documents 1878–1879.* Washington, DC: Government Printing Office, 1879.

_____. *Papers Relating to the Foreign Relations of the United States, Transmitted to Congress, with the Annual Message of the President, December 3, 1888.* Washington, DC: Government Printing Office, 1889.

United States Senate. *Index to the Executive Documents, 1870–71.* Washington, DC: Government Printing Office.

_____. *Index to the Executive Documents, 1878–1879.* Washington, DC: Government Printing Office, 1879.

_____. *Index to the Senate Executive Documents for the Third Session of the Fortieth Congress of the United States of America, 1868–69.* Washington, DC: Government Printing Office, 1869.

Uls, Errol Lincoln. *Brazil.* New York: Simon and Shuster, 1986.

Vacaresco, Helene. "Pedro II, Emperor of Brazil." *Contemporary Review* 86 (November 1904).

Vale, Brian. *Independence or Death: British Sailors and Brazilian Independence.* London: Tauris Publishers, 1822–1825, 1996.

Vieira, Hermes. *Princesa Isabel— Uma Vida de Luzes e Sombras.* 3rd ed. São Paulo: Edicioes GRD, 1990.

Vieira da Cunha, Ruy, preface and ed. *D. Pedro II Conselhos a Princesa Isabel de Como Melhor Governar.* São Paulo: Edições GRD, 1985.

Vieira da Silva, José Custodio. *The National Palace, Sintra.* London: Scala, 2002.

Viotti da Costa, Emilia. *The Brazilian Empire: Myths and Histories.* Revised ed. Chapel Hill: University of North Carolina Press, 1985.

Walzer, Michael. *Regicide and Revolution: Speeches at the Trial of Louis XVI.* New York: Columbia University Press, 1993.

Warren, Harris G. *Paraguay and the Triple Alliance: The Postwar Decade, 1869–1878.* Austin: University of Texas Press, 1978.

Wild, Anthony. *Coffee: A Dark History.* New York: W.W. Norton, 2004.

Williams, John Hoyt. *The Rise and Fall of the Paraguayan Republic, 1800–1870.* Austin: University of Texas Press, 1979.

Williams, Mary Wilhelmine. *Dom Pedro the Magnanimous.* Chapel Hill: University of North Carolina Press, 1937.

Wise, Stephen. *Though the Heavens May Fall: The Landmark Trial That Led to the End of Human Slavery.* Cambridge, MA: Perseus Books, 2005.

Wood, Eric. *The Boy's Book of the Sea.* New York: Funk and Wagnall, 1915.

Worcester, David. E. *Brazil from Colony to World Power.* New York: Charles Scribner's Sons, 1973.

Young, Henry Lion. *Eliza Lynch: Regent of Paraguay.* Great Britain: Anthony Blond, 1966.

Zweig, Stefan. *Brazil: Land of the Future.* New York: Viking, 1941.

Index